TEXTILES FOR SUSTAINABLE DEVELOPMENT

TEXTILES FOR SUSTAINABLE DEVELOPMENT

RAJESH ANANDJIWALA,
L. HUNTER,
RYSZARD KOZLOWSKI
AND
GENNADY ZAIKOV
EDITORS

Nova Science Publishers, Inc.
New York

For permission to use material from this book please contact us:
Telephone 631-231-7269; Fax 631-231-8175
Web Site: http://www.novapublishers.com

NOTICE TO THE READER

The Publisher has taken reasonable care in the preparation of this book, but makes no expressed or implied warranty of any kind and assumes no responsibility for any errors or omissions. No liability is assumed for incidental or consequential damages in connection with or arising out of information contained in this book. The Publisher shall not be liable for any special, consequential, or exemplary damages resulting, in whole or in part, from the readers' use of, or reliance upon, this material.

Independent verification should be sought for any data, advice or recommendations contained in this book. In addition, no responsibility is assumed by the publisher for any injury and/or damage to persons or property arising from any methods, products, instructions, ideas or otherwise contained in this publication.

This publication is designed to provide accurate and authoritative information with regard to the subject matter covered herein. It is sold with the clear understanding that the Publisher is not engaged in rendering legal or any other professional services. If legal or any other expert assistance is required, the services of a competent person should be sought. FROM A DECLARATION OF PARTICIPANTS JOINTLY ADOPTED BY A COMMITTEE OF THE AMERICAN BAR ASSOCIATION AND A COMMITTEE OF PUBLISHERS.

LIBRARY OF CONGRESS CATALOGING-IN-PUBLICATION DATA
Textiles for sustainable development / Rajesh Anandjiwala ... [et al.].
    p. cm.
Includes index.
ISBN-13: 978-1-60021-559-9 (hardcover)
ISBN-10: 1-60021-559-9 (hardcover)
1. Textile industry--Case studies. 2. Sustainable development. I. Anandjiwala, Rajesh D.
HD9850.5.T384   2007
330.4'7677--dc22   2006101911

Published by Nova Science Publishers, Inc. ✦ New York

CONTENTS

Contents vii

PREFACE

A conference with the theme "Textiles for Sustainable Development" was hosted and organized by CSIR Materials Science and Manufacturing of South Africa and the Institute of Natural s (INF), Poland under the FAO/ESCORENA European Cooperative Research Network on Flax and other Bast Plants. The conference was held from 23-27 October 2005 in Port Elizabeth, South Africa. The theme was particularly important and appropriate for developing countries in Africa and elsewhere. The conference was aimed at bringing together experts from the fiber, textiles, clothing, agriculture, composite and niche product areas to discuss recent progress, disseminate research and technical findings and to explore the role of future research in the economic development of South Africa in particular and the world at large. The conference was well attended by local and foreign delegates from industry, academia and research organizations. In all some 130 delegates from USA, Canada, UK, Germany, Czech Republic, Hungary, Poland, Portugal, Russia, Sweden, South Africa, Swaziland, Brazil, India, Iran, Pakistan, Cuba, etc., attended the conference. At the conclusion of the conference some experts and delegates expressed interest in the publication of the edited proceedings for the benefit of researchers and others. It was, therefore, decided to do so.

The conference covered following themes and cross-cutting research and development activities:

- Agronomy, economics and market trends for the production of natural fibers.
- Synthetic and natural fibers, their properties, processing and applications.
- Properties, performance and primary processing of natural fibers.
- Textile and clothing production processes and properties.
- Nanotechnology applications in fibers, textiles and clothing
- Comfort and health related applications of textiles.
- World trade and marketing of fibers, textiles and clothing.
- Modern and innovative textile processing techniques and technologies.

Based on the above themes, the present volume is broadly divided into five Parts according to the subject matter. Part 1 deals with Fiber Production and Properties, and developments in natural fibers and their evaluation. Part 2 is devoted to special textile measurement and metrology techniques, for example, the use of Near Infrared spectroscopy for the rapid assessment of properties of modified linen fabrics and the application of osmotic pressure for the evaluation of the quality and quantity of fiber in flax and hemp. Part 3 covers a wide range of conventional and novel textile processes and products, advances in the field of fiber reinforced composites and its importance in various new and advanced products. Part 4 is devoted to the application of nanotechnology in textiles, which is an emerging field cutting across different aspects of the entire textile production value chain. Part 5 provides general information including market trends and future opportunities.

The papers have been edited and revised without changing the technical content of the original papers submitted by the authors. Care has been taken to present the information in the form that will assist the research and educational institutes as well as the industry to gain a better understanding of existing and new trends in textile and related research. The authors are responsible for the accuracy and the content of their papers and are thanked for their contribution and permission to publish their papers.

No endeavour, such as this, can be handled without the dedicated support of many people. We wish to express sincere gratitude to our colleagues, both at the CSIR and the INF, who directly and indirectly assisted, advised and laboured with us in organizing the conference and preparing these proceedings. Special thanks are due to Kelly-Anne Matthews, Mary-Anne Sullivan, Sonia Slement and Catherine Stocker of the CSIR and Maria Mackiewicz-Talarczyk of the INF for their dedicated assistance throughout the process. We also wish to acknowledge the financial support of the managements of the CSIR, The Department of Trade and Industry (the dti), Advanced Manufacturing Technology Strategy of the Department of Science and Technology of South Africa and Trutzschler GmbH during the organization of the event. The support and encouragement of the INF, Food and Agricultural Organization of the United Nations (FAO) are also gratefully acknowledged.

We trust that the readers will find the information presented here both informative and useful.

R. D. Anandjiwala,
L. Hunter,
R. M. Kozlowski,
G.E. Zaikov

PART I
FIBER PRODUCTION AND PROPERTIES

In: Textiles for Sustainable Development
Editors: R. Anandjiwala, L. Hunter et al., pp. 3-11

ISBN: 978-1-60021-559-9
© 2007 Nova Science Publishers, Inc.

Chapter 1

PERFORMANCE OF FOUR EUROPEAN HEMP CULTIVARS CULTIVATED UNDER DIFFERENT AGRONOMIC CONDITIONS IN THE EASTERN CAPE PROVINCE, SOUTH AFRICA

Sunshine Blouw[a] and Monde Sotana[b]

[a] CSIR, P.O. Box 1124, Port Elizabeth, 6000, South Africa
[b] Döhne Agricultural Development Institute, Private Bag X15, Stutterheim,
4930, South Africa; sblouw@csir.co.za ; monde@dohne1.agric.za

ABSTRACT

The purpose of this work was to obtain information on the performance of four European hemp cultivars piloted at four different sites in the Eastern Cape (South Africa), by assessing the fiber content of each cultivar grown under different agronomic experimental design. The southern region of the Eastern Cape is characterized by long day-length periods compared to other regions in South Africa and it should be an ideal area for hemp cultivation in South Africa.

According to the objectives of the project, selected hemp straw samples from the four hemp pilot sites were investigated to determine their hemp fiber content. The experimental results gave information about the fiber yield in general and in accordance to the agricultural parameters as documented in the report on "Hemp cultivar adaptation trials in the Eastern Cape" by the Agriculture Research Council – Institute for Industrial Crops ARC-IIC. It also gave an indication of the best performing cultivars of the four piloted in the Eastern Cape Province.

After dew retting, the hemp fiber was extracted from the stems using a simple and relatively inexpensive decorticating turbine.

For each hemp cultivar piloted, the fiber yield was objectively evaluated in terms of both the long and short fibers. The relationships between the fiber content of the European hemp cultivars as determined by the agronomic experimental design was evaluated and used to establish the performance of the individual cultivars and how each adapted to the Eastern Cape conditions.

Keywords: European hemp cultivars; decortication; fiber content, dew retting, fiber quality..

INTRODUCTION

South Africa has a very high level of unemployment, hovering around 36%, and both the National and the Provincial Governments have initiated a number of programs aimed at creating conditions conducive for stimulating employment creation opportunities [1]. The Eastern Cape Provincial Government identified the establishment of a fiber agro-crop industry, e.g., flax, hemp and kenaf, as one such program that will help revitalise the agricultural potential of the province. Hemp imports (fibers, yarns and fabric) in South Africa for January – November 2003 amounted to close on U\$2million [2].

The growing popularity worldwide of this high value cash crop has resulted in great interest in the crop from farmers, agricultural organisations, industries and co-operatives in South Africa. The commercial production of this crop is labour intensive, and has great potential for job creation in rural areas. However, the ethical complexity, limited knowledge and expertise in the production and processing of this crop make it difficult for farmers and other entrepreneurs to benefit from the increasing demand for hemp products.

It is this recognition of the economic opportunities presented by hemp for emerging farmers and industries alike that led to the launch of a pilot initiative for hemp cultivation in the Eastern Cape Province in 1999/2000.

The Agriculture Research Council – Institute for Industrial Crops (ARC-IIC) and the Döhne Agricultural Development Institute were partners responsible for all the agronomic related activities, i.e., experimental design, planting, crop-care, harvesting and retting. For this purpose, four European hemp cultivars, namely; Novodsaska, Felina-34, Futura-77 and Kompolti were used in this research and piloted at four sites in the province.

Retted hemp straw was sent to the CSIR for the determination of the fiber yield of the cultivars grown under different agronomic conditions, in order to evaluate their performance and adaptation to conditions in the Eastern Cape Province. The results of the work are presented in this paper.

DESCRIPTION OF WORK CARRIED OUT

Agronomic Hemp Pilot Trials

The agronomic trials were undertaken on plots located at the two agricultural research stations, i.e., Addo and Döhne, as well as at two community sites (Libode and Qamata). At the Döhne research station the experimental trials covered:

- spacing and density[1], and
- weed control, both using only the Novodsaska cultivar.

---

[1] Density (density factor) means the seed quantity per unit area.

The experimental trials at Addo and the two community sites focused on hemp cultivar adaptation and performance when planted a month apart (see table1).

Table 1. Experimental agronomic parameters for hemp cultivar pilot trials in the Eastern Cape Province

Experiment 1. Hemp spacing and density trials at Döhne		
Objective: Determination of optimum row spacing , seeding rate, and population density		
Cultivar	*Spacing factor (cm)*	*Density factor (kg)*
Novodsaska	S1 = 12.5	D1 = 50
	S2 = 25	D2 = 80
	S3 = 55	D3 = 110
Experiment 2: Weed Control trials at Döhne		
Objective : To identify and select suitable herbicide and weed control methods for hemp		
Cultivar	*Treatment*	*Method*
Felina - 34 , Futura - 77 and Novodsaska	Chemical	Accotab, Basagran, Gallant Super, Afolan SC, Diuron, Frontier , and Dual S
	Non Chemical	Weed removal by hand
	Control	No weed removal
Experiment 3: Hemp cultivar adaptation trials Addo, Libode and Qamata		
Objective: To evaluate adaptation of hemp cultivars to Eastern Cape Province conditions		
Cultivar	*Seeding rate (kg) / hectare*	*Spacing (cm)*
Felina-34		
Futura-77	50	25
Novodsaska		

Fiber Extraction

Since hemp is a bast fiber crop, with the most valuable fibers contained within the bark of the stem, fiber extraction involves the separation of the bark from the core, a process known as decortication. The fibers were removed using the hemp breaker-scutching unit available at the centre. A random sample of 20 retted hemp stems (figure 1) from each cultivar grown under each of the different agronomic parameters, were weighed and decorticated by the crushing mechanism of the fluted steel rollers of the breaker.

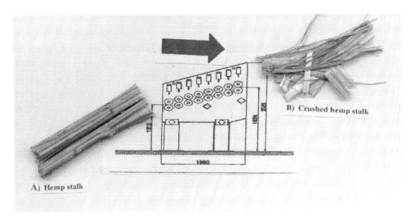

Figure 1. Hemp breaker used to crush retted hemp stems.

After successive cycles of crushing of the retted stems from the same sample, a steel comb was used to remove the plant debris still attached to the fibers. The weight of the sample fibers was then recorded in order to determine the total fiber content.

RESULTS AND DISCUSSION

The results of the total fiber yield of *European* hemp cultivars grown under different agronomic conditions in the Eastern Cape Province to determine cultivar adaptability and performance are given for all the parameter used.

Experiment 1. Hemp spacing and density trial at Döhne

Spacing (S) and seeding rate (D) combination	FiberYield (%)
S1D1 = 12,5cm ; 50kg	23.7
S1D2 = 12,5cm ; 80kg	20.1
S1D3 = 12,5cm ; 110kg	20.4
S2D1 = 25,0cm ; 50kg	19.6
S2D2 = 25,0cm ; 80kg	21.5
S2D3 = 25,0cm ; 110kg	21.2
S3D1 = 50,0cm ; 50kg	23.1
S3D2 = 50,0cm ; 80kg	19.6
S3D3 = 50,0cm ; 110kg	23.1

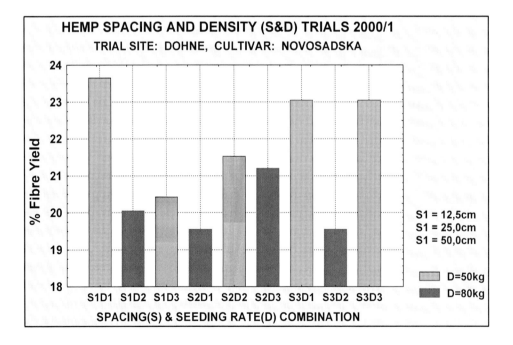

Figure 2. Fiber yield for different hemp spacing and density combinations.

There was a marginal variation in the total fiber yield, ranging from around 19.55 to 23.65% for the same cultivar grown under different spacing and seeding rate. The S1D1 spacing and density combination showed a higher fiber yield compared to the other combinations.

Experiment 2. Weed Control trials at Döhne

Treatment	Fiber Yield (%)		
	Novodsaska	Felina-34	Futura-77
Accotab	23.1	22.1	21
Basagran	24.5	21.6	20.3
Gallant Super	25.2	20.1	22.3
Afalon SC	24	20.5	20.6
Diuron	21.3	20.3	22
Frontier	20.7	19.9	20.4
Dual S	21.1	22.6	23.1
Control (weeded by hand)	24.1	22	20.3
Control (no treatment)	22.3	21	21.4

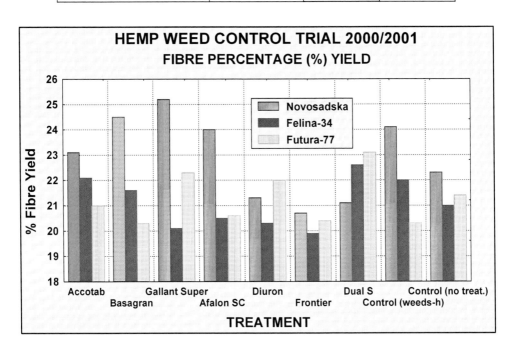

Figure 3. Table and graph on results of hemp fiber yield obtained under different weed control conditions.

The fiber yield of the different hemp cultivars grown under different weed control conditions, i.e., chemical, mechanical and no treatment, ranged from 19.9 to 25.2%. The different cultivars performed as follows:

- *Novodsaska* responded positively overall to most of the treatments, except for Diuron and Dual, with the fiber yield ranging from 20.7 to 25.2%.

- *Felina-34* fiber yield varied from 19.9 to 22.6%
- *Futura-77* fiber yield varied from 20.3 to 23.1%

These results show no significant difference in the fiber yield of the chemically treated and untreated cultivars. The treatment does not appear to influence the fiber yield of different hemp cultivars relative to the control experiments.

Experiment 3. Hemp cultivar adaptation trials at Addo, Libode and Qamata

HEMP CULTIVAR ADAPTATION TRIALS				
1st planting 2000				
CULTIVAR	Fiber Yield (%)			
	ADDO	DOHNE	LIBODE	QAMATA
Novodsaska (Yoguslavia)	24.3	17.7	23.8	24.1
F – 34 (French)	21.8	17.0	23.6	24.3
F – 77 (French)	22.3	19.4	25.0	22.7
Kompolti (Hungarian)	21.1	16.5	25.8	22.7

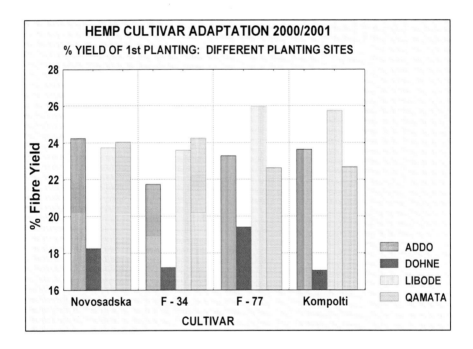

Figure 4(a). Fiber yield during hemp cultivar adaptation trials - 1st planting.

HEMP CULTIVAR ADAPTATION TRIALS (2000/2001)				
2nd PLANTING				
CULTIVAR	FIBER % YIELD			
	ADDO	DOHNE	LIBODE	QAMATA
Novodsaska (Yoguslavia)	22.8	17.5	25.0	22.4
F - 34 (French)	19.7	18.5	24.1	23.6
F - 77 (French)	22.4	19.0	25.3	22.4
Kompolti (Hungarian)	22.3	22.6	25.3	23.2

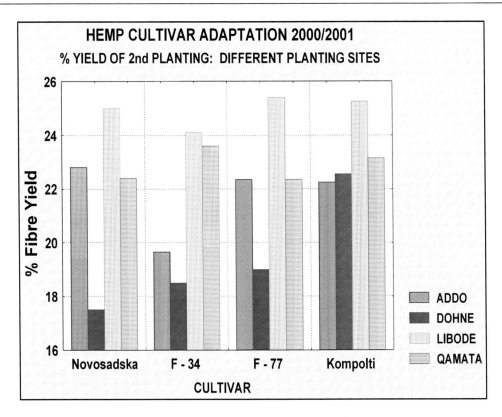

Figure 4(b). Fiber yield results for hemp cultivar adaptation trials – 2nd planting.

A comparison of the effect of different sowing dates, a month apart, on the performance (adaptability) of the different hemp cultivars piloted in the Eastern Cape was made on the basis of the fiber yield which ranged from 16.5 to 25.8.

There were no significant differences in the fiber yield of cultivars grown on the same pilot site but sowed on different dates. The fiber yield results from the Döhne pilot sites were lower for both sowing dates than those of the other three sites, except for Kompolti which performed better with the second sowing date.

CONCLUSION

The potential to develop a hemp industry in South Africa was investigated by the cultivation of four different cultivars under different agronomic conditions.

This study has shown that:

- Hemp can be grown successfully in South Africa, with a fiber yield comparable to that found in other countries.
- To achieve a slender hemp straw that will produce a high fiber yield, using minimum spacing and density combinations thereby resulting in an easy decortication process, the spacing and density combination found to be appropriate was 12,5cm and 50kg respectively.

- The application of herbicide did not cause any improvement in the fiber yield when compared to the untreated control.
- The most appropriate time of the year for the cultivation of hemp in the Eastern Cape Province is October – November.

FURTHER WORK

Further research on the best farming practices for the cultivation of hemp, i.e., crop care, harvesting method and retting process, by the agricultural research partners continues. Other cultivars sourced from different parts of the world will be evaluated in terms of their suitability for cultivation in the province and country.

The CSIR will continue to evaluate the fiber properties (physical and chemical) of the different hemp cultivars as well as undertaking product developmental via different spinning and nonwoven technologies.

ACKNOWLEDGEMENTS

The work reported has been undertaken as part of a wider investigation into "Feasibility of cultivation of hemp in the Eastern Cape Province" championed by the National Hemp Foundation consisting of the following partners:

- Agriculture Research Council-Institute of Industrial Crops, Rustenburg, for all activities related to agronomic research.
- Döhne Agricultural Development Institute, Eastern Cape Provincial Department of Agriculture, Stutterheim, for providing research and extension services for this initiative as well as supplying the CSIR with samples of hemp straw for fiber yield evaluation.
- The Eastern Cape Provincial Department of Economic Affairs, Environment and Tourism, for supporting this initiative.
- The communities of Qamata and Libode for their enthusiastic labour as well as providing security to prevent crop theft from the pilot sites.
- The CSIR for investing research funds in this research work and for fiber evaluation.

REFERENCES

[1]   Statistics South Africa, Labour Force Survey, March 2005
[2]   Booth, I; Harwood, R.J; Wyatt, J.L; Grishanov, S. A Comparative Study of the Characteristics of - Flax (Linum usitatissimum), De Montfort University, 2002.
[3]   Müssig, J; Martens, R. Quality Aspects in Hemp Production – Influence of Cultivation, Harvesting and Retting, *Journal of Industrial Hemp,* 2003, 8, Number 1,
[4]   Kaniewski, R; Konczewicz, W; Cierpucha, W. New Trends in Harvesting, Processing and Utilizing Hemp, *Natural s,* 2000, XLIV.

[5]   Shekhar Sharma, HS; Van Smere, CF. The Biology and Processing of Flax, M Publications, Belfast.

[6]   Garcia-Jaldon, C; Dupeyre, D; Vignon, MR. s from Semi-Retted Hemp Bundles by Steam Explosion Treatment, *Biomass Bioenergy*, 1998, 14, 251-260.

[7]   Kautto, K; Hakkarainen, E; Pasila, A; Pehkonen, A. Harvesting and Processing of Hemp, *Publication Agricultural Engineering*, 2001, 31, University of Helsinki.

[8]   Sankari, H.S. Comparison of Bast Yield and Mechanical Properties of Hemp (Cannabis sativa L) cultivars, *Industrial Crops and Products*, 2000, 11, 73-84.

[9]   ARC, CSIR, DALA, Progress Report on Hemp Research 2000/2001, National Hemp Foundation – a report, 2001

[10]   Mankowski, J; Rynduch, W. Cottonized Hemp Fiber as a Component of Blended Yarns, Proceedings of the 4th European Workshop on Flax, Rouen, 1996.

In: Textiles for Sustainable Development
Editors: R. Anandjiwala, L. Hunter et al., pp. 13-20
ISBN: 978-1-60021-559-9
© 2007 Nova Science Publishers, Inc.

Chapter 2

ANTIBACTERIAL COTTON FIBER

Judit Borsa and Katalin Lázár

Budapest University of Technology and Economics;
H-1521 Budapest, Hungary; jborsa@mail.bme.hu

ABSTRACT

New properties and functions were developed in cotton fibers by a slight carboxymethylation. The modified fiber has a slight acidic character and swells greatly in water to. In previous studies, a high sorption capacity and good soil release of such fibers were found. In the present work, the antibacterial effect of the modified fiber is presented. As the special properties belong to the chemically modified cellulose molecules, the modification is durable and can be used for various purposes.

Keywords: cellulose, cotton, antibacterial, carboxymethylation, swelling, adsorption, protective clothes, soil release.

INTRODUCTION

Due to its excellent properties, cotton fiber is widely used for clothing. During traditional textile finishing, cotton fabric can gain some new beneficial properties, such as dimensional stability, crease recovery etc. New functions can be developed for cotton fibers by special treatments, called *functionalisation*. Functionalisation of textile materials is one of the research and development priorities of the European Technology Platform for the Future of Textile and Clothing to develop special products and new textile applications for human and technical purposes. The Platform has been established for the transformation of the textile industry into a knowledge-based innovation driven sector.

Chemical modification of cellulose is a very promising method to develop special properties. Introduction of new functional groups into the cellulose molecule can significantly alter the physical and chemical characteristics of the fiber. The products of chemical

modification generally enhance the usefulness of cellulose because more desirable properties
are incorporated.

Recently many cellulose derivatives have been developed to meet certain areas of
applications. *Carboxymethylcellulose* is one of the classical cellulose ethers, its preparation
using monochloroacetic acid and sodium hydroxide

$$Cell-OH + Cl-CH_2-COOH + 2\ NaOH \rightarrow Cell-O-CH_2-COONa + NaCl + 2\ H_2O\ (1)$$

was patented in 1921 [5] already. Substitution of the proton in the hydroxyl groups of
cellulose by a bulky carboxymethyl group results in a less ordered structure of the fiber,
finally the modified cellulose can be dissolved in a dilute alkali medium or even in water. For
many years only water or alkali soluble carboxymethylcellulose of high degree of substitution
(DS > 0,5) has found widespread application in diverse industries.

Cotton cellulose, having only 5-15 carboxymethyl groups on its 100 monomer units (DS
= 0,005-0,015), has a fibrous character while its properties differ from that of the original
fiber. Both the ionic character and the supermolecular structure of the cotton cellulose vary
over a very wide range depending on the reaction parameters.

Research studies on the preparation, properties and application of fibrous
carboxymethylcellulose have been reviewed elsewhere [3].

The aim of this study is to *summarise our previous results on the slight
carboxymethylation* of cotton cellulose for a better understanding of the main tasks of the
modification and to *show new results on the antibacterial effect of specially modified fiber.*

PREVIOUS RESULTS ON CARBOXYMETHYLATED COTTON FIBER

The effect of the reaction parameters (concentration of reagents and duration of the
treatment) on some basic properties of cotton cellulose and *some possible applications* of
specially modified fiber were previously investigated. The concentration of the alkali applied
was sufficient for the cellulose I – cellulose II transition.

Effect of the Reaction Parameters

The Degree of substitution and some other properties of various carboxymethylated
cotton cellulose fibers were studied.

Degree of Substitution [11], Distribution of the Substituents [4]

Fibrous carboxymethylated cotton cellulose of various degrees of substitution (DS =
0,01-0,15) were produced. Higher reagent concentrations did not obviously result in a higher
degree of substitution. The accessibility and reactivity of various hydroxyl groups of cellulose
molecules in cotton fiber are different; hence the distribution of the substituents along the
molecule chain is not uniform. Highly substituted molecules can be dissoluted by the reaction
medium, hence the actual degree of substitution is the resultant of two competitive processes
(substitution and dissolution) [11].

Carboxymethyl groups were found in the whole cross-section of the modified fiber [4].

Accessibility of Slightly Carboxymethylated Cellulose Fibers [9, 10]

Accessibility of cellulose molecules, characterised by water retention value [9] and iodine sorption capacity [10], was generally increased by the modification. The degree of change was highly influenced by the reaction parameters. The effect of dissolution mentioned above was observed in the accessibility values as well: it was unexpected that accessibility (sorption capacity) of the modified fiber can be even less than that of the original fiber. There was no correlation between carboxyl content and accessibility, as can be seen when comparing the carboxyl content values (figure 1.) and iodine sorption capacity (figure 2.) of the same samples.

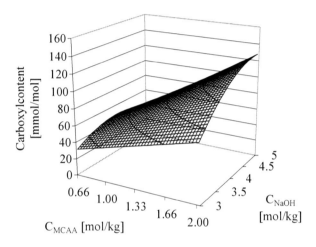

Figure 1. Carboxyl content of slightly carboxymethylated cotton fibers as a function of reagent concentration (70 °C, 20 min) [11].

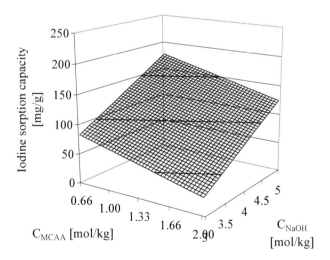

Figure 2. Iodine sorption capacity of slightly carboxymethylated cotton fibers as a function of reagent concentration (70 °C, 20 min) [10].

Some Possible Applications of Slightly Carboxymethylated Cotton Fiber

The high accessibility is the most promising property of the modified fiber. Cotton fiber, carboxymethylated using the proper technology, swells in water to a very high extent, it has a very high sorption capacity. Due to its properties, the fiber appears to be hydrogel coated, while the carboxymethyl groups can be found, not only on the surface of the fiber but in the whole cross-section as well.

Pesticide Protection [12], Soil Release [8]

Modified cotton fabric can absorb a large amount of pesticide, moreover, it can release the contamination easily in the laundry process [12]. Oily soils, as well, can be effectively removed from the modified fabric (figures 3 a and 3 b) [8].

As the special properties belong to the fiber, itself, the modification is durable and suitable for various purposes.

a.

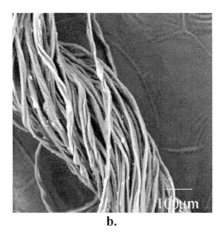

b.

Figure 3. Residual oily soil on untreated (a) and carboxymethylated (b) fibers after laundry [8].

ANTIBACTERIAL EFFECT OF CARBOXYMETHYLATED COTTON FIBER

Patient and medical staff safety has become a serious concern in recent years as the need for protection against microbial diseases has been realised. Apparel can reduce the transfer of microorganisms by creating a barrier between the infection source and a healthy individual. On the other hand, microorganisms may be transmitted between patients on the clothes of medical staff. One critical factor for the transmission of microorganisms from person to person or from the environment to a person (patient or health care worker) is the ability of the microbe to survive on an environmental surface [7], e. g. on textiles. The effects of fabric characteristics (thickness, yarn count, weight, pore size and oil and water repellency) have been widely investigated [6].

Traditional textiles can provide *passive protection* against bacteria: textiles impede the penetration of fluid transporting microorganisms (vehicles), but microorganisms remain viable. Antibacterial textiles provide an additional *active protection* by killing bacteria.

Experimental

The survival of Gram positive and Gram negative bacteria (*Staphylococcus aureus* and *Escherichia coli,* respectively – frequent species in nosocomial/hospital infections) was tested on untreated and carboxymethylated cotton fabrics according to the relevant AATCC test methods [1, 2]. Fabrics after ironing were tested, too. Bacteria soaked from the contaminated fabric were determined [1], the parallel stripe method [2] were used. The Quinn test presented in [1] was modified: in the original test, the contaminated textile is covered with agar, in our modified test, agar, containing nutrient and bacteria, was poured on the fabric. In some experiments, antiseptic dressing was used as positive control.

In order to study the role of acidic carboxyl groups on the antibacterial effect of the carboxymethylated cellulose, the survival of acidophyl bacteria (*Acetobacter)* was also investigated.

Results

Soaking: Just Immediately after contamination far less bacteria were soaked from the carboxymethylated fabric than from the untreated one. Moreover, after 24 hours there were no living bacteria in the soaking solution of the carboxymethylated fiber, while bacteria on the untreated fabric survived (for Escherichia coli see figure 4).

Parallel stripes method: There were no colonies of bacteria on the carboxymethylated sample even at the highest concentration of bacteria, while for the control samples bacteria could survive (for Staphylococcus aureus see figure 5).

Modified Quinn test: Bacteria could not survive on the modified fabric and on the positive control sample (antiseptic dressing). As antibacterial agents can diffuse from the dressing material, the antibacterial effect of the active agent around the antiseptic dressing can be observed. There is no such phenomenon in the case of the carboxymethylated fabric, because the fiber itself is antibacterial (for Escherichia coli see figure 6.).

Effect of ironing: Ironing of fabrics did not influence the antibacterial effect.
Survival of acidophyl bacteria: Survival of acidophyl Acetobacter was not hindered by both types of fabric (figure 7).

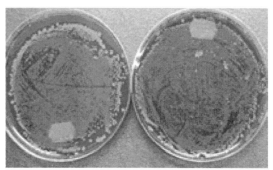

0 hours 24 hours untreated cotton

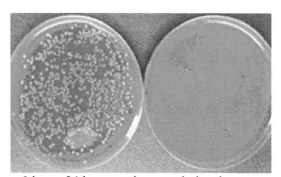

0 hours 24 hours carboxymethylated cotton

Figure 4. Survival of Escherichia coli on untreated and on carboxymethylated cellulose fibers (soaking method [1]).

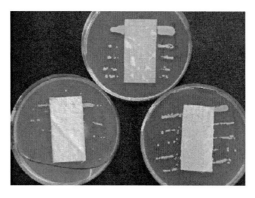

Figure 5. Survival of Staphylococcus aureus on various fabrics (parallel stripes method [2]) untreated: right – mercerised: left – carboxymethylated: above.

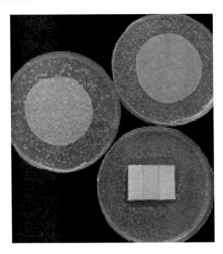

Figure 6. Survival of Escherichia coli on various fabrics (modified Quinn test [1]) untreated: left – positive control: bottom – carboxymethylated: above.

Acidophyl bacteria could produce many colonies on the carboxymethylated cellulose fiber as well (figure 7), hence it can be supposed that acidic groups have an important role on the antimicrobial effect of the modified fiber.

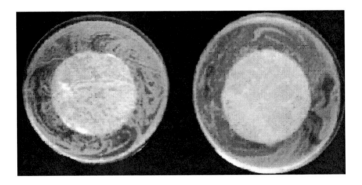

Figure 7. Survival of acidophyl Acetobacter on various fabrics (modified Quinn test [1]). untreated: left – carboxymethylated: right.

SUMMARY

Cotton fiber, carboxymethylated using the proper technology, swells in water to a very great extent, it has a very high sorption capacity. Due to its properties, the fiber seems to be hydrogel coated, while the carboxymethyl groups can be found not only on the surface of the fiber but in its whole cross-section.

The slightly carboxymethylated cotton fabric is effective against nosogenic bacteria, probably due to its acidic character. Chemical modification, as a permanent finish, can be used for the preparation of antimicrobial cotton fabric for hospital use, especially for patients having a depressed immune system.

ACKNOWLEDGEMENTS

Special thanks are due to the previous co-authors and to Dr. Ákos Sveiczer, Dr. Judit Zala, Ms. Katalin Kiss and Ms. Emőke Horváth. The Hungarian government supports OTKA 048701 and GVOP-3.2.2.-2004-07-0006/3.0 are also gratefully appreciated.

REFERENCES

[1]   AATCC (American Association of Textile Chemists and Colorists) 100-1982 test method

[2]   AATCC (American Association of Textile Chemists and Colorists) 147-1982 test method

[3]   J. Borsa, I. Rácz, Carboxymethylcellulose of Fibrous Character, a Survey, *Cell. Chem. Technol.*, 29, 657-663 (1995).

[4]   J. Borsa, V. Ravichandran, S. K. Obendorf: Distribution of the Carboxyl Groups in the Cross-Section of Carboxymethylated Cotton Fibers, *Journal of Applied Polymer Science* 72, 203-207 (1999)

[5]   Deutsche Celluloid Fabrik Eilenburg (credited to E. Jansen by E. Heuser), *German Patent.* 332.203 (Jan. 22, 1921).

[6]   K. K. Leonas, R. S. Jinkins: The Relationship of Selected Fabric Characteristics and the Barrier Effectiveness of Surgical Gowns Fabric, *American Journal of Infection Control* 25 (1) 16-23 (1997)

[7]   A.N. Neely: A Survey of Gram-negative Bacteria Survival on Hospital Fabrics and Plastics, *Journal of Burn Care and Rehabilitation* 21 (6) 523-527 (2000)

[8]   S. K. Obendorf, J. Borsa: Lipid Soil Removal from Chemically Modified Cotton, *J. Surfactants and Deterg.*, 4 (3), 247-256 (2001)

[9]   Rácz, J. Borsa: Swelling of Carboxymethylated Cellulose Fibers, *Cellulose* 4, 293-303 (1997)

[10] Rácz, J. Borsa, G. Bodor: Crystallinity and Accessibility of Fibrous Carboxymethylcellulose by Pad-Roll Technology, *J. of Applied Polymer Science* 62, 2015-2024 (1996)

[11] Rácz, I. Deák, J. Borsa: Fibrous Carboxymethylcellulose by Pad-Roll Technology, *Text. Res. J.* 65 (6), 348-354 (1995)

[12] Rácz, S. K. Obendorf, J. Borsa: Carboxymethylated Cotton Fabric for Pesticide Protective Work Clothes, *Text. Res. J.* 68, 69-74 (1998)

In: Textiles for Sustainable Development   ISBN: 978-1-60021-559-9
Editors: R. Anandjiwala, L. Hunter et al., pp. 21-37   © 2007 Nova Science Publishers, Inc.

Chapter 3

AVAILABILITY, PRODUCTION, MARKETING AND POTENTIAL APPLICATIONS OF NATURAL FIBERS OF BRAZIL

J.L. Guimarães[1], K.G. Satyanarayana[2] and F. Wypych[3]

[1] Usina Piloto de Tecnologia Química Universidade Federal do Paraná.
[2] CEPESQ – Centro de Pesquisa em Química Aplicada,Universidade Federal do Paraná,
Departamento de Química, CP 19081, 81531-990, Curitiba – PR – Brazil.
[1] jlguimaraes@ufpr.br; [2] kgssatya@quimica.ufpr.br; [3] wypych@quimica.ufpr.br

ABSTRACT

Brazil occupying fifth position in the world in terms of area, is endowed with abundantly available renewable resources, such as natural plant fibers and different types of starches. Despite the fact that most of these natural fibers are being used in conventional, automotive and textile industries, many are still underutilized. This paper discusses the availability of some of these fibers, their extraction methods, their characteristics, present applications and markets. Natural fibers have been gaining importance because of their unique properties, such as low density, biodegradability and low production costs for the diversified applications. Perspectives for the better utilization of these resources are also presented, which may lead to a whole spectrum of exciting and promising opportunities and challenges for their utilization.

Keywords: Renewable resources, plant fibers, polymers, production, marketing, societal applications.

INTRODUCTION

It is well known that natural resources play an important role, not only in the growth of the Gross Domestic Product (GDP) of any country, but also in the social and economic development of developing third world countries. There is a worldwide trend to use such resources to the maximum extent through new technologies and new products. This in turn creates new jobs, generating more income and thus improving the standard of living of the people in these countries. Brazil is no exception to this. With an area of approximately 520 thousand km^2 of arable land and occupying approximately 50% of the South American Continent, a population of 169,872,856 and GDP of 2.8 [36], Brazil is privileged also geographically to possess exceptional and favorable climatic conditions for the cultivation of a rich diversity of plants. This includes renewable resources for rs and natural polymers, such as sisal, jute, coconut, banana, curauá, and different types of starches as well as derivatives from sugarcane, rubber and cashew nut shell liquid.

Table 1 shows the agricultural production of various s natural fibers in Brazil for 2003 and 2004 while figure 1 shows some of the sources of natural fibers. The reason for the decrease in banana production is explained in the next section. With the high cost of exploration of reserves of non-renewable sources of materials and energy and the development of new technologies for the substitution of wood. Brazil has great possibilities for the commercial exploitation of these resources. The current thinking is to stimulate growth in these resources and technologies that lead to development and to a growth in employment and the national economy. Brazil has therefore been supporting RandD related to these resources through various agencies, such as Brazilian Agrofarming Research Corporation (EMBRAPA), Institute of Agronomy (IAC), Council of National Science and Technology (CNPq), etc.

Table 1. Statistical data for Agricultural Production (Tons) in Brazil [16]

Product (Tons)	Period		Variation (%)
	2003	2004	
Pineapple (thousand fruits)	14,06,128	14,33,710	+1.96
Rice	1,03,19,925	1,32,62,373	+28.51
Banana	67,74,985	65,00,554	-4.05
Sugar cane	38,98,49,400	40,96,36,390	+5.08
Coconut (thousand fruits)	19,00,571	19,54,369	+2.83
Jute	1485	2170	+46.13
Casava	2,21,46,801	2,40,20,449	+8.46
Sisal or agave	1,84,503	1,88,380	+2.10

Cultivated Area

In Brazil, agricultural policies have been receiving the government's special attention, though it has yet to meet the expectations of small farmers. Also, there are some cultures of plantations of high productivity developed in the country, probably due to farmers' own initiatives through agricultural cooperatives. The Brazilian company of Farming Research (EMBRAPA) has been contributing to the development of some of these new techniques and the improvement of different varieties of cultivation. One example is the increase in curauá (native of the north of Brazil) production. Besides, an increase in mechanization has contributed to the increase of the availability of fibers in the market although the percentage of fibers produced is low in relation to the total mass of the plants available. These natural fibers present a vast diversity of applications in view of their low production cost and , attractive properties, such as low density, sound absorption and strength. In most cases they contribute to the biodegradation and renewal of the ecological cycle. There has been a significant increase in the land cultivated for fiber yielding production, plantations in the country as presented in table 2. This is despite a lack of funds, which is noteworthy. The slight decrease in cultivated area for banana can be linked to the disease developed in the plants in the south-southeast coast, causing the producers to cut off the plants to avoid the progress of the disease, while a similar argument may apply in the case of coconut.

Table 2. Plantation area (ha) in Brazil [16]

Product	Period		Variation (%)
	2003	2004	
Pineapple	53,508	54,589	+2.02
Rice	31,86,822	37,31,854	+17.10
Banana	5,12,826	4,83,814	-5.66
Sugar cane	53,36,985	55,55,938	+4.10
Coconut	2,90,653	2,73,810	-5.7
Jute	1047	1406	+34.29
Sisal	2,18,015	2,22,662	+2.13
Curauá*	100	400	+400

* Estimated production.

Productivity

Table 3 presents the production of various plantation products in Brazil during 2003 and 2004. It can be seen that only pineapple production shows a negative variation. This can be related to the decrease in the area available for its cultivation and also due to the two types of pineapple cultivation practiced in the country. This is discussed in the next section.

Table 3. Production (kg/ha) of some plantations in Brazil [16]

Product	Period		Variation
	2003	2004	(%)
Pineapple (fruits/hectare)	26,279	26,264	-0.06
Rice	3238	3554	+9.76
Banana	13,211	13,436	+1.70
Sugar cane	73.047	73.729	+0.93
Coconut (Fruits/hectare)	6539	7138	+9.16
Jute	1418	1543	+8.82
Sisal or Agave	846	846	Nil

(a) Curauá pPlants [17]   (b) Luffa Cylindrica pPlant [18]

(c) Luffa Cylindrica fFruit [18]   (d) Piaçava pPlant [19]

(e) Malva Plant [20]

Figure 1. Photograph of vVarious sSources of nNatural fFibers.

Extraction and Availability of Fibers

Mostly mechanical methods are used for the extraction of these fibers. Some typical fibers unique to Brazil are Curauá, Luffa cylindrica and piaçava. Therefore, more details on their availability and extraction are given below.

The first typical source of natural fiber is the curauá plant - *Ananas erectifolius,* (figure 1(a)), which belongs to the pineapple family and a hydrophilous species from the Amazon region [17]. About 10,000 plants per hectare are grown. Each plant yields 50-60 leaves per annum. Each leaf of about 1-1.5m long, 5-4 cm wide and about 5 mm thick, yields about 5-8% of fibers on a dry weight basis. Curauá fibers are extracted using a machine called "periquita" (figure 2(a)) which is used for sisal fibers, followed by washing and then beating the leaves using a rod, after this they are kept in water for about 36 hours for "mercerizing" before they are again washed and dried [31,29]. These three fibers are shown in figure 2(d-f.) Curauá fibers rank third in an economical analysis and fourth in stiffness and are thus more competitive among the traditional fibers in the country [31,29,30]. There is a demand of 150 tons of curauá fiber while the production is only 8 tons [32]. Accordingly, steps were taken to enlarge the plantation area to more than 100 hectares in the municipal district of Santarém in the north of Brazil, by the end of 2001, with the support of BASA (Banco da Amazonia S/A) and of the Bank of Brazil. At present, the Curuai lake, located in the municipal district of Santarém, is the only place to market the curauá fiber. This place, with a population of about 150 families, has a plantation area of 50 hectares for cultivating this plant. Mercedes Benz, in partnership with the POEMA (Program of Poverty and Environment in the Amazon), has a great interest in this fiber with a potential demand of about 300 tons/year at a cost of US$ 0.35/kg [15]. The commercialization of this fiber tends to grow, once the demand for the curauá fiber reaches around 300 tons/month [10].

(a) Curauá [21]   (b) Malva [22]

(c) Piaçava [19]   (d) Curauá fibers [21]

(e) Malva fibers [22]   (f) Piaçava fibers [19]

Figure 2. Photographs of some natural fibers of Brazil and the processes of extraction.

On the other hand, Luffa is the generic name of a group of species known as "vegetable sponges", which are perennial and trailing herbs. Luffa Cylindrica, the largest produced in Brazil, is the most exploited as vegetable sponge of the eight species of these herbal plants. The fruit of the cylindrical luffa has a nucleus with structure similar to beehive surrounded by entangled fibers arranged multi directionally [2,31,38,39] (figure 1(b)). Luffa is an oblong-cylindrical, green, smooth fruit 15-25 cm long, with numerous black, grey or medium brown-clear and rough seeds. Despite an increasing production of these fibers, there is no scientific method of extraction, which is done manually. A small company in São Paulo exports this fiber to the USA and Europe mainly as hygienic scouring pads. The business is lucrative for the entrepreneurs who sell the fibers in the American market for US$0.60 per kg. Nevertheless, not much information is available in the literature regarding this fiber.

Piaçava (*Attalea Funifera*) fibers, also known as piaçaba/piassava, are extracted from the palm tree (figure 1c). This tree is grown in the Atlantic rain forests of Brazil (such as in Bahia, which accounts for about 90% of the national production of the fiber) and its natural occurrence is close to the coastal range, being concentrated in the latitude range of 13-17°S [3]. When correctly planted, it begins to yield economically from the seventh year. In a natural field, they grow an average of 300 plants per hectare, while in non-populated areas, a density of 1000 plants/ha can be encountered [19]. It needs low financial resources for planting, maintenance and exploration. Thus, it turns out to be an attractive agricultural option, with reduced risks and high income to the investor. For example, these fibers are extracted manually from the stalks which are picked using long knives as is done in the case of other palm fibers in India. The stalks are picked once a year, preferably between March and September, with a view to get longer and more flexible fibers of better commercial value and for greater longevity of the plant. Otherwise, fibers of inferior quality would result. Then the fibers are cleaned, brushed and sorted on the basis of length and tied into bales with variable weights. These fibers are 4 m long, of average width of 1.1 mm, stiff and waterproof. The bales containing continuous long fibers are marketed to countries, such as USA, UK, Portugal, Belgium, Holland, Germany and Argentina, while those containing shorter fibers, termed "stubs", are used in industrial brooms in the country. One piaçava plant yields between 8 to 10 kg of fiber/annum and its useful life can be up to 20 years, the medium productivity being 3 kg/plant/annum [19]. In the producing areas, the price received by the producer is about U$ 0.52/kg. This fiber industry is very profitable for all involved. A hectare of piaçava plantation costs about U$ 61.00, producing 3 tons on average, corresponding to an income of US$ 1122. It is observed that the income obtained by this plantation in the south of Bahia is better than that obtained with perennial cultures, such as rubber, cocoa, coconut, etc. The production of piaçava fibers has been increasing over the years, the present production being about 100,000 metric tons [3].

Another interesting fiber is derived from the malva plant (figure 1e), the Amazon region being the largest producer in the country. The production of this fiber is one of the economic bases of municipal districts, such as Manacapuru, about 84 km from Manaus [22]. The malva plant is planted in the meadows of rivers as it needs fertile land. In about eight months, it would reach a height of three meters. Extraction of the fibers from this plant is similar to that of jute, in that stems of the plants would be cut and tied into bunches. They are put inside the water for about 7-8 days to soften. Afterwards, the outer cover is pulled to separate the fibers, followed by drying in the sun (figure 2e). Expected production for this year is about eight thousand tons, which would be about 40% less than that of last year, due to the ebb tides of last year hindering the planting of the fiber. The producer receives US$ 0.45 per kg of fiber, with a subsidy of US$ 0.08 by the federal government through the National Company for Supply of Goods (CONAB), which is below the demand price of US$ 0.62. (July/2004 - price for 1 kg in the north of Brazil ranging from US$ 0.33 to 0.37 while the international cost is 0.31) [23].

Turning to the other conventional fibers produced in Brazil, sisal is an important leaf fiber of Brazil, accounting for about 50% of the world market in recent times and about a million people depend on this crop in the Northeast region of the country [30]. The annual production is still increasing, with 171,266 tons in 2002, 178,611 tons in 2003 [16] and 188,380 tons in 2004 [24], mainly from the Northeast of the country. It has an excellent commercialization opportunity. According to the FAO (Food and Agricultural Organization), the world production of sisal increased from 247,000 tons in 2003 to 251,600 tons in 2004, showing an increase of 1.8%. A part of this increase may be attributed to the action taken by Brazil, where a 5.2% growth occured in the production of sisal during this period. Estimates of the production of sisal during 2004-2005 indicated that it would be below 250,000 tons due to drought in countries, such as Kenya and Tanzania, which are the second and third largest producers of sisal, respectively.

The banana plant is another source of biomass and fiber that has been the subject of various studies in Brazil since it is the third largest producer of banana, after India and Ecuador [25]. Banana plant has a tree-like appearance, with its trunk/stem having a length from 3 to 9 m and diameter ranging from 200 to 370 mm. The stem contains long multi-cell fibers (of about 24% pseudo-stem) extending length-wise. Fiber is extracted manually from the stem by a simple low-cost fiber extraction process. A mechanical method was developed, using a decorticator which is similar to the one used for curauá fiber. It is reported to yield about 1.75 kg of fiber on dry weight basis/man hour, giving the cost of the fiber as US$0.89/kg [31]. Of the 6.6 million tons of biomass produced annually from banana plants, only 2% is used by artisans, particularly by coastal populations in the states of São Paulo and Paraná, while in countries such as India its use exceeds about 10%, in view of its use not only by artisans, but as a energy saver and for other industrial uses. The São Paulo state is the main producer of this fiber with about 95,000 tons per annum compared to a yield production of about 3×10^5 tons of fiber on 1.5 million acres in India. However, in the last 5 years, the banana culture is decreasing in the country, with increasing volumes of other renewable resources, the development of new technologies applicable to the automotive industry being the main objective of research in the northeast and southeast of the country [15,25].

Coir fibers have varied applications and the typical species of North of Brazilian were subjected to genetic modifications in order to be cultivated in the cooler areas, south and southeast of Brazil [15]. The Brazilian production of coconut is of the order of 1.5 billion fruits a year, with the northern part being the biggest contributor. For instance, the farm of Socôco, in Moju-Pará, broke the productivity record in the harvest of 1999-2000 with 140 fruits/tree of coconut plant [15], while the world record monitored by the Institut de Recherches pour les Huiles et Oleagineux (IRHO), is only 120 fruits/tree/annum in several countries of Asia and of Africa. The Program of Poverty and Environment in the Amazon (POEMA) enlarged its project for the use of coconut fiber, mainly in the production of accessories for the automobile industry. POEMATEC, a natural fiber industry in Brazil, has been using the German technology since its inception for the improvement of this fiber [15].

This industry has received investments of about US$ 3 million, in the form of equipment and technology development, half from Daimler-Chrysler, the Constitutional Fund for the financing of North of Brazil (FNO) and the Fund of Development of the State (FDE). This industry will have a capacity to process 75 tons of coconut fiber/month, and it will produce various products for the automotive and domestic sectors. It is reported that the demand for this fiber by Mercedes Benz will be about 60% of the capacity of the factory [15]. The use of the coconut husk represents an alternative of income for 700 families in 23 municipal districts of the State of Pará. It is reported that POEMATEC will produce 25 thousand tons of automobile parts, generating 50 jobs and profits of US$ 300,000 a year, while the goal is to reach 80,000 tons of fiber and the generation of 150 jobs [15]. The small producers will be supplying the husk of the dry coconuts to the small factories. Together they will be using about 1.2 million fruits/month, producing 8 tons of fiber that will go directly for the machines of POEMATEC. This industry will have a capacity to produce 100 thousand parts per month.

Pineapple is another source of fibers produced in Brazil, being which is the third largest producer of this fiber after Thailand and Philippines [1,31] accounting for about 7% of the fibers [1]. Nevertheless, it exports only 1% of the annual production of 1.4 million tons. Taking about 40 leaves per plant and each leaf weighing 0.065kg [2% fiber per leaf], the total quantity of fibers produced in 2002 was given as 74,528.16 tons, which amount to about 1.2 kg/ha with a total value of US$ 162 per hectare [1]. Thus the price of this fiber will be about US$ 0.31/kg. Two types of pineapple farming exist in Brazil. In the first, after the first crop, the plants are cut, leaving some stems for the next crop along with the fresh plantations in the remaining space. Although this brings down the investment, the yield is reduced. In the second method, only fresh plantations are cultivated. The cost of pineapple production in the Forest of Araguaia is US$ 0.02-0.04 per fruit, which represents 50% of the automated farming cost [15].

Among all the cultures that produce biomass and vegetable fibers, sugar cane is the one that has been receiving the greatest attention and incentives from the Brazilian government, Brazil being the second largest producer in the world [12]. This may be due to fact that in additional to the production of sugar and ethanol, it generates a host of residues, which can have several end uses instead of being discarded as waste. One of these residues is bagasse, which is composed of broken fibers resulting from the extraction of the sugarcane juice. This cane pulp has great potential which is discussed in Section 3. With the current production of sugarcane in Brazil, the country could almost produce the same amount of power (12 Mw) as that produced by the hydroelectric power station at Itaipu [world's second largest producer of hydroelectric power located at the border between Paraguay/Argentina and Brazil]. It is also reported [36] that Brazil is the third largest supplier of Ramie fibers, also producing about 938,000 tons of cotton fibers and 12,000 tons of wool. Availability of rs, such as *Luffa Cylindrica,* straws of wheat and rice, sugarcane bagasse and husks of rice and coffee though reported, are not quantified. The cost of all the plant fibers in Brazil is almost the same, which is about US$ 0.6/kg [29].

STRUCTURE AND PROPERTIES OF NATURAL FIBERS OF BRAZIL

The physical, chemical and mechanical properties of most of the natural fibers have been evaluated by different groups working in the area of natural fiber composites, although the data is not available in a comprehensive/consolidated manner [*See References 27,30,32,34-36* in 35,41]. Most of them have followed the same standard test methods [ASTM/Brazilian/German, etc] followed by others. For example, the chemical analyses of some of these fibers [4,6,7,37,38,40] have been according to TAPPI T19M, TAPPI T13m-54 or TAPPI T222 om-88, ABCPM11/77 or TAPPI T211-om-93, ABTCP M3/69, TAPPI T207-om-93 and TAPPI 212 om-98. (see table 4). However, Luffa Cylindrica fiber showed great variations in composition, as it depends on various factors, such as type of species and soil as well as climatic conditions. The values given represent the averages and are within the ranges reported for other natural fibers.

Various physical properties of these fibers have been determined [3,8,29,32,38-40,43]. Thus, the length (in mm) of microfibrils of sisal, sugar cane bagasse and pineapple are found to be 1-8, 0.8-2.8 and 1.56, respectively, with the diameter or width (in μm) 8-41, 7-10, 25-60 for sisal, curauá and Luffa Cylindrica, respectively.

The apparent density of the fibers was determined as per standard NBR 11936 or other test method and moisture content by thermogravimetry as per ASTM D2654 or other standards. These values (in $mg.m^{-3}$) for sisal, curauá, sugar cane bagasse and Luffa Cylindrica are 1.26, 0.92, 0.45 and 0.82, respectively. Similarly, the crystallinity indices of these fibers were calculated using the equation [37,38]: I_{Cr} = Crystalline Area/Total Area. In the case of sisal and Luffa fibers the standard Buschele-Diller and Zeronian methods weres used as in the case of curauá fiberes (in %). The values for sisal, sugar cane bagasse and Luffa Cylindrica being 72.2, 47 and 59.1% respectively.

Table 4. Chemical Composition of Plant Fibers of Brazil

Fiber	α-cellulose (%)	Hemicellulose (%)	Lignin (%)	Ash (%)	Extracts (%)	Ref.
Luffa-cylindrica	62	20	11.2	0.40	3.1	38,39
Sisal	74-75.2	10-13.9	7.6-7.98	0.87-3.00	6.0	4,37
Curauá	70.7	21.1	11.1	0.79	2.5-2.8#	29
Bagasse (sugar cane)	55.2	16.8	25.3	1.1	0.7-3.5*	14,40
Coir@	53	-	40.77	-		43
Pineapple	83	-	12	1	4	1
Rice straw	51-70 (28-48)		12-16	15-20	9-14*	Ref.27 in 33

From Unpublished work; *- Silica.

The thermal behavior of the fibers has been determined using DTA/TG and DSC techniques, with appropriate heating cycles (for example, in the case of sisal and Luffa Cylindrica fibers at 10°C/min between 293-873K and 223 to 693K respectively) [38].

Figures 3(a-c) shows some of these, indicating the degradation of some of the fiber components (cellulose, lignin, etc.). Endothermic peaks indicate loss of mass due to oxidative degradation of the cellulose and ashes. The higher the cellulose content the higher will be the degradation temperature. FTIR spectra of the fibers show characteristic axial vibrations from hydroxyl groups of cellulose (3430 cm^{-1}, signals from regions of C-H axial vibrations at 2990-2950 cm^{-1} and signals from hemicellulose at 1730cm^{-1} and of C-O at 1440cm^{-1} for piaçava) [3]. DSC curves show regions corresponding to cellulose (210-360°C in the case of sugar cane bagasse) and some lignin fragments for high temperature change and also thermal response due to chemical modification of the fibers. Even Raman spectroscopy is used for some of these fibers [11]. Figure 3d shows this, with almost similar profiles for all the fibers with a very weak and broadband at ~3300 cm^{-1}, indicating stretching of the O-H bond and a strong peak at 2950 cm^{-1} for the C-H stretching. Several peaks of typical cellulose structural unit are shown, with other bands at 1800-400 cm^{-1}, while the peak at 1600 cm^{-1} is attributed to vibrations of structures C=C of aromatics and aliphatics.

On the other hand, the tensile properties of the fibers have been evaluated following appropriate ASTM standards with the appropriate number of fibers tested, gauge length, load for testing, etc. Thus, the ultimate tensile strength (in MPa) and elongation (in %) values reported [3,8,29,32,37-40,43] for sisal, curauá, sugar cane bagasse, Piaçava, coir and pineapple fibers are 324-329 and 2-2.5, 439-495 (modulus of rupture) and 1.3-4.5, 222 and 1.1, 108.5-147.3 and 6.4-21.9 (for GL between 15-150mm.), 95-118, 23.9-51.4 and 180 and 3.2 respectively, while the Young's Modulus (in GPa) for these fibers (except sisal) are 10.5, 27.1, 1.07-4.59, 2.8 and 82, respectively. In the case of curauá fibers subjected to textile processing (carding, mat making), a linear decrease in strength was observed due to mechanical damages caused during such processes [15].

Similarly, structural evaluation of these fibers has been made using optical, scanning and transmission electron microscopy. Figure 4(a-d) shows some of these results, revealing cell like outer lignin rich layer around cellulosic inner fibrils. The effects of modifications of these fibers through oxidation and other treatments have also been studied.

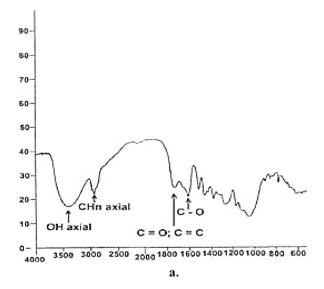

a.

Figure 3. Continued.

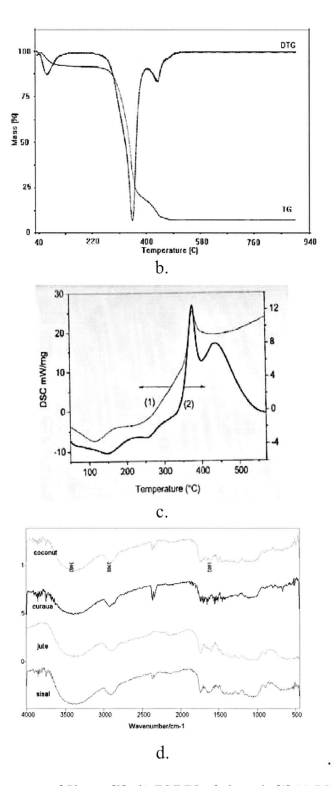

Figure 3. (a) FTIR spectrum of Piaçava [2]; (b) TG/DTG of pineapple [1] (c) DSC of Sugarcane Bagasse [40] and (d) FT-Raman spectra of nNatural fFibers of Brazil [11].

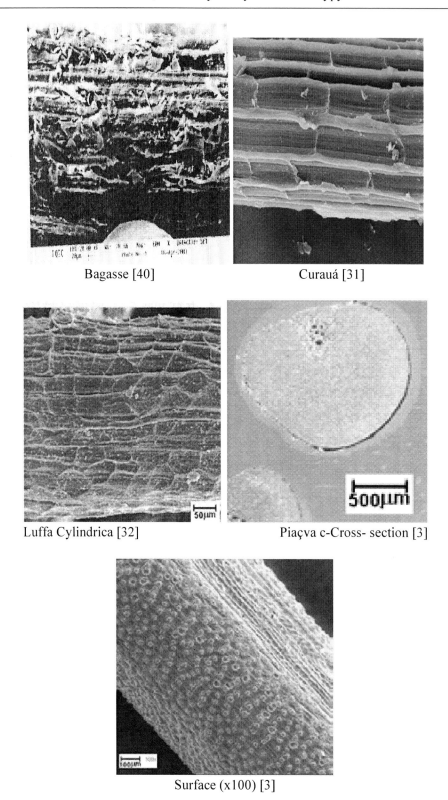

Bagasse [40]   Curauá [31]

Luffa Cylindrica [32]   Piaçva c-Cross- section [3]

Surface (x100) [3]

Figure 4. Morphology of some natural fibers of Brazil.

APPLICATIONS OF NATURAL FIBERS IN BRAZIL

All the natural fibers produced in the country have been used in conventional ways, such as domestic and industrial brooms, brushes, ropes, baskets, and to make fancy articles and carpets. Special uses of some of the fibers include;: wide use of Luffa cylindrica as scouring pads during bathing, in the industry for the manufacture of palm sole, inner soles for shoes, bolters, leather straps, filters for automobiles and other engines, bath gloves, foot rugs, hats, etc. [5]; Piaçava fibers [3], for stuffing in car seats, as ropes and for thermal insulation. It is also imported by Russia, USA and several other countries for use it in equipment for sweeping the snow [3,19]. Coir is used for making a wide variety of floor furnishing materials, as support for seats and seat covers in automobiles, and also in domestic use in mattresses/sofa beds and in gardening, etc [15]. Research and development efforts have been underway to find new applications for coir in view of the small percentage of this fiber being used in the applications mentioned above. It is also used as an alternative source of energy in industrial ovens, as buttons, cigar pipes, cane fists, and various decorative articles, including imitations for pearl and ivory. Similarly, research has been carried out to use them as oil absorbers [44], for stuffing in car seats, ropes and for thermal insulation.

Uses of sugar cane bagasse include raw material for paper manufacturing and cellulose, fertilizer for plantations, fuel for thermo electrical plants, raw material for the production of synthetic plastics not derived from petroleum [9,26]. Curauá fibers are used for hammocks and fishing lines by the indigenous population called "Indians", also as ropes, as nets for sleeping, etc [12]; Blankets/mats of sisal fabric are produced by compression, using an adhesive [31,36].

Currently, most of these fibers are used for automotive, textile industries along with composite technology with a higher demand being predicted for some of these (e.g. about 15,000 tons/year for curauá fibers) [36]. For example, blankets of Luffa-cylindrical have been successfully tried with advantages in the preparation of molded composites by compression or resin transfer (RTM); sisal blankets also facilitate the preparation of such materials, wherein one can evaluate interference in the fiber/matrix adhesion [33].

PERSPECTIVES

Some of the advantages of natural fibers in composite technology are [15,28,34,35]: environment friendly materials in all stages of production, processing and waste, renewability, lower energy inputs in production [4 GJ/tonne compared to 25-130 GJ/tonne for synthetic fibers], use of commonly known processing procedures, promotes employment generation during production and utilization, comparable technical properties in relation to glass fiber reinforced composites, acoustic insulation and absorption of vibration (good damping), natural polymers producing biodegradable composites while with synthetic polymers, on burning produce less CO_2, CO and other toxic gases, less abrasion to machines/tools and poses fewer health risks when inhaled during the processing of fibers and their composites. Some of the limitations of natural fibers include the large areas required for cultivation to produce the large amount of fibers, location based and sample based non-homogeneous properties, time consuming processing, necessity of pressure application while preparing composites, need for surface modification to get good compatibility with matrix materials, absorption of higher amounts of polymers and moisture, fire prone without the use of fire retardant and, last but not least, very moderate properties of the composites. However, it may be said that both of the above can be taken advantage of for increasing their utilization in view of the large areas of positiveon criteria compared to synthetic fiber composites. In addition, developing countries, such as Brazil, would become part of the global composite industry, as both developer and manufacturer, low fuel consumption for transport and the potential for local development of the entire production chain, starting from growth to marketing of products [42]. On the social front, a large number of jobs can be created and maintained in all the fiber producing areas, assuring the sustenance of a large number of families, both in rural and urban areas [27,28]. On the utilization front, these fibers can be used in both textile and non-textile applications, with most of these fibers being adapted to modern processing techniques to develop new items, for apparel, home furnishing, biodegradable non-wovens and geotextiles [28]. They require aggressive marketing of their socio-economic, health and ecological benefits to gain the attention of governments, local authorities, entrepreneurs and even authorities of international standards. It can be concluded that the cultivation and utilization of these fibers are a hidden treasure [28] and are the best options for the agriculture-economical diversification in Brazil in particular and in third world countries in general. To attain this, there is an urgent need for the systematic characterization of all these fibers for their structure and all types of properties, particularly for the fibers of Brazil, which at this juncture is very sparse.

CONCLUSION

Brazil possesses a large wealth of renewable resources, particularly of the plantation type, with large amount of unemployment. Some of the plantations are cultivated in a systematic manner, RandD for their growth and utilization are well supported by the government through many of its agencies leading to socio-economic development of the country. Forward looking, but limited, RandD is going on at various research and academic institutions in the country. However, further steps, which need to be taken, include the following:

- Strengthening of the agribusiness, utilising the best knowledge on markets, the collection and democratization of statistical data and strategic alliances with external capitals in the raw material improvement.
- Need for more investment in Science and Technology without any priority deviation from the agricultural productive sector, particularly for the development of the North and Northeast areas. These are the main producing areas of natural fibers, such as jute, coconut, sisal, curauá and pineapple, and depend on the creation of new opportunities for businesses and technological options.
- While the positive aspects of several NGOs stand out to guide the small producers and the small agribusinesses, discovering markets, offering new technological options and valuing the dimension of natural products, there is lack of appropriate funds. The existence of substantial resources of FNO, for instance, has not matched the effective implantation of agriculture-industrial units, due to the lack of larger

technological support on an appropriate scale, leading to risks for the entrepreneurs [15]. Other factors, such as the lack of regional infrastructure (electric power and well paved highways, low quality labor and technical support), lack of appropriate ports, agricultural inputs, airplanes, cargo ships, units of inspection, among others, pose great limitations for the implementation of plans, and increase the costs and risks in the various stages of the production chain.

ACKNOWLEDGEMENTS

The authors thank the Authors, Editors and Publishers [Wiley-VCH Verlag GmbH and Co KG, Germany] for their kind permission to use figures, tables and data from their papers. Funding by CNPq to Profs. KGS and FW are also acknowledged.

REFERENCES

[1]   Alexandre, M.E.O., Ladchumananandasivam, R., Veríssimo, S.A., Menezes, P.L., Batista, J.H. and Araújo, R.C. in Proc. in *2nd International Conference on Textile Engineering (SINTEX-2004)*, Eds: R.L. Sivam et al, Natal, in CD-ROM, Paper TTN-H-001, Paper TTN-H-004.

[2]   Almeida, A.L.F.S., Barreto, D.W., Calado,V. and Almeida, J.R.M., In Proc. 5th International Symposium on Natural Polymers and Composites – *ISNaPol.* 2004, pp 22-24.

[3]   Aquino, R.C.M.P., Monteiro, S.N. and Almeida, J.R.M., in Proc. ISNaPol 2004, pp 144-147 and 272-274, Sao Pedro, SP, Brasil; *J. Mater. Sci. Letters,* 20, 1017 (2001) and 21, 1495 (2003).

[4]   Amico, S.C., Mochnacz, S., Sydenstricker, T.H.D., Plastico Industrial, 2004, 67 - Março, 72. (*in Portuguese*), in Proc. *ISNA Pol.* 2004, pp 253-256.

[5]   Annunciado, T.R., Masters Degree Dissertation, Federal University of Paraná, Curitiba, 2005.

[6]   Boynard, C.A. and d'Almedia, J.R.M., Polym.Plast.Technol. and Engg, 39, 489 (2000); J. Appl. Polym. Sci., 87, 1927 (2003); *J. Mater. Sci. Lett.,* 18, 1549 (1999).

[7]   Caraschi,J.C. and Leao, A.L, Mol. Cryst. and Liq. Cryst., 353,449 (2000); in Proc.Wood -Plastic Composites, 1996, Madison, WI, 251; Leao, A.L Tan, I.H. and Caraschi, J.C, Proc. International Conference on Advanced Composites (ICAC), Hurghada, Egypt, 15-18 December 1998, 557.

[8]   Carvalho, L.H., Ladschmananandanansivam, R., Alexandre, M.E.D. and Cavalcanti,W.S., In *Proc. ISNaPol.* 2004, 176-178.

[9]   Cavani, C.S., Sanchez, E.M.S., Compósito Poliéster Insaturado-Bagaço de Cana-de-açúcar: Melhoria da Adesão matriz/fibra e Envelhecimento Acelerado, IX Encontro de Iniciação Científica e II Mostra de TCC, 2004, Campinas, SP, Brasil.

[10] Fabiana, G.B.; http://www.biodiversidadedaamazonia.com.br/curaua.htm.

[11] Ferreira,L.C., Trindade,W.G., Frollini, E and Y.Kawano, *ISNaPol.* 2004, pp 269-271.

[12] Filho, P.A. and Bahr, O., *Appl. Energy,* 77, 51 (2004)

[13] Giacomini, N.P., Leao, A.L and Neis, A.M., *ISNaPol.* 2000, pp. 386-392.

[14] Hoareau, W., Trindade, W.G., Siegmund, B., Castelan, A.R, Frollini, E., *Polym. Degrad. and Stabil.,* 86, 728 (2004).

[15] Homma, A. K. O., http://www.captu.ebmbrapa.br/pup_outros/rev.20011213_08pdf.

[16] http://www.ibge.gov.br/home/estatistica/economia/pam/tabela1pam_2001.shtm

[17] http://www.revistaagroamazonia.com.br/13-fibras.htm

[18] http://personales.ciudad.com.ar/ecoespon/portugues/principal.html

[19] http://www.ceplac.gov.br/radar/piacava.htm

[20] http://www.conab.gov.br/download/cas/semanais/Semana07a11022005/Juta%20-%200 7a11-02-05.pdf

[21] http://www.cnpa.embrapa.br/sisal/sisalcolheita.html

[22] http://globoruraltv.globo.com/cgi-bin/globorural/montar_texto.pl? controle =9042

[23] http://www.conab.gov.br/download/cas/semanais/Semana-23072004/Cjtjuta-23-Julho 04.pdf

[24] http://www.pt.org.br/assessor/cartlula.htm

[25] http://www.cpatu.embrapa.br/online/Circ.tec.27.pdf

[26] http://www.unica.com.br/pages/cana_origem.asp, Cana de açúcar, produtos e sub-produtos, União da Agroindústria Canavieira de São Paulo.

[27] http://www.rgt.matrix.com.br/jornaljr/agricola/agricola33.html, *Tronco da bananeira é matéria-prima para artesãs que transformam a palha em geração de renda*, Regional Agricola on Line, Edição n° 22, Abril, 2003.

[28] Kozlowski, R. Rawluk, M and Barriga, J., In *Proc. SINTEX* 2004 (see Ref.1 above for details).

[29] Leao, A.L. Rowell, R and Tavares, N, in 'Science and Technology of Polymer and Advanced Materials', [Eds.N.Prasad et al], Plenum Press, New York, 755-761, (1998).

[30] Martins, M.A., Joekes, I., Ferreira, F.C., Job, A.E. and Mattoso, L.H.C., In *Proc. ISNaPol.* 2004, pp 13-15.

[31] Proc. 2nd International Symposium on Natural Polymers and Composites – In *Proc. ISNaPol.* 1998, Atibaia, SP, Brasil.

[32] Razera,I.A.T., Trindade, W.G., Leao, A.L. and Frollini, E., In proc. *ISNaPol.* 2002, pp 507-514.

[33] Satyanarayana, K.G., "Agrobased s Of Brazil And Their Composites - An Overview", in Proceedings FAO/ESCOREA, 312-324 (2005).

[34] Satyanarayana, K.G., Wypych F. and Ramos, L.P., in *"Biotechnology and Energy Management"* (Eds. Ghosh et al), Vol.2, 2004, Allied Publishers, pp 566-606.

[35] Satyanarayana, K.G., Wypych, F., Ramos,L.P., Amico, S.C. and Sydenstricker, T. H.D., In *Proc. ISNaPol.* 2004, Sao Pedro, SP, Brasil, Paper N°.90.

[36] Satyanaryana, K.G., Wypych, F., Guimarães, J. L., Amico, S.C., Sydenstricker, T.H.D., and Ramos, L.P., Metals, *Materials and Processes,* 17 (3-4), 183-194, 2005.

[37] Sydenstricker, T.H.D., Mochnacz, S., Amico, S.C., *Polymer Testing,* 22, 375 (2003).

[38] Tanobe, V., Amico, S.C., Mazzaro, I., Sydenstricker, T.H.D., In Proc. 58° Congresso Anual da Associação Brasileira de Metalurgia e Materiais - ABM, Rio de Janeiro - RJ 2003. (*in Portuguese*).

[39] Tanobe, V., Sydenstricker, T.H.D., Amico, S.C., Gabriel, S., In Proc. XV Congresso Brasileiro de Engenharia Química/COBEQ, Curitiba - PR, 2004. (*in Portuguese*).

[40] Trindade, W.G., Hoareau, W., Razera, I.A.T., Ruggeiro, R, Frollini, E and Castelan, A., Macromol. Mater. and Engg., 289,728 (2004); In *Proc. ISNaPol.* 2004, pp 249-252.

[41] Toro Ind. e Com. Ltd., *Natural s,* International Publication, 1994.

[42] Wambua, P. Ivens, J. And Verpoest, I., *Compos. Sci.and Techn.,* 63,1259 (2003).

[43] Wieldman, G.A., Costa, C.Z. and Nahuz, M.A., In *Proc. ISNaPol.* 2000, pp. 488; In Proc. ISNaPol 2002, pp 488-492.

[44] Wiggers, D., Annunciado, T.R., Amico, S.C., and Sydenstricer T.H.D., In Proc. IV Encontro dos Programas de Recursos Humanos em Petróleo e Gás Natural do Paraná - *IVRAA,* Curitiba - PR 2004 (*in Portuguese*).

In: Textiles for Sustainable Development ISBN: 978-1-60021-559-9
Editors: R. Anandjiwala, L. Hunter et al., pp. 39-52 © 2007 Nova Science Publishers, Inc.

Chapter 4

NEWEST ACHIEVEMENTS IN CURAUA PROCESSING AND APPLICATIONS

A. Leão[1], M. Sartor[1], R. Kozłowski[2] and S. Manyś[2]

[1] UNESP Campus de Botucatu, Brazil and UNIMONTE - Santos, Brazil
[2] The Institute of Natural Fibers, Poznań, Poland

Keywords: Curaua, fiber composition, fiber properties, fiber processing, wrap spinning, ring spinning.

1. INTRODUCTION – CURAUA A NEWCOMER IN TEXTILES

In the textile world *curaua* is a new emerging fiber – yet not in Brazil – where it was used as a very strong fiber for hammocks and fishing nets.[1]. To widen the use of *curaua* and to find new applications for this natural cellulosic fiber in textiles we have to consider all parameters important in spinning and in yarn processing. The Ddata in table 1 show the similarities and differences between curaua and well-known vegetable fibers, such as flax, hemp, ramie, jute, sisal and abaca. It is apparent that, curaua is similar to all bast and leavef fibers in terms of length, strength and elongation but was generally coarser (similar to jute and sisal), yet stronger than the last two fibers.

The plant, CURAUA - *Ananas erectifolius* - is a hydrophylous species from the Amazon region. Its leaves are hard, erect and have flat surfaces. The leaves are about one meter long, or more, and 4 cm wide. The plant requires 2,000 mm or more of annual precipitation, preferring silil-humus soils, but also grows in clay-sillic soils. It is commonly used by the indigenous people as a favorite plant fiber for hammocks and fishing lines. Eight months old leaves can reach up 1.5m in length, and 50-60 leaves per year. The dry fiber content in leaves is about 5-8%. The fiber is commonly extracted by a primitive process called "forca" (hanger), washed and beaten with a circular rod and left in water in order to mercerize for 36 hours. They are again washed and allowed to dry. Natural Curaua fiber (wet) shows an average elongation of 4.5%, MOE (Modulus of Elasticity) of 10.5 GPa, and MOR (Modulus of Rupture) 439 MPa. Dry fiber (OD – oven dry) values are, respectively, 3.2%, 27.1 GPa, and 117 MPa. Cut and defibered the values are, respectively, 3.7%, 9.7 GPa, and 428 MPa.

Cut, defibered and dried (OD), the values are respectively 4.3%, 11.8 GPa, and 502 MPa. Curaua is very competitive among the traditional fibers, always ranking in the top three for economical analysis and top four for stiffness (TORO, 1994). It has been reported in a study using several agricultural fibers, such as jute, kenaf, abaca, sisal and henequen, that bast fibers composites have superior properties to leaf fiber composites.

The main advantages of composite materials based on natural fibers are:

- Replacement of man-made fibers (glass and asbestos). The final disposal of post-consumer products, based on glass fiber, faces environmental restrictions in many countries, and some even have forbidden its utilization, as for asbestos;
- Reinforcement of conventional thermoplastics and thermosetting resins by the natural fibers or polymers can reduce the demand for petroleum based products;
- Substitution of solid wood by plastics reinforced with wood or other natural polymers can help to reduce the deforestation in many areas, as well offering mechanical advantages over the traditional wooden products;
- Development of profiles in civil constructions which can be applied in niches, such as the replacement of aluminum in coastal cities;
- Enhancement of the fiber quality through better hybrids or varieties based on genetic knowledge directed towards the end use application, such as fiber percentage, mechanical strength, etc...;
- Increasing the agricultural productivity as well the quality of the fibers through better extraction processes;
- Development of new machines to process and industrialize the natural fibers in the field (reduced size, high quality and safety);
- Providing rural populations in economically deprived areas a new source of income and raw-materials;
- Low cost compared to man made fibers – the price per weight is much lower compared to its counterparts;
- Phytomass is totally utilized, although for many crop fibers a very low percentage are represented by the fiber itself, and the rest represents a new source of raw materials or feedstock for natural chemicals;
- Environmental friendly in terms of its production, harvesting, processing and recycling and final disposal;
- Renewability – by definition, a natural resource is renewable if its cycle can be completed in a period comparable to the human cycle
- Do not easily break when processed, which contracts with its counterparts, such as glass fiber, opening up possibilities of more intense processing;
- Release harmless residues when incinerated for energy recovery or just for final disposal, not presenting sulphur or heavy metals;
- Absorbs renewable carbon (green carbon), contributing to reduced climate changes;
- Automotive parts made from natural fibers are resistant against fractures, providing a high standard of passive safety in case of collision or fire;
- Non-abrasive when processed on conventional machinery;
- Low density/High specific modulus, representing one of the highest modulius, even higher than steel;

- High resistance, low elongation, desired for some applications;
- Low energy consumption when processed, due to its low temperature requirements and flexibility;
- Possible applications of higher levels of reinforcement (up to 90%) with new technologies, such as extrusion and injection molding;
- Environmental pressures for the greater utilization of Natural Renewable Resources, aiming to reduce the applications of man-made materials;
- Better efficiency in converting raw-materials into products when compared to other man-made fibers, through energy balance;
- Products are competitive based on Life Cycle Analysis (ISO 14.000);
- National strategy to create rural jobs in economically deprived areas;
- Good mechanical property relations: Weight versus Resistance, helping to reduce the fuel consumption in the automotive industry;
- Composites/*Ecomenes* – The concept of having a product that is ecological, but as well as economically competitive. Oikos (environment) – menes (way), a mixing of ecological and economics;
- Recyclability, since the composites based on natural fibers can be recycled many times without significant loss of mechanical properties;
- Greenhouse Effect is reduced by the utilization of natural fiber based products, since production is based on the cycle of green cCarbon, according to the Kyoto protocol; and
- Marketing – The market concept must be reviewed since the population considers lignocelullosics based composites as a piece of low technology, when in fact it is the opposite, since the products, in many cases, are produced on machinery developed to work with man-made products, such as polypropylene fibers.

The chemical constitution of curaua and alike fibers shows that:

- cellulose content in curaua is higher than in flax , hemp, jute, sisal and abaca- yet lower than in ramie and cotton;
- hemicellulose content is in curaua is twice as high as in jute and sisal, three times higher than in ramie and cotton, ca 25% higher than in flax and hemp; and
- lignin content is as high as in sisal and jute. It is five times that of flax, three times that of hemp and ten times that of ramie (figures 1-3).

Cellulose Content of Vegetable Textile Fibers

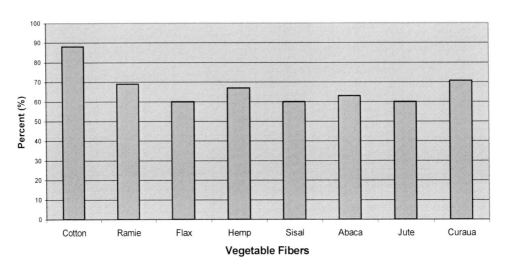

Figure 1. Cellulose Content of Vegetable Textile Fibers.

Hemicellulose Content of Vegetable Textile Fibers

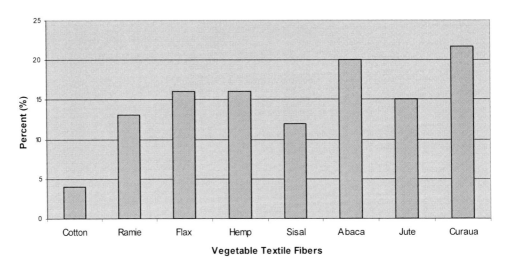

Figure 2. Hemicellulose Content of Vegetable Textile Fibers.

Lignin Content of Vegetable Textile Fibers

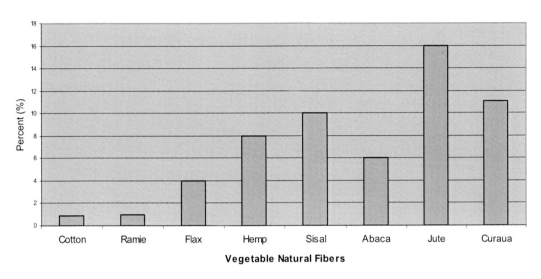

Figure 3. LIgnin Content of Vegetable Textile Fibers.

Table 1. Physical properties – decisive in spinning – of curaua and other cellulosic fibers

FIBER	LENGTH	FINENESS	BREAKING STRENGTH	ELONGATION
	(mm)	(TEX)	(cN / TEX)	(%)
CURAUA: • RAW FIBER Refined in flax system:	1500	28	48 – 51	1.8
• Hackled long fiber	1500	5.8	43.1	1.7 – 2.0
• Noils	612	4.8	40.2	1.7 – 2.0
FLAX	200 – 1400	1.5 – 2.7	40 – 80	2.5 – 3.0
HEMP	1000 – 3000	2.2 – 4.4	47	2.2
RAMIE	100 – 1800	0.6 – 0.8	59	3.7
JUTE	1500 – 3700	22 – 44	30	1.7 – 1.9
SISAL	600 – 1500	33 – 44	36 – 43	3.6 – 5.1
COTTON	30 - 45	0.1 – 0.3	26 - 43	8.0 – 10.0

 Similar

Different.

2. PROCESSING ROUTES TO BE CHOSEN

Fiber Refining

Raw, long and thick curaua fiber can not be spun without adjustment to existing textile machinery. Instead of long, energy-consuming breaking, cleaning and, refining lines, such as Laroche and, Bahmer, we have chosen new equipment, RCZ-120-3 developed by Rieter-Elitex, a Swiss/Czech Rep. textile machinery manufacturers.s makers.

The chosen equipment makes it possible to obtain the specific properties required for different spinning systems – fiber length, while the fiber is refined and dust removed. The machine can be used individually or can form an integrated line. It is equipped with metal particle detector, acoustic and luminous signaling, including the covering with vacuum regime in order to comply with safety and hygienic requirements. The machine is smart, small and low-energy consuming.

In our co-operation with Rieter-Elitex we have found it especially suitable for flax/hemp fibers and those results were decisive for our choice of RCZ-120-3 for curaua shortening/cleaning and refining. [2-4]

Spinning

    A. Traditional Spinning Systems:
    1. Long Staple Flax/Hemp System (figure 5)

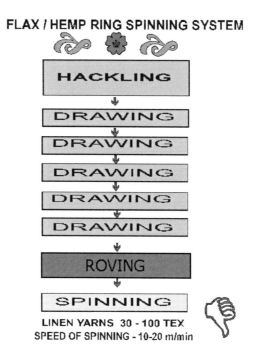

Figure 5.

Data presented in table 1 suggest that curaua might be processed by traditional long-staple machinery, built for fibers similar to curaua in length, strength and elongation. High linear density and stiffness represent the boundaries. Yet we do also realize this system is slowly being phased out because it consists of many individual operations which are not automated and represents the lowest known speeds of wet and dry spinning frames. It should be stated that although it is old and slow it provides excellent yarns not replaced until now by any other technique. But high costs lower the competitiveness of these yarns and products made from them.

2. Universal Long/Short Staple Ring Spinning (figure 6)

Accordingly to our experiences both the universal ring-spinning systems are future alternative routes for fibers such as flax/hemp. These fibers must be adapted before spinning. Vegetable fibers are processed on these systems in blends with wool, cotton and synthetic fibers. With the experiences developed at INF, we have chosen initially to use for curaua the long staple spinning route. It was also decided to prepare the rest of the fiber for future short staple spinning. [5-15]

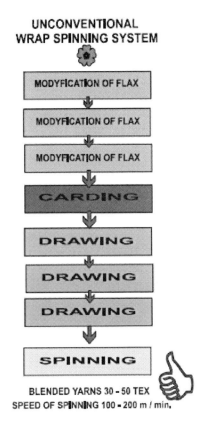

Figure 6.

In these two spinning techniques the delivery speed of the yarn is still borderline. It is higher than in the traditional flax/hemp system but considerably lower than for the unconventional spinning technologies.

B. Unconventional Spinning Systems.

From the unconventional spinning systems:

- OE-ROTOR
- AIR JET
- FRICTION
- WRAP TECHNIQUE (figure 7),

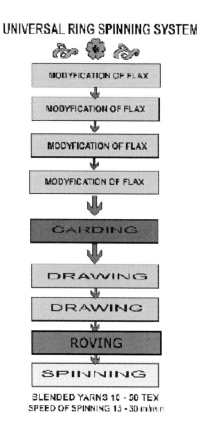

Figure 7.

The wrap-spinning technique was selected mainly because of the high stiffness of curaua fiber. In wrap spinning, parallel fibers are wrapped by a soft filament to form the yarn. That is why this technique is ideal for fibers which are stiff and difficult to twist. To some extent this is also true for flax and hemp [5,6,and 10]. The abovementioned feature, unique to the wrap-spinning process, could be for curaua an opportunity in modern, unconventional spinning.

It must be stated that in this first step in processing of curaua in textiles, only mechanical treatments have been studied, chemical/enzymatic or other processes being left for future investigations. Mechanical processing and the use of commercially produced textile machinery are considered easier to introduce in practice than chemical/enzymatic processes. This was considered essential during these very early stages of the new fiber, such as like curaua, in the textile world.

3. METHODS USED

The methods used in the processing of the curaua fiber are presented in figure 8.

These processing conditions were used for raw fiber traditionally produced in Brazil using the "Aforca" process.

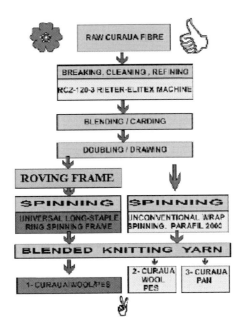

Figure 8. The I Step Technological Chart developed by INF and Rieter-Elitex for trials of Curaua textile processing.

4. RESULTS AND DISCUSSION

Curaua is a surprising fiber.

1. A Light-Microscope Picture of raw curaua fiber shows that though different in dimensions it is like "Islands in the Sea" Shingosen fiber.

So- Nihil Novi Sub Jove (figure 9).

2. The main textile properties of Curaua after RCZ-120-3 breaking/cleaning and refining were close to the requirements of the long staple universal ring spinning system, excluding the linear density of the fibers (figure 10). Yet RCZ-120-3 refined curaua fibers were ready to split further in the following stages of processing, namely carding/doubling/drawing

3. The Main Parameters of New Knitting Yarns With Curaua.

The main parameters of knitting curaua yarns produced by different spinning systems from two different blends of curaua and natural/wool/ as well as synthetic fiber (polyester and polyacrylic) are presented in figure11. In figure12 the parameters of these new yarns obtained in the first experiments when spinning curaua on commercial textile spinning systems, are compared with similar blended yarns made of linen, hemp and pineapple leafve fibers.

4. Application of curaua blended yarns in knitted apparel.

The new blended curaua yarns have been used in knitted apparel: blouses, dresses, skirts shown in Picture 1.

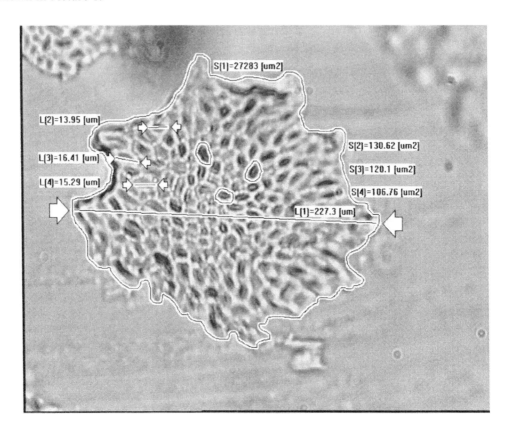

SINGLE CURAUA RAW FIBRE:
(TECHNICAL FIBRE)

DIAMETER L(1)   – 227.3 µm.
SURFACE AREA S(1) - 27283µm²

ELEMENTARY FIBRES:

DIAMETER:
L(2) – 13.95 µm.
L(3) - 16.41 µm.
L(4) - 15.29 µm

SURFACE AREA:
S(2) - 130.62 µm²
S(3) - 120.1 µm²
S(4) - 106.76 µm²

Figure 9. Light microscope picture of Curaua fiber.

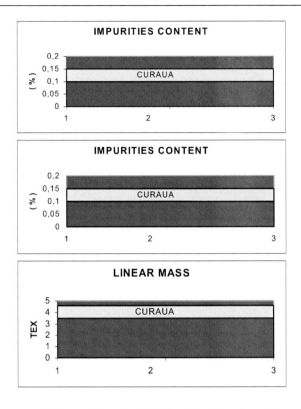

Figure 10. Main parameters of Curaua fiber after RCZ120-3 refining for Universal Ring Spinning.

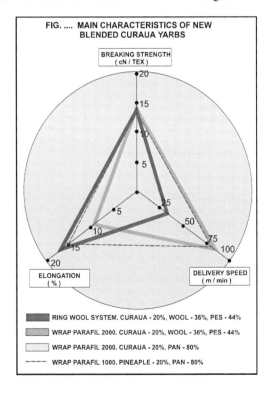

Figure 11. Main characteristics of new blended Curaua yarns.

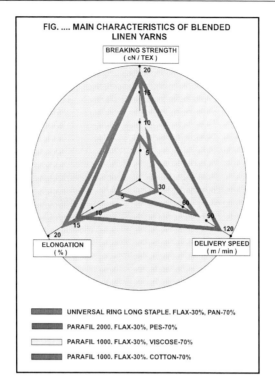

Figure 12. Main characteristics of blended linen yarns.

5. CONCLUSION

From investigations of curaua fiber conducted at UNESP and the Institute of Natural Fibers and first technological trials in curaua textile processing and applications conducted by INF in co-operation with the world recognized textile machinery makers, Rieter-Elitex, the following conclusions were drawn:

1. According to its light-microscopy picture, curaua resembles a natural "Islands in Sea" fiber, which though different in dimensions, is very much alike to Shingosen fibers of that type;
2. The main textile parameters of curaua, such as length, impurities content and linear density, can be adjusted by the RCZ-120-3 Rieter-Elitex breaking/cleaning/refining machine in line with universal ring or unconventional spinning systems;
3. Refined by the RCZ-120-3, curaua fiber is similar to flax/hemp modified fibers prepared to be spun oin other than traditional flax/hemp spinning machinery. Linear density of refined curaua remains relatively high but the fibers are ready to be split during further processes of doubling and drawing. It is also stiffer, which indicates the future need for treatments, such as enzymatic/plasma/corona/chemical treatments;
4. Refined by the RCZ-120-3, curaua fiber is a suitable component for blends with other natural fibers and synthetic fibers. Processes of blending, doubling and drawing can be conducted using conventional commercial machines;

5. Parameters of blended curaua yarns, obtained from two different blends and by two different spinning systems, show that these yarns have a high tenacity (14,6-12,8 cN/tex) and elongation (16,7%-7,8%), which are important in subsequent processing stages and result in positive product features;

6. The present results should be followed by further research to develop a wide array of different curaua yarns obtained by conventional, universal and unconventional spinning systems. Endless blending possibilities and different spinning techniques can offer a rich assortment of yarns with this New In Textile World – Curaua Fiber;

7. According to initial experiments at INF, the new curaua blend yarns can be used in the apparel sector. They are especially suitable for knitting. In knitted apparel, the refined curaua fiber, blended with other fibers, curaua has lost its stiffness, yet kept the comfort properties of natural cellulosic fiber.

6. REFERENCES

[1] Leão, A. and Tan, I. 1999. Tropical Natural Fibers. Presented at FAO Consultation on Fibers. Nov.15-16, 1999, *Poznań,* Poland.

[2] Kozłowski, R. and Manyś, S. 1997. Coexistence and Competition of Natural and Man Made Fibers. Proceed. of the 78th World Conference of the Textile Institute. May 25-26 1997, Thessaloniki, Greece.

[3] Kozłowski, R. and Manys, S. 1999. Green Fibers. Proceed. of the 79th World Conference of the Textile Institute. Feb. 10-13 1999, Chennai, India.

[4] Kozłowski, R.; Manyś S.; Kozłowska, J.; Helwig, M. 1998. Linen Knitted Apparels for All-Year Use. *Proceed. of Intern. Congress of IFKT.* Oct. 4-6 1998, Busto Arzizio, Italy.

[5] Weigelt, H. 1992. Claas Erntetechnik fur Nachwachsende Rohstoffe. *Proceed. of the Intern. Seminar.* July 9,1992, Harsewinke, Germany.

[6] Manyś, S., and Mazur E. 1996. Progress in Parafill, Linen Yarns and Products made thereof. Proceed. of 4th European Regional Workshop on Flax. Sept.25-29, 1996, Rouen, France.

[7] Kozłowski, R. and Manys S. 1995. The New Flax and Pineapple Leaves, Fibers, Cashmere and Angora in Short Spinning System. *Proceed. of Texan.* '95. Nov.19-22, 1995, Coinbatore, India.

[8] Kozłowski, R. and Manyś, S. 1998. Development in Flax/Hemp Processes for Improved Comfort. *Proceed. of world Textile Congress on Natural and Natural Polymers Fibers.* July 10-11, 1998. Huddersfield, England.

[9] Kozłowski, R. and Manyś, S. 1998. Cleaner Production of Textiles. *Proceed. of ERCP'98.* Oct.28-30, 1998, Lisboa, Portugal.

[10] Manyś, S.; Mazur, E.; Zimniewska M. 1998. World's Records in Bast Fibers Spinning and Knitting. May 25-27, 1998, *Liberec,* Czech Republic.

[11] Kozłowski, R. and Manys S. 1996. The Properties of Liquid Ammonia Treated Linen Fabric. *Proceed. of AATCC Intern. Symposium.* Sept. 25-29, 1996, Orlando, USA.

[12] Kozłowski, R. and Manys, S. 1999. Bast Fibers. Proceed. of the 5th Asian Textile Conference. Sept. 30-Oct.02, 1999, Kyoto, Japan.

[13] Kozłowski, R. and Manyś, S. 1995. New Flax and Pineapple Leaves Fibers Technology and End-Uses. *Proceed. ATC.* Sept. 19-21, 1995, Hong Kong.

[14] Manys, S; Mazur, E.; Zimniewska, M. 1998. Linen for Ill/Aged People – Linen Knitted Antibedsore Bedding. Proceed. of the 1st Nordic Conference on Flax and Hemp Processing. Aug. 10-12,1998, Tampere, Finland.

[15] Kozłowski, R. 1996. Look at Flax in 21st Century. Proceed. of 4th European Workshop on Flax. Sept. 25-29,1996, Rouen, France.

In: Textiles for Sustainable Development
Editors: R. Anandjiwala, L. Hunter et al., pp. 53-61

ISBN: 978-1-60021-559-9
© 2007 Nova Science Publishers, Inc.

Chapter 5

FIBER QUALITY OF HEMP GROWN ON THE SWEDISH ISLAND GOTLAND

Gunilla Östbom[1] and Bengt Svennerstedt[2]

1 Department of Domestic Science, Uppsala University, Trädgårdsgatan 14,
SE-753 09 Uppsala, Sweden. gunilla.ostbom@ihv.uu.se
2 Biofiber Technology Research Group, Department of Agricultural Biosystems and
Technology, Swedish University of Agricultural Sciences, P.O. Box 86,
SE-230 53 Alnarp, Sweden. bengt.svennerstedt@jbt.slu.se

ABSTRACT

Hemp, Cannabis sativa L, has been grown in Sweden for many years. During the last 40 years it has been prohibited to cultivate hemp but now it is possible for Swedish farmers to grow it again. Before the ban, Gotland, a limestone island in the centre of the Baltic Sea, was the last major growing area in Sweden. At that time the main crop was used for the production of rope. During later years, hemp has received increased interest as a sustainable crop and for a multitude of possible uses. Fabric made of hemp fibers for clothing coming from China can now be seen, but is the quality of hemp cultivated on Gotland also good enough for clothing textiles? This paper focuses on the strength and fineness of hemp fibers from five different varieties, grown on Gotland, at different locations and handled differently during the process from seed to fiber. The varieties were Beniko, Futura 75, Fedora 17, Felina 34 and USO 31. These varieties are generally available on the market and not especially for the soil and climate on Gotland. Therefore it is important to investigate the quality of the fibers.

Keywords: Textile, hemp fiber, strength, fineness.

INTRODUCTION

Hemp has been grown in Sweden at least since the Middle Ages, especially in the counties of Uppland and Gotland. During the 1700s and 1800s hemp growing was comprehensive since the Swedish navy needed strong raw material for ropes and other products. Hemp was also grown as a raw material for industry and handicrafts during the 1800s.

During the Second World War hemp cultivation again expanded very rapidly. In 1942 about 2000 ha were cultivated of which, 1000 ha on the Baltic island of Gotland and the rest on the Swedish main land. The soil of Gotland has a high content of calcium, which is favourable for hemp growth and fiber development. The humus-rich soils of the drained Gotland swamps also gave good hemp yields. At that time, two hemp processing industries were in operation in the country. Hemp fiber production remained relatively constant during the period 1940-1960. The hemp varieties cultivated in Sweden during this period, were Mona from Svalöv, Sweden, Schurig from Germany and Tiborszallas from Hungary. During the 1960s, however, competition from synthetic fibers became too strong and the last hemp processing industry in Sweden, situated on Gotland, was closed in 1965 (Nyström, 1995).

Because of the increasing drug problems during the 1960s a ban on all commercial hemp production, including cultivation and processing, was imposed in Sweden in 1968. In 1995 Sweden entered the European Union and at that time the Swedish ban on hemp production was changed. Experimental hemp cultivation under the supervision of scientific institutions was allowed under licence from the Swedish pharmaceutical authorities. After a period of discussion, commercial cultivation of industrial hemp was again allowed in Sweden in 2003. This year (2005) around 320 ha are being cultivated in Sweden, of which some 64 ha are on the island Gotland.

The parameters which mostly influence the spinning of textile fibers are strength, diameter, friction and length. These four factors, shown in fFigure 1, interact and if one factor is lacking, one or more of the others have to compensate. To be suitable for clothing and not only for coarser textiles, the fiber has to be finer than about 40 µm and down to about 10 µm in diameter. It also has to have adequate strength. There is no doubt that the friction and the length of hemp fibers, grown almost everywhere, are adequate to create a textile product. Of greater interest is the strength of hemp fiber, since the stronger the fiber, the finer it can be and the softer the fabric can be made. Fabrics made for hemp fibers for clothing, especially from China, can now be seen on the textile market but the question is whether the quality of hemp cultivated on the Swedish island Gotland is also good enough for clothing textiles?

OBJECTIVES

The aim of this study was to investigate whether fibers from industrial hemp grown on the Swedish island Gotland has sufficient quality to be used for textile products. Fiber strength and width/diameter, as two of the most important textile fiber quality factors, were therefore investigated.

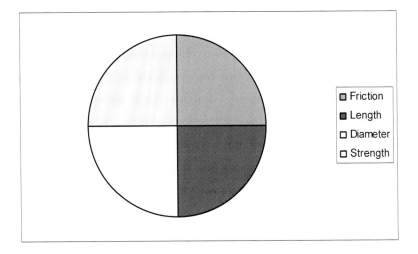

Figure 1. Fiber parameters influencing spinning.

MATERIAL AND METHODS

Retted Hemp

Hemp samples were randomly collected from several experimental plots on the island Gotland during the period 2003-2004. The following varieties were grown at the experimental plots: Beniko, Futura 75, Fedora 17 and Felina 34. The varieties were not specifically grown for textile use. After harvesting, the hemp fiber samples were treated in the traditional way by water retting (W) and dew retting (D). The water retted samples were kept in a lake for 8 days. The water temperature varied between 23-25°C. Dew retting was carried out on hemp samples in the field for 16 days. After drying, the samples were stored and tested.

Unretted Hemp

During late summer of 2004, hemp samples were collected from the research station Stenstugu on the island Gotland. Field trials with three varieties were made; the varieties Felina 34, Fedora 17 and USO 31 at a seeding rate of 30kg/ha (Ss), and one variety, Futura 75, in various seeding rates (Ss 15-25-30-35). All the fields were fertilized with 150 kg N/ha according to recommendations.

The second experimental plot was situated at the Rural Development School Lövsta and was cultivated with the variety Futura 75, at a seeding rate 25kg/ha. The plot was fertilized with manure (Lo). The third experimental plot was at a farmers field on the island Gotland. It was cultivated with Futura 75 and fertilized with 150 kg N/ha (uR) and with sewage sludge (mR). In both cases, the seeding rate was 25 kg/ha. The hemp samples were all dried, broken and combed before fiber strength and fineness testing.

Testing Methods

The fiber strength measurements were made on a Pressley fiber bundle tester at the Bio Technology Research Group, Swedish University of Agricultural Sciences, Alnarp, Sweden. Small bundles of combed fiber bundle samples were loaded until breaking and then weighed. The fiber strength is obtained by dividing the breaking load by the weight of the fiber bundle. The strength values are expressed in cN/tex. Each strength value is based on about ten tests. The fiber diameter (width) measurements were performed with the Fiber shape testing method at the Faserinstitut Bremen e.V., Germany. The diameter values are expressed in μm.

Number Index

A number index was calculated by dividing the mean value of fiber strength by the mean value of fiber diameter width.

RESULTS

Fiber Strength Measurements

Strength of Retted Hemp

Table 1. Fiber strength of hemp in samples taken from retted hemp stalks

No.	Variety and treatment	Mean (cN/tex)	Sd (cN/tex)	Lot	Mean (cN/tex)	Sd (cN/tex)
R1	Beniko water retted	39,3	6,5			
R2	Beniko water retted	43,4	10,1	W	43,1	9,1
R3	Beniko water retted	41,0	10,4			
R4	Futura 75 water retted	48,5	5,6			
R5	Futura 75 dew retted	44,3	9,8			
R6	Fedora 17 dew retted	40,0	9,5	D	40,6	8,5
R7	Felina 34 dew retted	38,4	7,1			
R8	Beniko dew retted	39,4	6,8			

W is the mean of the four water retted samples 1-4. D is the mean of the four dew retted samples, no 5-8. There was a small difference of about 6 % in strength between W and D. Futura 75 showed the highest value among all the samples, both among the water retted; 48,5 cN/tex and among the dew retted; 44.3 cN/tex samples.

Strength of Unretted Hemp

Table 2. Fiber strength of hemp samples taken from unretted, green hemp stalks

No.	Variety and treatment	Mean (cN/tex)	Sd (cN/tex)	Lot	Mean (cN/tex)	Sd (cN/tex)
G1	Felina 34	55,4	11,2			
G2	Fedora 17	53,7	6,5	Ss	54,1	8,1
G3	USO 31	53,2	6,2			
G4	Futura75,15kg/ha	43,9	5,1	Ss 15	43,9	5,1
G5	Futura75, 25kg/ha	50,7	8,4	Ss 25	50,7	8,4
G 6	Futura75, 30kg/ha	52,6	8,7	Ss 30	52,6	8,7
G 7	Futura75, 35kg/ha	50,3	5,0	Ss 35	50,3	5,0
G 8	Futura75, Lövsta I	50,3	2,8			
G 9	Futura75, Lövsta II	49,3	6,8	Lo	49,8	5,1
G10 t	Futura75, without sludge	49,2	12,0			
G10 m	Futura75, without sludge	57,0	19,8	uR	51,6	15,7
G10 b	Futura75, without sludge	48,0	15,6			
G11 t	Futura75, with sludge	47,5	8,5			
G11 m	Futura75, with sludge	53,6	13,2	mR	49,1	9,9
G11 b	Futura75, with sludge	46,2	5,4			

Ss is the mean value of samples G1-3. Lo is the mean of samples G8 and G9. The letters t, m, b after numbers G10 and G11 indicate from which part of the stalk the fibers were taken. t- top, m-middle and b-base. uR is the mean of the whole stalks from samples G10, hemp fertilized in a common way (without sludge). mR is the mean value of the whole stalk sample of no G11, hemp fertilized with sludge.

Strength of Retted and Unretted Hemp

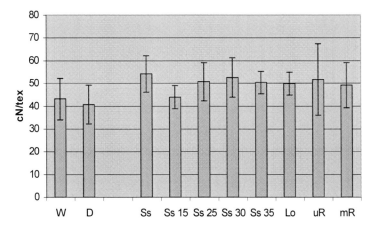

Figure 2. Mean strength values of fibers from both retted and unretted green hemp.

Figure 2 shows fiber values from tTables 1 and 2. The strength of the retted hemp fibers was around 41 cN/tex and that of green hemp fibers was around 51 cN/tex. The retted hemp being about 20 % weaker than green hemp.

Fiber Diameter Width Measurements

Diameter of Retted Hemp

Table 3. Median value of fiber diameter in retted hemp expressed in μm, with 95 % confidence level

No	Variety and treatment	Median (μm)	conf. lev./ med. +	conf. lev. / med. –	Lot	Median range (μm)
R1	Beniko water retted	28,4	0,98	0,91		
R2	Beniko water retted	26,6	0,94	0,91	W	26,6 -28,7
R3	Beniko water retted	28,7	1,37	0,9		
R4	Futura 75 water retted	26,6	1,35	0,94		
R5	Futura 75 dew retted	23,4	0,86	0,76		
R6	Fedora 17 dew retted	25,2	0,95	1,06	D	22,2 -25,9
R7	Felina 34 dew retted	22,2	0,94	0,83		
R8	Beniko dew retted	25,9	0,8	0,72		

W represents the whole group of water retted hemp and D the whole group of the dew retted stalks. Water retted had fibers had a lower fineness than the dew retted fibers. The median ranges did not overlap.

Diameter of Unretted Hemp

Table 4. Median value of fiber diameter in green hemp expressed in μm, with 95 % confidence level

No	Variety and treatment	Median (μm)	conf. lev. / med. +	conf. lev. / med. -	Lot	Median (μm)
G1	Felina 34	37,3	2,5	3		
G2	Fedora 17	49,6	3,2	2,88	Ss	37,3 -49,6
G3	USO 31	46,8	3,01	3,63		
G4	Futura75,15kg/ha	40,6	2,54	2,1	Ss 15	40,6
G5	Futura75, 25kg/ha	32,1	2,63	1,85	Ss 25	32,1
G6	Futura75, 30kg/ha	36,1	1,85	1,53	Ss 30	36,1
G7	Futura75, 35kg/ha	41,5	3,01	2,37	Ss 35	41,5
G8	Futura75, Lövsta I	35,7	1,93	2,05	Lo	35,7 -37,7
G9	Futura75, Lövsta II	37,7	3,26	2,29		
G10 t	Futura75, without sludge	24,4	1,3	1,67		
G10 m	Futura75, without sludge	41,3	3,36	2,67	uR	24,4 -41,3
G10 b	Futura75, without sludge	32,8	2,88	3,19		
G11 t	Futura75, with sludge	30,3	1,52	1,67		
G11 m	Futura75, with sludge	35,7	2,03	2,1	mR	30,3 -35,7
G11 b	Futura75, with sludge	31	1,94	2,68		

Ss represent the whole group of samples G1-3. Lo represents all of no. G8 and G9. The letters t, m, b after numbers G10 and G11 indicate from which part in the stalks, the fibers are coming, t-top, m-middle and b-base. uR is the median value and its variation, of the whole stalk from G10, for the hemp fertilized in a normal way, without sludge. mR is the median value and how its sample variation, of the whole stalks of no G11, hemp fertilized with sludge.

Diameter of Retted and Unretted Hemp

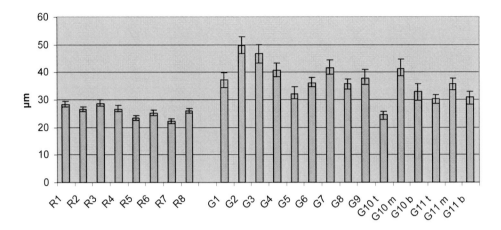

Figure 3. Median value of fiber diameter for both retted hemp fibers, R1-R8, and green hemp fibers, G1-G11, as well as the 95% confidence level.

The median diameter of retted hemp is about 26 µm and of green hemp about 36 µm, a difference of 10 µm or 28%.

Number Index of Retted and Unretted Hemp

Table 5. Number index

No	Mean Strength (cN/tex)	Mean diameter (µm)	Number index strength/diameter	Index with two digits
R1	39,3	35,8	1,097765363	1,1
R2	43,4	36,2	1,198895028	1,2
R3	41	37,4	1,096256684	1,1
R4	48,5	38,2	1,269633508	1,27
R5	44,3	33,7	1,314540059	1,31
R6	40	36,4	1,098901099	1,1
R7	38,4	33,5	1,146268657	1,15
R8	39,4	36,9	1,067750678	1,07
G1	55,4	56,9	0,973637961	0,97
G2	53,7	74,5	0,720805369	0,72
G3	53,2	71,1	0,748241913	0,75
G4	43,9	62	0,708064516	0,71
G5	50,7	60,3	0,84079602	0,84
G6	52,6	48,9	1,075664622	1,08
G7	50,3	63,3	0,794628752	0,79
G8	50,3	62,4	0,806089744	0,81
G9	49,3	67,9	0,726067747	0,73
G10 t	49,2	46,1	1,067245119	1,07
G10 m	57	64,6	0,882352941	0,88
G10 b	48	53,4	0,898876404	0,9
G11 t	47,5	53	0,896226415	0,9
G11 m	53,6	58,3	0,919382504	0,92
G11 b	46,2	50,9	0,907662083	0,91

DISCUSSION

In this investigation, the strength values of retted hemp fiber from the Swedish island Gotland varied between 38,4 and 48,5 cN/tex and the diameter varied between 22,2 and 28,7 µm. The strength values of unretted hemp varied between 43,9 and 57,0 cN/tex and the diametrer varied between 24,4 and 49,6 µm. The fiber strength results indicate that there is a 20 % loss inof strength for the retted samples compared to the unretted green samples and there is a 28 % decrease in width for the retted samples compared to the unretted green samples.

A small difference in strength between the dew retted and the water retted samples was observed, the dew retted being 6% weaker. Similarly the median fiber diameter of the dew retted hemp was lower. This indicates that the retting method affects fiber strength and dimension.

The Gotlandic hemp fiber quality results may be compared to by European standards. The Flax Standards A - J from France (long flax) specify fiber strength mean values in the range from 47 to 63 cN/tex and a mean fiber diameter from 19 to 25 µm (Müssig, 2005).

According to the French flax standard the retted hemp fiber samples do not fulfill the strength requirements but most of them were finer enough. Most of the unretted green hemp fiber samples are strong enough to fulfill the standard requirements but not fine enough.

The width results show that the unretted hemp fiber bundles are too coarse compared to the French flax standard. Unretted hemp is coarser but has the same fineness as retted hemp (Hobson, et al. 2000). According to that and the fact that it was strong enough it may satisfy the standard.

If the definition of a textile fiber is that it has to be finer than 40µm not to be uncomfortable toon the skin, Swedish hemp fiber should be suitable for certain textile purposes.

CONCLUSION

Comparing the results of the hemp growing in Sweden with the French flax standard, the hemp fiber grown on Gotland will not be suitable for qualities, such as linen products, but the hemp fiber will be suitable for other textile purposes. The investigated hemp was not grown specific for textile use but a few hemp samples complied with the French flax standards, indicating that there is a potential to produce Swedish hemp fibers with the qualities required for linen products through refinement of cultivation and treatment procedures.

ACKNOWLEDGMENTS

The financial support from the Royal Swedish Academy of Agriculture and Forestry is gratefully acknowledged. We also want to thank Dr Jörg Müssig, Faserinstitut Bremen e.V., Germany for his valuable testing work and support.

REFERENCES

[1]   Hobson, RN et al. 2000. Quality of fiber separated from unretted hemp stems by decortication. Silsoe Research Inst. Wrest Park Silsoe, Bedford, UK.

[2]   Müssig, J. 2005. Personal communication.

[3]   Nyström, O.1995. *Odling och beredning av hampa på Gotland 1942-1966. (Cultivation and processing of hemp on Gotland 1942-1966)* Gutabygd. Årsskrift för den gotländska hembygdsrörelsen. Gotlands Hembygdsförbunds förlag. Visby. Sweden.

In: Textiles for Sustainable Development   ISBN: 978-1-60021-559-9
Editors: R. Anandjiwala, L. Hunter et al., pp. 63-69   © 2007 Nova Science Publishers, Inc.

Chapter 6

IMPORTANT PLANT PARASITIC NEMATODES AFFECTING FIBER CROPS SUCH AS COTTON AND HEMP IN SOUTH AFRICA

Elizabeth R. van Biljon

ARC-Institute for Industrial Crops, Private Bag X82075,
Rustenburg 0300, South Africa; JeannievB@arc.agric.za

ABSTRACT

In South-Africa, Meloidogyne incognita race 2 is the only known root-knot nematode species that parasitizes cotton. Nematicide trials over three seasons gave an indication of the limiting effect that the mentioned nematodes have on cotton yield. Various single applications or combinations of applications were compared for their efficacy in the management of nematodes on cotton and to determine their effect on yield. When the lesion nematode species, Pratylenchus teres, was treated with nematicides a positive yield response was achieved. The response of the cotton to nematicide and bionematicides treatments gave an indication of the damage done by these nematodes and varied from a 3,7% response by a bionematicide treatment to a 39,5% by a fumigant plus nematicide treatment. M. javanica and M. incognita races 2 and 4 as well as P. teres, P. zeae and P. scribneri were found in association with hemp grown under South African conditions. Greenhouse trials demonstrated the effect of M. javanica on the following hemp cultivars: Kompolti, Uniko-B, Novosadska, F-17, F-75 and VIR-140. With the exception of the hemp cultivar VIR-140 all the cultivars evaluated were negatively affected by the presence of this nematode species. Continuance of the trial work is imperative to determine the effect of the other nematode species on the various hemp cultivars.

Keywords: Root-knot nematode, lesion nematode, *Meloidogyne*, *Pratylenchus*, yield response, cotton, hemp.

INTRODUCTION

Root-knot (*Meloidogyne* spp.) nematodes are among the most damaging and economically important pests of subtropical and tropical crops throughout the world. Two species of *Meloidogyne* are known to parasitize cotton, viz. *M. incognita* and *M. acronea*. Races 3 and 4 of *M. incognita* attack cotton, but only race 4 has been found on cotton in South Africa. *Meloidogyne* species became a limiting factor in cotton production in some of the irrigation schemes in South Africa as early as the 1970's [12]. A lesion nematode species, *Pratylenchus teres* Khan and Singh 1974 [2, 3], was first reported in that area in the 1995/96 season. Although the pathogenicity of this nematode species was not known, it was suspected that some of the nematode damage in the area could be attributed to this nematode species.

Nematicide trials over three seasons were used to calculate the limiting effect that the mentioned nematodes have on cotton yield.

Meloidogyne javanica and *M. incognita* races 2 and 4 are root-knot nematodes commonly associated with hemp in South Africa. *M incognita* and *M. javanica* are principally found in the warm temperate, tropical and subtropical regions of the world [18]. In a recent survey at hemp trial sites in the Eastern Cape, *M. javanica* was the only root-knot nematode species present at Addo, while both *M. javanica* and *M. incognita* were present at Bathurst and Fort Cox. Fort Cox had the highest lesion nematode (*Pratylenchus* spp.) numbers (53%) followed by Bathurst (25%) and Döhne (19)%, with Tsolo and Addo having 2 and 1%, respectively. P. zeae, *P. scribneri* and *P. teres* were the lesion nematode species found at these trial sites.

Nematode surveys done in the various hemp trials in the Eastern Cape indicated that various root-knot and lesion nematode species were present in the roots of the different hemp cultivars. Therefore trials were initiated to determine the damage potential of these species on hemp. In the first trial, the effect of the root-knot nematode species, *M. javanica,* was evaluated and the data wereas used to determine the response of the various cultivars to the presence of the mentioned nematode species.

DESCRIPTION OF THE ACTUAL WORK

Cotton Trials

During the 1999/2000, 2000/2001 and 2001/2002 seasons, field experiments were conducted on a trial site with a heavy *M. incognita* race 4 infestation at Jan Kempdorp in the Northern Cape Province of South Africa, to evaluate the efficacy of nematicides and bionematicides in the management of nematodes on cotton and to determine their effect on the yield.

The fields were ploughed and disked to obtain a fine tilth before commencing with the trials. The soil at the trial site was a light sandy soil (< 10% clay). The cotton cultivar NuCOTN 37B, was planted, with the exception of the 2000/2001 season when NuCOTN 35B was used.

Considering rainfall, the trials were flood-irrigated when necessary. Normal agronomic practices were used throughout the trials. All plants were treated identically with respect to cultivation, fertilization, insect control and harvesting.

During the three seasons various treatments, which included different nematicides, bionematicides or organic amendments, were used and compared to an untreated control treatment (table 1).

The experiments comprised randomized complete block designs with 10 treatments, replicated five times. The plots consisted of six rows, each row being five meters long. Seeds were spaced 0.20 meteres in the row. The four centre rows were used as the data rows to eliminate any side effects.

The actual nematode counts have not been included in this paper.

At harvest, the cotton in the data rows was picked and the yield per hectare as well as the response to the nematicide for each treatment calculated.

Table 1. The different treatments in the form of fumigants, nematicides, bionematicides or organic amendments used during the 3 seasons at the trials in Jan Kempdorp (Northern Cape Province, South Africa)

Treatment	
Fumigant	EDB
Nematicides	Aldicarb Oxamyl
Bionematicides	Pl-Plus®[1] Biostart 2000[2]
Organic amendments	RUM®[3]Chicken manure Chitin

[1] Pl-Plus® contains an isolate of the fungus *Paecilomyces lilacinus*

[2] Biostart 2000® contains three *Bacillus* spp. viz. *Bacillus chitinosporus, B. laterosporus, B. licheniformis.*

[3] R.U.M. ® is an earthworm derivative and a typical R.U.M. analysis is as follows:

N - 15%; P - 1.1%; K - 1.4%; S - 96 mg/ℓ; Ca - 44 mg/ℓ; Mg - 110 mg/ℓ; Na - 110 mg/ℓ; Cu - 0.1 mg/ℓ; Zn - 0.23 mg/ℓ; Mn - 0.49 mg/ℓ; Fe - 2.6 mg/ℓ; Bo - 0.16 mg/ℓ. R.U.M.® also contains some biological agents.

Hemp Trials

The hemp trials were executed in greenhouses at the premises of the ARC-Institute for Industrial Crops in Rustenburg, South Africa. During the 2003-2003 season the damage potential of the root-knot nematode, *M. javanica*, was evaluated on the hemp cultivars Kompolti, Uniko-B, Novosadska, F-17, F-75 and VIR-140.

The hemp seeds were sown directly in the pots. For the evaluation, plastic pots, containing 2700 g pasteurized soil, were used. The experiments were devised in a randomized split plot design with seven replications. The inoculum levels consisted of 1500 nematodes/pot and no nematodes/pot. An inoculum density of *M. javanica,* representing 1500 nematodes/2700 ml soil, was prepared from greenhouse cultures. The inoculum was applied to three holes, each 1 cm from each plant and 2,5 cm deep to three-week old hemp seedlings. Normal maintenance practices were followed.

The experiment was terminated at the senescence of the hemp plants. The plants were carefully removed from the pots and the roots separated from the shoots. The roots were washed, blotted dry and weighed. The dry aerial mass was determined.

Data were analysed using Genstat 5, computer statistical software, and subjected to a two-factor analysis of variance for inoculum level and cultivar. Means were compared using Tukey's multiple range test (P ≤ 0.05).

CONCLUSION

Cotton Trials

In the 1999-2000 season, the aldicarb-combination treatments gave a 39,5 and 28,1% nematicide response (table 2).

Table 2. The cotton yield (kg/ha) for the various treatments and the nematicide response (%) 1999 – 2000

Treatment	Yield[1] (kg/ha)	Nematicide response (%)
Untreated control	2173ab	-
EDB + aldicarb	3589d	39.5
Aldicarb + oxamyl EC	3024bcd	28.1
Oxamyl EC (O)	2635abcd	17.5
Biostart 2000[1] [Tr. A]	1761a	Negative
Biostart 2000 (Tr. A) + oxamyl EC	2432abcd	10.6
Biostart 2000 [Tr. B]	2318abcd	6.3
Biostart 2000 [Tr. B] + oxamyl EC	1892a	Negative
PL-Plus	2286abc	4.9
PL-Plus + oxamyl EC	3112cd	30.2
LSD$_T$ (P ≤ 0.05)	938	-

[1] Values within the column followed by the same letter are not significantly different according to Tukey's multiple range test.

During the 2000-2001 season, adicarb followed by the Biostart (AB2) treatment resulted in a yield increase of 39,7% when compared with the untreated control. All the aldicarb treatments yielded 1110 kg/ha or more with a 31,1 – 39,7% response to the nematicide (table 3).

For the 2001-2002 seasons, the aldicarb followed by R.U.M.(RA) resulted in a yield increase of 35,26% when compared with the untreated control. The aldicarb + Biostart (AB1) treatment yielded a 31,2% yield increase while the single aldicarb (A) and oxamyl (O) treatments resulted in yield increases of 26,9 and 30%, respectively. The use of R.U.M. added an additional 8.36% to the yield in the aldicarb + R.U.M. (RA) treatment. The aldicarb-combination treatments, therefore, resulted in a yield increase of more than 600 kg/ha (table 4).

**Table 3. The cotton yield (kg/ha) for the various treatments
and the nematicide response (%) 2000-2001**

Treatment	Yield[1] (kg/ha)	Nematicide response (%)
Untreated control	2464a	-
EDB + aldicarb	3574bcd	31.1
Chitin + Biostart 2000[1] (Tr. A)	2964abc	16.9
EDB + Biostart 2000 (Tr. A)	2712a	9.1
Biostart 2000 (Tr. A)	2968abc	17.0
Aldicarb + Biostart 2000 (Tr. A)	3643bcd	32.4
Biostart 2000 (Tr. B)	2886ab	14.6
Aldicarb + Biostart 2000 (Tr. B)	4089d	39.7
PL-Plus	2559a	3.7
Aldicarb + PL-Plus	3746cd	34.2
$LSD_T (P \leq 0.05)$	848	-

[1] Values within the column followed by the same letter are not significantly different according to Tukey's multiple range test.

**Table 4. The cotton yield (kg/ha) for the various treatments
and the response to the nematicide (%) 2001 - 2002**

Treatment	Yield[1] (kg/ha)	Nematicide response (%)
Untreated control	1691a	-
Aldicarb	2315abc	27.0
Biostart 2000	1989abc	15.0
Oxamyl EC	2414bc	30.0
R.U.M.	1766ab	4.2
Aldicarb + Biostart 2000	2459bc	31.2
Aldicarb + oxamyl EC	2295abc	26.3
R.U.M. + aldicarb	2612c	35.3
Chicken manure	1997abc	15.3
Aldicarb + chicken manure	2411bc	29.9
$LSD_T (P \leq 0.05)$	715.52	-

[1] Values within the column followed by the same letter are not significantly different according to Tukey's multiple range test.

It is known that both aldicarb and oxamyl stimulate plant growth in the presence or absence of nematodes [1, 14, 15, 16], but they are also effective nematicides as was observed in results obtained in various nematode trials [17]. Trials done in Mississippi in the U.S.A. also resulted in a similar high reduction in root-knot nematode numbers with the aldicarb and oxamyl treatments [11].

Results furthermore indicated that the damage done by *M. incognita* race 4 can be quite severe and that yield losses in sandy soils with a heavy *M. incognita* race 4 infestations can be as much as 40%. A certain number of root-knot nematodes in a sandy loam soil at a certain time of the year, might give rise to a certain percentage of yield damage e.g. 1000 root-knot nematodes in a kg of soil sampled in March in the San Joaquin Valley might only result in 68% of the normal yield potential [20].

Nematode damage was almost always overlooked in cotton production but during the past few years the role that these "hidden enemies" play, has become apparent. In Alabama, yield losses, due to the cotton root-knot nematode, ranged from 10 – 75%, depending on soil type and prevailing weather conditions [6]. In South Carolina, not every field was infested with damaging levels of nematodes, but in fields that were infested, yield losses ranged from barely detectable to more than 50 % [13]. In some Texas High Plains cotton fields, yields can increase by as much as 50 % when root-knot nematodes are controlled [10]. Field trials conducted in Pinal Coiunty, Arizona, to determine the impact of nematode control on the yield of upland cotton, resulted in increased lint production in 20 out of the 24 trials [8]. In 2004 the U.S. cotton industry lost an estimated $402 million to nematodes [7]. Beltwide cotton losses due to root-knot nematodes may exceed 50 % of the yield potential in severely affected fields [19]. The yield losses in cotton due to *Meloidogyne incognita* race 4 were 19.9 and 17.7% in Gabipur and Fatehabad (Haryana, India) respectively [9].

In none of the trials executed by ARC-ICC could any nematode effect be detected on fiber quality. It was, however, stated by an unknown author that depending on the stage of development of the infested crop, they could hamper the quality of the crop [21].

Hemp Trials

The biggest effect of inoculum levels on the dry aerial mass of tested cultivars was noticed in Novosadska (table 5). The hemp cultivar VIR-140 was not affected by the presence of the root-knot nematode, *M. javanica* (table 5).

Although a meaningful estimate of yield cannot be made in pot tests, it can, however, give an indication of the effect of nematodes on the test crop. The results obtained in this study indicated that the growth of hemp cultivars could be negatively influenced by the presence of the root-knot nematode species, *M. javanica*.

Little research has been done regarding the effect of nematodes on hemp. It was only the work of De Meijer, which gave an indication that nematodes can be problematic for hemp. De Meijer found that varying resistance levels (ranging from highly resistant to moderately susceptible) to the root-knot nematode, *M. hapla*, existed in various hemp cultivars [4, 5].

Table 5. The dry aerial mass (g) of the different hemp cultivars
at two inoculum levels of the root-knot nematode M. javanica
and the cultivar response to the nematode (2002-2003)

Cultivar	Plus *M. javanica*	Minus *M. javanica*	Cultivar response to nematode
Kompolti	3.90	7.42	-47.44
Uniko-B	9.26	9.72	-4.73
Novosadska	7.84	8.88	-11.71
F-17	8.74	11.86	-26.31
F-75	8.88	10.56	-15.91
VIR-140	7.90	6.18	+27.83

REFERENCES

[1] Barker, KR; Powell, NT. *Journal of Nematology.* 1998, 20: 432–438.

[2] Carta, LK; Handoo, ZA; Skantar, AM; Van Biljon, J; Botha, M. *African Plant Protection.* 2002, 8:13-2 4.

[3] Khan, E; Singh, DB. *Indian Journal of Nematology.* 1974, 4:199-211.

[4] De Meijer, *EPM. Euphytica.* 1993, 62:201-211.

[5] De Meijer, EPM. Diversity in Cannabis, Doctoral thesis, Wageningen Agricultural University, The Netherlands 1994.

[6] Gazaway, WS. Plant disease notes ANR-1012 1997.

[7] Hollis, PL. Cotton nematode losses continue, Delta Farm Press. Feb 11, 2005.

[8] Husman, S; Wegener, R; McClure, M; Schmitt, M. Nematodes and Their control In Upland Cotton, Arizona Cotton Report 2001.

[9] Singh, JRK; Vats, J; Rajesh and Vats Singh J. *Indian Journal of Nematology.* 2000, 30:1, 92 – 93.

[10] Lee, Jr, TA. "Testing, Treating For Nematodes: A Wise Production Practice," in Vegetable Production and Marketing News F. J. DAINELLO, Ed., (October 2001).

[11] Lawrence, GW; Mclean, KS; Diaz, AJ. "Nematode Management Investigations in Mississippi, 1997", Mississippi Agricultural and Forestry Experiment Station.

[12] Louw, I. "Nematode pests of cotton." in Nematology in Southern Africa, D.P. Keetch, J. Heyns, Ed., Science Bulletin, 1982, Department of Agriculture and Fisheries, Republic of South Africa.

[13] Mueller, JD. Cotton Nematode Control, Clemson University report, Edisto Research and Education Centre 1996.

[14] Ragab, SM. Journal of Agricultural Science. 1981, 97:731-737.

[15] Reddy, KR; Baker, DN; Reddy, KR. "Effect of Temik and temperature on growth development and photosynthesis of cotton," 1990, Clemson University and ASDA/ARS Crop Simulation Research Unit, Mississippi State University, P.O. Box 5248, Mississippi State, MS 39762.

[16] Reddy, KR; Baker, DN; Reddy, KR. "The impact of aldicarb on canopy photosynthesis of cotton", 1990, Clemson University and ASDA/ARS Crop Simulation Research Unit, Mississippi State University, P.O. Box 5248, Mississippi State, MS 39762.

[17] Van Biljon, ER. Proceedings World Cotton Research Conference-3 2003, 1:1439 – 1447.

[18] Taylor, AL; Sasser, JN. Biology, identification and control of root-knot nematodes (Meloidogyne species, 1978, International Meloidogyne project, North Carolina State University Graphics, 111 pp.

[19] Wrather, JA; Phipps, B; Milam, MR. "Cotton Nematodes in Missouri: Your Hidden Enemies," University of Missouri Extension 1993 – 2005.

[20] http://muextension.missouri.edu/explore/agguides/crops/g04259.htm

[21] Unknown, Integrated Pest Management for Cotton in the Western Region of the United States. Second Edition Publication 3305 – Published 1996 – ISBN 1-879906-30-9.

[22] Unknown, Cotton pests and diseases. http://r0.unctad.org/ infocomm/ anglais/ cotton/crop.htm

PART II
TEXTILE METROLOGY

In: Textiles for Sustainable Development
Editors: R. Anandjiwala, L. Hunter et al., pp. 73-80

ISBN: 978-1-60021-559-9
© 2007 Nova Science Publishers, Inc.

Chapter 7

HEMP SYS: DESIGN, DEVELOPMENT AND UP-SCALING OF A SUSTAINABLE PRODUCTION SYSTEM FOR HEMP TEXTILES: AN INTEGRATED QUALITY SYSTEMS APPROACH. HOW TO AFFECT HEMP FIBER QUALITY?

S. Amaducci[1], J. Müssig[2], A. Zatta[3] and F. Pelatti[3]

[1] Istituto di Agronomia e Coltivazioni Erbacee – Università Cattolica del Sacro Cuore
Via Emilia Parmense 84 29100 Piacenza Italy stefano.amaducci@unicatt.it,
[2] Faserinstitut e.V. – FIBER – Bremen Germany muessig@faserinstitut.de
[3] DiSTA – GRiCI – Bologna Italy

ABSTRACT

The European Community co-financed Project HEMP SYS aims at researching and developing an entire production chain for hemp based textiles, starting with the cultivation of the crop and finishing with the end-products. The innovative production chain herewith developed is based on green decortication of the hemp stems cut into 1 m long sections, and subsequent industrial microbiological retting of the scutched fiber. Considering the industrial demand for a consistent quantity of fiber of homogeneous quality, how quality is affected by a variation in the production factors along the production system is studied.

Field trials are carried out at multiple locations to determine the effect of Genotype x Environment x Management on hemp production. Different harvesting techniques, mechanical fiber separation methods, fiber preparation for further treatment are all evaluated. Fiber retting and fiber cleaning are carried out on a pilot plant set up in the framework of a regional research programme (www.toscanapa.it). Fiber samples are collected at different stages of transformation and are analyzed for quality characteristics. In this presentation, preliminary results from a selected combination of experiments will be presented and discussed.

Stem and fiber production increased with harvest time, but fiber-bundle finesses tended to be higher for the early harvest times (beginning of flowering). Plant density affected stem and fiber production in only a few cases, while fiber-bundle fineness tended to increase at higher densities.

Fineness of single fiber was also measured in portions of stem taken at different plant height in order to evaluate interplant variability of fiber quality. It was noted that the average fineness of the primary fiber tends to be higher in the lower and central portions of the stem.

The practical implications of these results are discussed, highlighting the strategies of quality control developed within the production chain proposed in the Hemp Sys Project.

Keywords: Cannabis sativa; hemp, fiber; genotype; plant population; retting; quality; fineness.

INTRODUCTION

Hemp Sys is a research and development project co-financed in the Fifth Framework Programme of the European Community for research, technological development and demonstration activities [1]. The main objective of this project is to promote the development of a competitive, innovative and sustainable hemp fiber textile industry in the EU by:

a. Developing an improved, ecologically sustainable production chain for high quality hemp fiber textiles coupled to an integrated quality system for stems, raw and processed fibers, yarns and fabrics based on eco-labeling criteria.
b. Providing a comprehensive economic assessment of EU and international fiber hemp markets, consumer requirements and EU-production costs and returns.
c. Disseminating as much as possible the knowledge generated using the latest information technologies.

Hemp fiber has a multitude of traditional applications. It was used to produce working clothes, curtains, carpets, nets, twines, shoes, but mainly ropes and sails [5]. Nowadays, in Europe, it is mainly used to produce pulp and paper, automotive and building materials, and only a very limited amount is available for the textile industry [7].

Hemp Sys aims to exploit the relative European lead in the field of long bast fiber processing into high value textile products, in order to find the higher added value for the hemp fiber. The main bottlenecks of this agro-production chain that are tackled in the frame of Hemp Sys are: lack of fiber of homogeneous and consistent quality, sub-optimal fiber processing (harvesting, decortication, de-gumming, fiber packaging); lack of fiber qualification system.

Optimal harvesting device should cut the stems at the base and above 2 m height and lay them in an ordered swath as for flax. The same device should also cut the stem in half so as to form two swaths of about 1 m width. This last operation could also be performed by another device. Further mechanical operations can then be carried out successfully with flax round balers and scutching machines (HempSys internal report). This harvesting strategy allows the fibers extracted from the base to be separated from those obtained from the apical portion. This system could therefore produce fiber of diverse quality and of improved homogeneity.

Stems must be removed from the field as soon as dried, in order to minimize microbial contamination.

De-gumming within the framework of HempSys is carried out through controlled microbiological retting.

Variation of fiber quality is minimized in all the processing steps, therefore fiber quality should depend mainly on agronomical and environmental factors affecting plant growth and consequently fiber formation.

Field trials were carried out at multiple locations, and stem and fiber samples were processed and analyzed onat both industrial and laboratory scale in order to evaluate the effect of different agrotechniques (location, genotype, plant population, sowing time, harvesting time, harvesting strategy) on fiber characteristics, such as fineness, strength, maturity, presence of secondary fiber and presence of pectin and lignin.

In this paper, some preliminary results from a selection of field experiments and laboratory analysis, are presented and discussed.

DESCRIPTION OF THE ACTUAL WORK

Field Trials

Field trials were carried out at A.U.B. (Azienda Università di Bologna) in Cadriano (32 m a.s.l.; 44°33' latitude; 11°21' longitude) during 2003 and 2004.

According to the USDA classification, the soil was loamy in both years, pH (in H_2O) 7.07 and organic matter content 1.5% in 2004, pH 8.01 and organic matter content of 1.91% in 2003.

Sowing took place on 16th April 2003 and 8th April 2004, using an experimental sowing machine (Vignoli), row distance was set at 13 cm and seeds were placed 3-4 cm deep.

The experimental layout was a completely randomised block design for the two varieties and the three densities, while three harvest times were split into the main plots. Main plots were 62,4 m^2 (6.24 m x 10 m).

The two varieties investigated, were the French monoecious Futura 75 and the Hungarian dioecious Tiborszallasi.

Target plant densities were: 120, 240 and 360 plants m^{-2}, named respectively D1, D2 and D3

According to the field protocol, three harvests were carried out at specific phenological stages: beginning of flowering, full flowering and end of flowering. In this paper, only data from the first two harvest times are presented.

Immediately after sowing, a 50 cm row of plants was randomly selected and every other day for a two week period, the number of emerged plantlets was counted.

Flowering measurements were carried out on the 25 marked plants in all the plots of one block. Inspection of these plants was performed weekly and the number of flowering plants was noted.

At each harvest time, 5 m^2 of crop per plot were cut at the base of the stem. Total biomass and number of plants were determined directly on the field. 20 plants per plot were brought toin the laboratory to be divided into stems and leaves; these were weighed and subsequently dried at 105° in order to calculate dry matter content. Plant height, diameter, flowering state and sex, when relevant, were determined on 100 plants. 5 plants of average weight were selected, dried at 60° and stored to determine pure fiber content.

Quality Analysis

Chemical Extraction and Opening of Fiber Bundles
Fiber extraction was carried out, according to Bredemann [4], in the laboratories of A.U.B. The fibers obtained were sent to the FIBER (Bremen, D), where they were stored for 24 h at 20°C and 65% relative humidity.

A handmade sliver, with a mass of 6 g m^{-1}, was produced for each fiber sample. The parallelised fiber-bundles were refined with a coarse separator. A self-developed laboratory coarse separator was used. This machine consists of a serrated cylinder (Ø 261 mm) and is fed by a rotating roll (Ø 32 mm). The distance from the feeding roll to the rotating serrated cylinder is 20 mm. The fiber transport after coarse separation was by air. The results of separation are comparable with industrial separation techniques [9].

Fiber fineness was determined with an image analysis system, called Fibershape [10].

Measurement of the fiber width distribution of the fibers and fiber bundles was done by preparing the fibers between two glass slides for color positives (Company Gepe type 69 01) after 24 h climatisation at 20°C and 65% relative humidity. For each sample, 4 slides were prepared and scanned on a Minolta Dimage Scan MultiPro at 4800 dpi. Scanner software Dimage scan 1.0 out of Photoshop 5.0 LE, was used to process the data. To measure the width of the prepared fibers and fiber bundles an adapted setup was developed (ALFM48Z5.D00).

Microscopic Determination
In 2003 and 2004, using the genotype Futura 75, thin cross sections were hand cut from the middle part of the 1st, 3rd, 5th and 7th internodes, immediately after harvest. The cross sections were coloured with toluidine blue and observed and photographed under Leitz Orthoplan light photomicroscope at 40, 100 and 250 times magnification [3]. These images were then processed with the UTHSCSA Image Tool IT Version 2.03 software in order to measure primary cell diameter and degree of maturity (calculated as percentage of lumen diameter on cell diameter) and to count the layers of secondary fiber cells.

RESULTS AND DISCUSSIONS

Plant Population Effect

In both years the plant population did not affect stem dry matter production, but it did affect stem morphology (table 1). This confirms the results obtained in other research studies, carried out in both the same [1] and different environments [5, 10]. Investigations, carried out in the frame of the Hemp Sys Project, showed that seed purchase price has a major impact on hemp cultivation costs. Therefore, high seed rates are justified only if fiber production and/or fiber quality is significantly influenced by plant population. However, pure fiber content was on average 16.2 % of total stem dry weight and it was not significantly influenced by plant population.

Table 1. Effect of plant population on stem dry weight (SDW),
fiber production, stem height (H) and diameter (D)

P. population	SDW (t ha^{-1})	fiber (t ha^{-1})	H (cm)	D (mm)
D1	11,4	1,9	198,8	6,4
D2	10,5	1,8	179,0	5,4
D3	10,2	1,8	169,4	5,0
Mean's	10,7	1,8	182,4	5,6

Mean fiber width, determined using Fibershape analysis carried out on fiber extracted from plants grown at different plant populations in 2003, was 20.4, 19.6, 18.8 µm, respectively, for densities 120, 240 and 360. A tendency for plants cultivated at the higher plant population to have finer fibers was noted. It should be noted that fibers measured with this systems are both single fibers and fiber bundles that resisted the chemical treatment and the passage through the coarse separator (figure 1). The width distributions of the hemp fibers and fiber bundles, as shown in figure 2, are skewed to the left, which is typical for bast fibers samples in which single fibers and bundles of different size are present.

Information of single fiber diameter was taken from direct measurements carried out on digital pictures of stem cross sections (figure 3). The tendency for increasing plant population to reduce fiber diameter was confirmed in both field trials (figure 4).

From the visual analysis of stem cross sections, it was observed that fiber maturity and presence of secondary fiber tend to increase at lower plant populations.

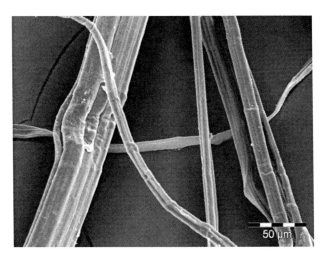

Figure 1. SEM picture of Tiborszallasi fibers after chemical and coarse separation.

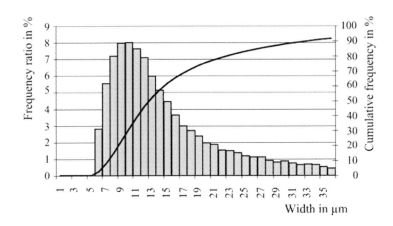

Figure 2. Width distribution of hemp fibers and fiber bundles measured with fFiber shape are typically skewed to the left.

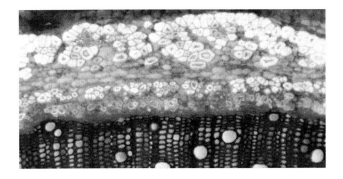

Figure 3. Digital picture of a hemp stem cross-section with primary fibers (top) and secondary fibers (bottom).

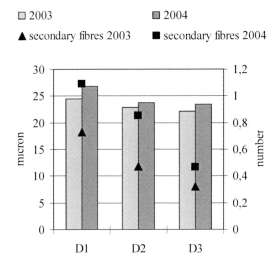

Figure 4. Effect of plant population on the diameter of primary fiber (columns) and number of layers of secondary fiber (symbols).

Plant Portion Effect

Harvesting strategies applied within the Hemp Sys Project are based on the idea of dividing the stem in two portions of approximately 1 m of length in order to use existing flax processing lines to scutch hemp stems. Fiber content and fiber quality were also determined in different stem portions in order to evaluate whether fiber quality changes along the stem.

In figure 5, the partitioning of stem dry biomass and fiber along the stem is presented. On average, more than 70% of stem dry matter and 74% of pure fiber are located in the basal portion (0-1 m).

Fibershape and microscopic analysis, carried out along the stem, showed that fiber diameter tends to decrease from the lower to the higher portions. Secondary fiber formation started in the lower plant portion and was absent in the upper portion of the stem. Fiber maturation also started from the basal portion and from there it proceeded to the upper part of the stem.

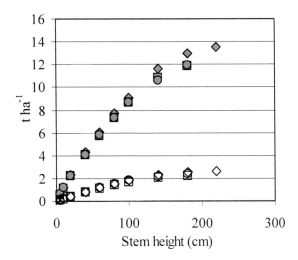

Figure 5. Partitioning of dry biomass (filled symbols) and pure fiber (open symbols) along the stem in the second harvest of 2004 of Futura 75: D1 (♦, ◊), D2 (■, □) and D3 (●, ○).

Genotype Effect

On average, stem production was statistically higher for Futura 75 compared to Tiboszallasie (respectively 11.9 and 9.5 t ha^{-1}). Fiber percentage in the stem, and thus the total fiber yield, was also higher in Futura (18.7 % and 15.4% for Futura and Tiborsallazie, respectively).

In 2003, despite its lower production in total biomass and in pure fiber, Tiborsallazie seemed to produce finer fiber compared to Futura (18.7 and 20.5 μm respectively).

Harvest Time Effect

Harvest time significantly influenced stem dry biomass production only in 2003, when Tiborsallazie had an early flowering, and as a consequence it was harvested earlier than usual. The average fiber production increased from beginning to full flowering by 24%.

Fiber finesses tended to decrease with time [8]. This was probably due to a more difficult mechanical separation of the fiber bundles, and not to an increased diameter of the single fiber, as was confirmed by the measurements carried out on stem cross sections. Secondary fibers increased significantly with harvest time.

CONCLUSION

Preliminary results from field trials and fiber quality determinations carried out within the framework of the HempSys Project, indicate that hemp fiber quality is affected by plant population, genotype, harvest time, and it varies within the stem. A pre-determined fiber quality can therefore be obtained through specific agronomical choices (seed density, variety, harvest time). Fiber quality can be further controlled by dividing the stem at harvest in basal and apical portions and keeping these portions separate during processing.

REFERENCES

[1]   Amaducci, S; Errani, M; Venturi, G. *Journal of Industrial Hemp,* 2002, 7, 33-60.
[2]   Amaducci, S. *Journal of Industrial Hemp,* 2003, 8, 79-83.
[3]   Bredemann, G. *Faserforschung,* 1942, 16, 14 – 39.
[4]   Backe, H. Der Hanfanbau. Berlin: Parey Verlag; 1936.
[5]   Cromack, H.T.H. *Industrial Crops and Products,* 1996, 7, 205-210.
[6]   Karus, M. European hemp industry 2001 till 2004: Cultivation, raw materials, products and trends [online]. 2004. Available from: URL: http://www.eiha.org
[7]   Keller, A; Leupin, M; Mediavilla, V; Wintermantel, E. *Industrial Crops and Products,* 2001, 13, 35-48.
[8]   Mussig , J. Untersuchung der Eignung heimischer Pflanzenfasern für die Herstellung von naturfaserverstärkten Duroplasten - vom Anbau zum Verbundwerkstoff -. Düsseldorf: D: VDI Verlag GmbH, 2001, (Fortschritt-Bericht VDI, Reihe 5, Grund- und Werkstoffe / Kunststoffe, No. 630), (ISBN 3-18-363005-2) .- manuscript, 214 pages.
[9]   Mussig, J; Schmid, H.G. In: Anderson, I.M. / Price, R. / Clark, E. / McKernan, S.: Microscopy and Microanalysis 2004, Press Syndicate of the University of Cambridge, 2004 (Proceedings to the Conference .- Microscopy and Microanalysis, Volume 10, Supplement 2, 2004) (ISSN 1431-9276 .- (2004)10+2;1-U), (Savannah, Georgia, USA, August 1-5, 2004) Cambridge, New-York, Melbourne, pp. 1332CD - 1333CD (2004)
[10] Van Der Werf, H.M.G.; Wijhuizen, M; De Schutter, *J.A.A. Field Crop Research,* 1995, 40, 153-164.

In: Textiles for Sustainable Development
Editors: R. Anandjiwala, L. Hunter et al., pp. 81-93

ISBN: 978-1-60021-559-9
© 2007 Nova Science Publishers, Inc.

Chapter 8

A REVIEW ON THE DEVELOPMENT OF RAPID ANALYTICAL TECHNIQUES FOR ASSESSING PHYSICAL PROPERTIES OF MODIFIED LINEN FABRIC

K. Kernaghan, T. Stuart, R.D. McCall and H.S.S. Sharma

Department of Applied Plant Science, School of Agriculture and Food Science, Queens University Belfast and Applied Plant Science Division, Department of Agriculture and Rural Development for Northern Ireland, Newforge Lane, Belfast, BT9 5PX, Northern Ireland, United Kingdom. S.Sharma@qub.ac.uk

ABSTRACT

The challenge of achieving good crease recovery (CR) performance for linen fabrics, without incurring unacceptably high reduction in abrasion resistance (AR), remains to be resolved. This publication reviews some of the research and the techniques employed in investigating the structural and chemical changes in flax fibers treated with crease recovery agents over the past eighty years. Also the decline of the linen industry in Europe is discussed to provide a background to this review. The techniques of spectroscopy and thermal analysis are discussed, with reference to multivariate analysis techniques, for predicting the fabric performance parameters, such as CR and AR. In addition, the possibilities of employing instrumental techniques during production are considered.

Key words: Creasing, abrasion, linen, spectroscopy and thermal analysis.

INTRODUCTION

It is ironic that just as a half-century era of cheap thermo-polymer fibers based on abundant low-cost petrochemical precursors appears to be ending, the traditional European linen industry -which could be a principal beneficiary-, has never been weaker. Although decimated by decades of contraction, a sector largely based on vertically structured groups still survived in recognizable form, as a critical mass of expertise until the late 1990s. It has since undergone relentless collapse, accelerated by the post 9/11 recession, leaving only one survivor, Linificio Canapificio Nationale, Bergamo, Italy along with several independent small and medium enterprises (SME) and a few specialist finishers, which fine-tune their processes in isolation. Whilst the economic climate for renewable bio-fibers may be improving, it is essential that unresolved technical questions be resolved, and a network of problem-solving support made available. A vital aspect of any expansion must be the re-acquisition of 'lost' expertise in entire industrial sectors; including quality assessment (QA), process equipment development and manufacture, spinning, weaving, dyeing and finishing operations, otherwise any investment will be jeopardized.

Review of Research

Established reference texts provide a comprehensive overview of fiber properties and performance [20, 45], yarn structure and properties [18] and textile performance [37], respectively. However, flax and linen receive only passing mention, at best. Of the principal textile fiber classes, cellulosics collectively exhibit the poorest response to creasing, with linen being markedly inferior in performance to cotton and rayon [2] (table 1). As a consequence, the development of reagents and processes for crease-resist finishing of cellulosic fabrics has attracted sustained research effort for over 80 years.

Table 1. The crease recovery performance of various types of fabrics [2]

Fabric	R (%)	Crease recovery angle (%)			
		OD	SC	Wet	MP
Wool	14	162	157	132	125
Linen	9	80	48	100	28
Cotton	7.5	99	95	100	63
Viscose Rayon	13	150	125	107	50
Polyester	~0.5	125	125	125	125

R- regain at standard conditions; OD- oven dry; SA- standard conditions (20°C, 65% RH); MP- minimum performance. Mean of warp and weft measurement (Method: Shirley, BS 3086). A perfect crease recovery performance is equivalent to 180°.

The theoretical background and process technology are broadly common to all cellulosics, and have been presented in standard references [4, 41, 69], as has the underlying organic chemistry, most notably by Mark and co-researchers, [38]. Accordingly, the general relationships between key physical performance parameters, such as crease-resistance, tensile/tear strength, and abrasion resistance, of treated cellulosic fabrics have been extensively examined and reviewed at length [2, 4, 38, 50, 52]. A vast range of products has been marketed for cotton/rayon, originating from many differing structural classes, and all systems utilized for linen have been modified variants of these. A range of process options is available: wet, moist, dry and combination cure systems exist [50, 40, 69] with specific applications to linens [4, 11, 47]. Whilst linen constituted a significant proportion of the total cellulosic finishing market, it was assured of some support from the RandD and technical services of the principal chemical suppliers: this no longer applies.

From a textile technology viewpoint, linen exhibits very high wet and dry tensile strengths, low elongation/elastic recovery, poor dry crease-recovery (CR) performance and resistance to abrasion in the wet state, all primarily consequences of its highly ordered structure. Of these, dry uncreasing ability determines how the fabric will withstand creasing in use and is most apparent to the end-user, although purely an aesthetic consideration. Since the early 80s, linen apparel fabrics have successfully exploited the 'creased look' cachet. But this is a limited, niche sector, and marketing specialists have long viewed the absence of crease-resist performance as the key factor restricting expansion of market share [3, 14, 59, 60]. Reviewing publications over the past 20 years, the lack of emphasis on fabric structure and finishing is evident, whilst a comprehensive range of instrumental analysis techniques have been employed to study flax fiber.

The accepted view based on cotton studies is that dry CR is mainly imparted by *intermolecular* covalent interactions between cellulose chains, their formation optimized by dehydration. Conversely, wet crease recovery relies on *intramolecular* bonding, in regions separated by swelling within the fiber [40, 41]. Water sensitive interactions may also bring about increases in fabric resilience in the dry state [63]. The principle can be demonstrated by swelling tests on treated cotton/rayon samples, but flax fiber exhibits a more complex response as shown by swelling characteristics of fiber treated with zinc chloride, lithium hydroxide and sodium hydroxide [53]. High dry/low wet crease recovery, due to hydrophobic interactions, was found in cotton fabric treated with mono-functional stearoyl chloride. Treatment with stearic acid alone did not bring about the same result so that some chemical reaction with cellulose was necessary [39].

Therefore, improvement of dry CR has always been the priority for linens, with dry cross-linking techniques, based on a pad-dry-cure process (at elevated temperatures), being the preferred route. In comparison to cotton or rayon, application of a given reagent/catalyst system to linen yields a lower degree of fixation, making afterwashing more essential. The finish is more susceptible to subsequent hydrolysis, and if formaldehyde-containing, yields significantly higher free/release formaldehyde levels, particularly in the Shirley determination. Attempts to counter this by enhancing fixation via increased catalyst, concentration, cure temperature or employing a more aggressive catalyst can rapidly reduce AR to unacceptable levels [11, 22, 24, 59] (table 2). A series by Lambrinou [29-36] constitutes the most comprehensive published study of application techniques, including effect of mercerization, response to laundering and test performance of treated fabrics. The basic requirements for dry CR and AR conflict to some extent and although the relationship is approximately inverse, it has since been found to be particularly complex for flax (and possibly for all bast fibers). Attempting to plot CR performance vs AR diagrammatically or graphically reveals an extremely non-linear relationship [24]. The 'tail' occurring over a short range of low add-on/ low cross-link densities was previously unrecorded. It is considered to be a consequence of the unique morphology of flax [19] and has been briefly discussed elsewhere [52, 54, 56]. The original investigators concluded that whilst treatment with a variety of reactant-type cross-linkers produced this effect, conventional resins did not, but more recent results have challenged this [41]. Such enhancement of AR may be of interest to specific sectors, e.g. table linens, but the matter has not been fully investigated and resolved to date.

Table 2.Effect of alternative catalysts on fabric performance [24]

Uncreasing[1] angle (°)				Formaldehyde (ppm)			
				Free	Free	Release	Release
Catalyst[*]	Dry	Wet	AR		FAW		FAW
15% MgCl$_2$	111	137	145	450	73	560	220
10% Mg(NO$_3$)$_2$	120	139	95	1910	84	790	390
15% Mg(NO$_3$)$_2$	123	140	48	2070	71	830	305
10% Zn(NO$_3$)$_2$	134	139	38	100	61	370	360
Control	62	105	890	---	---	---	---

[*]All hexahydrates (6H$_2$O); [1]mean values of warp and weft; AR- abrasion resistance (modified Martindale); FAW- fabric afterwashed; Free- determined by Shirley, and Release- determined by AATCC (112/1978) methods respectively.

For optimal response, linens should be mercerized prior to CR treatment, as fabric resiliency is essential [11, 59, 60], but this requires specialist expertise and equipment. The fabric or weave structure also has considerable influence on uncreasing performance. Plain-weave constructions exacerbate creasing in cellulosics [21] and are - unfortunately for the finisher - predominant in linens [11, 24]. A potentially major problem affecting easy-care performance is solute migration. This phenomenon has been identified in cottons, where reagent has been found to aggregate at the crowns of yarns, the region of a fabric construction most subject to heating and evaporative loss during the curing process [1, 26]. The problem is especially marked in linens due to the complex morphology of the flax fiber, as it is longitudinally heterogeneous, having nodal regions and internodal regions, in addition to the fibrillar structure and axial lumen. The nodes are known to be where cellulose solvents and enzymes attack preferentially, where gaseous and liquid exchange is thought most likely to occur [7, 23] and undergo elongation during normal tension mercerization [53].

By the mid-1960s linen researchers had concluded that the most promising approach for significant advances in performance lay in so-called intra-fiber differential treatments [11, 6, 61]. Employing physical, chemical or combined approaches to deliberately generate non-uniform distribution of cross-links within fibers, similar studies on cotton have yielded much more published information [21]. However, numerous attempts to localize reagents mitigate the loss in tensile strength and AR from migration have been described. These include chlorinated carrier solvent-based application, and solvent vapor curing [11]; a range of chemical, UV, X- and γ-ray induced radical grafting studies [62]; the addition of soluble polyester activator compounds to pad liquors [50, 59, 60] and a comprehensive study of novel polymer approaches [5]. The effects of low liquor add-on techniques, foam and vacuum slot application respectively [4] have also been investigated. Of these, only the foam treatment and polyester additives were considered to confer improvements and be viable, the others yielding a balance of results similar to conventional pad dry cure techniques.

The poor AR and tensile strength of treated fabrics haves been attributed to loss of elasticity within nodes due to cross-linking, and an alternative approach was aftertreatment to hydrolyse or otherwise disrupt cross-links in the more accessible regions. Post-mercerization or other treatments of aminoplasts can achieve this but reduce the dry CR [11, 59, 60]; the available data (largely patents) having been reviewed [50]. Such aftertreatment of reactants is generally impractical, but liquid ammonia treatment has been shown to be effective on linen [28]: the effect requires further investigation. Evaluation for finish distribution was usually by staining and optical sectioning, occasionally scanning electron microscopy (SEM), along with conventional physical testing. The availability of techniques, such as environmental SEM and Fourier transform infrared (FT-IR) microscopy, should help to quantify these effects.

SPECTROSCOPY

Innovation has generally been led by cotton research and commercial research and development (R and D) laboratories, as evidenced in O'Connor [46]. IR spectroscopy, for example, has been utilized for decades in the evaluation of fixation, response to laundering/hydrolysis and analysis of competing products. Very extensive work on cotton finish development from Yang [70] onward, employed FT-IR, while Gilbert and Kokot [15, 16] applied chemometric techniques, diffuse reflectance infrared Fourier transform spectroscopy (DRIFT) and FT-Raman to results. Originally developed for other processes, the potential of spectroscopy for textile applications was recognized some time ago [17, 48]. Early applications for cottons included quantifying degree of mercerization, and concentration of sizing compounds on warp yarns by Centebexel [50]. At present, available quality control procedures during production are limited to observing the change in fiber or fabric, for example, length and cross-section using labor intensive physical tests. Faughey and Sharma [8] have investigated the use of visible and near infrared spectroscopy (Vis-NIRS) for measuring changes in key quality parameters and this application has been followed up with the recent report on the development of Vis-NIR calibrations for monitoring fiber quality during production using the partial least squares regression method [58]. Preliminary results also suggest that infrared spectroscopy could be useful in fabric finishing, notably in assessing crease recovery and abrasion resistance performance [43, 44].

Quality evaluation, using FTIR (figure 1) and Vis-NIR (figure 2), can be used for assessing fabric quality [42], particularly modification in the non-cellulosic fractions, mainly as a result of pre-finishing treatments, such as mild scour followed by bleaching. Cross-linking applications (e.g. dimethylol urea) significantly improves crease recovery in linen relative to untreated linen, and increasing the concentration to 5 % rate of application improves the crease recovery performance at the expense of resistance to abrasion [56]. This effect has long been observed for all cellulosics [59]. In addition, bleaching the fabric appears to have a major detrimental effect on abrasion resistance, but conversely it gave the best material for crease recovery treatment [43]. These changes resulting from of cross linking can be detected as shifts in a number of NIR spectral bands, especially 1400 – 1550 nm, 1880 - 1920 nm and 2020 - 2500 nm. In addition, the use of mid-infrared spectroscopy to determine degree of cross-linking, which is linked to crease recovery and abrasion performance for linen, has been demonstrated [42]. Mercerization had a major effect on improving the abrasion resistance. Previous reports have suggested that caustic treatment generally yields only moderate improvements in abrasion resistance, but performance can be aided by the improved cover i.e. the degree of evenness of yarn spacing, thickness and weight/m^2. This process involves considerable weft shrinkage in linens. Resistance to abrasion is sensitive to fabric construction and degree of shrinkage permitted. This observation was derived from work on both traditional yarn- and piece-bleached fabrics and further investigation is required. Crease-recovery performance is principally dependent on the degree of chemical cross-linking and this parameter should correlate with specific bonding changes, confined to localized regions of the spectrum. However, some contribution from the fabric construction is inevitable, as this influences abrasion resistance and to a limited extent, the un-creasing capabilities. Recent work carried out in the Department of Applied Plant Science has shown that visible and near infrared spectra can be used for classifying linen fabric treatments. Boil, bleach and mercerization processes impart spectral shift in the visible-NIR spectral range [43]. In future, Vis-NIR tools may prove to be invaluable for predicting process requirements of woven fabric with unknown process history. Calibrations for this type of application can be generated quickly in contrast with the warp yarn break model [10], as the process steps are limited.

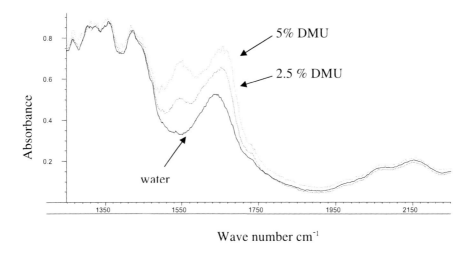

Figure 1. Overlays of FT-IR spectra of bleached linen treated with water, 2.5 % and 5 % (DMU) [43].

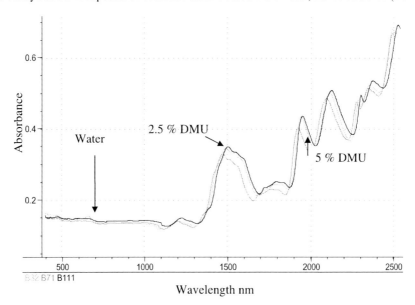

Figure 2. Overlays of Vis-NIR spectra of bleached linen treated with water, 2.5 % and 5 % (DMU) [43].

THERMAL ANALYSIS

The use of thermogravimetric analysis (TG) has been demonstrated by Sharma and co-workers [9, 51] to predict flax fiber parameters, such as quality in relation to yarn production and flax fiber fineness. Derivative thermograms of linen fabric samples display two active regions of high rate of weight loss at 200 - 400°C and 400 - 600°C (figure 3). The effects in these regions are referred to as peak 1 and peak 2, respectively. Figure 3 illustrates the ability of thermal analysis to detect the presence of cross-links between cellulose molecules, created by treating the fabric samples with dimethylolurea (DMU) for improving crease recovery [44]. The main components of flax fibers are cellulose, hemicelluloses, pectins and lignins [13]. These components have been stated to combust individually in particular temperature ranges, pectin at 200°C-290°C, hemicellulose at 243°C-305 °C, alpha cellulose at 240 °C - 360°C, and straw lignin at 410°C-600 °C [57]. Peak 1 can be interpreted as being primarily from a cellulose origin whilst Peak 2 is regarded as being caused mainly by combustion of secondary products from the combustion associated with Peak 1 in association with any contribution from other fractions, such as lignin, rather than combustion of these fractions alone [12]. Previously reported observations [9, 55] on flax fibers have demonstrated that changes occurring in the combustion peaks, such as their temperatures, widths, areas and heights, can be related to physical and quality aspects of the fibers. Differences in the thermograms have also been reported [57] in relation to heating rates employed and the technique used to prepare samples. This publication also suggested that improved resolution might be expected at lower heating rates.

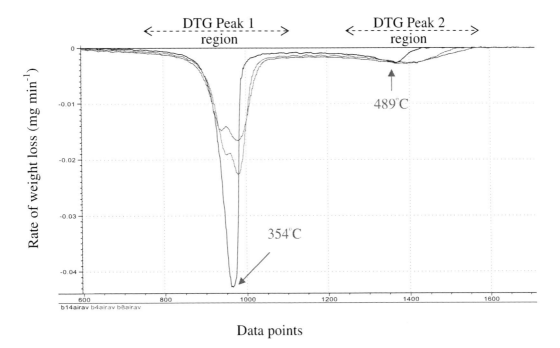

Figure 3. Overlays of derivative thermograms of bleached linen treated with water (black), 2.5 % (green) and 5 % (DMU) (red) combusted in air at 20 °C min $^{-1}$ heating rate (McCall unpublished data).

Thermal data obtained has generally been investigated using multivariate analysis techniques, such as principal component analysis, to identify the significant thermal parameter. Statistical modelling methods, such as partial least squares regression analysis, have been used to establish equations that can be used to predict fiber, yarn and fabric parameters. Thermal techniques, although not particularly rapid, are nonetheless much more rapid than conventional physical measurement techniques. In addition, they provide structural and chemical information and do not require pre-conditioning before analysis.

A differentiation must be made between instrumental techniques that offer potential for research and development in laboratory applications, and those compatible with routine analysis. Although it is clear that a proven suite of techniques and chemometric packages is currently available to assist both the near-market and long term requirements, given the beleaguered state of the industry, it is doubtful if fundamental research into finish development is a first priority. Commercial linen finishers now operate on a small scale, prioritizing degree of fixation and batch-wise consistency. Even the provision of instrumental systems, now essential for QA purposes, will require collaboration between academic groups and widely scattered SMEs. The development of optimized finishes and associated predictive models for physical performance in crease recovery, abrasion resistance and tensile strength testing would constitute a major advance but demand external funding.

A series of publications have detailed the application of SEM, X-ray microanalysis, elemental analysis, thermal analysis and spectroscopy to CR and AR finished fabrics, and the application of chemometrics to develop predictive models for dry crease recovery and abrasion resistance [43, 56]. Recent studies on linen treated with DMEU have shown that amorphous and superficial regions of the flax fiber were made inaccessible to cellulase, DRIFT spectra confirming this finding. DSC was employed to analyze the process itself, and the influence of a catalyst [64]. Batch-wise variation was shown to occur during methylolation of ethylene urea to form dimethylol ethylene urea (DMEU), with DSC proving superior to FT-IR and melting point determination in assessing reagent purity. When DMEU is used as a cross-linking agent, prolonged exposure to elevated temperatures (during extended curing) may result in deleterious side-reactions resulting in flawed or imperfect textiles [65]. Predominance in other sectors has led to the availability of robust proven equipment, which has seen extensive application to the flax industry, ranging from assessment of fiber fineness during mechanical processing [58] to prediction of weaving performance in yarns [10]. The logical extension of established methodologies to finishing is ongoing.

Applications

An important consequence of the demise of vertical groups is a growing prevalence of global sourcing for fiber (tow, sliver and roving) by spinners; yarn (unbleached, bleached and dyed) by weavers; fabrics (grey, bleached, dyed and finished) by garment manufacturers, and the necessity to outsource specialist bleaching, dyeing and finishing services. Spectroscopy can be used for the identification and quantitative estimation of the presence, chemical nature (essential in proper desizing), level and uniformity of sizing agents and lubricants. The detection and/or identification of applied biocides, some of which are known to interfere with dyeing, in addition to health and safety implications, is also possible. Top quality linen apparel is frequently produced in small batches. On bought-in fabrics, the instrumental verification of physical performance and identification of any crosslinking agent present, is necessary to ensure meeting permissible formaldehyde levels for specific markets. This would enable flexible manufacturing and improved response times without recourse to third-party physical testing. In view of anticipated growth in demand for flax fiber in non-textile applications, such as composite manufacture, production and supply in the form of a compositionally and physically uniform staple are essential for end-users. An NIRS based system for the analysis of fiber fineness, composition and, level of additives, would be readily achievable on the basis of current published work.

Development and Optimization of Finishes

As a precursor to any development work on finishes, more basic research on the effect of finish distribution is essential if significant improvement over current performance is sought. However, the entire industry, let alone finishers, does not possess the technical resources for such work. Given the current size of the market, collaborative input from finish manufacturers will be modest, if any. Trask-Morrell and co-workers [66-68] emphasized the application of techniques, such as TGA, TGA-MS and DSC, as cost-effective rapid filter or screening techniques for the investigation of cotton reagent and catalyst systems. Such innovative approaches would be essential for work on linen.

Alternative Approaches to Improved Fabric Properties

It must be accepted that achieving twice the current performance of dry crease recovery and abrasion resistance with 100% linen may not be technically or economically feasible. Accordingly, during the 1960s and 70s much effort was expended in developing and optimizing blends and unions with a variety of regenerated and synthetic fibers. Fabrics offering enhanced performance whilst largely retaining the characteristics of pure linen became commercially available, and brief details have been summarized in various publications. Linen/polyester blends containing 15% polyester were found to improve abrasion resistance considerably in dry cross-linked samples with the pre-mercerized pieces producing the best results [36]. Linen/rayon mixtures have shown potential as the properties of rayon - high extensibility, low strength and excellent crease resistant behavior with urea-formaldehyde resins compliment those found in linen [24]. Post-mercerization of resin-treated samples has also shown promise [61]. In general, precise monitoring is essential to prevent damage to one or other component during bleaching and dyeing finishing operations. However, predictive models could be developed for blends to incorporate characteristics of components using spectral and thermal results.

In reality, any increase in demand for linen fabrics will highlight the paucity of modern equipment now available, and to avoid the financial risk of investing in dedicated machinery, it is probable that non-linen spinners will seek to utilize linen fiber compatible with short-staple spinning systems. The best known of these developments are the steam explosion process [25] and Linron [24]. Fabrics from such fibers, alone or in blends, would represent an anomalous class in performance and response to finishing, requiring specific databases.

Ongoing work by cotton breeders includes a radical approach to fiber durability, employing genetic modification to generate polymers within the fiber lumen. Given the very different primary function of flax (bast) fibers, acting as stressed structural members within the plant stem, such an approach is less feasible. Breakthroughs in durable press finishing, along with the new applications for flax outlined above, will help to stabilize the flax and linen market, freeing it from the fluctuations inherent in a fashion-driven industry

CONCLUSION

The incessant rise and future uncertainties in petroleum pricing, an increasing environmental awareness at government level, and current rural diversification initiatives are all factors which are potentially very beneficial for renewable bio-fibers, and particularly the bast fibers. In conjunction with such global trends, the identification of key advances in quality assurance and/or efficiency developed by other industries, and their adoption in a coordinated manner could revitalize a moribund sector. It is undeniable that the linen industry has generally shown great reluctance to collaborate on technical research and development, whether internally or with external academic researchers. Having now contracted to a point where it barely retains the necessary critical mass to survive, it cannot afford not to exploit forthcoming opportunities and must embrace modern techniques. Real time spectral data acquisitions, during either on-line or off-line assessment, will open up new frontiers for interpretation and utilization of the hardware. The finishing industry needs a rapid technique for assessing quality in order to control and optimize the process. The approaches outlined are not speculative, but available and have already been proven and are established procedure in other manufacturing sectors, including the cotton industry, and key aspects have been satisfactorily demonstrated on flax fiber and fabrics. Additionally, such methods would help circumvent any shortage of skilled technical and laboratory staff arising as a result of market expansion.

REFERENCES

[1]   Aboul-Fetouh, MS; Miles, LWC. *Textile Research Journal,* 1968, 38, pp. 176.
[2]   ANON. Progress Research Report, Lambeg Industrial Research Association (LIRA), Lambeg, UK, 1982, 1, pp. 26 -27 .
[3]   ANON. A for the Future. Report of the Linen Task Force. 1985, *IDBNI,* Belfast, pp. 179.
[4]   ANON. Linen Research and Developments 1980-1986. Textile Institute, Manchester, Publication, 1988, pp. 47.
[5]   Archibald, LB. Project Report IDB 1A: Feasibility study in the use of polymerisation methods to improve the crease-resistance of flax. 1987, *LIRA,* Lambeg, pp. 145.
[6]   Archibald, LB; Hanvey, *J. Personal communication.* (1985).
[7]   G. Buschle-Diller, G; Zeronian, SH; Pan, N; Moon, MY. *Textile Research Journal,* 1994, 64, pp. 270.
[8]   Faughey, GJ; Sharma, HSS. *Journal of Near Infrared Spectroscopy,* 2000, 8, pp. 61.

[9]   Faughey, GF; Sharma, HSS; Mccall, RD. *Journal of Applied Polymer Science,* 2000, 75, pp. 508.

[10] Faughey, GF; Sharma, HSS. *Journal of Near Infrared Spectroscopy,* 2002, 10, pp. 151-163.

[11] Finlay, AR. Crease-resist Finishing of Fabrics Containing Linen. Technical Report. 199, *LIRA,* Lambeg, 1975, pp. 12.

[12] Fisher, T; Hajaligol, M; Waymac, B; Kellogg, D. *Analytical and Applied Pyrolysis Journal,* 2002, 62, pp. 331.

[13] Focher, B; Marzetti, A; Sharma, HSS. "Changes in the Structure and Properties of Flax During Processing" in The Biology and Processing of Flax, H.S.S. SHARMA, C. Van SUMERE, Eds., M Publications, Belfast, 1992, pp. 329-342.

[14] Franck, RR. "The History and Present Position of Linen" in The Biology and Processing of Flax, H.S.S. Sharma, C. Van Sumere, Eds., M Publications, Belfast, 1992, pp. 1-10.

[15] Gilbert, C; Kokot, S. *Microchimica Acta,* 1997, 14, pp. 185.

[16] Gilbert, C; Kokot, S. *Vibrational Spectroscopy,* 1995, 9, pp. 161.

[17] S. Ghosh. *Textile World,* 1985, 135, pp. 45.

[18] Goswami, BC; Martindale, JG; Scardino, FL. Textile Yarns, John Wiley, NY, 1977, pp. 473.

[19] Gray, J; Riley, J. Personal communication. (1985).

[20] Happey, F. Applied Science, Academic Press, London, UK, 1978, pp. 562.

[21] Harper, RJ. Durable Press Cotton Goods. Merrow Publication Ltd., Watford, UK, 1971, pp. 54.

[22] Heap, SA; Hunt, RE; Rennison, PA; Tattersall, R. U-F Resin in the Treatment of Textiles, in Chemical Aftertreatment of Textiles, H. MARK, N.S. Wooding and S.M. Atlas, Eds., Wiley, New York, 1971, pp. 267 –317.

[23] Hock, CW. *Journal of Research Natural Bureau of Standards.* (U.S. Dept of Commerce), 1942, 29, pp. 41.

[24] Kernaghan, K. "Physical Properties of Linen and Their Influence on Finishing" in The Biology and Processing of Flax, H.S.S. SHARMA and C. Van SUMERE, Eds., M Publications, Belfast, 1992, pp. 475-500.

[25] Kessler, RW; Becker, U; Kohler, R; Goth, B. *Biomass and Bioenergy,* 1998, 14, pp. 237-249.

[26] Kokot, S; Komatsu, K; Meyer, U; Zollinger, H. *Textile Research Journal,* 1975, 45, pp. 673.

[27] Kokot, S; Yang, C; Gilbert, C. *Analytica Chemica Acta,* 1996, 332, pp. 105.

[28] Kratz, G; Funder, K. *Melliand Textilberichte,* 1987, 68, pp. 775.

[29] Lambrinou, I. *Melliand Textilberichte,* 1970, 51, pp. 815.

[30] Lambrinou, I. *Melliand Textilberichte,* 1970, 51, pp. 930.

[31] Lambrinou, I. *Melliand Textilberichte,* 1970, 51, pp. 1241.

[32] Lambrinou, I. *Melliand Textilberichte,* 1975, 56, pp. 277.

[33] Lambrinou, I. *Melliand Textilberichte,* 1975, 56, pp. 787.

[34] Lambrinou, I. *Melliand Textilberichte,* 1982, 63, pp. 526.

[35] Lambrinou, I. *Melliand Textilberichte,* 1982, 63, pp. 528.

[36] Lambrinou, I. *Melliand* Textilberichte, 1983, 63, pp. 419.

[37] Lyle D. Performance of Textiles, J Wiley, NY USA 1977 pp 579.

[38] Mark, H; Wooding, NS; Atlas, SM. Chemical Aftertreatment of Textiles, Willey, NY, 1971, pp. 634.

[39] Matschat K; *Textil-Rundschau,* 1961, 16, pp. 580.

[40] Marsh JT. Self Smoothing Fabrics, Chapman and Hall, London, 1962, pp. 399.

[41] Marsh JT. An Introduction to Textile Finishing, Chapman and Hall, London, 1966, pp. 588.

[42] Mccall RD; Kernaghan, K; Sharma, HSS. *Journal of Applied Polymer Science,* 2001, 82, pp. 1886.

[43] Mccall, RD; Sharma, HSS. "Application of Spectroscopy for Assessing Linen Treated with a Crease Recovery Agent", in Near Infrared Spectroscopy: Proceedings of the 11th International Conference, A.M.C. Davis, A. Garrido-Varo, NIR Publications, Norwich, 2004, pp. 1027-1032.

[44] Mccall, RD. The Surface Characteristics of and Analysis of Flax s, PhD thesis, Queen's University Belfast, Belfast, 2003, pp 241.

[45] Morton, WE; Hearle, JWS. Physical Properties of Textile s, Textile Institute, Manchester, UK, 1997, pp. 708.

[46] O'Connor, RT. Instrumental Analysis of Cotton Cellulose and Modified Cotton Cellulose, Marcel Dekker Inc. New York, 1972, pp. 479.

[47] Optiz, MD. Textil Praxis, 1972, 27, pp. 166.

[48] Ranford, SL; Hammersley, MLJ; Acker, VC. Wool Technology and Sheep Breeding, 1986, 34, pp. 147.

[49] Ruys, L; Van Lancker, M; Saey, A. *Melliand Textilberichte,* 1993, 74, pp. 358.

[50] Ryan, JJ. "Wash and Wear Fabrics", in Chemical Aftertreatment of Textiles, H. Mark, N.S. Wooding, S.M. Atlas, Eds., Willey, New York, 1971, pp. 417-464.

[51] Sharma, HSS; Kernaghan, K. *Thermochemica Acta,* 1988, 132, pp. 101.

[52] Sharma, HSS; Van Sumere, CF. The Biology and Processing of Flax, M Publications, Belfast, UK, 1992, pp. 572.

[53] Sharma, HSS; Fraser, TW; McCall, RD; Shields, N; Lyons, G. *Journal of the Textile Institute,* 1995, 86, pp. 539.

[54] Sharma, HSS. " and Yarn Qualities and Their Relationship to Fabric Characteristics" in Producing for the Market, J. Boyazoglu, R. Kozlowski, H.S.S. Sharma, L. Rosenberg, C. Morvan, C. Sultana, 1996, Fourth Regional Workshop on Flax, University of Rouen, France, pp. 397-408.

[55] Sharma, HSS; Faughey, G; McCall, RD. *Journal of the Textile Institute,* 1996, 87, pp. 249.

[56] Sharma, HSS; McCall, RD; Kernaghan, K. *Journal of Applied Polymer Science,* 1999, 72, pp. 1209.

[57] Sharma, HSS; Whiteside, L; Kernaghan, K; Mccall, RD. Quality assessment of from 2000 flax crop using derivative thermogravimetry and near infrared spectroscopy, in Natural Fibers Special edition: Proceedings of the Second Global Workshop – Bast Plants in the New Millennium, A. Bozzoni, R. Krell, R. Kozlowski, A. Atanassov, A. Balabanova, R. Koeva, M. Tubach, eds., Institute of Natural s, Poznan, 2001, pp. 42-53.

[58] Sharma, HSS; Reinard, N. *Applied Spectroscopy,* 2004, 58, pp. 1431.

[59] Sloan, FRW. Journal of the Society of Dyers and Colourists, 1997, 113, pp. 46.

[60] Sloan, FRW. Journal of the Society of Dyers and Colourists, 1997, 113, pp. 82.

[61] Sloan, FRW. Personal communication, (1998).

[62] Spencer-Smith, JL. Lambeg Research Review, *LIRA,* Lambeg, 1969, 4, pp. 4.

[63] Steele, R. *Textile Research Journal,* 1960, 30, pp. 37.

[64] Stuart T; Eggins, B; Stewart, D. *Cellulose Chemistry and Technology,* 2001, 35, pp. 371.

[65] Stuart, T; Crangle, A; Wilson, R; Stuart, D. *Cellulose Chemistry and Technology,* 2001, 35, pp. 545.

[66] Trask-Morrell, BJ; Andrews, BAK. *Journal of Applied Polymer Science,* 1991, 42, pp. 511.

[67] Trask-Morrell, BJ; Andrews, BAK. *Textile Research Journal,* 1992, 62, pp. 144.

[68] Trask-Morrell, BJ; Andrews, BAK; Graves, EE. *Textile Colorist and Chemist.* 1990, 22, pp. 23.

[69] Trotman, ER. The Dyeing and Chemical Technology of Textile s, C. Griffin, High Wycombe, 1984, pp. 587.

[70] Yang, CQ. *Textile Research Journal,* 1991, 61, pp. 433.

In: Textiles for Sustainable Development   ISBN: 978-1-60021-559-9
Editors: R. Anandjiwala, L. Hunter et al., pp. 95-102   © 2007 Nova Science Publishers, Inc.

Chapter 9

APPLICATION OF OSMOTIC PRESSURE FOR EVALUATION OF QUALITY AND QUANTITY OF FIBER IN FLAX AND HEMP

Wanda Konczewicz and Ryszard Kozlowski

Institute of Natural s; ul. Wojska Polskiego 71 B, 60-630 Poznan, Poland;
wanda@inf.poznan.pl, sekretar@inf.poznan.pl

ABSTRACT

The research covered the effect of the osmotic pressure on the evaluation of the yield of fiber of Polish flax cultivars - NIKE, ARTEMIDA, Belgian flax cultivar - ELISA and Polish hemp cultivar BIAŁOBRZESKIE. The experiments were conducted by using the following processing conditions: temperature 25-35°C, duration of process: from 72 to 96 h for flax and from 72 to 168 h for hemp, with constant, regular and controlled water flow. The parameters of the fiber obtained according to this method are characterized by color and fineness.

Keywords: osmotic degumming, flax fiber, hemp fiber, fiber yield.

INTRODUCTION

There are many commonly known methods for plant fiber degumming which allow for separation of the fiber from the woody part, and removal of non-cellulosic components, such as pectin, hemicellulose, lignin, waxes and fats. Separation of non-cellulosic components from the fiber can be achieved by preliminary processing the raw materials: straw (dew retting, water retting, etc.) and enzymatic, chemical or physical processing of the fibers [3-9]. The various methods of plant fiber degumming is shown in figure 1.

Proper extraction methods result in fiber with the required length, fineness and strength as well as high purity, optimal efficiency and homogeneity. The extraction of fibers from fibrous plants is carried out mainly by mechanical processes.

At the INF, research concentrates on new methods of fiber degumming which can provide higher quality of raw material. An example of such a method is the extraction of fiber using the natural physical laws: water diffusion, osmosis and osmotic pressure [1-2]. Utilization of physico-chemical phenomena, especially osmosis, occurring inside the fibrous plants when they are exposed to water, permits extraction of fibers without affecting their natural features. The parameters of the fiber obtained according to this method are characterized by an adequate fineness and color.

In particular, the application of osmotic degumming of fibrous raw materials, produces uniform fiber and enables the objective evaluation of the quantity and the quality of the fibers in the plant. Specifically, this is important for evaluating progress in breeding new cultivars of fibrous plants.

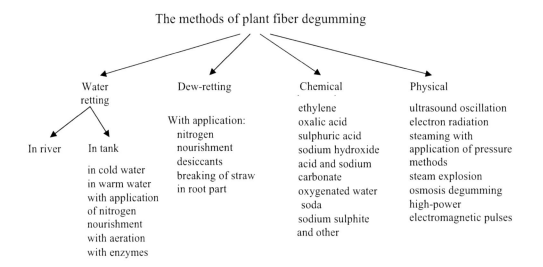

Figure 1. Degumming of plant fibers.

EXPERIMENTAL

The raw material used for the experiment was the straw of Polish flax cultivars – NIKE and ARTEMIDA, Belgian flax cultivar ELISA and Polish hemp cultivar BIAŁOBRZESKIE.

Samples of flax straw of uniform length, thickness, color and posture health condition were taken and assessed for quality, according to the requirements of Polish standard PN-P-80103.

The middle part of the plant, with a nominal length of 50 cm, was taken for the experiment (i.e. the top part with branches and capsules and the bottom part with roots were thrown away).100g samples of the raw material were used for the tests.

The experiments were conducted by using the following process conditions process: temperature 25-35°C, duration of process: from 72 to 96 h for flax and from 72 to 168 h for hemp, with constant, regular and controlled water flow.

After degumming, the straw was dried. Then the straw was scutchedscotched, separatinge the fiber from the woody part, using the KL-13 apparatus and the total fibers content determined.

Then the fiber was hackled manually and subjected to metrological testing. The fiber fineness (tex) and breaking tenacity (cN/tex) were measured. Chemical analyses were performed to establish the cellulose, hemicellulose, lignin, pectin, wax and fat content as well as the degree of polymerization of the cellulose.

RESULTS AND DISCUSSION

Application of Osmotic Degumming for the Objective Evaluation of the Quantity and the Quality of Flax Fibers

The results of the evaluation of the three flax fiber cultivars are presented in table 1.

The results of the flax fiber yield (%), fiber fineness (tex) and fiber tenacity (cN/tex) are shown in figures 2, 3 and 4, respectively, whereas the results of the chemical analysis are given in table 2.

Table 1. Evaluation of the flax straw from three flax cultivars: NIKE, ELISA and ARTEMIDA

	NIKE	ELISA	ARTEMIDA
Length of straw [cm]			
- nominal	74	65	68
- total	93	72	85
Thickness [mm]	1.5	1.12	1.27
Color [%]			
- yellow	95	-	-
- dark yellow	-	-	65
- green yellow	-	100	-
- bronze	5	-	35
Healthy stems[%]	100	100	100
Straight straw[%]	100	100	100
Grade of straw	I	I	I

The fibers obtained were characterized by color, handle, fineness and breaking tenacity relative to the corresponding values of the initial raw material.

As can be seen in figure 3, the fiber fineness varied according to the cultivar. The fineness of fiber from the Nike cultivar was 4-5 tex while that from the remaining two cultivars ranged from 2.8-2.9 tex. On the other hand, the breaking tenacity (figure 4) of fiber from the Nike cultivars (53 cN/tex) was lower than that of the fibers from the other two cultivars (59 cN/tex). The values presented in table 1 and figure 3 show that finer degummed fiber can be obtained from thinner straw. For instance, the 1.5 mm thick straw of the Nike cultivar gives a fiber fineness of 4-5 tex whereas the 1.12 mm thick straw of the Elisa cultivar produced a fiber fineness of 2.5-3.5 tex.

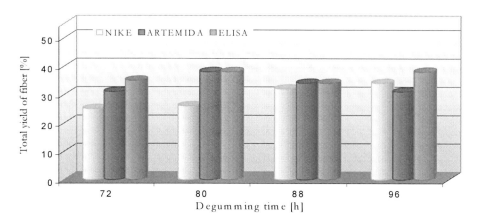

Figure 2. Effect of degumming time on flax fiber conent.

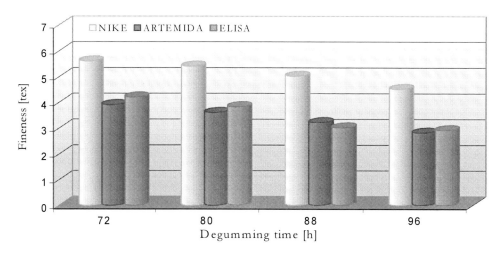

Figure 3. Effect of degumming time on flax fiber fineness.

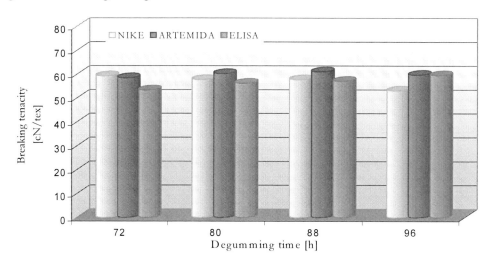

Figure 4. Effect of degumming time on flax fiber breaking tenacity.

Table 2. Chemical composition of hackled flax fibers from three cultivars:
NIKE, ELISA, ARTEMIDA

	NiKE	ARTEMIDA	ELISA
Cellulose [%]	80.5 – 82.3	78.8 – 80.8	79.4 – 82.4
Hemicellulose [%]	13.3 – 14.7	14.0 – 14.5	12.5 – 14.3
Lignin [%]	1.7 – 2.2	2.2 – 2.9	1.7 – 2.8
Pectin [%]	1.8 – 2.2	1.0 – 1.6	1.9 – 2.6
Waxes and fats [%]	0.4 – 1.0	1.6 – 2.6	1.0 – 1.3
Polymerization degree	2680 – 2910	2630 - 2910	2680 - 2900

The total fiber yield in the case of all the cultivars tested, using osmotic degumming, was above 30%, whereas the reported values for regular water retting vary from 20-25% [8].

The chemical composition (table 2) shows that the osmotic degumming had no negative effect on the chemical parameters, the cellulose content being high – about 80%. The high degree of cellulose polymerization, ranging from 2630 to 2910, shows that no degradation of cellulose has occurred. The results of the chemical analysis of fiber from the three flax cultivars were similar. This shows that the osmotic degumming causes no changes in the natural properties of the flax fibers.

The results of the fiber yield, fiber fineness, fiber tenacity and chemical analysis show that there is a strong correlation between the fiber and the initial material used for all the flax cultivars tested in this study.

Application of Osmotic Degumming for the Objective Evaluation of the Quantity and Quality of Hemp Fiber

The raw material used for the experiment was hemp straw having the following characteristics:

- total length of straw   215 cm
- nominal length of straw   195 cm
- thickness   6.9 mm
- color   green yellow 100%
- healthy stems   100%
- Grade of straw   I

The results of fiber yield (%), fiber breaking tenacity (cN/tex) and fiber fineness (tex) are presented in figures 5, 6 and 7, respectively, whereas the results of the chemical analysis are presented in table 3.

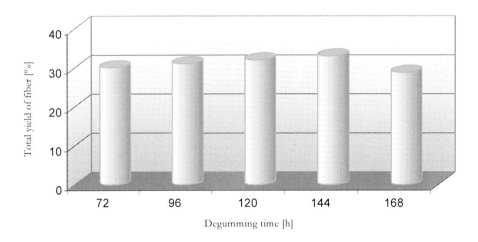

Figure 5. Effect of degumming time on total hemp fiber content.

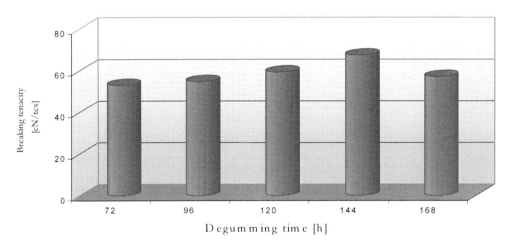

Figure 6. Effect of fiber degumming time on hemp fiber breaking tenacity.

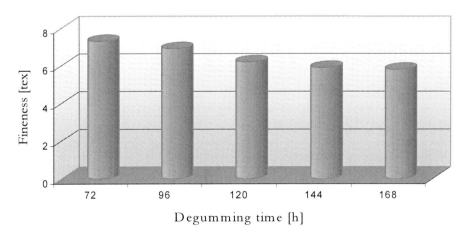

Figure 7. Effect of degumming time on hemp fiber fineness.

Table 3. Chemical composition of hemp fiber

Degumming time (h)	Cellulose (%)	Hemicellulose (%)	Lignin (%)	Pectin (%)	Polymerization degree
72	79.98	14.27	3.18	2.02	2713
96	77.50	15.59	4.53	1.95	2739
120	77.77	16.59	3.51	1.81	2841
144	77.27	15.83	3.88	1.83	2908
168	79.42	15.38	2.03	1.80	2865

The results presented in figures 6 and 7 show that the increase in degumming time improves the properties of hemp fibers, such as fineness and breaking tenacity.

The best properties, fiber fineness of 5.9 tex and breaking tenacity of 67.35 cN/tex, were obtained with the 144-hour osmotic degumming process.

The results of the chemical composition of the hemp straw indicate that the increase in the degumming time results in lower pectin and lignin contents, these being lowest after 168 hours of degumming (see table 3). However, the cellulose content remains high, between 77.27 – 79.98 %. The hemicellulose content, reaches a maximum of 16.59 % after 120 hours of degrumming.

The degree of polymerization remains high, varying from 2700 to 2900, which proves that none of the natural fiber properties are affected by the degumming process.

This method was subsequently used for the objective evaluation of the yield of fiber for the from Polish cultivar SILESIA. The experiment helped to determine the influence of the plant density and harvesting time on the hemp fiber content. Hemp cultivation occurred under 8 different sowing densities: 0.5, 5, 10, 15, 30, 40, 50 and 60 kg/ha and three periods of harvesting; half flowering stage, beginning of seed maturity and at 50% seed maturity.

CONCLUSIONS

- The osmotic pressure method of degumming allows the objective evaluation of the amount and quality of fiber in plant fiber straw. It is especially important for breeding new plant fibers.
- Application of osmotic degumming of bast fiber provides homogeneous, fine and strong fibers, and optimal yeield with a soft handle and natural color.
- Similar results were obtained for all the three flax cultivars (NIKE, ELISA, ARTEMIDA) indicating the same level which means that the method employed does not change the natural properties of the fibers. Evaluation of the straw quality, fiber efficiency as well as the fiber properties indicate a good correlation between the initial raw material and the fiber obtained as an output product of the process.

REFERENCES

[1]   A. Allam, R. Kozlowski, and W. Konczewicz, "Degumming of fibrous plants based on osmotic pressure phenomenon" in *International Conference of FAO European Research Network on Flax and Allied Plants for Humanity Welfare.* Cairo, Egypt, December 8–11, 2003

[2]   A. Allam, R. Kozlowski, and W. Konczewicz, "Application of Osmotic Pressure in Degumming of Flax" in *Proceedings of Conference "Bast Fibrous Plants on the Turn of Second and Third Millennium"*. Natural s, Special Edition 2001/2. Shenyang, China, September 18-22, 2001, V/10, p.382

[3]   R. Kozlowski, J. Batog, W. Konczewicz, M. Mackiewicz-Talarczyk, M. Muzyczek, N. Sedelnik, and B. Tanska, "Latest state – of art in bast fibers bioprocessing" in *11th International Conference for Renewable Resources and Plant Biotechnology*. Poznan, Poland, June 6-7, 2005

[4]   R. Kozlowski, J. Batog, and W. Konczewicz W., "Bioprocessing of bast plants s and by-products: degumming, osmotic and enzymatic treatment" in *Proceeding of the International Symposium an Kenaf Development and Products Show*. Beijing, China, August 19-21, 2003

[5]   R. Kozlowski, R., J. Batog, and W. Konczewicz, "Enzymatic treatment of bast fibrous plants, s and by-products" in *International Conference of FAO European Research Network on Flax and Allied Plants for Humanity Welfare*. Cairo, Egypt, December 8– 11, 2003

[6]   R. Kozlowski, J. Batog, W. Konczewicz, J. Kozlowska, and N. Sedelnik (2001). Overview of current activities relative to bioprocessing of bast plants, s and by products. Part I. *Natural s*. 45, pp.85-92.

[7]   R. Kozlowski, J. Batog, W. Konczewicz, J. Kozlowska, and N. Sedelnik (2001). Overview of current activities relative to bioprocessing of bast plants, s and by products. Part II. *Natural s*. 45, pp. 93-100.

[8]   R. Kozlowski (1970). Proces roszenia lnu z dodatkiem mocznika na tle klasycznego sposobu, ze szczegolnym uwzglednieniem lotnych kwasow tluszczowych w plynie roszeniowym i w pazdzierzach, wydzielanych gazow, zwiazkow azotowych oraz niektorych wlasnosci wlokna, przedzy i tkanin [Retting flax with addition of urea compared with the classical method, with particular consideration to volatile fatty acids in retting fluid and shives, produced gases, nitrogen compounds and some properties of , yarn and fabrics]. PhD dissertation. Poznan, Poland

[9]   R. Kozlowski, J. Tabisz, (1967). Sposob roszenia slomy lnianej z dodatkiem mocznika. [The retting method for flax straw with the use of urea]. Biblioteczka dla Praktykow. IPWL. [Practitioners' Library]. 3, p.67.

In: Textiles for Sustainable Development
ISBN: 978-1-60021-559-9
Editors: R. Anandjiwala, L. Hunter et al., pp. 103-115   © 2007 Nova Science Publishers, Inc.

Chapter 10

COMPARISON OF COTTON YARN STRENGTH PREDICTION METHODS

Dana Křemenáková and Jiří Militký

Textile Faculty, Technical University of Liberec, Liberec 461 17,
Czech Republic; dana.kremenakova@vslib.cz , jiri.militky@vslib.cz

ABSTRACT

Yarn mechanical properties are important for prediction of fabric mechanical behavior and estimation of yarn complex quality. The majority of models for yarn prediction are based on the fiber characteristics only. These models are valid for restricted range of fibers and yarns. In this contribution, the prediction of one-component cotton yarn strength, based on the knowledge of fibrous bundles strength (HVI) and correction factors for fibers orientation and yarn packing density, is described. This model is compared with models of Neckar [1], Solovev (described in [1]) and Pan [3], [4], [5].

Keywords: Yarn packing density, fiber bundle strength, utilization of fiber strength in yarn.

INTRODUCTION

The An enormous number of methods and their modifications hasve been proposed for characterization of cotton fibers. These methods can be used for predicting the influenceon of fiber properties influence on the properties (strength) of yarns. Generally, the cotton yarn strength is dependent on the fiber parameters of fiber (fiber strength, fineness and fiber uniformity mainly), parameters of yarn formation (yarn fineness, twist etc.) and spinning technology. The theoretical predictive models are based on either the mechanisms of yarn formation or the concept of strength utilization factors i.e. lowering of fiber strength due to bundle creation, orientation, number of fibers bearing load and limit arrangement of fibers in yarns. Models of this type are not based directly on measured properties and the degree of fit is usually low in comparison with classical regression type models. On the other hand, these models have better prediction ability and are based on the logical arrangements of variables.

STRENGTH UTILIZATION FACTORS

Relative yarn strength σ_y is frequently expressed as the product of relative fiber strength σ_f and correction factor ϕ_{fy} expressing the utilization of fibers strength in the yarn.

$$\sigma_y = \sigma_f \phi_{fy} = \sigma_b \phi_{by} = \sigma_f \phi_{fb} \phi_{by} \tag{1}$$

Utilization of fibers strength in yarn is a product of fiber strength utilization in the bundle ϕ_{fb} and utilization of bundle strength in the yarn ϕ_{by}. The σ_b denotes bundle strength. These factors are computed according to the various relations. One of simplest empirical relations for relative yarn strength σ_y was derived by Solovev [1].

$$\phi_{fy} = f_n f_l f_\alpha \psi \tag{2}$$

Factor f_n expresses the influence of fiber number, f_l is a factor of the fiber length influence, f_α is a factor of the yarn twist influence and ψ is a factor of the technology influence. Factors are limited from above by the value 1, and therefore are decreasing of relative fiber strength. Relation (2) can be simply used for the prediction of ring combed and carded cotton type yarn strength. The main problems are the selection of suitable constants and use of critical twist coefficients. On the other hand, this equation includes the main fiber characteristics, such as fineness, length and strength and as well as the yarn parameters of yarn..

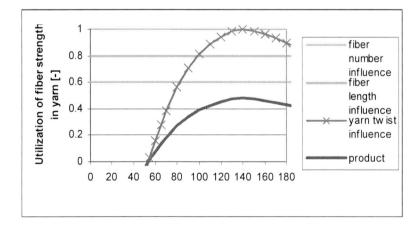

Figure 1. Utilization of fiber strength in yarn and their factors according to Solovev[1].

Neckar [1] proposed another products formmodel:

$$\phi_{fy} = \varphi \phi \chi \varpi \qquad\qquad (3)$$

where φ is the influence of fibers inclination, ϕ is the influence of fiber curling, χ is the influence of fiber slipping and ϖ is the influence of fiber migration. Relations for the computation of these factors are given in the book by Neckář book [1] and were tested in the work [2]. This relation leads to the overestimation of strength for low twist yarns [1]. The Iinfluence of critical twist coefficient is not included. The main shortcoming of this model is the necessity to know plenty ofmany material and technological parameters.

Pan [3], [4], [5] selected fiber strength distribution as a Weibull two-parameter type. The mean fiber strength, the mean bundle strength and corresponding standard deviations are defined in [3]. For large bundles, where the number of fibers in the yarn cross-section is more that 100, is bundle strength approachinges to a normal distribution (Daniel's result [3]). We derived a Ssimple approximate relation for the utilization of fiber strength in a bundle we derived [2].

$$\phi_{fb} = u^u \exp(-u)/\Gamma(1+u)_{; \ u=0,909 \ \frac{v}{\sigma_f}} \qquad\qquad (4)$$

In eqn. (4) the symbol $\Gamma()$ is a gamma function and $\frac{v}{\sigma_f}$ is the variation coefficient of fiber strength. It is shown that utilization of fiber strength in the bundle is a function of the variation coefficient of fiber strength only. In figure 3 is the solid line has been computed according to Pan's [3] relations and while the dashed line is computed by an approximate relation (4). For example, cotton fiber strength variation coefficient of 30 - 40% corresponds to a utilization of fiber strength in the bundle of 0,54 - 0,60. In figure 23 the point of 35% fiber strength variation coefficient and 0,56 utilization of fiber strength in the bundle is marked by a circle.

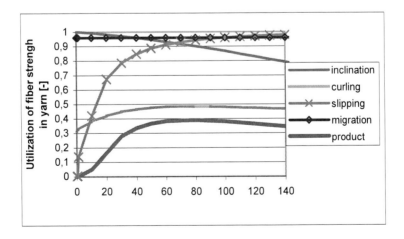

Figure 2. Utilization of fiber strength in yarn and their factors according to Neckar [1] .

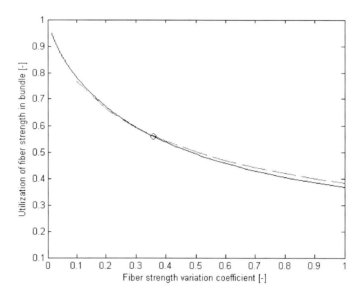

Figure 3. Utilization of fiber strength in bundle.

Utilization of bundle in yarn was derived by Pan [3]:

$$\phi_{by} = V_f n_\beta \tag{5}$$

Volume ratio V_f and orientation factor n_β as correction factors are here used here. The random distribution of helical angles of fibers is used for computation of orientation factor n_β. Migration of fibers is negligible. Fiber volume fraction V_f is computed from equation:

$$V_f\left[-\right] = 0,7(1-0,78\exp(-0,195K_y)) \tag{6}$$

where K_y is twist coefficient described by relation

$$K_y\left[cm^{-1}tex^{1/2}\right] = 10^{-2}\sqrt{T\left[tex\right]}Z\left[m^{-1}\right] = \alpha\left[m^{-1}ktex^{1/2}\right]\sqrt{1000}/100 \tag{7}$$

In eqn. (7) is T is yarn fineness, Z is yarn twist and α is twist coefficient. Orientation factor η_β is a function of helix angle β_D and yarn Poisson ratio η [3]:.

$$\eta_\beta = \frac{2\beta_D\left(1-\eta\right)+\left(1+\eta\right)\sin 2\beta_D}{4\beta_D} \tag{8}$$

Helix angle β_D is defined according to equation [6]:

$$\beta_D = arctg\left(10^{-1} K_y \sqrt{\frac{4\pi}{\rho V_f}}\right) = arctg\left(\alpha \sqrt{\frac{4\pi}{\rho V_f}} / \sqrt{10^3}\right) \tag{9}$$

where α is twist coefficient in [m^{-1}ktex$^{1/2}$], ρ is fiber density in [kgm^{-3}]. The Poisson ratio η has the form [3]:

$$\eta = \frac{\sin^5 \beta_D}{2\left(1 - \cos^3 \beta_D\right)\left(\frac{1}{2}\beta_D - \frac{1}{4}\sin 2\beta_D\right)} \tag{10}$$

Correction factors and utilization of bundle strength in yarn areis shown ion figure 4. Volume fraction is used as a factor describing inter-fiber slippage. The influence of critical twist coefficient is here not included here.

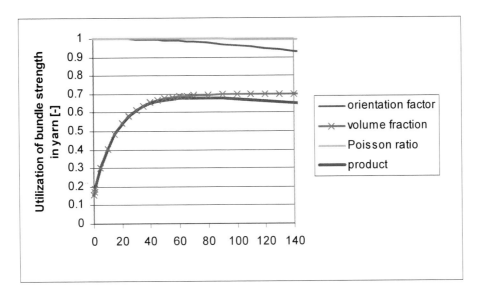

Figure 4. Utilization of bundle strength in yarn, and corresponding factors defined by Pan [3].

COTTON SINGLE FIBER AND BUNDLE STRENGTH

For measurement of cotton bundle strength, a set of devices, e.gi.e. Pressley, High Volume Instrument and Stelometer, can be used. Single fiber strength is usually measured on dynamometers or special devices as the Vibroscope and Vibrodyne set or the Mantis apparatus [13]. For evaluation of relative strength it is possible to measure fiber fineness (HVI, Afis, gravimetric method), too. Fiber fineness and strength are measured simultaneously on setthe Vibroscope and Vibrodyne set or on the Mantis. Many different principles lead to different results. The Wweakest links principle is used for explaining of the of gauge length influence on fiber strength,. fFiber strength is being a decreasing function of gauge length. The Rrelation between single fiber strength and bundle strength is shown in figure 5 [7]. The Rrelative single fiber strength was being measured on the Vibrodyne. Relative bundle strength was measured on the Pressley apparatus, with a zero gauge length and on the HVI with a 3,2 mm gauge length. Relative bundle strength was evaluated by using of the Pan model [3] as well. Paradoxically, the bundle strength is higher than the single fiber strength due to the different measurement principles. For the prediction of cotton yarn strength it is therefore better to use bundle strength as measured on High Volume Instrument (HVI).

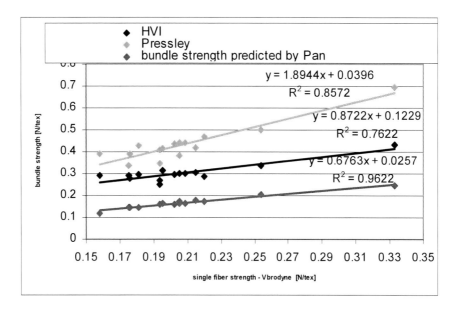

Figure 5. Relation between single fiber strength and bundle strength.

COMPARISON OF METHODS FOR YARN STRENGTH PREDICTION

A Ccomparison of the Solovev (2), Neckar (3) aand Pan (5) models is shown on the in figure 6,.the Solovev (2) and Neckar (3) models representing the utilization of fiber strength in the yarn. Utilization of bundle strength in yarn is calculated from eqns. (4) and (1). The Eeffective utilization of bundle strength in the yarn was evaluated as a ratio between cotton bundle strength σ_{HVI} (measured by HVI) and measured yarn strength σ_y :.

$$\phi_{by} = \sigma_{HVI} / \sigma_y \qquad (11)$$

The rRing spun, rotor spun, compact spun and Novaspin spun (new technology developed in VÚB Ústí n/O.) combed and carded cotton yarns were prepared. Novaspin yarn is produced at rates comparable with rotor yarn but have properties are similar to the ring yarn [9]. The pilot plant variety of Novaspin yarn was used. Characteristics of these yarns are described in table 1. The curves in the figure 6 were computed for a yarn fineness of 20 tex. The Eeffective utilization of bundle strength in the yarn was evaluated for yarns with fineness from 7,2 tex to 29,5 tex. Seven of the yarns have the same fineness (20 tex). Effective utilization of bundle strength in the yarn lies in the interval 0,35 – 0,55, and values are systematically lower than thate model curves. The Iinfluence of yarn production technology on the effective utilization of bundle strength in the yarn is visiblecan be seen from the in figure 6. The smallestlowest effective utilization of bundle strength in the yarn is for the rotor yarns and the highest is for the compact yarns and for some types of ring or Novaspin yarns.

Table 1. Experimental yarns characteristics and properties
(predicted/measured – 95% confidence interval)

Cotton technology	Fineness [tex]	Twist [m⁻¹]	Packing density [-] P/M	Diameter [mm] P/M	Tenacity [N/tex] P/M
MII combed ring	7.23	1193	0.527/ 0.417-0.481	0.107/ 0.104-0.113	0.207/ 0.167-0.175
MII combed ring	7.24	1307	0.543/ 0.414-0.454	0.106/ 0.104-0.113	0.216/ 0.150-0.161
MII combed ring	9.88	1189	0.589/ 0.464-0.502	0.119/ 0.117-0.126	0.224/ 0.206-0.218
MII combed ring	10.11	1117	0.531/ 0.410-0.452	0.126/ 0.124-0.134	0.204 0.196-0.203
MII combed ring	11.5	1066	0.528/ 0.428-0.476	0.135/ 0.127-0.145	0.213/ 0.178-0.188
AI combed ring	14.23	1023	0.530/ 0.374-0.416	0.150/ 0.151-0.165	0.136/ 0.128-0.133
AI combed ring	16.59	925	0.519/ 0.399-0.483	0.164/ 0.129-0.169	0.133/ 0.119-0.124
AI carded ring	19.42	889	0.491/ 0.411-0.457	0.182/ 0.162-0.190	0.122/ 0.159-0.166
AI combed ring	19.95	843	0.511/ 0.411-0.437	0.181/ 0.164-0.193	0.131/ 0.138-0.142
AI combed ring	20.07	944	0.531/ 0.405-0.452	0.178/ 0.159-0.201	0.146/ 0.162-0.168
AI carded ring	25.83	790	0.471/ 0.411-0.437	0.214/ 0.201-0.219	0.117/ 0.132-0.137
AI carded ring	28.46	658	0.447/ 0.393-0.424	0.231/ 0.199-0.234	0.116/ 0.146-0.155
AI rotor	19.43	940	0.447/ 0.441-0.474	0.191/ 0.170-0.180	0.110/ 0.104-0.108
AI rotor	19.82	888	0.455/ 0.406-0.450	0.191/ 0.163-0.194	0.112/ 0.107-0.113
AI rotor	29.48	681	0.408/ 0.385-0.419	0.246/ 0.216-0.238	0.103/ 0.107-0.113
AI combed Novaspin	9.43	1232	0.562/ 0.492-0.527	0.119/ 0.113-0.121	0.212/ 0.194-0.205
AI carded Novaspin	20.10	802	0.454/ 0.388-0.424	0.193/ 0.167-0.189	0.114/ 0.145-0.153
AI carded Novaspin	29.42	652	0.439/ 0.392-0.431	0.237/ 0.201-0.235	0.113/ 0.146-0.151
MII combed compact	7.35	1262	0.573/ 0.444-0.487	0.104/ 0.106-0.113	0.230/ 0.196-0.207
MII combed compact	11.79	1059	0.564/ 0.453-0.499	0.502/ 0.134-0.142	0.229/ 0.218-0.226
AI combed compact	20.05	977	0.572/ 0.433-0.466	0.171/ 0.177-0.193	0.157/ 0.163-0.169

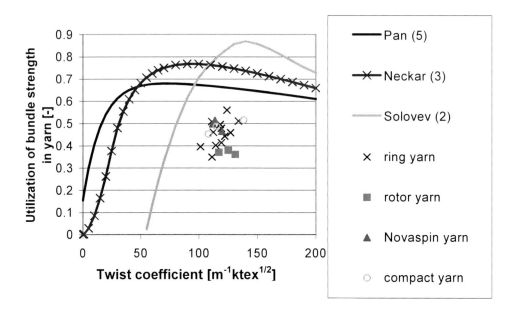

Figure 6. Predicted and effective utilization of bundle strength in yarn.

IMPROVED PREDICTION OF COTTON YARN STRENGTH

Based on the careful inspection of the above mentioned models, the modified relation for prediction of cotton yarns strength σ_c is proposed

$$\sigma_c = \sigma_{HVI}\phi_{by}^* = \sigma_{HVI}\mu\eta_{\beta}^* \tag{12}$$

where σ_{HVI} is fibrous bundle strength, measured on HVI, and ϕ_{by}^* if is a factor of bundle strength utilization in the yarn. Via packing density μ, the influence of spinning technology oninto strength prediction is included. The Ccorrected orientation factor n_{β}^* is computed from equation derived by Pan [3].

Packing density expresses in fact the fiber compactness in the yarn. The Ppacking density computed from cross section analysis is the relative for portion of fiber area in to area of yarn [10]. Limit packing density is defined from by the closest arrangement of fibers in the cross section. The Eempirical limit of packing density is about 0.8 [1] or about 0.7. [3]. Packing density varies as a function of distance from the yarn center [9], [11], [12]. In plenty manyof applications is the radial course of packing density is replaced by a constant value or by two linear portions. As examples we can mention Koechlin's theory of yarn diameter and van Wyk's approach to inter- fibrous pressure corrected by Neckar by using of the limit packing concept [1]. Neckar [1] derived a relation between packing density μ and yarn fineness T, yarn twist Z, fiber density ρ , material and technology characteristics M and limit packing density μ_m in the form:

$$\frac{\left(\dfrac{\mu}{\mu_m}\right)^{5/2}}{\left[1-\left(\dfrac{\mu}{\mu_m}\right)^3\right]^3} = \frac{M\sqrt{\pi}}{2\mu_m^{5/2}\sqrt{\rho}}\left(ZT^{1/4}\right)^2 \tag{13}$$

Suitable values of M for ring and rotor cotton yarns (ρ = 1520 kgm-3) are have been published [1]. Values of M for compact and Novaspin cotton yarns were evaluated from previous experiments [10] and are given in [2]. Packing densities of ring, rotor, compact and Novaspin cotton yarns, computed from equation (13), are presented ion figure 7. The Hhighest packing density corresponds to the compact combed yarns. Lower packing density result for ring combed, compact carded, Novaspin carded and Novaspin combed yarns. The Llowest packing density is for the rotor yarns, due to the fiber arrangement.

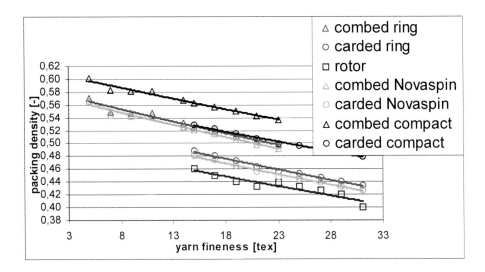

Figure 7. Predicted yarn packing density.

Corrected orientation factor η_β^* and corrected Poisson ratio η^* are computed with corrected angle β_D^* according to eqns. (8) and (10):

$$\beta_D^* = arctg\left(\alpha\sqrt{\frac{4\pi}{\rho\mu}}\,/\,\sqrt{10^3}\right) \tag{14}$$

Comparison of predicted utilization of bundle strength in yarn computed from eqns. (5) and (12), with effective utilization of bundle strength in yarn (11) is shown ion the figure 8. Effective utilization of bundle strength in yarn is evaluated only for ring yarns defined in table 1. The corrected relation (12) is closer to the experimental value. The iInfluence of yarn technology and yarn fineness (connected with optimal twist) is demonstrated inon the figure 9. The Mmaximum utilization factor is for the compact yarn,. Lower utilization factor is forthat of ring and Novaspin yarns being lower with the and the lowest values are being for the rotor yarn. Combed yarns have always have a -higher utilization factor in comparison withthan carded yarns.

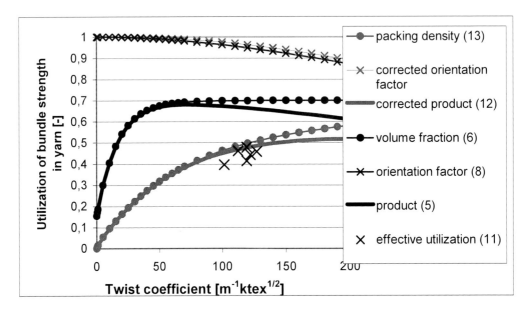

Figure 8. Predicted (5), (12) and effective (11) utilization of bundle strength in yarn.

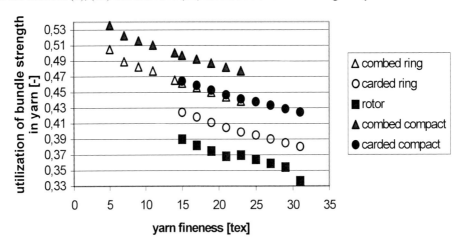

Figure 9. Utilization of bundle strength in yarn, according to eqn. (12).

Relative prediction errors of yarn strength and 95%th confidence intervals are shown oin the figure 10. Yarns are arranged into groups according to the specific technology, and from with fineness increasing from left to the right is increasing fineness. Zero values ion figure 10 are for mean values of yarn strength. Limit of 95%th confidence interval $\pm\delta_r$ are expressed as relative values:

$$\delta_r = 100\left(\eta_m - \eta_{conf}\right)/\eta_m \tag{15}$$

where η_m is mean measured value of yarn strength and η_{conf} is lower or higher limit of 95%-th confidence interval.

Relative prediction error δ is defined by the relation:

$$\delta = 100\left(\eta_p - \eta_m\right)/\eta_m \qquad (16)$$

where η_p is predicted value (i.e. value computed from model). The Rrelative errors of yarn strength prediction, computed from relation (15) and Pan equation (16), are shown on thein figure 10. Modified relations for computation of bundle strength utilization in yarn are sensitive toon the spinning technology and lead to a lower error. It is clear that prediction for fine yarns is worse (systematic overestimation) in comparison with than for coarse yarns (systematic underestimation). The extra low strength of rotor yarn and higher strength of compact yarn is are not sufficiently adequately explained by relations (12). One of the reasons is the higher sensitivity of the packing density computation from equation (13) on the yarn twist factor. Twist factors for coarser yarns areis generally lower. The predicted packing density is therefore lower as well.

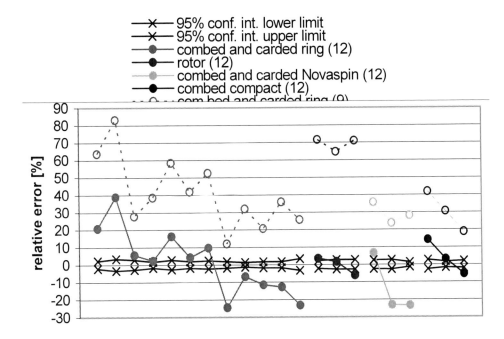

Figure 10. Relative prediction errors of yarn strength, solid lines are for model (12) and dashed lines are for model (5).

CONCLUSION

It is clear that for the strength prediction of cotton type yarns it is quite sufficient to use equation (12). The yarn strength is here a product of cotton fiber strength, determined from HVI, and corrected fiber strength utilization in the yarn. The packing density includes to the prediction the influence of spinning technology in the predictionas well. The fFurther improvement of the model requires proper evaluation of the critical twist factor. By using of this factor it will be possible to evaluate the maximum utilization of the fibrous bundle in the yarn.

ACKNOWLEDGEMENT

This work was supported by the research project "Textile Center" of Czech Ministry of Education LN00B090 and project 1M4674788501.

REFERENCES

[1]   Neckar, B.,Yarn. "Forming, structure and properties", *SNTL,* Praha 1990, (in Czech).
[2]   Kremenakova, D, "Modeling of cotton yarn geometry and strength" Report of Research Center of Textiles, Faculty of Textile Engineering, *TU Liberec.* 2004, (in Czech).
[3]   Pan, N. "Development of a Constitutive Theory for Short fiber Yarns", PART IV, The Mechanics of Blended Fibrous Structures. *Textile Res. J,* V.87, 467-483.1995.
[4]   Pan N., "A Detailed Examination of the Translation Efficiency of Fiber Strength into Composites Strength", *Journal of Reinforced Plastics and Composites.* Vol. 14, 2-28 1995.
[5]   Pan N." Theoretical Determination of the Optimal Fiber Volume Fraction and Fiber Matrix Property Compatibility Polymer Composites",,*Polymer Composites*, V.14, p.85-93.
[6]   Hearle, J., W., S., Grosberg, P., Backer, S.: Structural Mechanics of Fibers, *Yarns and Fabrics.* John Wiley and Sons, New York 1969.
[7]   Krupincova, G., "Relationship between cotton fiber single strength and bundle strength, Report of Research Center of Textiles, Faculty of Textile Engineering, *TU Liberec.* 2004, (in Czech).
[8]   Neckar, B., "Morphology and structural mechanics of fibrous assemblies", Faculty of Textile Engineering, *TU Liberec.* 1998, (in Czech).
[9]   Kremenakova, D.,Vikova, M." Influence of production technology on yarn and woven fabric structure and properties., Report of Research Center Textile, Faculty of Textile Engineering, *TU Liberec,* 2004, (in Czech).
[10] Kremenakova, D. et al." Internal Standards" Research Center of Textiles, Faculty of Textile Engineering, *TU Liberec,* 2004.
[11] Kremenakova, D., Rubnerova, J.," Comparison of methods for yarn packing density evaluation." 30th Textile Research Symposium at Mt. Fuji, Shizuoka, Japan 2001. Proceding, p. 201-210.
[12] Kremenakova, D., Novackova, J., Voborova, J." Compact yarn Structure and properties." 5th International Conference TEXSCI'03., Technical University of Liberec, June 2003.

[13] Thibodeaux,D.,P., Hebert, J.,J., Abd. El-Gawad, N., S., Moraitis, J., S."Relating Bundle Strength to Mantis Single Fiber Strength Measurement."*The Journal of Cotton Science,* P. 2-62-67, (1998).

In: Textiles for Sustainable Development
Editors: R. Anandjiwala, L. Hunter et al., pp. 117-129

ISBN: 978-1-60021-559-9
© 2007 Nova Science Publishers, Inc.

Chapter 11

COTTON FIBER QUALITY INDEX

Jiří Militký

Textile Faculty, Technical University of Liberec, Liberec 461 17,
Czech Republic; jiri.militky@vslib.cz

ABSTRACT

Quality is a very frequently used word in industry as being synonymous for a good product. According to the general definition, quality is characterized by several properties expressing the ability of a product to fulfill the functions it was designed for. The degree of quality (complex criterion) is often expressed as a utility value U. The method for complex evaluation of cotton fiber performance based on this idea is presented. This approach is compared with some other complex criteria such as fiber geometric factor. The results of HVI measurements are used as input data. The program QCOTTON, written in MATLAB, is briefly mentioned. The application of complex criterion is demonstrated on the simulation based examples.

Keywords: Cotton quality, Utility value, HVI measurements, Simulation results.

INTRODUCTION

Quality is a very frequently used word in industry as synonymous for a good product, technologies etc. Strictly speaking, this word is frequently misused or misinterpreted. In some cases, the word "quality" is used for expressing consistency, reliability or economy of production. Especially in textiles it is necessary to define quality very tightly because textile products can be used for various applications (ranging from clothing to wipes). One general definition of quality is:" "Quality expresses the ability to fulfill end-use requirements"". Therefore before speaking about quality, it is necessary to specify the potential target application of a textile.

The quality of the textile fibers is dependent on the aims of the evaluation:

- *Fiber producers:* Quality means the achievement of required technological parameters (geometrical evenness, fineness, shrinkage, mechanical and physical parameters etc.).
- *Textile producers:* Quality means the ability to fulfill requirements of technological operations and processability (friction, surface properties, cohesion, selected mechanical and physical properties and evenness).
- *Consumers:* Fiber quality is hidden in the properties and comfort of fabrics (hand, wearing comfort, thermal comfort, moisture, transport properties etc.).

Natural fibers: Controlled changes of properties are very difficult (selection, breeding, gene manipulation) and therefore the quality is oriented to the processability, yarn characteristics (especially strength) and blending potential.

Chemical and synthetic fibers: By varying the fiber geometry (fineness, cross section profile, texturing) and spinning conditions (rate of production, drawing degree, temperature, forming conditions) it is possible to markedly change the majority of properties. The chemical modification is another way to change properties. The general definition of quality according to the intended utilization can be used here for ranking and classification.

According to the general definition, quality is characterized by several properties expressing the ability of a product to fulfill the functions for which it was designed. The degree of quality (complex criterion) is often expressed as a utility a value U [6]. The general quality of textiles is characterized by many different utility properties R_i (i=1,...m). These are such properties that make it possible for the product to fulfill its functions. Utility value $U \in <0, 1>$ combines in a certain way partial quality properties [1-2].

The purpose of the paper is to describe the complex evaluation of cotton fiber quality based on this concept. The results of HVI measurements are used as input information. The application of complex criterion is demonstrated on simulation based examples.

COTTON FIBER QUALITY

In 1907 an international group of cotton industry representatives recommended that uniform cotton standards be established to "eliminate price differences between markets and make the farmers more cognizant of the value of their products". In response to requirements of standardization the cotton grade standards and cotton classification systems were developed and authorized by the US Dept. of Agriculture.

The cotton classification is now the system of standardized procedures for measuring the raw cotton properties (physical attributes) that affect quality of processing (spinning mainly) and quality of products (yarns). The classification system for US cottons is described on the internet (http://www.cottonic.com/CottonClassification).

There exists many standard and HVI techniques for the characterization of cotton fibers. It is known that there are some differences in the principles of measurement and the results of AFIS and HVI spectrum apparatus. The differences exist between measurements of fiber strength based on the bundles concept or single fiber concept as well [8]. Despite these differences, it is possible to specify basic cotton fiber properties having a potential influence on the cotton yarn strength [9]:

- Fiber length (expressed as upper half mean *UHM* [mm]),
- fiber length uniformity (expressed as uniformity index *UI* [%]),
- fiber strength (as bundle strength *STR* [cN/tex]),
- fiber elongation at break (*EL* [%])
- fiber fineness and maturity (expressed by micronaire reading (*MIC* [-]),
- short fiber content (*SF* [%]),
- trash content *TR* [%].

The importance of these properties is generally dependent on the spinning technology. The relative weight *b* of the above listed properties (as relative importance percentages divided by 100 and then standardized - sum of weighted values should be one) are given in table 1.

Table 1. Contribution of cotton properties to yarn strength

Property/ weight	Rotor yarn	Ring yarn
UI [%]	0.20	0.22
MIC [-]	0.16	0.17
UHM [mm]	0.14	0.24
STR [g/tex]	0.28	0.22
EL [%]	0.09	0.06
SF [%]	0.06	0.06
TR [%]	0.07	0.03

The values in the table 1 were derived from pie charts presented previously [9]. The main problem with the utilization of the above mentioned properties for quality characterization is the multivariate character of information, various units and lack of transformation to the utility scale.

One of the first attempts to create aggregated criterion of cotton yarn quality was the *FQI* index expressed by the following relation [10]:.

$$FQI = (fiber\ strength*length)/fineness \qquad (1)$$

Korickij [4] introduced the so called geometric properties index, *IG*, defined for LVI measured properties by the relation:

$$IG = 0.1*L_m*UI*(1-SF/100)*MAT*(FI)^{-0.5} \qquad (2)$$

where L_m is the cotton weighted mean length, FI is fiber fineness and MAT is maturity. For HVI measured properties, *IG* is expressed as:

$$IGa = \frac{UHM*UI*(100-SF)}{10000*\sqrt{MIC}} \qquad (3)$$

or

$$IG = \frac{UHM * UI * (100 - SF) * MAT}{1000000 * \sqrt{FI}} \qquad (4)$$

The relation (3) is very approximate because the micronaire is a combination of fiber fineness and maturity. The relationship between fiber micronaire and fineness for US cottons is shown in figure 1.

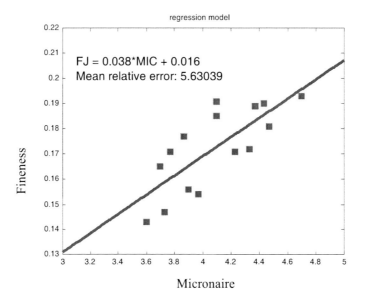

Figure 1. Relation between cotton fiber fineness and micronaire.

The index, IG, correlates with yarn mass unevenness by the empirical relation [4]:

$$CV = \frac{100 * A_2}{I_g \sqrt{T_P}} \qquad (5)$$

where $A_2 = 11.7$ for long staple cottons and $A_2 = 14.7$ for medium staple cottons. TP is yarn fineness. Index IG correlates with yarn strength variation coefficient CVP by empirical relation [4]:

$$CV_P = \frac{100 * A_3}{I_g * \sqrt[4]{T_P}} \qquad (6)$$

where $A_3 = 3.85$ for long staple cottons and $A_3 = 4$ for medium staple cottons.
    Cotton yield during spinning is expressed by the relation:

$$B = 95.4 - 2.9 * TR \qquad (7)$$

A complex quality index, *IK*, expressing the spinning ability of cottons is then defined as a combination of *IG* and *B*, including the cotton fiber price *C*.

$$I_K = A_4 * B * I_g^4 / C \qquad\qquad (8)$$

where $A_4 = 0.0108$ for long staple cottons and $A_4 = 0.0141$ for medium staple cottons. These relations were derived from Russian cottons, LVI measurements and contain a number of dimensional parameters. The fiber strength of US cottons (Texas cottons 1990) is not significantly correlated with parameter *IG* as shown in the figure 2.

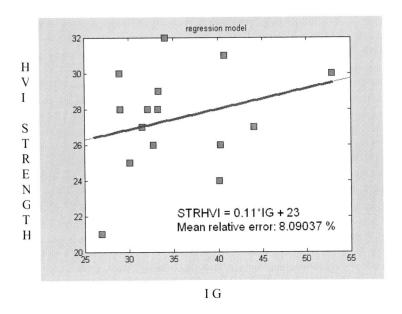

Figure 2. Correlation between cotton fiber strength and *IG*.

The yarn geometry index is therefore not to be used for the prediction of cotton fiber strength. The main problem with the Korickij approach is its dependence on the cotton properties used for empirical evaluation and no inclusion of individual fiber properties of importance.

Our approach, based on the utility function concept, is more general and can be easily modified in future (the properties of cotton depends on time, progressively improving due to breeding and genetic manipulation)

UTILITY VALUE CONCEPT

Evaluation of quality, based on complex criterion, is closely related to the well-known problem of complex evaluation of variants [2]. For complex evaluation of variants, the *X* matrix of the (n x m) order is available containing for individual $V_1,.....V_n$ variants (*X* matrix rows) the values of selected $R_1,.......R_m$ characteristics (*X* matrix columns).

The x_{ij} element of the matrix thus expresses the value of the j - th characteristic of R_j for the i-th variant of V_i. The aim is to sort individual variants in the order of their importance. In economics, several different methods are used in this field and most of them are based on preferential relations [2]. A special technique is the so called "useful effect method" or "base variant method". Base variant practically represents an ideal state where individual characteristics get optimum values.

By means of o_j (j = $1,...m$) values for individual characteristics of a base variant, dimensionless standard quantities u_{ij} are calculated. If the increase of the R_j characteristic is accompanied by an increase in quality, the standard quantities are calculated according to the relation:

$$u_{ij} = \min(\frac{x_{ij}}{o_j}, 1) \qquad (9)$$

In the opposite case, the multiplier and the divisor are interchanged. As $U(R) = U(u)$ is an aggregating function, a suitable weighted average is used. Generally, the question may arise whether a suitable aggregating function really exists [1].

Modification of this approach for expressing textile quality is demonstrated in the work of Militký [6]. The procedure for the prediction of cotton fiber quality from the point of view of the yarn strength is described in sequel.

Let we have K utility properties R_1 ,...,R_K (cotton fiber properties selected in the table 1). Based on direct or indirect measurement, it is possible to obtain some *quality characteristics* $x_1,...,x_K$ (mean value, variance, quantiles etc.). These characteristics represent utility properties. Functional transformation of quality characteristics (based often on the psycho-physical laws) lead to partial utility functions:

$$u_i = f(x_i, L, H) \qquad (10)$$

Where, L is value of the characteristic for only just unacceptable cotton (u_i = 0.01) and H is the value of the characteristic for an only just fully acceptable product (u_i = 1)

Utility value U (quality index) is the weighted average of u_i with weights b_i

$$U = ave(u_i, b_i) \qquad (11)$$

Weight b_i corresponds to the importance of the given utility property [3] and is closely related to the area of application of the cotton.

Using the weighted geometric mean as an average has the following advantages:

- For zero values of u_i, U = 0. This means that an unacceptable utility property cannot be replaced by combinations of other utility properties.
- The geometric mean is, except for not constant u_i, always lower than the arithmetic mean. This reflects an evaluation based on the concept that the values of utility

properties close to unsatisfactory cottons are more important for expressing the quality than those close to the optimum cotton.

•

Basic steps of utility function computation are:

- Selection of characteristics x_i corresponding to utility properties R_i,
- Determination of preferential functions $u(x_i)$ expressing "partial quality" for the chosen utility property,
- Assessment of the importance of individual utility properties, via weights b_i,
- Proper aggregation, i.e., determination of the U function.

In the case of cotton fiber quality, the utility properties and weights are already selected (see. table 1). For aggregation, the weighted geometric mean can be used and therefore only the preferential functions $u(x_i)$ have to be proposed. A partial utility function is in fact a psycho-physical variable expressing the sensation of quality induced by (measured) characteristics of cotton properties. Schematic representation of transformation of measurements to preferential functions is shown in figure 3.

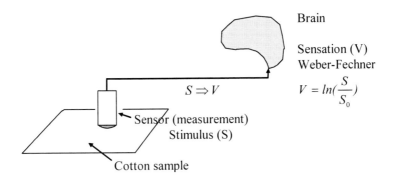

Figure 3. Transformation to the psycho-physical scale, S0 is threshold value (sensitivity limit).

The computation of preferential functions is dependent on the measurement scale and property type.

Ordinal characteristics - in this type of scale, classification has been introduced, but differences are not quantified. Grades are awarded by the comparison with etalons. Usually the higher is the grade; the higher is the partial textile quality. Standardization is carried out by the relation:

$$W_j = \min\left(\frac{x_j - L_j}{H_j - L_j}, 1\right) \qquad (12)$$

where L_j is the value of a only just unsatisfactory cotton (inadmissible value) and H_j is the value of an absolutely satisfactory cotton. Partial utility functions are calculated by the relation:

$$u_j = W_j^{\beta} \qquad (13)$$

where β is a coefficient expressing the nonlinearity of the transformation:

- $\beta > 1$, it is a convex transformation.
- $\beta < 1$, it is a concave transformation
- $\beta = 1$, it is a linear transformation.

Suitable is the selection $\beta < 1$ that expresses the fact that any improvement near the unsatisfactory product will affect the quality much more than any improvement near a quite satisfactory product (see. figure 4). This type of partial utility function can be used for cotton price as well.

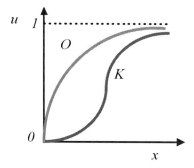

Figure 4. Transformation for ordinal variable (O) and cardinal variable (K).

Cardinal characteristics - are usually expressed in physical units. There are two types of cardinal characteristics:

- *One-side bounded characteristics* are those where after the H_j value has been exceeded, utility does not change any more (fiber strength, length, etc.). After standardization, the partial utility function is computed, e.g., by using the Harrington preference function
- *Two-sides bounded characteristics* are those where on both sides from "the optimum" partial utility decreases. (e.g., fiber micronaire)

The nonlinear transformation to preference functions for cardinal utility values has been given [6]. For practical application to express the quality of cotton fibers it is sufficient to replace standardization and nonlinear transformation to the partial utility function by the piecewise linear transformation.

For *one side bounded properties,* quality is a monotone increasing or decreasing function of quality characteristic x and therefore the piecewise linear transformation has the form shown in figure 5.

For the case of LB (lower is better), property limits were selected according to the known ranges as e.g. published in [9]

Trash content *TR [%]*	$L = 6$	$H = 2$
Short fiber content *SF [%]*	$L = 18$	$H = 6$

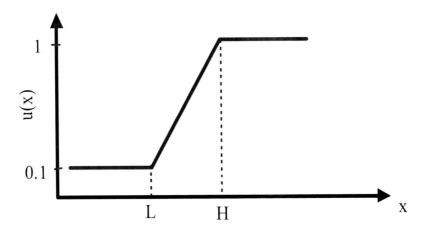

Figure 5. Transformation for one side bounded cotton properties (L is the lower limit and H the upper limit).

For the case UB (upper is better), property limits were selected according to the known ranges ase.g. published in [9]

Strength HVI *STR [g/tex]*   *L = 23*   *H = 31*
Length *UHM [mm]*   *L = 25*   *H = 32*
Uniformity index *UI [%]*   *L =77*   *H = 85*
Elongation *EL [%]*   *L = 5*   *H = 7.7*

For *two side bounded properties,* quality is a monotone decreasing function of the property value x on both sides from the optimal (constant) region and therefore has the piecewise linear transformation form as shown in figure 6.

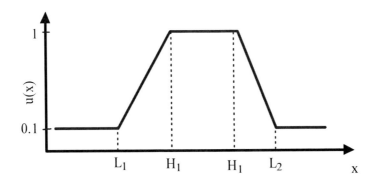

Figure 6. Transformation for two side bounded cotton properties (L_1, L_2 are lower limits and H_1, H_2 are upper limits).

For this case, limits were selected according to the known ranges as , e.g. published in [9]

Micronaire *MIC [-]*   *L1 = 3.4, H1 = 3.7*   *L2 = 5, H2 = 4.2*

The weighted geometrical average U, characterizing cotton fibers quality is then simply calculated from the relation:

$$U = \exp\left(\sum_{j=1}^{m} b_j * \ln(u_j) \right) \qquad (14)$$

When forming the aggregating function *U* from experimentally determined values of individual utility properties, the statistical character of the x_j quantities should be considered and the corresponding variance *D(U)* should also be determined.

PROGRAM *QCOTTON*

Program *QCOTTON*, written in MATLAB, is based on the above procedure. The technique described in [5] has been applied for computation of the statistical characteristics of cotton fiber utility function. This technique is based on the assumption that for each utility property R_j, the mean value x_j and variance s^2_j are determined by a standard treatment of the measured data. The procedure of the statistical characteristics of utility value U estimation is divided into the following parts:

I.   Generation of $x^{(k)}_j$ (*j=1,.....m*) values having normal distribution with mean values x_j and variances s^2_j. The pseudorandom number generator built in MATLAB is used.
II. Calculation of the utility value $U^{(k)}$ using the relation (14).
III. The steps I and II are repeated for *k=1,.....n* (usually *n=600* is chosen).
IV. Construction of a histogram from the values $U^{(k)}$ (k=1,.....n) and computation of the estimators of *E(U)*, *D(U)*.

SIMULATION RESULTS

The influence of micronaire changes and upper half mean length changes to the utility value of some ideal cotton fiber is shown in figure 7.

As expected, an increase in *UHM* leads to a better quality, expressed by the *U* value. The micronaire influence is more complex, because the lower values indicate immature cottons and the high values too coarse cottons. The distributions of *U* for the idealized case, where the relative errors of measurement CV are 3 % for all properties, are given in figure 8.

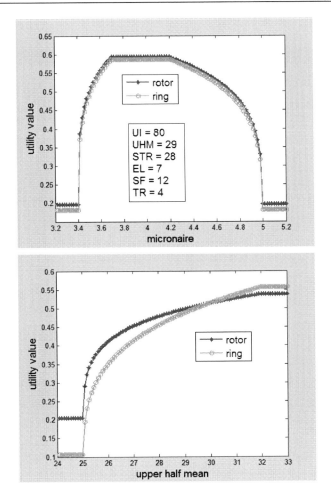

Figure 7. Influence of *MIC* and *UHM* on utility value.

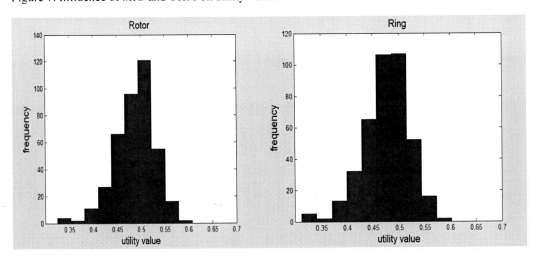

Figure 8. Distribution of U values for measurements with a 3 %precision.

There are visible differences between the U values for rotor and ring yarn weighting coefficients.

Complex criterion (weights; rotor):

Mean		lower limit	upper limit
0.49	¨	0.4.86	0.494

Complex criterion (weights; ring):

Mean		lower limit	upper limit
0.479	¨	0.4.75	0.484

The differences between both types of weights are not so high but the confidence intervals do not overlap and the conclusion is "this cotton is significantly better for rotor yarn production".

CONCLUSION

The procedure described for the evaluation of cotton quality (utility value) can be very simply modified for other selected properties or other sets of weights. This is important for future cotton varieties. Based on preliminary results it will probably be necessary to solve problems with some cotton varieties having a low micronaire due to fineness and relatively high strength. For these cases it will be necessary to add restrictions to the L_1 and H_1 values.

ACKNOWLEDGEMENT

This work was supported by the research project "Textile Center" of Czech Ministry of Education LN00B090 and project 1M4674788501

REFERENCES

[1]   Arrow K.J. Community Choice and Individual Values, Praha 1971 (in Czech)
[2]   Černý M; Gluckhaufová D; Toms M. Methods for Complex Evaluation of Variants, Academia Praha 1980, (in Czech)
[3]   Dobrov G.M. Expert Estimates in Scientific Prognoses, Kiev 1977
[4]   Korickij K.I. Technological economic estimation and design of textile materials quality, *Legkaja Industria,* Moscow 1983 (in Russian)
[5]   Meloun M; Militký J; Forina M. Chemometrics in Instrumental Analysis, Ellis Horwood, London 1993

[6]   Militký J. Statistical properties of complex quality indices, Proc. Conf. STAQUAREL 80, Praha 1980, (in Czech)

[7]   Militký J. MATLAB Program for Complex Quality Evaluation, National Textile Centre Rept., Liberec 2004

[8]   Militký J; Křemenáková D; Krupincová G; Ripka J. Proc. 2nd. Int. Text. Conf, - *Magic World of Textiles,* Dubrovnik 2004

[9]   Rasked E.S. Technical seminar at the 61 plenary meeting of the Int. Cotton Advisory Committee, Cairo, October 2002TRC 19, No10, June 1983

PART III
PROCESSING AND PRODUCTS

In: Textiles for Sustainable Development   ISBN: 978-1-60021-559-9
Editors: R. Anandjiwala, L. Hunter et al., pp. 133-145   © 2007 Nova Science Publishers, Inc.

Chapter 12

BIODEGRADABLE/COMPOSTABLE COMPOSITES FROM LIGNOCELLULOSIC FIBERS

Gajanan Bhat[1], M.G. Kamath[1] and D. V. Parikh[2]

[1] Department of Materials Science and Engineering;
The University of Tennessee, Knoxville, TN 37996, email: *gbhat@utk.edu*;
[2] USDA, New Orleans, LA, and D. Mueller, University of Bremen, Germany

ABSTRACT

The Iincreased importance of renewable resources for raw materials and recyclability/biodegradability of the product at the end of the useful life are demanding a shift from petroleum-based synthetics to agro-based natural fibers in automotive interiors. Natural fiber composites can contribute greatly to the automotive manufacturer's final goal of weight and cost reduction. The approach in this research has been to evaluate lignocellulose-based nonwoven composites for automotive and other similar applications. The effect of different lignocellulose and binder fiber compositions on the structure and properties of the resulting composites will be discussed.

These ligno-cellulose fiber-based composites can be safely disposed of after their intended use without polluting the environment. It is shown that by suitably blending cotton and flax or kenaf, with an appropriate thermoplastic biodegradable fiber in the right proportion, a moldable automotive nonwoven-based composite can be produced. Cellulose acetate, biodegradable copolyesters and other thermoplastic polymers/fibers will function as the binder fibers, eliminating the use of any non-biodegradable synthetic or a chemical binder. Recent studies indicate that nonwoven composites with good tensile properties can be produced from such blends. These composites have shown good promise in tensile properties, and further experiments are being conducted with different combinations of cotton/flax or cotton/kenaf and different thermoplastic biodegradable binder fibers. The composite samples fabricated by thermoforming of nonwoven batts prepared from fiber blends are being evaluated for their physical and acoustical properties. Issues related to blending of different components and adhesion between different matrix and fibers are discussed.

Keywords: natural fibers, composites, biodegradable, compostable, nonwovens, cellulosics.

INTRODUCTION

Composites are produced from two or more distinct materials to achieve a combination of their best properties. Generally the composites are made up of just two phases, namely matrix and dispersed phase [1]. Matrix is the continuous phase that completely surrounds and holds the dispersed particles or fibers in place. In a fiber-reinforced composite, the dispersed phase is made up of fibers, the mechanical characteristics of which are enhanced by reinforcement.

Fibers possess a large length to diameter ratio and spatial orientation which provides a potential for reinforcement efficiency. These fiber-reinforced polymer composites gained prominence as they replaced structural materials, such as wood or metal, due to their high strength and stiffness on weight basis.

Properties of the fiber-reinforced composites are determined by the fiber diameter, length, orientation (parallel or random), surface roughness, crimp, level of consolidation, and level of adherence to the binders. The polymeric matrix material binds and holds the fibers together. When load is applied, it is transmitted and distributed to the fibers. The matrix, which is ductile in nature, sustains only a small portion of the applied load. Further, these matrix polymers protect the fibers, from surface damage or environmental attack, and prevent crack propagation. Ease of fabrication, excellent properties and relatively lower cost make the composites very popular.

Today's composites contain synthetic fibers, which are not recyclable or biodegradable and pose difficulty in disposing at the end of their useful life. This has triggered a need for biodegradable composites. Enhanced biodegradability is achieved by replacing glass fibers with the lignocellulosic fibers, such as cotton, kenaf, flax, hemp, and jute. Such natural fiber reinforced composites are known as green composites [2]. Furthermore, these green composites are efficient sound absorbers and reduce noise in the automotives. However, to achieve total biodegradability even the binder should consist of a biodegradable polymer.

If biodegradable fibers were chosen to substitute many of the existing composites, the finished products would not pose disposing problems [3, 4]. To accelerate this process of switching to recyclable and biodegradable constituents, legislations in Europe have contained specific directives on the end-of-life of vehicles [5] that promotes the use of environmentally safe products. The directive, which came into effect at the turn of this century, predetermines the deposition fraction of a vehicle to 15% for the year 2005, and then gradually reduced to 5% for the year 2015 [6].

Natural fibers are good substitutes for reinforcing parts having a large area and complex geometry, such as door trims [7]. Moreover, these composites meet crash safety requirements and favorable crash behavior with no sharp edges at the rupture point. These composites have an important inherent quality that provides excellent z-directional properties that minimizes delamination problem. These natural fiber based composites made with biodegradable melt blown fabrics as binders [8-10] possess many of the required properties that are comparable to the traditional polypropylene based composites. Further, flax fiber composites are generally stronger, but somewhat brittle, due to the inherent properties of the fiber. Incorporation of cotton is likely to increase the impact resistance of these structures that will make such composites suitable for many more applications.

Natural Fibers

Natural fibers are found in nature or are produced from naturally available materials from plant and animal sources. Asbestos is an inorganic natural fiber which was used as insulation material. The majorities of the natural fibers are plant based and belong to the lignocellulosic category. Cotton is a natural lignocellulosic fiber that contains about 85% cellulose and low lignin (only about 1%). Flax, kenaf, jute, hemp, coir and sisal are other types of lignocellulosic fibers that contain lower amounts of cellulose and higher (5 to 20%) amounts of lignin compared to cotton. Generally, they are coarser and stronger than cotton.

Flax has properties similar to that of cotton, but better strength and modulus. Flax is a bast fiber from the plant, *Linum usitatisimum* [11]. Kenaf is another bast fiber produced from a cane like plant, *Hibiscus cannabinna,* which grows 12 to 15 feet in just seven months. Kenaf has been identified as a very promising fiber source as a substitute for fiberglass and some synthetic fibers. Today, kenaf is considered as a commercial crop in the USA.

Binder Fibers/Polymers and Biodegradability

In order to produce nonwoven fabrics from natural fibers, it is generally blended with a synthetic binder fiber or a polymeric chemical binder. At present, the most common synthetic binder fibers are polypropylene fibers and bicomponent fibers that are not biodegradable, thus posing difficulty in disposal. Many of the biodegradable synthetic fiber forming polymers are still at the development stage and very few are commercially produced. Cellulose acetate (PCA or CA) is a modified cellulosic fiber made from cheaper renewable sources, such as wood pulp or cotton linters. The thermoplastic nature of CA makes it a suitable binder fiber that can undergo thermal calendaring, and blends of cotton/CA can produce good quality nonwoven fabrics that are compostable at the end of their useful life [12].

Other promising candidates for thermoplastic and biodegradable binder fibers are the recently developed materials in the market, such as Eastar (PTAT) from Eastman Chemical Company [13], Poly Lactic Acid (PLA) from Dow-Cargill [14], and Biomax (BioPET) from Dupont [15]. PTAT is petroleum-based product with a melting point close to 120°C. Similarly, Biomax is petroleum based hydro/biodegradable polyester with a melting point of 200°C. PLA is an agro-based biodegradable polymer that is produced from cornstarch. PLA fiber has a melting point of 175°C and tensile properties comparable to that of polyester fibers [16]. One more type of biodegradable binder fiber that we acquired for our research was poly vinyl acetate (PVAc).

EXPERIMENTAL

Fibers

This research was carried out by acquiring lignocellulosic fibers and binder polymers from various available sources. Experiments were carried out to produce composites using lignocellulosic fibers and various binders as matrix. Fibers, such as kenaf and flax, were also used along with cotton in the composites to derive certain property advantages. Lignocellulosic fibers investigated include cotton, kenaf and flax. The binder materials investigated include, PTAT (Eastar) fiber provided by Eastman Chemical Company, BioPET (Biomax) biodegradable polyester fiber from Dupont, and cellulose acetate (CA) from Celanese Acetate. The later stage of the research was concentrated on presently available binder fibers, namely: PLA, PVAc, and BioPET.

Composite Preparation

As shown in Figure 4, Fiber Mix Type composite was made from fiber blends. A uniform blend of lignocellulosic fibers and binder fibers was used to produce fiber mix composites, wherein the composition is expected to be uniform throughout the product. When this mixed fiber mat is heated under pressure in the hot press, bonding takes place between binder fibers and the natural fibers. The design of the experiments involved the production of composite samples under various process parameters, such as bonding time, temp and pressure for various compositions. Bonding conditions were based on the melting temperature range as observed from the Different Scanning Calorimetry (DSC) results.

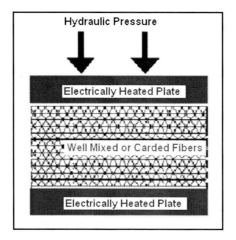

Figure 4. Schematic for the preparation of fiber mix composites.

Fibers were well mixed by hand, and dry laid using air jets, or carded, where possible, to produce webs/fleece before making composites. Initially a few samples of composites were made to establish the procedure. Table 1 shows the various sets of mixed fibers produced. A Hollingsworth card (at Star Lab Inc. Knoxville) was used to make 300mm wide webs from small amount (200 g) of fiber samples.

These mixed fiber webs were subjected to thermal bonding in the hot press. Experiments were conducted specifically with the raw cotton to keep the cost low, and with various biodegradable binder fibers. Conventional PP fiber was used as control in most of the experiments.

Table 1. Details of Fiber Mixture

Sample No.	Binder	Cotton	Kenaf	Flax
1	50	50		
2	50	25	25	
3	50	25		25
4	50		50	
5	50			50

Keeping the binder content constant at 50%, the mixtures of cotton, flax and kenaf in the desired proportions were prepared in the laboratory by hand mixing followed by air laying. These mixed webs were subjected to thermal bonding at hot plate temperatures of 20°C above the melting point of the binder, 1 bar pressure and for 5 minutes.

Characterization Methods

The samples produced in the experiments were analyzed for physical properties and structure after conditioning the samples for at least 24 hours under standard laboratory conditions, of 21°C ± 1°C and 65% ± 1% relative humidity [17].

Diameter and denier of the fiber samples were examined under an Olympus optical microscope or scanning electron microscope (SEM), and diameter was measured using the image analysis software. Since the cross section is not circular in all fibers, the second largest dimension is reported as diameter. The fiber denier was calculated from 20 readings of the diameter and the fiber density. Fiber denier was also calculated by measuring the mass of a known length of manufactured fiber and then converting it to mass in grams per 9000 meters. Density of the fiber samples was measured using the Density Gradient Column and values from literature were taken if the density was out of the range. Differential Scanning Calorimetry (DSC) of the polymers and fibers was carried out on a Mettler DSC821. The sample was placed in a 40 micro liter volume standard aluminum crucibles with lid. In order to vent the trapped air, three pinholes were made in the lid. Nitrogen at 200 cc per minute was used as the carrier gas in all the samples. A heating rate of 10°C per min was used while running the DSC.

For natural lignocellulosic fibers, individual fiber tenacity and elongation values were taken from the literature. Since fiber bundle behavior is important in composites, a tensile test was carried out on a bundle of fibers containing 20 s with 25mm gage length. Tensile properties of the fibers and composites were measured using a United Tensile Tester with test conditions described in ASTM [17]. Composite samples (up to 50 kg breaking load) were tested as nonwoven fabrics, wherein samples were cut to 25mm width, 125mm length and tested at 75mm gage length. A uniform extension rate of 25mm per minute was maintained in all cases. The average of four readings was taken for evaluation. In the case of thicker composite samples (breaking load more than 50kg up to 2500kg), the MTI Pheonix Tensile Tester Model 386 was used. The average of four readings was used in the analysis.

A 3-point bending method was used to determine the flexural strength of composites. Test was carried out according to ASTM D178 using MTI Phoenix Tensile Tester. Sample size was 25mm long, 25mm wide placed on the 3-point setup 75mm gage length (distance between lower pins) and the test conducted at 2mm per minute compression rate. The bending load at 5% strain was entered and the average of four readings used in the evaluation.

Tinius Olsen Impact Tester Model 899 was used for testing the impact properties of the composite samples. The specimen dimension for Izod testing is 63mm x 12mm and sample thickness typically 3mm to 12mm. Specimens were notched using a Tinius Olsen specimen notcher Model 892. The mass and the drop height determine the potential energy of the hammer and built in software calculates impact strength that is expressed in Joules (Nm) per m^2 cross-section area of the sample. Samples were taken at random. The average of four readings was used for evaluation.

SEM pictures were obtained using the Hitachi and Leo 1525 surface scanning electron microscope in the back scatter mode, with Gemini column, with the system vacuum of $\sim 1.3 \times 10^{-5}$ torr. Fiber surface, cross-section, uniformity, fiber pull out, melt flow over the fiber etc. were observed from the SEM pictures. For the cross-section, the samples were carefully cut by a sharp blade with one hit to get a neat cut. A minimum of two specimens of the same sample were placed on the platform and observed. For surface observation, a wafer-thin sample was placed on the platform. The samples after the tensile test (fractured) were prepared in a similar way to the cross-section specimens.

RESULTS AND DISCUSSION

Natural Fibers

The properties of the natural fibers are summarized in table 2. It can be seen that cotton is a fine fiber with convoluted surface. Cotton is the most popular natural fiber because of its natural soft and cool feel, comfort and moisture absorption properties. Whereas kenaf and flax fibers are coarser than cotton, they possess higher tenacity and lower elongation compared to cotton. Kenaf exhibits a lower apparent density due to several pores and voids in its structure. Equilibrium moisture level is about 7% for all these fibers. The cellulose content is the highest in cotton.

Table 2. Properties of Lignocellulosic Fibers

	Unit	Cotton	Kenaf	Flax
Linear density	dtex	0.8 to2.5	2.6 to4.1	0.8 to3.4
Fiber length	mm	12 to 38	12 to 50	12 to 75
Tenacity	cN/dtex	22 to 34	35 to 77	32 to 78
Breaking elongation	%	6 to8	4 to 5	3 to 5
Specific Gravity	-	1.54	--	1.51
Moisture Content	%	7	7	7
Cellulose Content	%	80 to 90	60 to 64	75 to 79

The tensile properties of the bundles of 20 fibers are presented in figure 2. Individual fiber strength as well as the interaction among fibers play a role in the bundle strength. Surface roughness or convolutions reduce slippage during tensile testing. It can be seen, that bast fibers, such as kenaf and flax, are coarser than cotton, exhibit higher fiber bundle tenacity and lower elongation compared to that of cotton. Cotton has surface convolutions and a bean like cross section (figure 3). Both kenaf and flax exhibited higher tenacity as well as surface roughness. Flax fiber properties are closer to that of kenaf than to that of cotton.

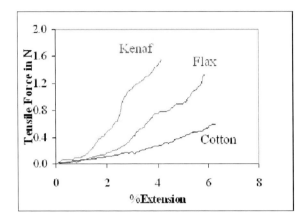

Figure 5. Tensile properties of a lignocellulosic 20 fiber bundle.

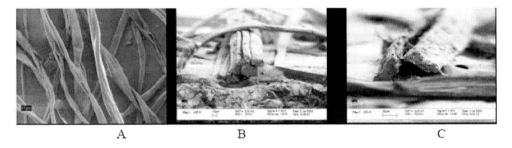

| A | B | C |

Figure 6. SEM pictures of cotton (A), flax (B) and kenaf (C) [400X].

Binder Fibers

Properties of the binder fibers are summarized in table 3. It can be seen that PLA, PVAc and BioPET fibers are coarser and have higher specific gravity compared to conventional PP binder. PLA exhibited higher tenacity and lower elongation compared to PVAc and Biomax. The moisture level is slightly higher than that of PP for all biodegradable binders. However, it is negligible compared to the moisture in natural fibers.

Results from the DSC scans of different binder fibers (figure 4) are shown in table 3. The melting point of PLA is very close to that of PP, around 170°C, and can thus be a good substitute binder that is biodegradable, whereas PVAc and BioPET have higher melting point of about 200°C. Moreover, higher temperature causes damage to cotton, leading to yellowing and some odor. The longer the duration the greater the odor is. All the web samples were dried in the oven for about 2 hours at 90°C under vacuum to remove moisture, before being subjected to thermal bonding.

Table 3. Properties of Binder Fibers

	Unit	PP	PTAT	BioPET	PVAc	PLA
Linear density	dtex	3.3	4.4	5.7	7.4	13.7
Fiber length	mm	35	20	12-50	50	12-50
Tenacity	cN/dtex	45	22	22	25	38
Breaking elongation	%	30	35	11	10	6
Specific Gravity	-	0.9	1.38	1.38	1.28	1.26
Moisture Content	%	0.5	0.6	0.6	1.5	1.8
Peak Melting Temp	°C	163	110	201	199	171

Tensile Properties

In fiber mix composites, the well-mixed fibers behave as one single material until the binders separate from the cotton fibers or the fibers break at the final stage of fracture. They showed good bonding between cotton fibers and the binder fibers all through the cross section, thus resulting in improved tensile strength (figure 5). All the composites were processed under identical conditions and the products had a basis weight of about 400 g/m^2. The fibers were uniformly mixed, laid and bonded to have desired flexibility. During tensile testing, the entire composite initially takes the load, then, gradually the load is taken by the cotton fibers until it breaks. This can be clearly seen in the SEM picture (figure 8) as the fibers were projecting from the fractured sample.

Raw cotton was used in all experiments since it is economical which is desirable in the automotive industries. In fact, lower grades of cotton and recycled cotton materials are widely used to lower the cost.

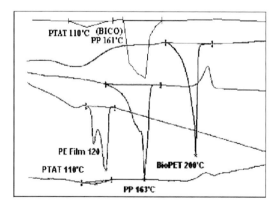

Figure 4. DSC scans of binder fibers.

With flax and kenaf fibers, it was difficult to produce carded webs, as they were not suitable for the carding machine that we used. The fibers were well mixed using an opener, air laid and then webs were formed by hand. These webs were consolidated using the hot press. Experiments were carried out with the biodegradable binders, such as BioPET, PLA, and PVAc. A substantial increase in tensile strength and a slight reduction in extension were noticed when flax or kenaf is present in the blend for all binders. The tensile properties of the composites produced with PLA binder are shown in figure 5.

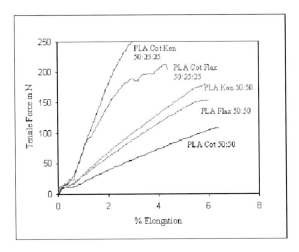

Figure 5. Tensile properties of biodegradable PLA - lignocellulosic fiber composites.

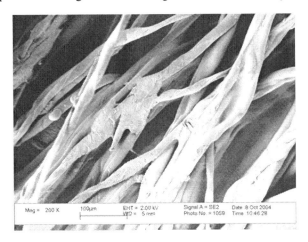

Figure 6. Adhesion between binder fiber and lignocellulosic fibers.

The SEM photographs in figure 6 show good bonding of the binder fibers with the natural fibers in the composites. As desired, the melting and flow of the binder fiber over the cellulosic fibers takes place to form good bond. The random distribution of fibers can be seen from the photograph in figure 7. This is true for all three binder fibers. Moreover, it is apparent that as the percentage of kenaf or flax increases, the tensile strength increases and the elongation decreases. This trend is the same for all binders. The SEM picture of the sample after tensile fracture (figure 8) indicates that fiber pullout and breakage occurred.

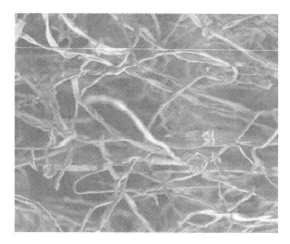

Figure 7. Random orientation of lignocellulosic fibers and binder fibers in the composites.

Figure 8. SEM picture of composite after tensile fracture.

Flexural and Impact Properties

The flexural strength of the composites containing intimately mixed fibers is shown in figure 9. Flexural strength is the ability of the product to bend under load. In the three point bending test, the load is at the center when the sample is supported at the ends. Generally, cotton composites have low flexural strength. As can be seen in figure 9, kenaf and flax add stiffness to the cotton based composites and thus lead to higher flexural strength for all binders. Moreover, it can be seen that kenaf provides a greater stiffness to the cotton composite than flax. Webs of the same weight are hot pressed at different pressures to obtain composites of varying thickness. Flexural strength increases with an increase in consolidation which reduces the thickness of the composite. Similarly, in the impact tests, blending with kenaf or flax (~10%) increases the impact strength of the cotton composites substantially (figure 10).

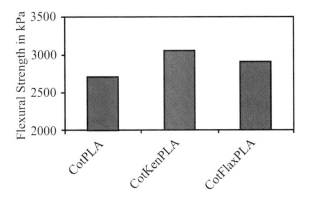

Figure 9. Flexural strength of composites.

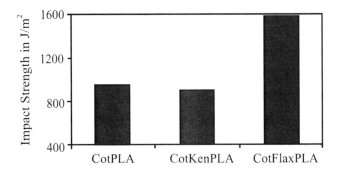

Figure 10. Impact strength of composites.

CONCLUSION

Studies on the structure and properties of fibers showed the ability of natural lignocellulosic fibers, such as like cotton, kenaf and flax, to form a good bond with thermoplastic polymers, such as PTAT, BioPET, CA, PLA, and PVAc. Fiber surface convolutions and roughness are desired properties in making composites as they act like ratchets in action, which gives rise to desired flexibility and elongation. In addition, they reduce slippage when tensile load is applied. Kenaf and flax possess higher tenacity as well as surface roughness which give higher strength to the composite. Further, intimate blending of the binder fibers with the natural fibers is the key to making a composite with good properties. The melting and flow of the binder fiber over the cellulosic fibers takes place and appears to provide a good bond. This observation is true with most of the biodegradable binder fibers investigated in this study. The increase in tensile strength due to the addition of kenaf or flax is substantial (even at 10% level). There is, however, a marginal drop in elongation.

The studies showed that there exists optimum temperature, time, and pressure of curing. The optimum temperature for bonding in a hot press is approximately 20°C above the melting point of the binder. Three point bending test results showed that adding 10% kenaf or flax to PLA-cotton composites, increases flexural strength substantially. This shows that kenaf and flax act like stiffeners. Notched Izod impact test results showed that the impact strength of PLA binders is higher than that of PP. Moreover, blending kenaf or flax (~10%) with cotton increases the impact strength of the composites substantially. Finally, on the basis of these studies, it is obvious that viable composite parts containing lignocellulosic fibers, such as cotton, kenaf, and flax, can be produced with thermoplastic binder fibers that are biodegradable/compostable, and possess the required properties that are comparable to the traditional polypropylene based composites.

ACKNOWLEDGMENTS

    The authors would like to thank Cotton Inc., Cary, NC for financial support, and DuPont, Eastman Chemical Company, Maverick Enterprise, Starlab, Vifan and Foss Manufacturing for their support in the preparation of, or providing, raw materials used in this study.

REFERENCES

[1]   Callister, WD. An Introduction to Materials Science and Engineering. 4th Edition. New York: John Wiley and Sons, Inc.

[2]   Parikh, DV. *Textile Research Journal.* 2002, 72(8), 668-672.

[3]   Mueller, DH; Krobjilowski, A; Schachtschneider, H; Muessig, J; Cescutti, G. Proceedings of INTC 2002, Atlanta, GA, Sept. 2002.

[4]   Muessig, J, Proceedings, 4th International Wood and Natural Fiber Composites Symposium, Kassel/Germany, April 10-11, 2002

[5]   N.N., Directive 2000/53/EC of the European Parliament and the Council of end-of-life vehicles, *Office Journal of the European Communities,* 2000, ABl. EG Nr. L 269 S. 34L 269/34.

[6]   Leaversuch, R. Plastics Technology [online] Available from URL: www.plasticstechnology.com

[7]   Philipp, K. Technical Textile. *Natural fiber reinforced composites,* March 2004.

[8]   Mueller, DH; Krobjilowski, A. Proceedings of the Ninth TANDEC Annual Conference, Knoxville, TN, 1999.

[9]   Mueller, DH; Krobjilowski, A. Proceedings of the INTC-International Nonwovens Technical Conference, Dallas, Texas/USA, September 26-28, 2000.

[10]   Mueller DH; Krobjilowski, A. *International Nonwovens Journal,* Spring 2001, Volume 10, No.1, pages 11-18.

[11]   [Online] Available from URL: http://www.hemopology.org/current%20history /1996520hemp%20composites.html

[12]   Bhat, GS; Duckett, KE; Suh, H. Proceedings of the 1999 INDA Conference, 1999.

[13]   Product Literature on Eastar, Eastman Chemical Company, Kingsport, TN.

[14]   Ecological Fiber Made from Corn, [online] Available from URL: http://www.kanebotx.com/english/new/corn.

[15]   [online] Available from URL: www.dupont.com/packaging/products/biomax.html.

[16]   Dugan, J. Novel Properties of PLA, [online] Available from URL: www.fitfibers.com

[17] Standard Test Methods for Nonwoven Fabrics D1117-95.

In: Textiles for Sustainable Development   ISBN: 978-1-60021-559-9
Editors: R. Anandjiwala, L. Hunter et al., pp. 147-159   © 2007 Nova Science Publishers, Inc.

Chapter 13

THE EFFECT OF COARSE EDGE ON WORSTED SPINNING PERFORMANCE AND YARN PROPERTIES

Anton F. Botha and Lawrance Hunter

CSIR Division of Textile Technology, PO Box 1124,
Port Elizabeth, 6000, South Africa; afbotha@csir.co.za, LHunter@csir.co.za

ABSTRACT

The inter-relationship between fiber, yarn and fabric properties is both important and complex, and considerable research has been undertaken in this area. Nevertheless, an area which has received little attention is that concerning the effect of relatively coarse fibers, or more specifically the coarse edge (CE), generally defined as the percentage fibers coarser than 30μm, on processing behavior and yarn and fabric properties, except for the well known effect on handle and scratchiness. The introduction of instruments, such as the OFDA and the Laserscan, which can routinely measure CE, makes it possible to study its effect in more detail.

Studies aimed at identifying and quantifying the effect of CE, are complicated by the high correlation between CE and mean fiber diameter (and it's CV). In an attempt to establish the effect of CE on spinning performance and yarn properties, analyses were carried out on the results previously obtained when close on 400 different wools (mostly merino) were processed into yarn on full scale worsted machinery and the spinning performance and yarn properties measured. Multiple regression analyses were carried out to establish the quantitative relationships between all the main fiber properties, including CE, on the one hand, and the spinning performance and yarn properties on the other hand. It was found that CE has no significant effect on predicting spinning performance and most of the yarn properties, except for yarn neps and yarn hairiness.

Keywords: Coarse edge, spinning performance, yarn properties, fiber diameter distribution, mean fiber diameter.

INTRODUCTION

There is today, a growing trend towards softer and more comfortable garments, with consumers becoming increasingly demanding in terms of these and other quality aspects. There are many aspects of fabric properties which contribute to comfort, including warmth, softness, weight, ability to absorb moisture, handle, drape and especially prickle and itch (discomfort). Wool garments are superior in a number of these areas, particularly with respect to comfort, but the discomfort of prickle and itch can occur when wearing wool garments.

The importance and quantitative effect of mean fiber diameter on wool processing performance and yarn and fabric properties have been widely researched and documented [2, 3]. So too, the effect of fiber diameter on fabric handle and prickliness has been widely researched and documented, it being shown that it is essentially those fibers coarser than about 30μm, referred to as the coarse edge (CE), which are responsible for the sensations of prickliness and also discomfort [5]. In contrast to this, relatively little work has been done on the effect of fiber diameter distribution, notably CE, on processing performance and yarn and fabric properties. A complicating factor in any such an investigation relates to the very high correlation between CE and mean fiber diameter (MFD), making it very difficult to isolate their respective effects.

In the 1970s and 1980s the South African Wool and Textile Institute (SAWTRI) of the CSIR carried out comprehensive trials to quantify the effect of wool fiber properties on worsted processing performance, yarn and fabric properties [2, 3]. From this work, several empirical prediction equations were derived. Nevertheless, at that time information was not available on the CE and its effect could not be investigated. It was therefore decided to measure the CE of the various lots processed then and to undertake statistical analysis in order to determine its effect on spinning performance and yarn properties.

EXPERIMENTAL

About 400 raw wool lots, covering South African merino and related sheep breeds and ranging widely in fiber diameter and staple length, were processed on full-scale worsted machinery into 734 ring-spun yarns. Details of the raw wool and tops are given in table 1 and of the yarns in table 2. Fiber diameter distribution, in particular the CE, was measured on all top samples, using the fiber diameter analyser (FDA-200), 8000 snippets per sample being measured. The yarns were comprehensively tested, using standard test methods and instruments. The spinnability of the lots was measured by the Mean Spindle Speed (MSS) at break test [1], which gives a rapid and accurate means of assessing the spinning potential of wool. Multiple regression analyses (involving various combinations of independent variables as shown in table 3) were carried out on the results so as to quantify the effects of the various fiber physical properties, in particular CE, on the spinning performance and yarn properties. As mentioned before, the high correlation (96.8%) between CE and mean fiber diameter (figure 1) makes it difficult to separate the effects of these two parameters. To overcome this, a new parameter, namely the Coarse Edge Ratio (CE_R), which is independent of D (R^2=0.024), was developed and included together with D in the regression analysis and its effect established independently of either CE or D. In essence, using CE_R will indicate whether a higher or lower CE relative to the "norm" for a certain D, has any effect on spinning performance or yarn properties.

Table 1. Summary of the wool fiber properties

Properties	N	Mean	Minimum	Maximum	Std.Dev.
Diameter (μm) (D)	±400	22.4	18.0	32.8	2.6
CV of Diameter (%) (CV_D)	±400	23.6	19.3	27.7	1.7
Coarse Edge (% fibers > 30μm) (CE)	±400	8.9	1.6	62.8	10.3
Hauteur (mm) (H)	±400	60.0	33.0	115.0	12.6
CV of Hauteur (%) (CV_H)	±400	46.7	20.6	66.3	7.3
% Fibers < 25mm (Sh)	±400	10.0	0.0	27.0	5.8
Tail Length (L 5%) (mm) (Tail)	±400	100.1	64.8	170.6	17.6
Duerden Crimp Ratio (De)**	±400	0.9	0.7	1.7	0.1
Staple Crimp (crimp/cm) (Cr)**	±400	3.9	1.9	6.5	0.9
Resistance to Compression (mm) (Rc)	±400	16.5	12.9	24.7	2.2

** - Measured on the raw wool.

Table 2. Range of yarn properties

Properties	N	Mean	Minimum	Maximum	Std.Dev.
Tex	734	34.9	16.8	53.3	12.1
Number of Fibers in Yarn Cross-section (NoF)	734	65.6	21.0	143.0	26.9
Twist Factor (Teurns/cm x $tex^{0.5}$) (Tf)	734	31.5	26.9	45.3	5.9
Irregularity (CV%)	734	18.0	12.3	28.1	2.9
Thin Places per 1000m	724	141	0	1547	198
Thick Places per 1000m	731	79	0	681	96
Neps per 1000m	730	29	0	452	37
Breaking Strength (cN)	734	234.2	79.0	414.0	97.7
Extension at Break (%)	734	15.6	5.9	34.0	5.5
Hairiness (hairs/m) (Hair)	734	40.6	14.0	93.0	12.8
Tenacity (cN/tex)	734	6.6	3.6	8.7	0.8
Classimat Faults 1	734	788	33	35802	1976
Classimat Faults 2	734	51	2	1276	75

Table 3. Description of Models

A	Tex	Crimp	De*	D	CV_D	CE/CE$_R$**	H	CV_H	Sh25	Tail*	
B	Tex	Crimp	De*	D	CV_D		H	CV_H	Sh25	Tail*	(CE Excluded)
C	Tex	Crimp	De*	D		CE/CE$_R$**	H	CV_H	Sh25	Tail*	(CV_D Excluded)
D	NoF	Crimp	De*			CE/CE$_R$**	H	CV_H	Sh25	Tail*	(NoF includes D and CV_D)
E	NoF	Crimp	De*				H	CV_H	Sh25	Tail*	(CE Excluded)

* - De and Tail were replaced by Tf in the regression analyses involving yarn properties.
** - CE was replaced by CE$_R$ in the regression analyses involving MSS and yarn properties.

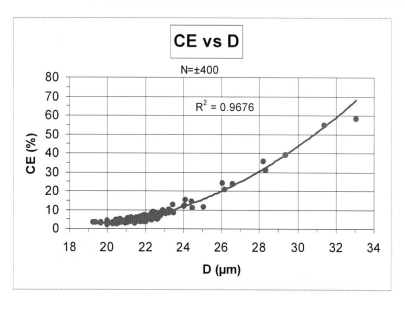

Figure 1. Relationship between CE and D for tTops.

RESULTS AND DISCUSSION

Spinnability

Through various analyses it was found that the multiquadratic regression analyses gave the best correlations for spinnability (MSS) and the predicted results were normally distributed. The results pertaining to the various predication equations for MSS are summarized in table 4. As expected, spinnability was largely influenced by the number of fibers in the yarn cross-section (NoF), yarn linear density (Tex), mean fiber diameter (D) and Hauteur (H). It was decided to develop formulae, firstly using the yarn linear density (Tex) and the mean fiber diameter distribution (D, CV_D and CE (also changed to CE_R)) and secondly using the number of fibers in the yarn cross-section (NoF) and CE (changed to CE_R). Various models were explored to see what effect, independent of mean fiber diameter, CE and CE_R had on MSS. CE or CE_R was either included as an independent variable or excluded and the option of excluding CV_D, but keeping CE or CE_R, was also investigated. In all these cases the aim was to see what effect, if any, CE and CE_R had on spinnability.

As can be seen from table 4, all five prediction equations for MSS basically display the same trend, with a higher yarn linear density (Tex) or more fibers in the yarn cross-section (NoF) coupled with a lower mean fiber diameter (D) and higher Hauteur (H) leading to improved spinnability, confirming earlier work [3]. In some cases, certain other fiber properties also become significant, although their overall contribution was mostly small. For example, an increase in crimp tended to be associated with a decrease in spinnability and so too a decrease in CV_H, as found previously [3]. Very high percentage fits were obtained for the multiquadratic regressions, as shown in table 4, with R^2 x 100, ranging from 85.3 to 86.7%. Nevertheless, many terms were required to obtain such high percentages. It was decided to exclude all fiber properties which contributed less than 1% to the total fit. In this case (8 terms in table 4) the percentage fit ranged from 79.1 to 83.1%, although the trends were generally similar. Including CE, at best only improved the percentage fit marginally. CE_R gave similar, if not the same, results as CE (table 4). Introducing CE in place of D does not change the correlation coefficient significantly, and it can be concluded that, once D is taken into consideration, neither CE nor CE_R improves the correlation coefficients significantly. Thus CE and CE_R have little, if any, effect on spinnability. This is illustrated in figures 2 and 3, which shows spinnability as a function of Hauteur for various levels of CE and CE_R, no significant effect being apparent for both CE and CE_R on spinnability. Both figures confirm the effect of Hauteur on spinnability, namely that an increase in Hauteur generally improves spinnability, although the effect levels off and possibly even reaches a turning point at a Hauteur beyond about 80mm.

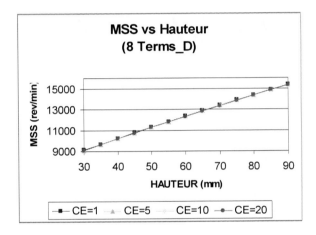

Figure 2. Effect of Hauteur and CE on MSS (multi-quadratic D).

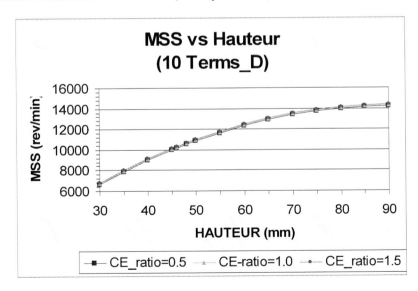

Figure 3. Effect of Hauteur and CE_R on MSS (multi-quadratic D).

Table 4. Summary of the mMulti-qQuadratic rRegression eEquations for MSS (N=702)

	Model	Regression Equation	%R² 8 Terms	%R² 16 Terms
Tex	A	$10739.63+0.46(Tail)(Tex)-1.99(CE)(Tail)-1070.12(D)+1242.91(Tex)-23.27(Tex)^2+9.50(Tex)(CE)+4.76(D)(H)+0.64(CVH)^2$ 40.1　28.4　2.4　2.6　2.3　3.2　2.1　1.8	83.0	86.7
	B	$7354.77-0.94(Tail)(Tex)-52.07(D)^2+15.44(Tex)-29.16(Tex)^2+124.44(H)+0.80(CV_H)^2+75.77(Tex)(D)$ 40.1　28.1　4.2　2.8　2.0　2.3　3.1	82.6	85.3
	C	$10739.63+0.46(Tail)(Tex)-1.99(CE)(Tail)-1070.11(D)+1242.91(Tex)-23.27(Tex)^2+9.5(Tex)(CE)+4.76(D)(H)+0.64(CV_H)^2$ 40.1　28.4　2.4　2.6　2.3　3.2　2.1　1.8	83.0	86.7
NoF	D	$2625.53+2.03(NoF)(H)+2.17(CV_H)(NoF)-0.09(CE)(Tail-10.85(CV_H)(Cr)+11.75(H)(Cr)+2.88(Sh)^2+17.2(Sh)(Cr)-0.14(H)^2$ 72.2　5.6　0.32　0.24　0.22　0.17　0.18　0.13	79.1	86.3
		$-26889.8-1.4(NoF)(H)+1.0(CV_H)(NoF)+4.1(CE_R)(NoF)-0.8(NoF)(Sh)-8.7(NoF)+932.0(NoF)+430.3(H)^2-2.10(H)^2+4.7(Sh)^2-20.4(Sh)(Cr)$ 72.2　5.6　0.57　0.14　0.13　3.2　1.1　0.59　0.76　0.63	85.0	-
	E	$-8428.60+1.02(NoF)(H)+2.61(CV_H)(NoF)-67.72(De)(CV_H)+60.56(De)(H)+601.94(NoF)-7.32(NoF)^2$ 72.2　5.6　0.27　0.18　0.09　3.6	82.0	86.1

Yarn Properties

Similar statistical models, as those applied above for MSS at break, were used to establish the effect of CE on the yarn properties. Through various analyses it was found that the log-log regression analyses gave the best correlations for the yarn properties and the predicted results were normally distributed. The results and contribution of the various independent variables to the total percentage fit are summarized in table 5. Only the most important yarn properties will be discussed, with the emphasis on the effect of CE.

Yarn Evenness and Tensile Properties

Similar trends were observed for all the yarn evenness related properties. As shown in table 5, CE had no statistically significant effect on these properties, the number of fibers in the yarn cross section (NoF) contributing most to the overall fit. As also found previously, mean fiber diameter (D) or number of fibers in then cross-section contributed the most to explaining yarn evenness and tensile properties [4]. Examining the graphs in more detail, figure 4 clearly illustrates that there is a sharp decrease in yarn irregularity as NoF increases from 20 to about 40. After this, there is a slower deterioration decrease in yarn irregularity. From figure 4 it can clearly be seen that once the effect of D (NoF is a function of D) is taken into consideration, there is no practically significant effect of CE on irregularity.

For frequencies of thin and thick places, the trends were similar to those for irregularity, although the total percentage fit was lower, CE having no significant effect on the frequencies of thin and thick places.

For the yarn tensile properties, CE did not have a statistically significant effect on the prediction of breaking strength, Tex, NoF and mean fiber diameter playing the dominant role in the prediction equation. Figure 5 illustrates that CE_R had little effect on breaking strength, once the effect of D is taken into consideration. Neither CE nor CE_R has a consistent or practically significant effect on yarn breaking strength. In summary, the results obtained above confirm previous findings [2,3,4], as illustrated in figure 6, which shows the average contribution of the various wool fiber properties towards explaining yarn evenness and tensile characteristics.

Yarn Neps

A decrease in CE increased the frequency of neps, the effect being larger for shorter fibers (figure 8), fewer fibers in the yarn cross-section (figure 7) and lower D (figure 8). In the case of normal commercial spinning, CE could therefore have a small, but significant effect on the frequency of neps.

Table 5. Average percentage contribution of the various fiber properties to the overall percentage fit (R^2) in predicting the yarn properties

Dependent Variables	Mod.	Total %R^2	Contribution of Independent Variables (%) (N=734)												Most Significant Regression Equations
			CE	CE_R	NoF	Tex	Tf	D	H	Cr	Rc	CV_D	CV_H	Sh25	
Irregularity (%)	D	85.1	*	0.17**	79.2**	*	0.58	*	3.6**	*	1.3	*	0.11**	NS	$10^{1.96} NoF^{-0.37} H^{-0.16} Rc^{-0.15} Tf^{-0.074} CE_R^{-0.033} CV_H^{-0.033}$
	E	84.9	*	*	79.2**	*	0.58	*	3.6**	*	1.3	*	0.12**	NS	$10^{1.93} NoF^{-0.37} H^{-0.15} Rc^{0.16} Tf^{0.073} CV_H^{-0.034}$
	D	84.2	0.46	*	79.2**	*	0.58	*	3.6**	0.29	*	*	NS	NS	$10^{2.0} NoF^{-0.36} H^{-0.16} Tf^{0.076} CE^{0.024} Cr^{0.053}$
Thin Places per 1000m	D	81.1	0.51	0.25	75.1**	*	0.59	*	4.0**	*	0.81	*	NS	0.12**	$10^{0.35} Rc^{-1.66} H^{-2.49} CE^{-0.21} Sh25^{-0.11} Tf^{0.92} NoF^{-4.58}$
	E	80.6	*	*	75.1**	*	0.59	*	4.0**	*	0.81	*	NS	0.12**	$10^{10.51} Rc^{-1.55} H^{-2.28} Sh25^{-0.11} Tf^{0.92} NoF^{-4.51}$
Thick Places per 1000m	D	75.2	1.2	0.16	63.6**	*	NS	*	9.2**	*	1.2	*	NS	NS	$10^{8.76} Rc^{1.21} H^{-2.25} CE^{0.24} NoF^{-2.72}$
	E	73.8	*	*	63.6**	*	NS	*	9.2**	*	0.96	*	NS	NS	$10^{8.940} Rc^{1.21} H^{-2.25} NoF^{-2.72}$
Breaking Strength (cN)	A	96.7	0.02	*	*	93.6	0.05	1.8**	0.98	NS	*	NS	NS	0.22**	$10^{1.07} D^{-0.83} CE^{0.03} H^{0.262} Tf^{0.061} Tex^{1.21} Sh25^{-0.033}$
	D	91.3	*	0.34**	73.3	*	0.29	*	12.0	5.4**	*	*	NS	NS	$10^{0.49} NoF^{1.11} CE_R^{-0.14} H^{0.54} Cr^{-0.58} Tf^{0.1}$
	E	90.9	*	*	73.3	*	0.29	*	12.0	5.4**	*	*	NS	NS	$10^{0.61} NoF^{1.11} H^{0.60} Cr^{-0.53} Tf^{0.15}$
Extension (%)	D	70.5	0.34**	0.94	49.4	*	3.3	*	9.6	*	7.0**	*	0.89**	NS	$10^{0.37} NoF^{0.68} Rc^{-0.74} CE^{-0.035} H^{0.56} CV_H^{-0.20} Tf^{0.40}$
	E	70.2	*	*	49.4	*	3.3	*	9.6	*	7.0**	*	0.89**	NS	$10^{0.37} NoF^{0.70} Rc^{-0.72} H^{0.53} CV_H^{-0.213} Tf^{0.40}$
Neps Per 1000m	C	42.3	*	0.25**	*	30.0**	NS	0.41	9.3**	*	0.37**	*	0.27	1.7	$10^{5.70} H^{-1.57} Sh25^{0.15} Tex^{-1.81} D^{0.51} CE_R^{-0.32} CV_H^{0.68} Rc^{-0.78}$
	D	45.5	3.7**	*	20.1**	*	NS	*	19.5**	*	0.54**	*	1.5	1.4	$10^{7.67} Rc^{-0.74} H^{1.93} CE^{-0.37} Sh25^{0.12} CV_H^{0.74} NoF^{1.80}$
	E	41.4	*	*	20.1**	*	NS	*	19.5**	*	0.16**	*	0.20	1.4	$10^{7.901} Rc^{-0.627} H^{-2.301} Sh25^{0.155} CV_H^{0.483} NoF^{-1.585}$
Hairiness (Hairs/m)	D	80.8	5.9	*	10.5	*	26.5**	*	0.13**	34.3**	*	*	0.4**	3.0	$10^{3.22} Cr^{-0.83} CE^{0.15} Sh25^{0.069} Tf^{-1.03} NoF^{0.30} CV_H^{-0.11} H^{-0.083}$
	D	72.2	30.4	*	8.9	*	23.9**	*	NS	*	7.0**	*	NS	2.0	$10^{3.343} Rc^{-0.820} CE^{0.27} Sh25^{0.06} Tf^{-0.07} NoF^{0.237}$
	E	40.3	*	*	0.66	*	25.1**	*	0.98	*	11.9**	*	1.6	NS	$10^{3.41} Rc^{-1.0} CV_H^{0.24} H^{0.15} Tf^{-0.96} NoF^{0.079}$

NS– Not significant   * - Omitted in regression   ** - An increase in the fiber property causes a decrease in the yarn property in question.

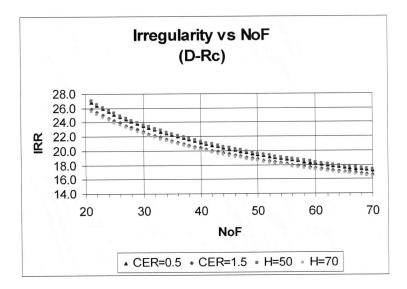

Figure 4. Effect of NoF, CE$_R$ and H on Iirregularity (model D_Rc)/.

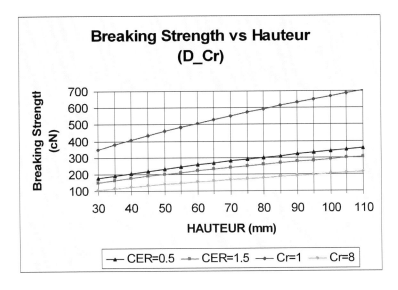

Figure 5. Effect of H, Cr and CE$_R$ on bBreaking strength (model D_Cr).

Yarn Hairiness

The regression results for yarn hairiness are shown in table 5. It can be seen from this table and figures 9 and 10 that yarn twist factor and staple crimp (or resistance to compression (Rc)) had the main effect on hairiness, the latter confirming previous findings [4]. As illustrated in figure 11, an increase in CE or fiber diameter also had an adverse effect on hairiness summarises the contribution of the various fiber properties towards change in yarn hairiness. Figure 9 shows that an increase in staple crimp frequency reduces hairiness significantly. Figure 10 shows that a wool with high CE levels, will produce more hairy yarn and, thus when worn next to the skin, could feel prickly, especially those wools with CE greater than 5%.

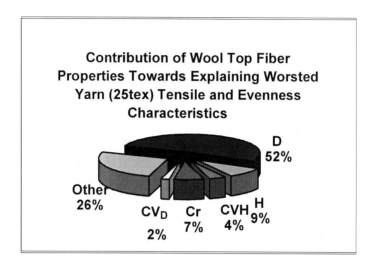

Figure 6. Percentage contribution of the various fiber properties towards explaining the observed variations in yarn tensile and evenness characteristics (averaged over 50 and 25 tex yarns [4]).

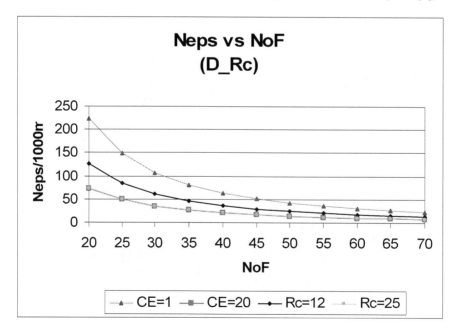

Figure 7. Effect of NoF, CE and Rc on nNeps (model D_Rc).

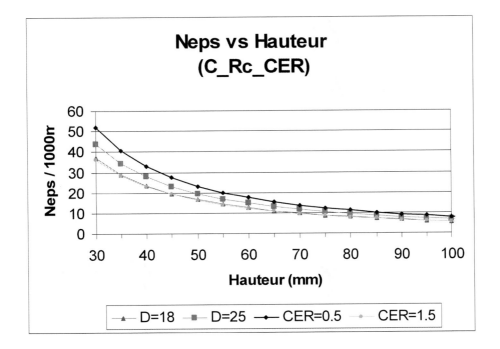

Figure 8. Effect of H, D and CE$_R$ on nNeps (model C_Cr).

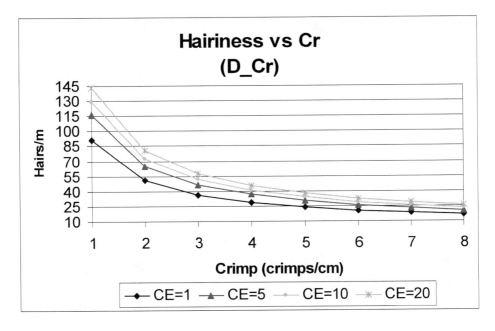

Figure 9. Effect of Cr and CE on hairiness (model D_Cr)

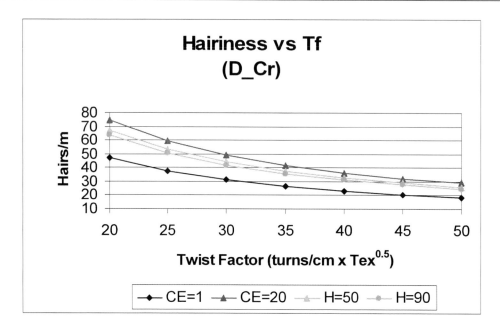

Figure 10. Effect of Tf, CE and H on hairiness (model D_Cr).

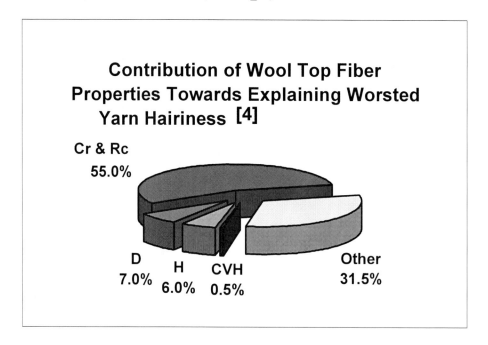

Figure 11. Contribution of wool top fiber properties towards explaining worsted yarn hairiness [4].

CONCLUSION

Five different statistical models were applied to determine the effect of CE on spinning performance and yarn properties. It was shown that, within the ranges covered here, neither CE nor CE_R had a statistically significant or consistent effect on spinnability and most of the evenness and tensile yarn properties. Nevertheless, for yarn neps and yarn hairiness both CE and CE_R had a practically significant effect. A 1% absolute change in CE resulted in a change of 1 nep per 1000m of yarn and 1.6 hairs/m.

REFERENCES

[1]   Turpie, DWF. *SAWTRI Techn. Report,* 1975, No. 240.
[2]   Hunter, L. Proc. 6th International Wool Text. Res. Conf.: Pretoria, 1980, 1, 134.
[3]   Hunter, L. SAWTRI Special Publication, 1987, Wol 78.
[4]   Hunter, L; Turpie, DWF; Gee, E. *SAWTRI Techn. Rep.,* No. 502. 1982.
[5]   Garnsworthy, RK; Gully, RL; Kandiah, RP; Kenins, P; Mayfield, RJ; Westerman, RA. *CSIRO Div. Of Wool Tech. Rep.* G64 (1988). Also published in Aust. Text., 8 (4), 26 (1988).

In: Textiles for Sustainable Development ISBN: 978-1-60021-559-9
Editors: R. Anandjiwala, L. Hunter et al., pp. 161-171 © 2007 Nova Science Publishers, Inc.

Chapter 14

HIGH PERFORMANCE IN SEWING – GUARANTEEING SEAM QUALITY THROUGH CONTROL OF SEWING DYNAMICS

M.A.F. Carvalho and F.B.N. Ferreira

University of Minho, Textile Engineering Department, Azurém / 4800-058,
Guimarães, Portugal; migcar@det.uminho.pt, fnunes@det.uminho.pt

ABSTRACT

To maintain an acceptable level of competitiveness of the apparel industry in developed countries in an open market after 2004, manufacturers should be able to achieve reduced quantities, short delivery dates, and an increasing number of styles in production and an increasing level of quality specifications. In this environment, machine set-up acquires a great relevance.

Therefore, the development of intelligent sewing machines in order to reduce human intervention during adjustment situations, detect operating anomalies and adjust automatically accordingly, thereby guaranteeing high quality levels, is of increasing importance.

The dynamics of the seam have been investigated, through the study of the tensions and consumption of the sewing threads during the formation of the stitch.

Keywords: thread tensions, thread consumption, monitoring, control, sewing..

INTRODUCTION

The apparel industry is known for its traditional high manual labor content, as most of the operations needed for the assembly of any garment involve considerable handling time (60-80%). At the same time, the operators have only a very basic education, with supervisors being in most of the cases normal operators promoted for good services to the company. Style and material variation is an increasing characteristic of the sector, where diversity is common place.

Most machine manufacturers and some of the most important apparel companies have developed costly semi-automated machines/workstations, enabling a considerable reduction in handling times. Nevertheless, because of market needs the quality levels and the flexibility of the production processes assume increasing importance? Short runs and high variability of styles make this type of solution not justified in most cases. On the other hand, although this type of machine allows high levels of efficiency foron the operations involved, they normally have no continuity in terms of the production flow, resulting in a reduced utilisation of the machine capacities during the day.

The constant change of styles and materials requires the presence of maintenance operators to set up machines according to the new sewing conditions. This results in a loss of productivity and can take a considerable amount of time to prepare all machines, as the resources are normally limited to one or two operators. Most machine operators haven't enough knowledge to set up their own machines, resulting in considerable dead time every time a style changes. With these needs in mind, we believe in the importance of developing a solution to control seam quality and to create a capability for machines to self adjust according to the type of material being used, thereby greatly reducing these dead times.

To be able to reduce garment defects we must monitor the sewing process, know when a thread breaks, when the interlacing failed during stitch formation, and when thread consumption is not within the correct values to obtain a balanced stitch, and that the material is properly fed to guarantee a regular stitch density, and that the needle is in perfect condition, without marking the material or breaking the yarns during its penetration. All this information is important to guarantee seam quality during the assembly of the whole garment.

The continuous search for reduced labour costs as a result of achieving competitive prices and good profit margins require that the companies that want to continue producing must adopt management solutions that allow them to increase productivity through the optimization and flexibility of their production processes in order to be able to respond quicker to market demands and to specialize in the production of high valued products. Efficiency will be the key for their survival.

In this environment, flexible sewing machines with a capability to re-adjust to new materials and different sewing conditions are of great importance.

THE SEWING RIG

Figure 1 shows the sewing rig used in this research project and which was developed at the University of Minho during the past 13 years by its multidisciplinary group of researchers involving three departments of the University, namely the Textile, Electronics and Mechanical Departments [1-7].

Even though the results presented here refer only to the overlock sewing machine and its most commonly used stitch type – the 504, a lockstitch machine is already at the testing phase, thereby covering the two most widely used machines in the sewing industry.

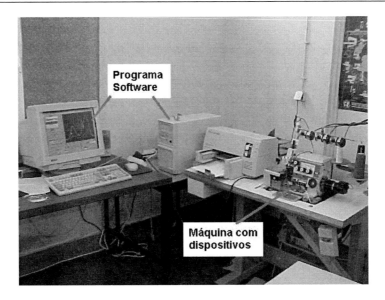

Figure 1. Sewing rig.

Data collection devices (sensors, cantilever beams, strain gauges, piezoelectric, encoders and an *LVDT - Linear Variable Differential Transformer)* were strategically positioned on the sewing machine for the acquisition of information about the development of the tension, determination of the thread consumption of each thread, evaluate the development of needle bar and presser foot bar force and measure the presser foot displacement during the formation of one stitch. With a software program installed on a PC it is possible to perform several tasks, with an increasing automation as the research continues, control rules are defined and relevant information identified.

Figure 2 presents the system used for the analysis of the collected data, namely the definition of zones where the tension peaks are generated in the needle thread during one stitch (one complete cycle).

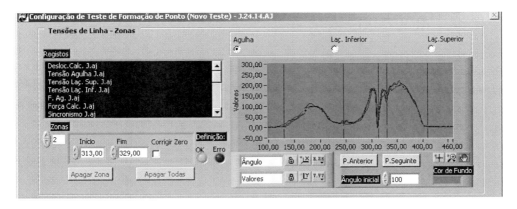

Figure 2. Panel for definition of zones for the analysis of needle thread tension.

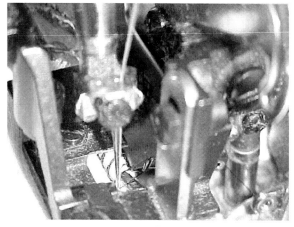

a.

b.

c.

Figure 3. Position of the elements involved in stitch formation during the second tension peak in one machine cycle for the three threads (aA – P2Ag (305°) Needle thread; bB - P2Li (305-320°) Lower Looper thread; cC - P2Ls (340 - 345°) Upper Looper thread).

TYPICAL VARIATION OF PARAMETERS BEING STUDIED

In this paper special attention is given to thread tension and thread consumption.

For each signal acquired, a detailed analysis was done in order to understand its importance during the stitch formation. Therefore, the second tension peak observed in each thread was chosen for analysis because it occurred at an important phase of stitch formation and also gave good results when a statistical analysis was done, namely in terms of the variation coefficient.

Figure 3 shows the position of the elements involved in stitch formation during the second tension peak in one machine cycle. The second needle thread tension peak occurs when the needle is descending and the loop formed by the needle thread is released from the lower looper. At this moment, the lower looper is moving to the left and its thread is being released from the upper looper.

The thread consumption ofin each thread was also studied under different sewing conditions. Figure 4 represents the consumption variation ofby the sewing stitch for the range of sewing stitches performed with the stitch balanced and when changing the pre-tension in the needle thread (loose and tight). It is possible to detect, as expected, that the thread consumption is a function of the pre-tension applied in the string tensioners. It was also found that a compensation of the consumptions between the threads occurs in order to maintain the total consumption constant.

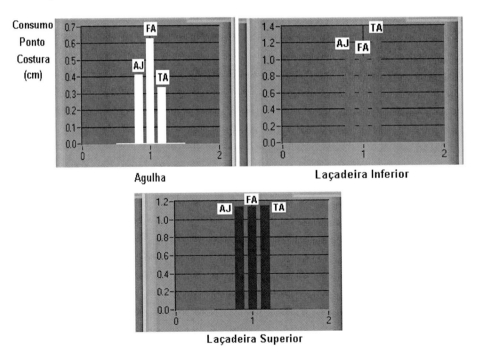

Figure 4. Consumption variation ofby the sewing stitch for the three threads for the range of sewing stitches performed with the stitch balanced (AJ), loose (FA) and tight (TA) in the needle thread.

A formula to determine the theoretical consumption for the stitch type 504 was also developed. This formula was then introduced in the program being used to determine the theoretical thread consumption.

With an accurate analysis of the stitch construction (represented in figure 5) the following formulae to determine the consumption of each thread was defined:

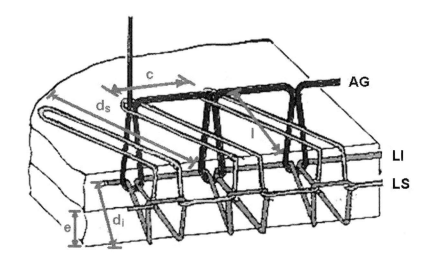

Figure 5. Overlock stitch type 504.

$$C_{Ag} = c + 2e \qquad\qquad (1)$$

$$C_{Li} = e + 2 * \sqrt{\left[(1/3 * c)^2 + 1^2\right]} + 2c \qquad\qquad (2)$$

$$C_{Ls} = e + 2 * \sqrt{\left(c^2 + 1^2\right)} + c \qquad\qquad (3)$$

Therefore, the total thread consumption for one stitch can be obtained using the following formula:

$$C_T = 4e + 2 * \sqrt{\left[(1/3 * c)^2 + 1^2\right]} + 4c + 2 * \sqrt{\left(c^2 + 1^2\right)} \qquad\qquad (4)$$

Where:

C_T - Total thread consumption; C_{Ag} - Needle thread consumption; C_{Li} - Lower Looper thread consumption; C_{Ls} - Upper Looper thread consumption; e - material thickness; c - Stitch length (distance between two contact points between the lower looper thread and the needle thread); 1 - Stitch width; $\sqrt{\left[(1/3 * c)^2 + 1^2\right]}$ (d_i) - Diagonal distance between the bottom material margin and the needle penetration point; $\sqrt{\left(c^2 + 1^2\right)}$ (d_s) - Diagonal distance between the top material margin and the needle penetration point.

PRE-TENSION VARIATION IN EACH THREAD
IN THREE DIFFERENT STRUCTURES

With the variation in pre-tension in each thread, it was possible to evaluate, for the structures *jersey*, *rib* and *interlock* (knitting material produced with the same type of yarn: 100% combed cotton 24Ne and tightness factor (K)), the variation of each of those tension peaks.

It was found that the tension values developed in one thread depend not only on the pre-tension of that thread but also on the tension of the other two threads, once there is an interaction between them resulting from the contacts developed during their interlacing for stitch formation.

When we change the pre-tension in the needle thread, the following equations are obtained for the second tension peak in the three material structures:

Jersey
$$P2Ag = 162.7189 - 1.03469 * T_{Ag} + 0.004191 * T_{Ag}^2 - 0.997997 * T0_{Li}$$
$$+ 0.014909 * T0_{Li}^2 + 0.185908 * T0_{Ls} - 0.177333 * T0_{Ls}^2 \tag{5}$$

Rib
$$P2Ag = 270.572 + 0.155838 * T_{Ag} + 0.001173 * T_{Ag}^2 - 12.8576 * T0_{Li}$$
$$+ 0.172295 * T0_{Li}^2 + 3.315022 * T0_{Ls} - 0.354216 * T0_{Ls}^2 \tag{6}$$

Interlock
$$P2Ag = 159.0966 - 1.43897 * T_{Ag} + 0.004835 * T_{Ag}^2 + 1.472724 * T0_{Li}$$
$$+ 0.002697 * T0_{Li}^2 - 7.04048 * T0_{Ls} - 0.808179 * T0_{Ls}^2 \tag{7}$$

Where:

T_{Ag} – Pré-tension in needle thread; $T0_{Li}$ – Tension in lower looper thread at the moment occurs the second peak occurs in the needle thread; $T0_{Ls}$ – Tension value in the upper looper thread at the moment the second peak occurs in the needle thread.

The regression equations obtained for the needle thread enable the prediction for the three structures, with 95% of confidence, the tension in each of the tension peaks for a certain needle thread pre-tension.

Figure 6 represents the tension variation for the needle thread, in the three structures *jersey*, *rib* and *interlock*, with variation in the needle thread pre-tension and with the tension values in the other threads.

From the graph it can be observed that the tension varies in each of the main tension peaks independently of the structure.

The above equations can be used in future to control the needle thread tensions. Similar studies were carried on for the looper threads.

The use of these formulaes has also revealed the in importance in defect detection, namely during the occurrence of skipped stitches, once the equations responds efficiently in a situation where the value of tension in one of the threads is zero (resulting from a thread break or an imperfection in the interlacement between the threads).

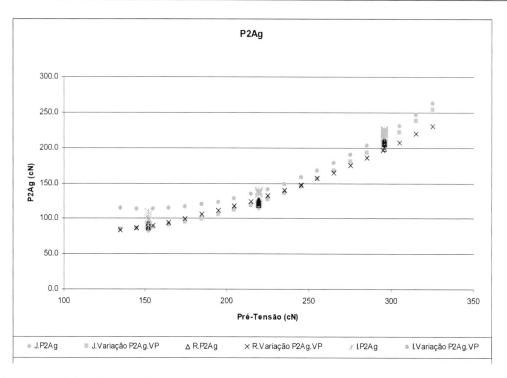

Figure 6. Variation in the needle second peak thread tension thread as a function of the needle thread pre-tension and the tension generated in the other threads (VP) for the *jersey*, *rib* and *interlock* *structures*.

STITCHECK PARAMETER AS A SEAM QUALITY CONTROL ELEMENT

Considering the information previously mentioned and the fact that the seam quality is directly related to the pre-tension and the thread consumption for each thread, in a balanced or adjusted stitch the looper threads must cross in the center of the edge of the material being sewn and the needle thread must hold the seam efficiently conferring the required resistance and elasticity of this stitch type.

Using the second tension peaks from each thread and its consumption, a factor, designated as *Stitcheck* was developed. It disclosed important characteristics and made it possible to quantify a balanced stitch to characterize an unbalanced stitch, this being essential in a situation of control with automatic machine set-up in terms of balancing the stitch. Figure 7 plots this parameter for the jersey structure *jersey* different and shows pre-tensions in each of the three sewing threads. This parameter allows one to identify well defined zones, in accordance with the different sewing conditions. A well defined zone can therefore be observed for the balanced stitch, where the pre-tension values for the three threads are ideal. It is also apparent that for each type of pre-tension variation, the *Stitcheck* value is unique, allowing the different zones of the unbalanced stitch to be defined.

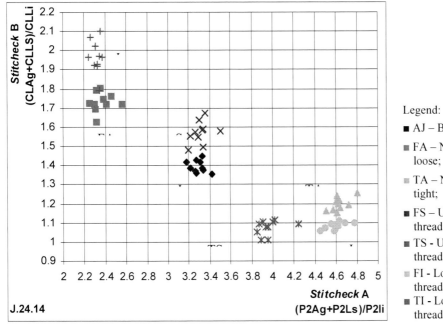

Figure 7. The *Stitcheck* parameter for the *jersey* structure.

Table 1 presents, for each of the situations of pre-tension set-up, the limits for both the *xx* (thread tension peak relationship) and *yy* (thread consumption relationship) *axes.*

Table 1. *Stitcheck* variation for the material structure *jersey*

Sewing Conditions	Axis *xx*	Axis *yy*
AJ - Balanced stitch	3.18 - 3.43	1.36 - 1.45
FA - Needle thread loose	2.26 - 2.56	1.62 - 1.80
TA - Needle thread tight	4.51 - 4.81	1.15 - 1.26
FS - Upper looper thread loose	3.20 - 3.50	1.48 - 1.57
TS - Upper looper thread tight	3.85 - 4.25	1.01 - 1.11
FI - Lower looper thread loose	4.45 - 4.77	1.06 - 1.11
TI - Lower looper thread tight	2.25 - 2.37	1.79 - 2.10

Based on the results presented in table 1, the values referring to the second thread tension peak that produce values for *Stitcheck* (both in terms of the thread tension relationship – axisle *xx* and thread consumption relationship – axisle *yy*) inside of the balanced stitch zone were determined for each thread.

It was found that to obtain values of the parameter *Stitcheck*, corresponding to balanced stitches, the thread tension in the second peak in the needle thread must be within the range 117.4 to 128.0 cN, 16.6 to 27.2 *cN* for the upper looper thread and 42.0 to 45.2 *cN* for the lower looper thread (table 2).

**Table 2. Second pPeak thread tension range to obtain
a balanced stitch in the *jersey* structure**

Sewing Conditions	Second Peak Thread Tension (cN)
Needle Thread	117.4 - 128.0
Upper Looper Thread	16.6 - 27.2
Lower Looper Thread	42.0 - 45.2

To be able to find a linear regression and define the equation representative of the *Stitcheck* parameter values, the variable points were adjusted for the equation type $y = (a + bx) / (c + dx)$.

The regression equation was obtained by adjusting the curve to the ideal points in the curve, represented in figure 8, for each type of machine set-up studied. The equation obtained was:

$$y = (0.281725 + 0.0846611x)/(-0.058401 + 0.147779x) \qquad (8)$$

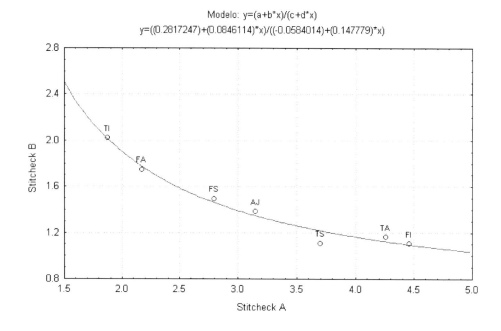

Figure 8. Curve representing the *Stitcheck* parameter values for the *jersey* structure.

DESCRIPTION OF THE ACTUAL WORK

Presently, this research group is in the process of evaluating the proposed control equations, using step motors positioned directly in each thread pre-tensioner. We are also testing other types of material and other parameters, such as: different sewing threads, different needles and machine speed variation.

Other types of sensors are being studied to reduce the cost of applying these devices in the industry.

As mentioned before, a Lockstitch sewing machine is being equipped with the same devices and software and the same research procedures will be carried out soon.

CONCLUSION

We found that with the *Stitcheck* parameter we can accurately control the quality of each seam on the *overlock* sewing machine. Its use, together, with the knowledge gained during the study of tension variation in each thread involved in stitch formation, has revealed the possibility of controlling, in real time, the seam quality, identify non-ideal situations in terms of thread adjustment and amend it accordingly. The system has also has the capability to detect the most frequent sewing defects, such as: thread breakage, skipped stitches and overlapping seams.

REFERENCES

[1]   Ferreira, FBN. A Study of Thread Tensions on a Lockstitch Sewing Machine, PhD thesis, 1991, University of Leeds, Leeds.

[2]   Ferreira, FBN; Carvalho, MAF. Advanced Machines for Advanced Products, Proceedings of the 4th AUTEX Conference, World Textile Conference, *ENSAIT, Roubaix* (2004).

[3]   Carvalho, MAF. Estudo das Tensões nas Linhas na Máquina de Costura Corta-e-cose, Tese de Mestrado, Universidade do Minho, *Guimarães* (1996).

[4]   Carvalho, MAF; Ferreira, FBN. Automatic Seam Control and Qualification on Sewing Machines, Proceedings of the IASTED International Conference - Measurement and Control, Pittsburgh (2001).

[5]   Carvalho, MAF; Ferreira, FBN. On-Line Seam Qualification and Control in a Sewing Machine, Proceedings of the IFAC Workshop on Manufacturing, Modelling, Management and Control – MIM 2001, Prague (2001).

[6]   Carvalho, MAF. Estudo das Relações entre os Parâmetros de Controlo, Propriedades dos Materiais e Condições de Regulação numa Máquina de Costura Corta-e-Cose, Tese de Doutoramento, Universidade do Minho, Braga (2003).

[7]   Carvalho, MAF; Ferreira, FBN; Silva, MEC. Ajuste Automático em Máquinas de Costura e Controlo On-line da Qualidade da Costura, *XXI CNTT,* Natal (2004).

In: Textiles for Sustainable Development   ISBN: 978-1-60021-559-9
Editors: R. Anandjiwala, L. Hunter et al., pp. 173-179   © 2007 Nova Science Publishers, Inc.

Chapter 15

LIQUID AMMONIA TREATMENT OF LINEN AND COTTON/LINEN FABRICS

Emília Csiszár[1], Barbara Dornyi[1], Péter Somlai[2] and István Sajó[3]

[1] Budapest University of Technology and Economics, Department
of Plastics and Rubber Technology, H-1521 Budapest, Hungary
[2] Pannon-Flax Linen Weaving Corp. H-9027 Győr, Hungary
[3] Chemical Research Center of the Hungarian Academy of Sciences,
H-1025 Budapest, Hungary; ecsiszar@mail.bme.hu

ABSTRACT

Liquid ammonia treatment (water-based process) was applied in a large-scale production for improving the quality of 100 % linen and cotton/linen fabrics. The results prove that the swelling treatment has several positive effects on the properties of the linen-containing fabrics, reducing their major disadvantages. Liquid ammonia treatment is very effective in improving wrinkling, dimensional stability, and resistance to abrasion. Significant improvement in easy care properties can also be achieved, especially for the heavier, more loosely constructed fabrics. Furthermore, the water-based swelling process affects the crystalline structure, accessibility and surface properties of the substrates.

Keywords: liquid ammonia treatment, linen fabrics, cotton/linen fabrics, mechanical properties, easy-care properties, fine structure.

INTRODUCTION

Liquid ammonia has been used to improve the aesthetic properties, strength and abrasion resistance of cotton yarns, sewing threads and fabrics since 1967 [10]. Liquid ammonia treatment induces intracrystalline swelling of cellulose and it has considerable influence on the rate and degree of conversion of the subsequent heterogeneous cellulose reactions. Two alternative technologies exist for liquid ammonia treatment today. They differ from each other especially in the procedure used to remove ammonia after the swelling stage. In the water-based process, ammonia is removed from the swollen substrate by means of hot water. In the dry-steam process, ammonia is removed by dry volatilization followed by steaming. The removal techniques alter both the physical properties and fine structure of the treated celluloses [1, 14].

For fabrics, liquid ammonia treatment can be used as a final finishing process or as a pre-treatment for the subsequent finishing operations. The commercial processes are generally applied to cotton products and the improvements that are conferred to cotton textiles by liquid ammonia treatment are widely documented in the literature [3, 8, 11, 13]. The swelling process is very effective in enhancing certain end-use properties, such as dimensional stability, tensile strength, resistance to abrasion, crease recovery, as well as handle and appearance. Although a number of studies and comprehensive reviews have been published regarding the swelling with liquid ammonia, most of them concentrated on cotton and only a very few publications focused on the liquid ammonia treatment of linen and linen-containing fabrics [4, 9, 15].

Linen has a more environmentally-friendly image than cotton, and has several extremely advantageous features, such as excellent tensile properties, high tenacity, "cool-handle" and good comfort and appearance. Along with its many positive qualities, linen fabrics have some disadvantages, such as low wrinkle recovery and dimensional instability, poor abrasion resistance, high stiffness and low resilience. Various finishes developed for linen can improve some of these less desirable qualities [6]. Our starting assumption is that liquid ammonia treatment can also be an appropriate technology for producing linen and linen containing woven fabrics with excellent easy-care and wearing properties, as well as for producing high quality and luxurious linen tablecloths and apparel textiles.

The objective of this work was to evaluate the effects of liquid ammonia, as a final finishing treatment, on the properties of linen and cotton/linen woven fabrics. Fabrics, from different stages of the finishing process were treated with liquid ammonia (water-based process) in a large-scale production process. Research discussed in this paper [5, 7] was concerned, first by changes in fabric structure; second by the improvement in easy-care, wear and hand-related properties; third by the changes in abrasion resistance and tensile properties; and finally with the evaluation of the finishing step applied prior to the liquid ammonia treatment.

EXPERIMENTAL

Fabric Selection

Six 100 % linen plain weave fabrics from different stages of finishing (i.e. scouring /S/, bleaching /B/, or dyeing /D/), and six cotton/linen (warp/weft) combination fabrics were chosen for the investigation. Table 1 gives the basic characteristics of the all-linen and cotton/linen fabrics, and also the designations used in this paper. Fabric weights ranged widely, from relatively lightweight to medium-weight (130-242 g/m^2). Fabrics were treated with liquid ammonia under industrial mill conditions (water system). The fabrics remained taut in the warp and they were not stretched in the weft direction.

Testing

Fabric samples, before and after liquid ammonia treatment, wereas tested using the appropriate recognized ISO and ASTM standards. Fabric weight, fabric sett, fabric width and air permeability were chosen to characterize the changes in fabric structure by the liquid ammonia treatment. The latter was measured using Metefém FF12 air permeability equipment according to ISO 9237:1995. The Cusick Drape Tester and Shirley Stiffness Tester were used to determine drape coefficient [2] and flexural rigidity (ASTM D1388), respectively. The hand of the untreated and liquid ammonia treated fabrics was compared by means of subjective evaluation, using postgraduate students of the department. Dry and wet CRA were measured according to ISO 2312:1972 and reported as the sum of both warp and weft directions. The ISO 5077:1984 standard was used for determining dimensional change due to washing and drying. For assessing the appearance of the fabrics after domestic washing and drying, the ISO 7768:1985 test method was applied, rating the washed fabrics with a scale from five to one. The breaking load and elongation of the fabrics at rupture were also measured by the ravelled strip test (5 cm width) on an Instron Tester Model 5566 (ASTM 1682). Abrasion resistance, expressed as the number of cycles to failure, was determined with a Martindale Tester, Model 404, according to ISO 12947-2:1998. The CUENE fluidity of the fabric samples was measured and converted to the degree of polymerization according to the Hungarian Standard (MSZ 14301/1-76). Color evaluation was performed according to the CIELab color space by using a Hunterlab Color QUEST (D65/10°) colorimeter.

Changes in fine structure were assessed by x-ray diffraction, moisture regain, iodine sorption and water retention. Morphological changes were characterized by scanning electron microscopy. Water retention was determined by soaking the fabrics in distilled water for 24 hours, followed by centrifuging using 2000 g for 10 minutes and drying. The water retention values were calculated from the weights of a sample just after centrifuging and after drying, and expressed as the percentage of water on a dry basis. Moisture regain of the samples was determined by exposing triplicate samples, previously dried over P_2O_5 for 5 days, to an atmosphere of 65 % rh at 25 °C for 5 days. Iodine sorption was measured according to Nelson et al [12]. Five parallel determinations were made and averaged.

X-ray diffraction patterns were obtained on a Philips model PW 3710 based PW 1050 Bragg-Brentano parafocusing goniometer, using CuK_α radiation (λ= 0.15418 nm), graphite monochromator and proportional counter. The XRD scans were digitally recorded with a step size of $0.04°$ and evaluated using profile fitting methods.

Surface morphological investigations were made on a JEOL 5500 LV electron microscope in high vacuum mode, with a secondary electron detector. The accelerating voltage was 20 kV and the working distance 20-21 mm. The samples were fastened to the copper sample holder by adhesive carbon tape. The surface of the samples was coated to obtain a 5 nm thick Au-Pd metal film.

Table 1. Characteristics of the linen and cotton/linen fabrics

100 % Linen				Cotton/Linen (warp/weft)			
Weight (g/m²)	Weave	Finishing[a]	Design.[b]	Weight (g/m²)	Weave	Finishing[a]	Design.[c]
130	plain	Bleaching	L-B130	140	Plain	Dyeing	CL-D140
145	plain	Dyeing	L-D145	144	Plain	Scouring	CL-S144
174	plain	Bleaching	L-B174	146	damask	Dyeing	CL-D146
201	plain	Dyeing	L-D201	148	damask	Bleaching	CL-B148
220	plain	Bleaching	L-B220	203	damask	Bleaching	CL-B203
242	plain	Scouring	L-S242	204	Plain	Scouring	CL-S204

[a] Finishing step prior to liquid ammonia treatment. [b] Based on the abbreviation of the fiber (L), the finishing step (B, D, S) and the fabric weight. [c] Based on the abbreviation of the fibers (CL), the finishing step (B, D, S) and the fabric weight.

RESULTS AND DISCUSSION

Mechanical Properties

Liquid ammonia treatment is effective in improving the very poor wrinkling and creasing properties of linen-containing fabrics and has also significant effect on the tensile properties. Figure 1 shows a characteristic curve of linen fabrics, representing the changes in the selected properties due to liquid ammonia treatment. Values are based on the values of the non-treated fabrics (100%), in terms of smoothness (S), crease recovery angle (CRA) and breaking load (BL).

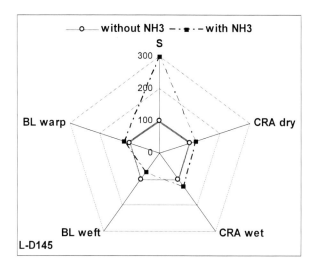

Figure 1. Changes (%) in smoothness (S), crease recovery angle (CRA) and breaking load (BL) of linen fabric (L-D145) treated with liquid ammonia.

The wrinkling of the fabrics after washing is evaluated by means of the AATCC Smoothness Appearance Replicas. The replicas are graded from 1, with the most wrinkled, to 5, which have a virtually smooth appearance. Although the evaluation is subjective with respect to wrinkling, we have found excellent reproducibility. Light-weight linen fabrics exhibit a greater degree of wrinkling after washing than the heavier fabrics. Liquid ammonia treatment significantly reduces the wrinkling and produces smoother fabric surfaces. For the heavier linen fabrics, the final wrinkle evaluation grade is 3.5; the liquid ammonia treatment is therefore successful in reducing the wrinkling of the heavier, loosely constructed linen fabrics and in improving their washing performance. For cotton/linen fabrics, the liquid ammonia treatment has a more significant effect, producing fabrics with final evaluation grades of 3,5-4,5. Thus, the other drawback of linen-containing fabrics, i.e. difficult to iron, has been overcome by the water-based liquid ammonia treatment.

Creasing is the major disadvantage of linen clothing, preventing them from being used for high quality garments. Results prove that if the linen fabrics with average dry and wet crease recovery angles (CRAs) of 92-119 ° and 82-137 °, respectively, are treated with liquid ammonia, the average angles increase significantly. However, the final CRAs are inferior remain low (maximum dry and wet angles: 180 and 195 °, respectively) and the performance of the linen fabrics to creasing remains unsatisfactory. It is obvious from the results that the applied water-based liquid ammonia treatment has a greater effect on the wet crease recovery properties (32-70° increase) than on the dry crease recovery (5-61° increase) of the linen fabrics. These observations are consistent with the concept that in the water based liquid ammonia process, the wet crease recovery angle is markedly increased, while the dry crease recovery angle is only slightly increased [4]. Data also show that the untreated cotton/linen fabrics have much better crease recovery properties which can be further improved by liquid ammonia treatment. Nevertheless, the performance of the liquid ammonia treated cotton linen/fabrics is still unsatisfactory.

The effect of liquid ammonia treatment is also reflected in the tensile properties of the fabrics. The results prove that the liquid ammonia treatment has a noticeable effect on the breaking load of the linen fabrics, the warp direction showing a breaking load increase of about 5-29 %. Nevertheless, in the weft direction, reduction of about 14-29 % can be observed. Similar results apply to the cotton/linen fabrics. Calculation of the breaking load of the individual yarns (N/yarn) in the fabrics reveals that the warp yarns in the liquid ammonia treated fabrics are stronger than their non-treated counterparts. Thus, the greater tension applied in the warp direction during the liquid ammonia process is beneficial, resulting in stronger yarns, whereas liquid ammonia treatment markedly weakens the weft yarns.

Fine Structure

The water-based swelling process, applied under industrial mill conditions, affected the crystalline structure, accessibility and surface properties of the linen-containing fabrics. X-ray diffraction showed that the ratio of crystalline to amorphous regions was not changed, but a partial recrystallization occurred in the crystalline part. The cellulose I was converted to moderately crystalline, but stable, cellulose III, resulting in mixed cellulose I and III lattices in the linen substrates. Changes in the crystalline structure led to increased moisture regain and iodine sorption values. Accessibility of the ammonia treated linen fabrics to liquid water, as measured by water retention, however, was significantly lower than that of the untreated controls. Significant differences between the cotton (warp) and the linen (weft) constituents of the cotton/linen combination fabrics were found only in terms of water retention. While the liquid ammonia treatment caused a significant decrease in the water retention of linen, there was no significant change in that of the cotton fibers [7].

Figures 2(a) and 2(b) show typical effects of liquid ammonia on the surface topography of the linen fibers. A longitudinal view of a linen fiber from one of the control fabrics (LB 220) reveals a larger number of small particulates on the fiber surfaces (figure 2(a)). These surface features are affected by the liquid ammonia treatment, the particulates disappearing, the surface becoming smoother and the fiber rounder and swollen (figure 2(b)).

Changes in the surface of cotton from the cotton/linen fabric are also obvious and substantial. The cotton fiber from the liquid ammonia treated fabric can be characterized by its smooth surface and rounded shape. It is convoluted, but to a lesser extent than that in the non-treated fabric.

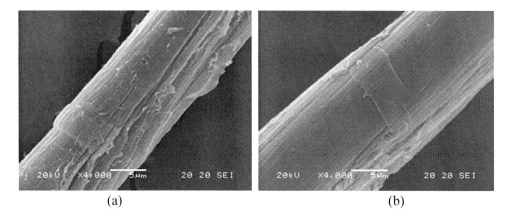

(a)   (b)

Figures 2. Electron photomicrographs at 4000× of untreated (a) and liquid ammonia treated (b) linen fibers obtained from L-B220 all linen fabric.

CONCLUSION

Liquid ammonia treatment is a well known swelling process used in cotton finishing for enhancing certain end-use properties, such as dimensional stability, tensile strength, resistance to abrasion, crease recovery, as well as handle and appearance. Our detailed study proves that liquid ammonia treatment can also be beneficial for finishing linen-containing fabrics.

Linen-containing fabrics are desirable because of their comfort and wear properties, whereas shrinkage, wrinkling and poor abrasion resistance of the fabrics present problems in their general acceptance. Our report discusses the effect of liquid ammonia as a final water-based finish on the mechanical and wear properties, as well as on the fine structure of linen and cotton/linen fabrics. Several trends are evident:

1. Liquid ammonia treatment strengthened the warp yarns and weakened the weft yarns, and increased the breaking elongation, especially in the weft direction.
2. Dimensional stability and appearance after washing of the liquid ammonia treated linen and cotton/linen fabrics improved significantly.

3. The applied water-based treatment had a markedly positive effect on wet crease recovery whereas the dry crease recovery improved only slightly.

4. The swelling treatment did not cause any measurable improvement in fabric drape but had a positive effect on the subjectively by assessed characteristics of the fabrics, producing linen and cotton/linen fabrics with attractive appearance and luxurious hand.

5. The water-based swelling process, applied under industrial mill conditions, affected the crystalline structure, accessibility and surface properties of the substrates.

ACKNOWLEDGEMENTS

This project has been partially financed by the OMFB-ALK−00169/2000 and OTKA T42927.

REFERENCES

[1]   Bertoniere, NR; King, WD; Rowland, SP. *J. App. Polym. Sci.,* 1986, 31, 2769.

[2]   Booth, JE. Principles of Textile Testing. 1969, Chemical Publishing Company, Inc. New York, pp. 287-289.

[3]   Bredereck, K; Buschle-Diller, G. *Melliand Textilberichte,* 1989, 70, 116.

[4]   Bredereck, K; Commarmot, A. *Melliand Textilberichte,* 1998, 79, 64.

[5]   Csiszár, E; Dornyi, B; Somlai, P; Bors, A. AATCC Review, 2006, 6(7), 44-49.

[6]   Csiszár, E; Somlai, P. AATCC Review, 2004, 4, 17.

[7]   Dornyi, B; Csiszár, E; Somlai, P; Sajó, I. *Textile Res. J.* (in print)

[8]   Greenwood, PF. *JSDC,* 1987, 103, 342.

[9]   Kozlowski, R; Manys, S. *Textile Asia,* 1997, 28, 55.

[10] Ladish, CM; Cheek, L. *Cellulose Chem. Technol.,* 1984, 18, 535.

[11] Meyer,C. *Int. Textile Bulletin,* 1999, 45, 68.

[12] Nelson, ML ; Rousselle, MA ; Cangemi, SJ ; Trouard, P. *Textile Res. J,* 1970, 40, 872.

[13] Rowland, SP ; Nelson, ML ; Welch, CM; Herbert,JJ. *Textile Res. J.,* 1976, 46, 194.

[14] Stevens, CV; Roldan-Gonzalez, LG. "Liquid Ammonia Treatment of Textiles" in Handbook of Fiber Science and Technology, Vol. I. Chemical Processing of Fibers and Fabrics, Fundamentals and Preparation, Part A., M. LEWIN, S.B. SELLO, Eds., Marcel Dekker Inc., New York, N.Y., pp.167-203 (1983).

[15] Troope, W. The Liquid Ammonia Treatment of Fabrics. Areas of Application. Book of Papers, Conference on the Liquid Ammonia Treatment of Cellulosic Textiles, Shirley Institute, Didsbury, Manchester, England, pp. 40-46 (1970).

In: Textiles for Sustainable Development   ISBN: 978-1-60021-559-9
Editors: R. Anandjiwala, L. Hunter et al., pp. 181-188   © 2007 Nova Science Publishers, Inc.

Chapter 16

THE DESIGNING OF MULTIFUNCTIONAL FIBROUS STRUCTURES FOR TECHNICAL APPLICATIONS

Mario de Araujo, Raul Fangueiro and Maria Jose Geraldes [1]
School of Engineering, The University of Minho, Campus de Azurem,
4800-058 Guimaraes, Portugal; Phone: +351253510291;
Fax: +351253510293; E-mail: mario.araujo@det.uminho.pt

ABSTRACT

This paper describes a quick prototyping unit for fibrous multifunctional structures that has been set-up at the University of Minho, which provides for the fast development of technical samples for a variety of special applications, mainly in the areas of health and well being, sports goods, personal protection, techno-fashion, civil construction and building industries, composite materials, and so on.

The unit works in a systematic way through the areas of conceptualization, design and simulation, development, manufacturing and testing of technical and intelligent textile materials and structures, providing solutions for technical problems.

New structures are developed for specific applications where special requirements are needed. Examples of the novel products developed are provided.

Keywords: multifunctional structures, intelligent materials, nanotechnologies, finite element aAnalyses, simulation, modeling, specialty products, mass customization.

INTRODUCTION

Mass customization has been defined as the organizing principle of business in the 21st Century. Because it is characterized by small batch production (short runs), timely delivery, competitive cost, and a move away from centralized manufacturing, mass customization is

---

[1] Prof. Maria Jose Geraldes is currently at the University of Beira Interior, Dep. of Textile Science and Technology, Covilha, Portugal

fast becoming the *modus operandi* of companies seeking to obtain or maintain a competitive edge in today's marketplace.

Mass customization is characterized by total market segmentation (1 customer per segment) and can be viewed as the quick and personalized design, manufacturing and delivery of products. In the case of textiles, customization includes personalizing the fiber, the yarn, the fabric, the finishing, the accessories, the style of the garment, the delivery and so on.

Many specialty products have to be customized for technical reasons, to suit a particular application or customer, i.e. vest to monitor the vital functions of the human body (needs fitting and tuning of sensors in a customized way).

The rapid prototyping of fibrous multifunctional structures is viewed as a model for customizing specialty products for technical applications i.e. making samples. It may, of course, also be used for the development of advanced fashion products (techno-fashion).

The technologies involved include advanced CAD systems, FEA (finite element analyses), testing of mechanical properties, permeability, conductivity, microscopy, as well as small scale computer controlled manufacturing of specialty yarns (fancy yarn twister), specialty non-woven fabrics (60 cm wide non-woven line), specialty woven fabrics (two 100 cm wide rapier looms with multiple weft insertion, one of which has an electronic Jacquard and the other with special weft insertion to handle difficult yarns), specialty warp knitted fabrics (100 cm wide electronic Raschel machine), specialty weft knitted fabrics (two 120 cm wide electronic Jacquard flat machines with special feeding units to handle difficult yarns), specialty braided fabrics (vertical and horizontal machines) and hybrid structures. Specialty finishing and surface treatments, coating and lamination are also possible to develop on a small scale.

MULTIFUNCTIONAL FIBROUS STRUCTURES

The development of multi-functional textile structures and systems may be approached in two ways:

1. Developing structures with well defined geometrical areas, each having a different pre-defined property;
2. Developing structures, which, on the whole, have an array of different pre-defined properties.

Developing Functional and Multifunctional Textile Materials

In textile material science the approach to developing functional materials can be divided into two areas:

1. The development of functional fibers to be used in the fabrication of the textile structures;
2. The development of functional finishing forbe applying to, or embedding in, the textile structure.

In each case the objective is to develop specific properties, which will enable these materials to better perform a particular task in the final product.

Examples of these are the development of special intense odors (ex. insect repellents, perfumes, etc), anti-bacteria, anti-mildew, water repellency, water proofing, wind proofing, breathability, color change (ex. thermochromic, photochromic, electrochromic), heat creation and exchange (ex. phase change), shape change (ex. shape memory), high strength, high or low stiffness, low density, high electric conductivity, high thermal insulation, high absorption, high permeability and so on.

Some of these materials may be active or passive. In passive materials their characteristics are quite stable (ex. Young's modulus). However, in active materials there is a change of characteristics (ex. color, heat creation and exchange, electric conductivity) in response to an external agent (ex. temperature, magnetic field).

It should be stressed that a particular material may have, normally, only one specific *but robust* functionality. To have a single material that is a *"jack-of-all-trades and a master of none"* and has all sorts of functionalities does not seem to be the way ahead. However, if a variety of specific functions are desired for the final product, molecular blending, particle blending and fiber blending may be one way to develop multifunctional materials and products for a number of applications.

For other applications, however, other methods are sought for. This is the case with the current work, which follows a different path in the development of multifunctional textile products: i.e. the development of multifunctional textile structures and systems from single-function and multi-function material elements.

Nanotechnologies

There are limits to the classical technologies used to develop textile materials. However, with the advent of nanotechnologies (10^{-9} m) it is possible to create and develop super-materials in which the performance is many-times that of the classical ones (ex. increasing the strength of a rope exponentially whilst decreasing its linear density exponentially). This is done by designing materials, at the very essence of matter: the atom and the molecule. With nanotechnologies it is becoming possible to produce nanofibers and nanoparticles with specific super-properties. These may be used to manufacture extremely strong and extremely light textile structures, since specific properties, such as the modulus of elasticity of the fibers may be extremely high and the density extremely low. If fibers can be produced with the diameter of a macromolecule, then the axial alignment of the molecule in the fibers can be perfect and the modulus of elasticity much increased. Furthermore, increasing the surface to volume ratio would lead to a decrease in the number of flaws of critical dimension and hence to increased fiber strength. With such fibers it would be possible to develop super-structures with extremely high strength, stiffness, toughness, permeability and so on, at extremely low densities.

Nanoparticles could be embedded to enable super-properties in all types of active materials. Here, increasing the surface to volume ratio would lead to higher specific surface area and hence to increased area of interface or contact between two media.

Some of the applications may include: multi-functional filters (dust, bacteria, virus), ballistic products, fiber reinforced composites, surface modified textiles, membranes for lamination and coatings, medical and well-being textiles, techno-fashion and so on.

Developing Multifunctional Fibrous Structures

The basic concept of developing multi-functional textile structures is one of assembling different types of robust high performance material elements (ex. fibers, particles, microcapsules, additives, and so on) in a particular pre-defined way to perform various specific tasks.

The use of yarn and fabric engineering design concepts is essential, together with the most advanced yarn and fabric forming and finishing technologies.

Starting with functional materials A, B, C, D, E…..these may be assembled as shown in figures 1, 2, 3 and 4.

As concerns linear multifunctional structures, the possibilities are many. However, examples of the two fundamental ways of developing these are given below:

- Multifunctional linear structure with a homogeneous effect, as shown in figure 1.
- Multifunctional linear structure with a localized effect, as shown in figure 2.
-

The examples given in figure 1 may be possible to achieve by twisting and braiding.

Figure 1. Schematic diagram of multifunctional linear structures with a homogeneous effect (shown in cross-section).

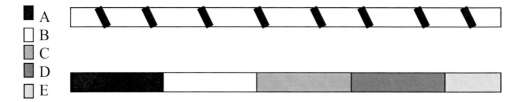

Figure 2. Schematic diagram of multifunctional linear structures with a localized effect (shown lengthwise).

The examples given in figure 2 may be possible to achieve by spraying, space printing and wrapping techniques.

With respect to planar multifunctional structures, there are also two fundamental ways of developing these:

- Multifunctional planar structures with a homogeneous effect or layered structures, as shown in figure 3.
- Multifunctional planar structures with a localized effect or patchwork structures, as shown in figure 4.

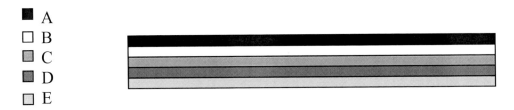

Figure 3. Schematic diagram of multifunctional structures with a homogeneous effect or layered structure (shown in cross-section).

The example given in figure 3 may be possible to achieve by knitting (ex. plaiting, sandwich fabrics), weaving (ex. multi-layered, spacer fabrics), non-woven technologies, coating, printing, laminating and combinations of these.

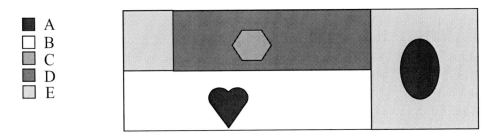

Figure 4. Schematic diagram of a multifunctional structure with a localized effect or patchwork structure (technical face shown).

The example shown in figure 4 may be possible to achieve by knitting (ex. intarsia, Jacquard), weaving (ex. interchangeable double fabrics, Jacquard, multiple weft insertion), embroidery, printing, spraying, flocking and combinations of these.

Combinations of the various approaches are also possible.

Depending on the application, the most suitable materials, structures and technologies to achieve them should be selected.

In this context, fabric structure takes on a new dimension as weaves and stitches have to be studied in the context of combining different functionalities (rather than color or pattern). In this way, fabrics with novel properties may be developed, the patterns of which may take the form of electrical circuits, transistors, resistors, capacitors, sensors, actuators and so on. The scaling down of all these components may be achieved through the development and application of nanotechnologies.

SETTING UP A SPECIFICATION FOR A HEALTH MONITORING TOP

The structure being developed for use in apparel for the purpose of monitoring the vital functions of the human body should also be comfortable, washable, flexible, tough, waterproof and windproof

In order to achieve good thermo-physiological comfort, the structure should keep the body dry, at constant temperature and be able to breath in order to transfer the body's excessive moisture. It should be able to support sensors, a display, a CPU, a transponder and a power supply in order to monitor the vital functions of the human body, communicate and be positioned by GPS.

There are several ways to achieve this depending on the application, the individual wearer and the environmental conditions.

An example of a design of a three-layered structure is as follows:

- 1ST LAYER: an open structure made of cotton to be worn close to the body in order to form a pleasing microclimate near to the skin and good water vapor transmission. Liquid moisture should be wicked away from the body via micro fiber polyester channels. An elastomeric fiber should be used in a low percentage for snugness;
- 2nd LAYER (at the 1st layer/ 3rd layer interface) sandwiched between the 1st and 3rd layers is placed a structure of micro fiber polyester to transfer vapor and liquid water and embed the electrically conductive fiber circuitry to supply electric current from a power supply to the sensors, display unit, CPU and transponder. The sensors and the display unit have micro-antennas for wireless communication with the CPU which also includes a micro-antenna, thus forming a network. The signals from the sensors are processed in the CPU and the measured values are displayed in the display unit and sent by wireless means wherever required. The transponder enables positioning by GPS. This layer could be bulky and embedded with micro-encapsulated PCM (phase change material) with a melting point of 28°C in order to create a thermal barrier between the human body and the atmosphere (passive and active).
- 3rd LAYER: a nylon structure could be used for toughness and hard wear; porous for moisture diffusion and anchored by micro fiber polyester channels to the 1st and 2nd layers in order to wick liquid moisture away from the human body. It could be coated with micro-porous breathable PTFE for water- and wind-proofing.

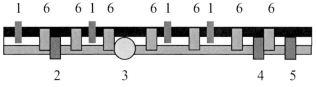

1 6   6 1 6   6 1   6 1   6   6

2   3   4   5

■ 1st layer composed of 5% spandex and 95% cotton
□ 2nd layer composed of 95% polyester microfibers + metal fibers + PCM
▨ 3rd layer composed of nylon + PTFE

1 - sensors with micro-antenna; 2 – display with micro-antenna; 3 – transponder; 4 – CPU with micro-antenna; 5 – power supply (ex battery); 6 – moisture transfer channels;

Figure 5. Schematic diagram of a multifunctional structure with embedded electronics for health monitoring (cross-section).

From a product design point of view, it may be *more practical* to embed the wearable electronics in accessories, such as wrist watches and belts, rather than clothing. However, the above example does show the possibilities of multifunctional structures.

Figure 6 shows a variety of multi-layered structures produced in a flat-bed knitting machine.

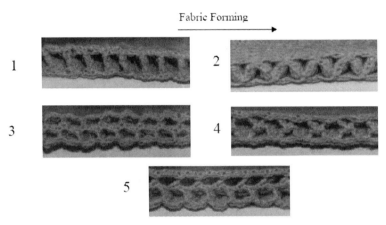

(1) Rectangular core structure (connecting layer: rib)
(2) Triangular core structure (connecting layer: interlock)
(3) Honeycomb core structure (connecting layer: jersey combined with rib)
(4) Triple face structure 1 (connecting layers are not alternated)
(5) Triple face structure 2 (connecting layers are alternated)

Figure 6. Multi-layered sandwich fabrics produced on a flat-bed knitting machine.

Example of a Layered Structure Developed to Maximize Thermo-Physiological Comfort

In the example shown in figures 7, 8 and 9 the objective is to develop a structure with maximum thermo-physiological comfort in the wet state, according to specified reference values of some thermal properties: high thermal resistance and low thermal absorption.

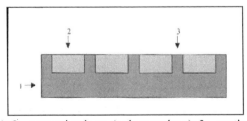

1 – absorbing layer (cotton); 2 – separation layer (polypropylene); 3 – suction channel (cotton)
Figure 7. Schematic diagram of a two layer structure with suction channels, 1 – absorbing layer (cotton);

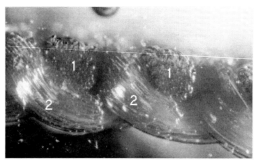

1 – suction channels (cotton); 2 – separation layer (polypropylene)

Figure 8. Microscopic view of the suction channels.

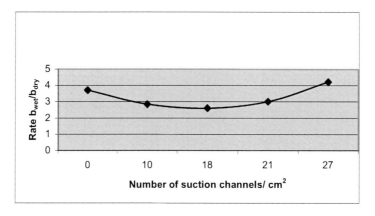

Figure 9. Optimized number of suction channels.

CONCLUSION

The quick prototyping unit set-up at the University of Minho has been an invaluable tool for the development of novel multifunctional fibrous structures, thus contributing to the fast development of technical samples for a variety of special applications.

The thinking behind the development of multifunctional structures has been systematized, providing a variety of possible solutions for solving specific problems.

Examples are given of multifunctional structures that are being developed for specialty products.

REFERENCES

[1]   Geraldes, MJ, Experimental Analyses of Functional Knits in the Wet State, PhD Theses, University of Minho, 1999
[2]   Fangueiro, R. Optimization of the Development of Weft-Knitted Preforms for Composite Materials, PhD Theses, University of Minho, 2002.

In: Textiles for Sustainable Development   ISBN: 978-1-60021-559-9
Editors: R. Anandjiwala, L. Hunter et al., pp. 189-198 © 2007 Nova Science Publishers, Inc.

Chapter 17

DEVELOPMENT OF HEMP FIBER REINFORCED POLYPROPYLENE COMPOSITES

Hajnalka Hargitai[1], Ilona Rácz[1] and Rajesh Anandjiwala[2]
[1]Bay Zoltán Institute for Materials Science and Technology;
H-1116. Budapest, Fehérvári u. 130. Hungary
[2] s and Textiles, Material Science and Manufacturing, CSIR;
Port Elizabeth 6000, South Africa

ABSTRACT

Nonwoven mats from hemp and polypropylene fibers in various proportions were produced and hot pressed to make composite material. The effect of hemp fiber content and anisotropy in the nonwoven mats resulting from the carding technology were examined on the basis of the three-point bending, tensile and impact properties of the resultant composite materials. Because of the hydrophilic nature and poor dimensional stability of cellulosic fibers due to swelling, the effect of water sorption on mechanical performances was also investigated. Optimal mechanical properties were achieved in composites made from 40-50 % of hemp fiber by weight. As was expected, better mechanical properties were found in the specimens cut from the composite sheets parallel to the direction of carding. A large decrease in three-point bending properties was noticed after immersing the composite samples in distilled water for 19 days, whereas the impact strength increased. Double carding of the raw materials resulted in a decreased anisotropy in the composite material.

Keywords: hemp fiber reinforced polypropylene, nonwoven mat, mechanical properties, water sorption kinetics

INTRODUCTION

Natural fibers, such as flax, hemp, jute and kenaf, have received considerable attention as an environmentally friendly alternative to glass fibers in engineering composites [1, 2]. These plant fibers have a number of techno-ecological advantages over traditional glass fibers since they are renewable, can be incinerated, leading to energy recovery, are less harmful in terms of safety and health (e.g. skin irritation) and cause less abrasive wear to processing equipment, such as extruders and molds. In addition, they exhibit excellent mechanical properties, especially when considering their low density (1.4 g/cm^3 versus 2.5 g/cm^3 of glass) [3-5]. Although natural fibers have a number of ecological advantages over glass fibers they also possess a number of disadvantages, such as lower impact strength, higher moisture absorption which brings about dimensional changes thus leading to micro-cracking, as well as poor thermal stability, which may also lead to thermal degradation during processing [6-8].

Up to now most of the studies in the area of natural fiber composites have been focused on the use of polypropylene as a matrix. Polypropylene offers a number of favorable characteristics for high volume applications because of its low price, high toughness and low density. Moreover, polypropylene can easily be processed, recycled and upgraded via the use of glass fillers which haves successfully bridged the gap between the commodity polypropylene composites and the engineering thermoplastics [1, 9, 10]. Using hybrid-nonwovens as semi-finished products, made from a blend of natural and thermoplastic fibers, provides a good basis for high product quality. By mixing the two composite components before consolidation, a proportionate distribution and a good wetting of the reinforcing fibers are ensured [11, 12].

In earlier studies, short fiber reinforced flax-PP composites were prepared, and the best properties occurred at a fiber content of 20-30% [6]. A slight effect of water uptake on the mechanical properties was observed [13]. Experiments were also carried out on flax-PP nonwoven composites. A strong effect of water was found on the dimensional and mechanical properties, and the best properties were observed at 30-50 % of reinforcement by weight [14].

In this study, the effects of hemp fiber content and anisotropy of the nonwoven mat, resulting from the carding technology, on the properties of polypropylene composites, were studied. The effect of water uptake on mechanical performance was also investigated.

EXPERIMENTAL

Materials, Preparation

Nonwoven fleeces of polypropylene fibers (75 mm long, 11 dtex) and hemp fibers (from Nagylak, Hungary) were prepared in different blend ratios.

The fibers were blended manually in the desired ratios of 30, 40, 50 and 70 % hemp by weight. After carding, the thin layers were bonded on a needle punching machine. The technological parameters were maintained constant for all samples. Blended mats, containing 40% hemp by weight, were also produced by double carding the reinforced polypropylene before needle punching. Composite sheets were then prepared by hot pressing the hybrid mats at a temperature of 190°C. The test specimens were cut by means of a TRUMPF CO$_2$ laser cutting equipment in the machine and cross-machine directions of the carding machine, respectively.

Testing Methods

The test specimens were stored in distilled water at room temperature (23±2°C) for about 450 hours (19 days). Each day the samples were dried by means of a paper towel and the increase in weight was measured.

Tensile tests were performed on a ZWICK tensile tester according to the MSZ ISO 527 standard, 5 repetitions being done on each sample.

The three point bending test was carried out on a ZWICK bending tester according to the MSZ ISO 892-78 standard. The specimens were tested in both dry and wet states (after immersion in distilled water for 19 days), 5 repetitions being done on each sample.

The impact strength was tested on ZWICK equipment according to the MSZ ISO 180 standard. The test was carried out in both dry and wet states, 5 repetitions being done on each sample.

All the above tests were carried out at 23±2°C and the dry state tests were performed at an RH of 65%.

RESULTS AND DISCUSSION

Water Sorption and Swelling

The water sorption characteristics were affected by the fiber content of the composites. The well-separated water sorption curves indicate the large effect of the fiber content on sorption characteristics. In contrast with the short fiber reinforced structures of earlier studies [9], the water uptake of the nonwoven composites is not a linear function of the square root of time, as shown in figure 1.

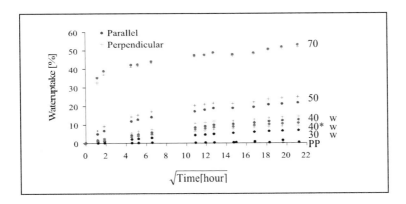

Figure 1. Water uptake, parallel and perpendicular to the direction of carding, as a function of the square root of time (* double carded sample).

At a higher natural fiber content, a higher water uptake is observed, differences being found even after the first day of immersion in water. For example, the weight of the composites increased by 2.4%, 6%, 13% and 42%, for hemp fiber contents of 30%, 40%, 50% and 70%, respectively. The rate of water absorption decreased significantly after the fifth day, saturation being achieved from 17 to 19 days in the case of composites containing the lower hemp fiber content, whereas saturation did not occur in the case of the composites containing 50% and 70% of hemp.

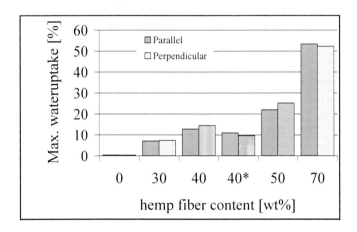

Figure 2. The maximum water uptake, parallel and perpendicular to the direction of carding, as a function of fiber content, (* double carded sample).

For assessing the influence of anisotropy resulting from carding, specimens from the composite sheets were cut both parallel and perpendicular to the direction of carding. The real effect of anisotropy on water uptake was found for 50% hemp in the reinforced composite, samples cut perpendicular to the direction of carding showing 5% higher water uptake than those cut in parallel. Almost 53% water uptake was measured at the highest fiber content of 70%, whereas only 7% water uptake was observed in composites containing 30% hemp fiber as shown in figure 2. Composites prepared by double carding showed about 1 to 5% lower water uptake than those prepared by single carding. Previously it was found that short fiber reinforced injection molded composite samples (20% flax fiber by weight) picked up only about 1% water after 31 days immersion [9].

The thickness of the composites increased by 18% for the composites containing 70% hemp and by 6, 8, and 10% for the composites containing 30%, 40%, and 50% hemp, respectively. The effect of double carding was minimal, reducing the thickness only about 1 to 2%.

Mechanical Properties

The Young's modulus and the tensile strength values of the composites are shown in figure 3(a).

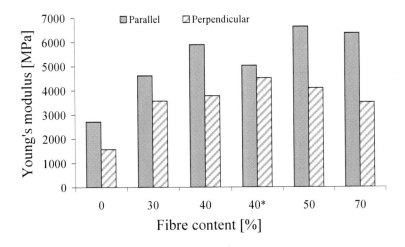

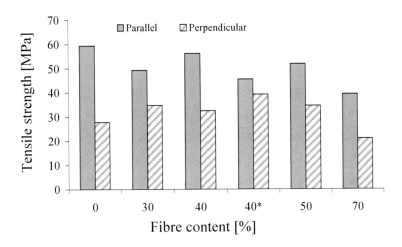

Figure 3(a). Young's modulus (left) and tensile strength (right), parallel and perpendicular to the direction of carding, as a function of fiber content (* double carded sample).

In general, the Young's modulus of the composite materials increased with an increase in fiber content – reaching a maximum value at 50% hemp fiber content and then decreasing slightly for 70% hemp fiber content. The modulus was almost two and a half times higher at 50% hemp fiber content than at 0% (i.e. pure PP) as shown in figure 3(a). Relative to single carding, double carding decreased the modulus by about 5% in the parallel direction and increased it by about 20% in the perpendicular direction. Some 20-40% lower values were found in the perpendicular direction than in a parallel direction. Figure 3(b) illustrates the anisotropic behavior in the tensile parameters of the composite materials. The ratio of the tensile parameter in the parallel direction to that in the perpendicular direction indicates the extent of anisotropy, a value of one means isotropicity. Double carding resulted in a less anisotropic composite material, which is indicated by the lower difference between the properties measured in parallel and perpendicular directions as shown in figure 3(b). The reduction in the modulus is attributed to poor adhesion of fibers to the polymer matrix resulting from poor wetting of fibers by the polymer. The un-wetted or poorly wetted fiber bundles can be easily pulled out of the composite matrix due to a lack of cohesiveness.

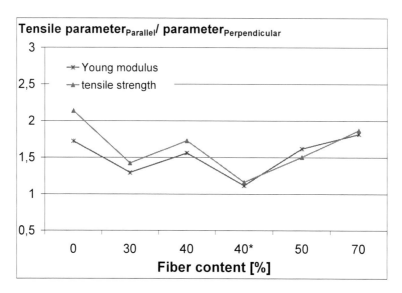

Figure 3(b). The ratio of tensile parameters, parallel and perpendicular to the direction of carding, as a function of fiber content.

Tensile strength in the parallel direction tended to decrease with increasing hemp fiber content (a maximum decrease of 34 % at 70% of hemp) as can be seen in figure 3(a), whereas in the perpendicular direction a different trend was found, the tensile strength showing a maximum value with increasing hemp content, also being about 20-40% lower than that in the parallel direction. Since the fibers lay perpendicular to the direction of load, they cannot act as load bearing elements in the composite matrix structure which is a potential defect and could cause failure. Double carding produced similar effects in strength and modulus, producing a higher strength in the perpendicular direction but a lower strength in the parallel direction relative to that of the single carding as shown in figure 3(b).

In the parallel direction, the modulus (figure 4.), calculated from the three-point bending test increased continuously as a function of fiber content, and was two and half times higher for the highest fiber content (70%) than that of the pure PP, whereas in the case of the perpendicular direction, no significant increase was found above 30% hemp fiber content. Double carding had a positive effect in both directions. The bending modulus decreased dramatically after 19 days immersion in water, for example, by 10-40% at 30-50% of hemp fiber content, and by 77% at the highest hemp fiber content, being 35% lower than that for the PP. In the perpendicular direction, a similar tendency occurred. For example, the values in the wet state were 30-60% lower than those in the dry state.

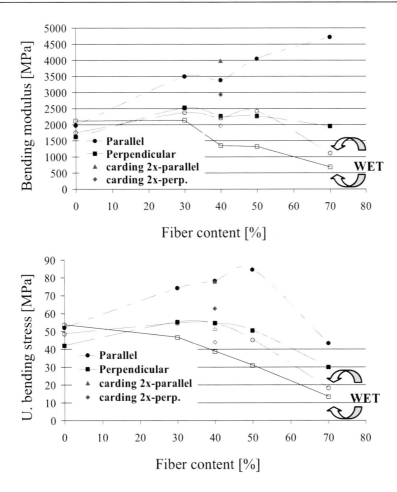

Figure 4. Bending modulus (left) and ultimate(U) bending stress (right) parallel and perpendicular to the direction of carding, as a function of hemp fiber content, tested in both dry and wet states.

The ultimate bending stress (calculated from the stress-strain curve at 10% deflection) showed a maximum, the maximum increase (63%) being found at 50% hemp content, as shown in figure 4. At the highest hemp content the lowest values were observed and which were even lower than that of pure PP, and almost half that at the lowest hemp content. As in the case of the other properties, lower values were found in the perpendicular direction. The ultimate bending stress of the double-carded composites was higher than that for the single carding. Similarly to the bending modulus, a higher decrease (28-60%) in bending strength can be seen in the wet state. The ultimate bending stress was 25-30% lower in the perpendicular direction than in the parallel direction.

Figure 5 shows the results for the Izod impact test. The impact strength of the dry composites increased with increasing hemp content, being 4 and 5 times higher at 50% and 70% hemp content than at 0% (i.e. PP alone). Similarly to the other properties, a higher impact strength was found in the machine (parallel) direction than in the cross-machine (perpendicular) direction. The impact strength decreased by about 25-30% in both directions due to double carding.

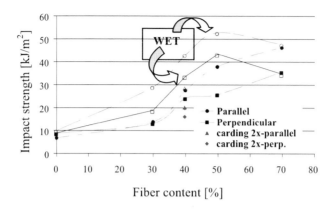

Figure 5. Izod impact strength, parallel and perpendicular to the direction of carding, as a function of fiber content, tested in both dry and wet states.

In contrast to the other characteristics, 110, 56, 40% higher impact strength was exhibited by the composite samples after immersion in water for 19 days as the hemp fiber content increased from 30 to 50%. The samples containing 70% hemp had the same impact strength in the wet and dry states.

CONCLUSION

The effect of hemp fiber content on the properties of hemp-PP nonwoven mats was investigated. Tensile, three point bending and impact tests were carried out in both the dry and wet states in order to study the effect of hemp fiber content and structural anisotropy resulting from carding. The sorption characteristics and swelling of the composites were also investigated. The results of this study can be summarized as follows:

- The water uptake increased significantly with time of immersion, up to 19 days, the maximum water uptake was lower at all hemp fiber content levels than was the case for the flax-PP composites previously reported [14]. The strongest anisotropic effect was observed at 50% hemp fiber content, as was found for the flax reinforced systems.
- On the basis of the mechanical tests, a hemp fiber content of 40-50% appeared to be optimal.
- The bending properties of the wet composite samples were much lower than those of the dry samples, being the same or lower than that of PP, while the impact strength was significantly higher.
- Lower values for the mechanical properties were found in the direction perpendicular to carding compared to those in the direction parallel to carding, the water uptake being approximately the same in both directions.
- Composites from double-carded mats showed a higher water resistance, and better bending properties than those made from single carded mats. In the case of the tensile properties, double carding produced higher values in the perpendicular direction but lower values in the parallel direction compared to single carding, which

indicates that the composites were less anisotropic. A 25-30% decrease in impact strength was produced by double carding.

- •
- •

ACKNOWLEDGEMENTS

Support by the Hungarian Ministry of Education (NKFP 3A/0036/2002) and by the Hungarian Science and Technology Foundation (DAK-2/03) and National Research Foundation of South Africa under the Science and Technology Bilateral Exchange Programme is gratefully acknowledged.

REFERENCES

[1] Peijs, T; Melick, HGH; Garkhail, SK; Pott, GT; Baille, CA. "Natural--mat-reinforced thermoplastics based on upgraded flax s for improved moisture resistance", Proceedings of the European Conference on composite Materials: *Science, Technologies and Applications,* (Visconti, C. ed.), 3-6 June, Vol. 2, 1998, Woodhead Publishing, ECCM-8 pp 119-126.

[2] Oksman, K; Nilsson, P. "Thermoplastic composites based on natural s", Proceedings of the European Conference on composite Materials: *Science, Technologies and Applications,* (Visconti, C. ed.), 3-6 June, Vol. 2, 1998Woodhead Publishing, ECCM-8, pp 133-140.

[3] Young, RA. "Utilization of Natural s: Characterization, Modification and Application", *Lignocellulosic-Plastic Composites* (Rowell, R. M., Schultz, T. P., Narayan, R. eds.), 1997, VSP, Sao Paulo, Brazil, pp. 1-21.

[4] Rowell, RM. "Composite materials from agricultural resources", Research in industrial application on non-food crops, I. plant s (Olesen, Ole, Rexen, Finn, Larsen, Jorgen, eds.), Proceedings of a seminar, Copenhagen, Denmark. Lyngby, Denmark Academy of Technical Science, 1995, pp 27-41.

[5] Bledzki, AK; Gassan, J. "Natural reinforced plastics", Handbook of Engineering Polymeric Materials (Cheremisinoff, N. P. Ed.) Marcel Dekker, 1997, New York, Basel, Hong Kong, pp 787-809.

[6] Rowell, RM. "A new generation of composite materials from agro-based fiber", Proceedings of the 3rd international conference on frontiers of polymers and advanced materials - *Polymer and other advanced materials: emerging technologies and business opportunities* (Prasad, P. N., Mark, James, E., Fai, Ting Joo, eds.), January*, 1995.*

[7] Hatakeyama, H; Hatakeyama, T; Nakamura, K. "Relationship between hydrogen bonding and water in cellulose", *Journal of Applied Polymer Science: Applied Polymer Symposium,* Vol. 37, 1983, pp. 979-991.

[8] Sanadi, A; Caulfield, DF; Jacobson, RE. "Agro-Fiber/Thermoplastic Composites", Paper and Composites from Agro-Based Resources (Rowell, R. M. et al. Ed.), 1997, Lewis Publishers, New York, p. 377.

[9]   Hargitai, H; Rácz, I. "Development of flax fiber reinforced polypropylene composites", 7. Internationale Tagung Stoffliche Verwertung Nachwachsender Rohstoffe, Chemnitz, Germany, 2000.

[10]   Czvikovszky, T; Hargitai, H; Rácz, I; Csukat, G. "Reactive compatibilization in polymer alloys, recyclates and composites", *Nuclear Instruments and Methods in Physics Research,* B151, 1999, pp. 190-195.

[11]   Köhler, E; Bergner, A; Odenwald, S. "Forming of hybrid nonwovens made from natural and thermoplastic fibers", Proceedings of 2nd International Wood and Natural Composites Symposium, Kassel, Germany, 1999, p. 19-1.

[12]   Wielage, B; Köhler, E; Odenwald, S; Lampke, Th; Bergner, A. Kunststoffe, Vol. 89, 1999, pp. 60-62.

[13]   Hargitai, H; Rácz, I. "Influence of water on properties of cellulosic reinforced polypropylene composites", *International Journal of Polymeric Materials,* Vol. 47, 2000, pp. 667-674.

[14]   Hargitai, H; Rácz, I."Development of flax-PP composites", Proceedings of Fourth Conference on Mechanical Engineering, Budapest, Hungary, Springer Verlag Hungarica, Vol.1, 2004, pp. 87-90.

In: Textiles for Sustainable Development   ISBN: 978-1-60021-559-9
Editors: R. Anandjiwala, L. Hunter et al., pp. 199-210   © 2007 Nova Science Publishers, Inc.

Chapter 18

COMPATIBILITY OF COTTON/NYLON AND COTTON/POLYESTER WARP-KNIT TERRY TOWELLING WITH INDUSTRIAL LAUNDERING PROCEDURES

Adine Gericke, L Viljoen and R. de Bruin
Department of Chemistry and Polymer Science, University of Stellenbosch,
Private Bag X1, Matieland Stellenbosch, South Africa, 7602; agericke@sun.ac.za

ABSTRACT

Large institutions, such as hotels and hospitals, often use specialized industrial laundries for laundering sheets, towels or uniforms. The main purpose of this study was to determine the effect of industrial laundering procedures on the durability of cotton warp knitted towels with a synthetic ground structure of either nylon or polyester. The durability of cotton/nylon and cotton/polyester terry towelling fabric samples that were subjected to repeated industrial laundering procedures, was compared by measuring the tensile strength of fabric samples after 50 washing cycles and 50 washing/tumble-drying cycles. The difference between the tensile strengths of the cotton/polyester and cotton/nylon terry towelling samples after washing alone was not significant. The tensile strength of the cotton/nylon samples, however, was significantly less than that of the cotton/polyester samples after tumble-drying. It was concluded that industrial laundering procedures, especially tumble-drying, have a more detrimental effect on the durability of the nylon ground structure than on the polyester ground structure of warp-knitted terry towelling fabrics.

Keywords: towelling, warp knit terry, laundering, tensile strength, durability.

INTRODUCTION

Large institutions, such as hotels and hospitals often use specialized industrial laundries for laundering sheets, towels or uniforms. Continuous washing machines, used by industrial launderers faced with large amounts of relatively uniform laundry, are designed for efficient water and energy use. The laundering process involves interaction of numerous physical and chemical effects on the laundry.

A growing demand and the quest for improved efficiency have led South African towel manufacturers to faster and more economical production methods. Cotton warp-knitted terry towels with a synthetic ground structure are becoming more popular because of the high production speed [1] and added advantage of enhanced durability because of the synthetic component that can be incorporated into the structure [14].

Warp-knitted terrycloth is manufactured on a Raschel warp-knitting machine, using three sets of warp yarns [6][14][22]. The ground structure of pillar stitches, similar to chain stitching, is formed by the first set of warp yarns. Pillar stitches of adjacent rows are not connected. A second set of warp yarns isare looped into this base structure in the weft direction – each set connecting four adjacent rows of pillar stitches – adding stability and strength in the weft direction to the structure. The third set of yarns, referred to as the pile yarns, forms the pile loops. When warp knitting terrycloth, one needlebar is replaced with a point or pinbar, around which the pile yarns are overlapped when the pile loops are formed [22][25]. An illustration of the structure is shown in figure 1 (the length of the pile yarns is not depicted according to scale in the illustration).

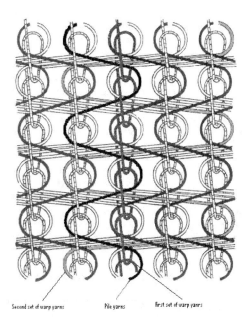

Second set of warp yarns   Pile yarns   First set of warp yarns

Figure 1. Illustration of warp knitted terry towelling fabric structure [8].

In practice, the ground yarns of warp-knitted terrycloth fabrics can differ in composition to that of the pile [22]. Synthetic fibers, such as like nylon and polyester, are mostly used in the ground structure – adding stability and strength [34]. Even though the percentage of synthetic fibers in the structure are is often less that 5%, but even such a small percentage can have a significant effect on the properties of the knitted fabric, as it can enhance the tensile strength without affecting the absorbency negatively. Cotton is generally used as pile yarn because of its excellent absorbency. The second set of warp yarns is often also cotton, to keep absorbency as high as possible, but also because cotton is reasonably priced and actually increases in strength when wet [14][22]. Such fabrics can be described as cotton-polyester or cotton-nylon mixtures.

According to American and European law, it is not compulsory for manufacturers of textile goods to indicate the synthetic component on the label of a product if it is less than 5% [14]. The same practice is applied in South Africa. A label may thus indicate 100% cotton, even though a synthetic component is present. As inferred from the structure of the warp knitted terrycloth (figure 2), the synthetic component plays a vital role in the durability of the towels, especially where breaking strength in the warp direction is concerned.

Care of textile fabrics plays an important role in their expected durability [6][21]. It is thus of utmost importance that the care procedures followed by industrial launderers are compatible with the fiber content and fabric construction of the laundered items.

Industrial launderers generally make use of continuous washing machines, referred to as continuous batch tunnel washers (CBTDs) [5][10]. These machines are designed to remove soiling, contamination and micro-organisms from large quantities of dirty linen. It usually entails a pre-wash, main wash and rinse, followed by tumble drying. Pre-weighed loads of laundry pass through a number of compartments (typically ten to twelve) in which they are pre-washed, washed and rinsed. A CBTD machine usually works with an internal counter-flow current system in which the wash load moves forward in the machine while the water flows in the opposite direction.

Chemical additives are added automatically to the appropriate compartments and steam can be injected into the main wash compartments to achieve the required high temperature levels. Stains and soil are removed through a combination of mechanical action, time and temperature control, detergent action and de-staining agents, which can include bleaches. For thermal disinfection, the achievement and maintenance of the required temperature areis critical.

According to the Fabricare Association [5], the most important factors that influence effective cleaning, and also the durability of the textiles being laundered, are temperature, time, level of wash liquid (dip), mechanical action during washing, additives, the tumble drying process, etc. Of these, temperature, additives and tumble drying are of particular relevance to this study.

Control of *temperature* during each phase of the laundering process is necessary, because on the one hand, temperature has a direct influence on effective soil and stain removal, and on the other, certain fabrics are sensitive to prolonged exposure to high temperatures. Control over temperature is also important when using hypochloritde bleaching agents, as bleaching at too high a temperature can damage certain fibers. In the hospitality and medical industries however, temperature plays an important role in the disinfection process. Here it is important that the critical temperature is reached to ensure effective disinfection [5]. According to Steyn [27], a washing temperature of higher than 54 °C is necessary to ensure effective elimination of micro-organisms in household laundering. In industrial laundries, a temperature of at least 71°C for three minutes or 65°C for ten minutes is recommended as safe time/temperature combinations for thermal disinfection. Additional time should be allowed for adequate penetration in large laundry loads. It is usually preferable to employ a higher temperature range to ensure thorough disinfection, and temperatures up to 80°C are often reached within certain areas in the machine [3][5].

Cotton is not thermoplastic and will not melt in the presence of heat [29]. Normal exposure to elevated temperatures, as found in routine care procedures, will not degrade cotton. White fabrics can be washed in hot water (95°C), but for colored fabrics temperatures higher than 60°C are not recommended [12]. Temperatures in the tumble dryer should not exceed 93°C to prevent the acceleration of fiber degradation [30]. The melting point of nylon varies between 215 °C and 260 °C, depending on the type of nylon [14]. Owing to its thermoplastic nature, and also because nylon does have a tendency to weaken slightly when wet, wash temperatures not exceeding 50°C and moderate drying temperatures are recommended [6][14][29].

Additives during laundering can include detergents, alkalis and bleaching agents.

Synthetic detergents are usually alkaline and are used to remove or suspend soil, reduce the effect of hard water or lower the surface tension of water with the purpose of enhancing soil removal. A pH-value of higher than ten in a detergent solution enhances the effectiveness of the wash process [5].

An alkaline medium will not damage cellulose fibers – even at high temperatures, so all detergents on the market can be used to wash cotton fabrics. Both nylon and polyester, as used in the ground structure of the terrycloth towelling fabrics, have excellent resistance to alkaline wash mediums. Polyester can be damaged by strong alkalis, but has good resistance to weak alkalis such as that found in detergents [6][14][29].

During the rinse phase, the remaining detergent and suspended soil are removed through dilution. A weak acid solution can be added to neutralise the alkalinity of the wash liquid. CSellulose fibers, like cotton, are damaged by strong acids, but even weak acids can degrade the fibers if not removed properly during rinsing [33]. Polyester has excellent resistance to acids, but nylon is sensitive to hydrochloric acid and isare damaged if exposed to sulphuric acid [14][29][20]. The effect of extended exposure to weak acids, especially in the wet state, could be questioned [20].

Bleaches are used to remove stains. The choice of a suitable bleaching agent is dependent on fiber type. The temperature of the washing liquid and the concentration of the bleaching agent should be carefully controlled, as degradation takes place more easily at higher temperatures and concentrations. Cotton is highly sensitive to, and can be degraded by, extensive use of chlorine bleach, whereas polyester is unaffected. Chlorine bleach is also known to cause damage and discoloration in nylon fabrics [14][29].

Tumble drying is the standard method of drying laundry during industrial laundering procedures. The size of the load in the dryer, the mechanical action, time and temperature have an effect on the amount of abrasion, and therefore degradation, that textile fabrics are exposed to [14]. Deans [4] wrote that tumble drying is not a homogenous process. Both the distribution of textile items in the drum and the variation in the temperatures of the air, sides of the drum and textiles being dried are dependent on textile fabric type, moisture content and packing density of the load. He explains that the nature of the textiles in the load influences the amount of moisture that migrates to the surface as well as the cohesion of items in the bundle.

The durability of textile goods is determined to a large extent by the wear and toughness of the textile yarns [31]. Durability is defined as the preservation of the physical integrity, appearance and functionality of a product under normal circumstances of usage [14][21]. This has led to the question of whether there is a difference in the effect of industrial laundering procedures on durability of the cotton/nylon and cotton/polyester warp knitted terrycloth towels.

AIM OF THE STUDY

The main purpose of the study was to compare the durability of cotton warp knitted terrycloth with a nylon ground structure with that of cotton warp knitted terrycloth with a polyester ground structure after exposure to industrial laundering procedures. In order to do so, the cotton/nylon and cotton/polyester terrycloth samples were first analysed to determine their comparability. Secondly, the durability of the fabrics was compared after exposure to industrial washing as well as to washing and tumble drying.

RESEARCH PROCEDURE

Cuprammonium fluidity tests were done on the cotton from both the unwashed cotton/nylon and cotton/polyester terrycloth samples to determine possible chemical damage to the cotton fibers as a result of the manufacturing process. The fluidity of both textile samples was <1 and the degree of polymerisation (GP-values) >3000, which showed that no chemical damage had taken place at that stage (CSIR Manufacturing and Materials Technology Centre for Fibers, Textiles and Clothing, 2004).

In order to describe the test samples and determine the similarity (and therefore comparability) of the cotton/nylon and cotton/polyester terrycloth, the percentage fiber composition, the structural properties, mass per unit area, as well as tensile strength of the unwashed cotton/nylon and cotton/polyester terrycloth were determined.

Samples were exposed to laundering procedures representative of that currently used in industrial laundries, which included washing in a continuous washing-machine and tumble drying. Test samples were exposed to 50 wash and 50 wash/tumble dry cycles and were washed and tumble dried together with other laundry. Wash bundles consisted of towels only and weighed 35kg per bundle. The laundering procedures were conducted under supervision of the researcher to ensure strict control.

Each bundle of washing was weighed in advance (35 kg) to ensure the correct loading level and corresponding concentration of wash additives during the washing process. Wash bundles were loaded in compartments on a conveyor belt that fed into the washing-machine. The continuous washing-machine used in this study consists of twelve different compartments into which washing additives are added in different stages. In the first two compartments (pre-wash area) of the machine, the temperature does not exceed 30°C. In the next two compartments, still in the pre-wash area, a temperature of 78°C is reached. The main wash area, consisting of compartments five to eight, maintains the 78°C temperature. In the rinse area, the temperature gradually decreases in the ninth and tenth compartments to 55°C and 45°C, respectively. In the last two compartments, there are again no specified temperatures to be reached. The procedure is computer-controlled to ensure adherence to specified processes and temperatures.

After washing, the excess water is pressed from the laundry and it is transported via a conveyor belt to a tumbler (not a tumble dryer) to separate the washing items from each other. The samples that were only washed were loaded directly back into the washing-machine, while the samples that were also tumble dried were transported to the tumble dryer.

The industrial tumble dryers were set to reach a maximum temperature of 120°C. During the study, temperature strips were used to measure the actual temperature inside the tumble dryer. Temperatures between 104°C and 110°C were measured. A load of towels took between 30 and 45 minutes to dry, depending on the size of the load.

In order to compare the durability of cotton/nylon and cotton/polyester warp knitted terrycloth, the tensile strength of the test samples in the warp direction was determined after exposure to 50 wash- and 50 wash/tumble dry cycles according to the SABS-standard test method. Ten specimens per terrycloth sample exposed to a specific treatment combination, were tested to ensure a representative average. All samples were conditioned according to standard procedures for 24 hours under controlled atmospheric conditions prior to testing. The tensile strength tests were only done in the warp direction because the nylon and polyester ground structure (pillar stitches) runs only in this direction. Adjacent rows of pillar stitches are not directly intertwined, but bound to each other by means of a second set of cotton warp yarns (figure 2). Since the purpose of this study was the comparison of the nylon and polyester components of the warp knitted terrycloth, it was not relevant to compare the tensile strength of the two sets of samples in the weft direction. The dimensional stability of the test samples was determined to establish whether adjustments to the tensile strength results would be necessary.

Fluidity tests were done on cotton from the laundered cotton/nylon and cotton/polyester terrycloth samples to determine if there was any chemical damage to the cotton fiber.

Textile Testing Methods

Before any tests were done, all test samples were conditioned according to standard procedures for 24 hours under controlled atmospheric conditions (20 ± 2°C and 65 ± 2% relative humidity). The fiber composition of the cotton/nylon and cotton/polyester textile samples was determined according to the ISO 1833-standard test method. The structural characteristics were compared by analysing the knitted structures under a microscope. The average stitch density of the textile samples was determined according to the SABS-method 1120. The average weight of the unwashed cotton/nylon and cotton/polyester terrycloth samples was determined according to the SABS-method 79.

The average tensile strengths of the cotton/nylon and cotton/polyester warp knitted terrycloth samples were compared through conducting tensile strength tests according to the SABS-method ISO 13934-1 on an Instron Universal Testing Machine (Model 4444) after the industrial laundering procedures were completed (50 washing and 50 washing/tumble dry cycles). The dimensional stability of the warp knitted terrycloth was measured and calculated according to the SABS-method 960.

Data Analysis

To compare the results of the tensile strength tests, a two-directional cross-classification variance analysis (ANOVA) was used with fiber content and laundering procedure as factors [23]. The main effects were directly interpreted if the interaction effects were not significant; otherwise various one-directional ANOVAs were done at each of the levels of industrial laundering procedures to determine if the tensile strengths differ significantly. A Bonferroni multiple comparison procedure was used to determine where the differences between levels of the main effects were. Throughout this study a 5% significance level was used. The fiber content included cotton/nylon and cotton/polyester for the purposes of the analyses. The care procedures included unwashed, washed, and washed/tumble dried.

RESULTS AND DISCUSSION

The main purpose of this study was to compare the durability of cotton/nylon and cotton/polyester warp knitted terrycloth towel fabrics that have been exposed to industrial laundering procedures. The tensile strength results of samples that were washed 50 times or washed and tumble dried 50 times were compared to the tensile strength of the unwashed samples, as any change in tensile strength serves as a direct indication of a change in textile structure, implicating a change in durability [21].

Description of Test Samples

Fiber Composition
The average nylon content of the cotton/nylon terrycloth samples was 4,40%. The cotton/polyester terrycloth samples had an average of 4,43% polyester. The difference in synthetic content of the two groups of samples was small enough for the synthetic components to be considered as similar in proportion.

Structural Characteristics
The knitted structure of both groups of terrycloth samples was identified as warp knitted terrycloth in which three sets of warp yarns were used, similar to those in figure 4.1. From the microscope analysis it was clear that the pillar stitches that formed the ground structure of the fabric were synthetic. The other two sets of yarns, namely the second set of warp yarns and the pile threads, were both cotton. In terms of the stitch density, the cotton/nylon terrycloth samples had an average of 48,2 wales and 65,8 courses per 10cm, while the average number of wales and courses per 10cm in the cotton/polyester terrycloth samples were 46,3 and 62,7 respectively. The cotton/nylon terrycloth samples therefore had a slightly higher knit density than the cotton/polyester terrycloth samples. The average mass of the untreated cotton/nylon and cotton/polyester terrycloth samples were 560,1g/m2 en 522,2g/m2, respectively. The average tensile strength of cotton/nylon terrycloth samples before treatment was 296,24N and that of cotton/polyester was 297,84N. A variance analysis (ANOVA) was done on the above-mentioned results to statistically determine the significance of the differences, after which the

cotton/nylon and cotton/polyester warp knitted terrycloth samples were considered comparable in terms of structural properties for the purpose of the study.

Durability of Cotton/Nylon and Cotton/Polyester Warp Knitted Terrycloth Samples after Industrial Washing and Wash/Tumble Drying

Of the samples that were washed only (not tumble dried), the average tensile strength of the cotton/polyester samples was 260,82 N, while that of the cotton/polyester terrycloth samples was 273,82 N. The average tensile strength of cotton/nylon terrycloth samples exposed to 50 wash/tumble dry cycles, was 222,04 N and that of cotton/polyester samples 275,43 N. These results are illustrated in fFigure 4.2. A two-directional ANOVA was done on tensile strength against laundering procedures. The interaction was significant ($p < 0.01$); and thus one-directional ANOVA's are given at each level of laundering in tables 4.2 and 4.3.

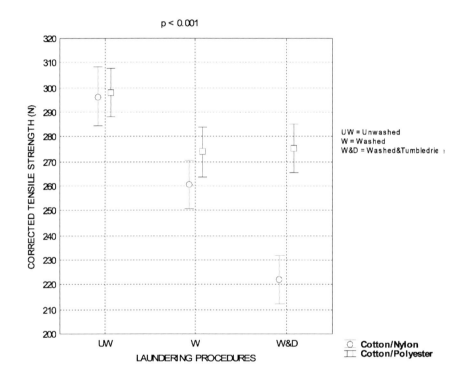

Figure 2. Comparison of the tensile strengths of unwashed (UW), washed (W) as well as washed and tumble dried (W and D) cotton/ nylon and cotton/ polyester warp knitted terrycloth samples.

Table 1. Variance Analysis of Average Tensile Strength of Terrycloth Samples Washed 50 Times

TENSILE STRENGTH				
SOURCE OF VARIANCE	SK	VG	GK	F	P
Fiber content	2538	1	2538	5.907	0.018199
ErrorFault	24922	58	430		

**Table 2. Variance Analysis of Average Tensile Strength
of Terrycloth Samples Washed and tumble Dried 50 Times**

TENSILE STRENGTH				
SOURCE OF VARIATION	SK	VG	GK	F	p
Fiber content	42756	1	42756	62.537	p<0.001
ErrorFault	39655	58	684		

The tensile strengths of both cotton/nylon and cotton/polyester warp knitted terrycloth samples that were washed 50 times, are lower than those of the untreated samples, but only the decrease in average tensile strength of the cotton/nylon terrycloth samples is significant (p < 0.05). Statistical analyses confirmed that there is no significant difference (p > 0.05) between the average tensile strength of cotton/nylon and cotton/polyester terrycloth samples that were exposed to 50 washing cycles. In the case of cotton/nylon towels, this greater decrease in tensile strength can probably be attributed to the fact that nylon fibers expand/swell and weaken slightly in water as the hydrogen bonds in the amorphous areas of the fiber break when water molecules are absorbed. The thermoplastic nature of nylon also causes it to deteriorate during strenuous laundering procedures at high temperatures [6]. A temperature of 78°C is reached during the washing process that is much higher than the recommended temperature, [6][14][29]. The temperature reached during tumble drying, was also as high as 110°C, and in this case the exposure was lengthier.

The reason for the decrease in the tensile strength of the cotton/polyester terrycloth towels can probably not be attributed to the polyester component, as there is no significant difference between the wet and dry strength of polyester fibers. The abrasion resistance and strength of polyester are not influenced by the presence of water and it should remain stable after repeated washes [12][14][18][33]. It is highly improbable that the alkalinity of the detergents caused the decrease in tensile strength, as literature shows that polyester fibers are only degraded by strong alkaline solutions.

The tensile strengths of the cotton/polyester terrycloth samples that were washed 50 times and those that were washed and tumble dried, did not differ significantly (p > 0.05). The tensile strength of the cotton/nylon terrycloth samples did, however, decrease significantly. This decrease in tensile strength was highly significant (p < 0.001). There was also a highly significant difference (p < 0.001) between the tensile strengths of the cotton/nylon and the cotton/polyester terrycloth samples after the 50 wash/tumble dry cycles.

In terms of the results of the cuprammonium fluidity tests, the fluidity value of the cotton in the cotton/nylon terrycloth samples changed from <1 to 5,5 and the degree of polymerisation (GP-value) thereof, from >3000 to 1848 after being washed 50 times and tumble dried. According to the laboratory report this value is comparable to normal damage during washing and bleaching during manufacturing. In contrast to this, the fluidity value of the cotton in the cotton/polyester terrycloth samples changed from <1 to 19,6 and the GP-value from >3000 to 854 after being washed 50 times and tumble dried. According to the laboratory report, these values are comparable to strenuously bleached cotton that points to definite chemical damage [3]. The difference in the extent of damage of the cotton in the cotton/nylon and cotton/polyester terrycloth samples is difficult to explain, as they were exposed to the same laundering procedures. The difference in values can be attributed to the fact that the cotton used in the two samples could have differed in terms of a variety of factors, such as maturity and fineness of the fibers, which could have an effect on the amount of chemical damage during the laundering process.

As a result of the fluidity test results it could be expected that the cotton/polyester should be weaker than the cotton/nylon (which was not the case). It can therefore be expected that the most important cause of the difference in tensile strength in the washed and tumble dried samples can be attributed to degradation of the synthetic yarns in the ground structure and not to the cotton pile yarns or the second set of cotton warp yarns.

The significant decrease in the strength of the cotton/nylon terrycloth after the 50 wash/tumble dry cycles can probably be ascribed to the swelling and weakening of the nylon fibers when exposed to the severe friction action with concurrent high temperature during the tumble drying process. The fact that the tensile strength of the cotton/polyester terrycloth samples after the 50 wash/tumble dry cycles remained nearly unchanged is a good indication of the good abrasion resistance and resiliency of polyester, enabling it to withstand repeated and lengthy tumble drying cycles.

CONCLUSION

The purpose of the study was to compare the durability of cotton warp-knitted terrycloth with a nylon ground structure with that of cotton warp-knitted terrycloth with a polyester ground structure after exposure to industrial laundering procedures. Samples exposed to typical laundering processes were compared. There was a similar decrease in the tensile strengths of both the cotton/nylon and the cotton/polyester terrycloth samples after the 50 wash cycles. The tensile strength of the cotton/nylon warp-knitted terrycloth towelling samples decreased significantly more than that of the cotton/polyester samples after the cycles that included washing as well as tumble-drying. It can therefore be concluded that industrial washing procedures have little or no effect on the strength of the nylon and polyester ground structures of warp-knitted towels, but that the tumble-drying process has a significantly greater degrading effect on the nylon componentcontent of the cotton/nylon terrycloth fabric.

According to the literature, the tumble-drying temperatures for synthetic fabrics should be kept low to average. Although the temperature setting of the industrial tumble-dryer was 120 °C, temperatures between 104 °C and 110 °C were measured. Even such temperatures were clearly too high for the fabrics containing nylon and, as a result, adversely affected the nylon component of the cotton/nylon warp-knitted terrycloth towelling samples.

In the light of the results of the fluidity tests, on the cotton from the cotton/polyester fabrics, the important role that the polyester yarns in the ground structure play in ensuring durability of warp knitted terrycloth is underscored. The fact that the cotton content of these samples showed chemical deterioration (which should translate into a deterioration in tensile strength) would lead to the expectation that the tensile strength of the samples would be lower than that of their cotton/nylon counterparts. In fact, the opposite was found. When the results of this study, namely that the tensile strength in the warp direction of the cotton/nylon terrycloth samples was lower than that of the cotton/polyester terrycloth samples after 50 wash cycles and significantly lower after 50 wash/tumble-dry cycles, and the results of the fluidity tests are taken into account, it is clear that the polyester component plays a significant role in maintaining the tensile strength of the samples during the laundering procedures.

It is important for towel manufacturers to take note of the fact that industrial laundering procedures, and specifically tumble-drying, appear to have a much greater detrimental effect on cotton/nylon than on cotton/polyester warp-knitted terrycloth towels. The fiber content of textile products plays a critical role in their durability and required care procedures. The importance of indicating the correct fiber content on labels of textile goods, even if it is less than 5%, is clearly indicated in this study. It is strongly recommended that manufacturers of textile goods in South Africa should accurately indicate the fiber content of textile goods on labels. In this way industrial laundries and/or consumers can take note of the fiber content and adapt the care procedures accordingly.

REFERENCES

[1]   Anand, SC; Smith, HM. Comparative performance of woven and warp-knitted towelling fabrics. 1994, *Kettenwirk-Praxis* 28(3):62-68.

[2]   Barrie, D. How hospital linen and laundry services are provided. *Journal of Hospital Infection,* 1994, 27(3):219-235.

[3]   CSIR Manufacturing and Materials Technology Centre for s, Textiles and Clothing. 2004. Laboratory Test Report. Port Elizabeth, South Africa.

[4]   Deans, J. The modelling of a domestic tumbler dryer. *Applied Thermal Engineering,* 2001, 21(9):977-990.

[5]   Fabric Care Research Association, 1993, *Washing technology.* SDML Consultancy and Training (RSA).

[6]   Hatch, KL. *Textile science,* 1993, New York. West Publishing Company.

[7]   Hegde, RR; Dahiya, A; Kamath, MG. Nylon fibers. Retrieved 30 August 2004. http://www.engr.utk.edu/mse/pages/Textiles/Nylon%20fibers.htm.

[8]   Innovative Technology Makes Its Mark, 2004, Instruction sheet for Raschel warp-knitting machine: *Wirkbau-Superpol* 14123.

[9]   Isaacs, M. DuPont nylon undergoes renewal at 60. *Textile World,* 1998, 148(11):41-46.

[10]   Jakobi, G; Löhr, A. Detergent and textile washing: Principles and practice, 1987, New York. Cambridge.

[11]   Johnsondiversey. 2004. Wadeville.

[12]   Joseph, ML. Essentials of textiles. 4th ed. USA, 1988, Saunders College Publishing.

[13]   Kadolph, SJ. Quality assurance for textiles and apparel, 1998, New York. Fairchild Publications.

[14]   Kadolph, SJ; Langford, AL. Textiles. 9th Ed, 2002, New Jersey. Pearson Education.

[15]   Kefford, C. What the textile exporter to the US and EU should know. Textiles Unlimited, 2001, 2(2):2.

[16]   Lloyd, J; Adams, C. Domestic laundering of textiles. Textiles, 1989, 18(3):72-79.

[17]   Lord. The serviceability of bed sheets in institutional use. *Journal of the Textiles Institute,* 1971, 62:304-327.

[18]   Mason, RW. Decades later, polyester forges new image. *Textile World.* 1999, 149(1):57-60.

[19]   Mccurry, JW. Towel mills modernize to compete. *Textile World,* 1999, 149(5):26-40.

[20] McIntyre, J.E. Synthetic s: nylon, polyester, acrylic, polyolefin. Cambridge. Woodhead Publishing Ltd. 2000

[21] Merkel, RS. Textile product serviceability, 1991, New York. Macmillan Publishing Company.

[22] Miller, E. Textiles: Properties and behaviour in clothing use, 1992, 4th ed. London. Batsford Academic and Educational.

[23] Milton, JS; Arnold, JC. Introduction to Probability and Statistics, Principles and Applications for Engineering and the Computing Sciences, 1990, McGraw Hill International. New York.

[24] Patel, P. Finishing of terry towels. *Journal of the Textile Association,* 1998, 58(5):195-197.

[25] Spencer, DJ. Knitting technology, 1983, Oxford. Pergamon Press.

[26] Steadman, RG. Cotton testing. *Textile Progress,* 1997, 27(1):1-36.

[27] Steyn, HJH.. Die invloed van wasmiddels en wastemperatuur op die groei en afsterwing van *Escherichia Coli.* 1994, PhD Thesis. University of the Free State.

[28] Taylor, MA. Technology of textile properties: An introduction, 1981, 2nd ed. England. Forbes. Publications Ltd.

[29] Tortora, PG. Understanding textiles. 4th ed. 1992, New York. Macmillan Publishing Co, Ltd.

[30] Ulrich, MM; Mohamed, SS. Effect of laundry conditions on abrasion of mercerized DP natural blend cotton/PET. *American Dyestuff Reporter,* 1982, 71(7):38-41.

[31] Trotman, ER. Dyeing and chemical technology of textile s, 1984, 6th ed. London. Charles Griffin and Company.

[32] Verryne, T. Cotton SA. Pretoria, 2003

[33] Wingate, IB; Mohler, JF. Textile fabrics and their selection. 1984, 8th Ed. New Jersey. Prentice-Hall.

[34] Wiska, Towel, 2003, Retrieved 19 July 2003. http://www.wiska.co.id/e_towel.htm.

[35] Wooten, HL. What's new in terry towel preparation? *Textile Chemist and Colorist,* 1979, 11(6):136-138.

In: Textiles for Sustainable Development   ISBN: 978-1-60021-559-9
Editors: R. Anandjiwala, L. Hunter et al., pp. 211-226   © 2007 Nova Science Publishers, Inc.

Chapter 19

KINETIC STUDY OF POLYPROPYLENE NANOCOMPOSITE THERMAL DEGRADATION

Sergei M. Lomakin[1]*, Irina L. Dubnikova[2],
Svetlana M. Berezina[2] and Gennadi E. Zaikov[1]
[1] N.M. Emanuel Institute of Biochemical Physics of
Russian Academy of Sciences, 119991 Kosygin 4, Moscow, Russia,
[2] N.N. Semenov Institute of Chemical Physics of
Russian 119991 Kosygin 4, Moscow, Russia

ABSTRACT

Polypropylene has wide acceptance for use in many application areas. However, low thermal resistance complicates its general use. The new approach in thermal stabilization of PP is based on the synthesis of polypropylene nanocomposites. This paper discusses new advances in the study of the thermal degradation of polypropylene nanocomposite. The observed results on thermal degradation of polypropylene nanocomposite are interpreted by means of a proposed kinetic model, and predominant role of the one-dimensional diffusion reaction type. According to the kinetic analysis, polypropylene nanocomposites demonstrated the transcendent thermal and fireproof behavior as compared with neat polypropylene.

Keywords: Charring; diffusion; flammability; kinetics; nanocomposite; polypropylene; thermal degradation.

* Correspondence to: Sergei M. Lomakin, N.M. Emanuel Institute of Biochemical Physics of Russian Academy of Sciences, Moscow, Russia, Kosygin 4, 119991, mailto:lomakin@sky.chph.ras.ru

INTRODUCTION

Polypropylene (PP) was the most important synthetic stereo-regular polymer to achieve industrial importance. Today PP represents the fastest growing material for technical end-uses where high tensile strength coupled with low-cost are essential requirements. However, the relatively low thermal resistance and flammability of PP complicate their usage in many fields of applications. The new approach in the thermal stabilization of PP is based on polymer nanotechnology [1-2].

Over the past decade, polymer nanocomposites have received considerable interest as an effective way for developing new composite materials, and they have been studied widely. Because of the larger surface area and surface energy of the additives when individual particles become smaller, it is not an easy task to obtain homogeneously dispersed organic / inorganic composites when the additives are down sized to nano-scale [3]. Melt intercalation has been successful in preparing polymer clay nanocomposites [4]. Recently, the thermal degradation behavior of nanocomposites based upon PP-organoclay was studied by Zanetti, Camino *et. al.* using isothermal and dynamic thermogravimetry [5]. They suggested that the oxygen charring action and scavenging effect in the nanocomposite increase as the volatilization proceeds and that in the nanocomposite a catalytic role is played by the intimate polymer-silicate contact that may further favor the oxidative dehydrogenation-cross-linking-charring process.

This silicate morphology may act as an efficient barrier to oxygen diffusion towards the bulk of the polymer. Surface polymer molecules trapped within the silicate are thus brought into close contact with oxygen to produce the thermally and oxidative stable charred material providing a new char-layered silicate nanocomposite acting as an effective surface shield [5]. In the present study, a routine set of TGA analytical data was generated to provide the kinetic analysis of the thermal degradation in air of PP nanocomposite based on layered organoclay (Cloisite 20A). The results obtained in this study provided additional evidence of the diffusion-controlled character of thermal degradation of PP nanocomposite caused by the catalytic-charring effect of nanosilicate clay.

Experimental

Synthesis

Polypropylene (PP) produced by the Moscow petroleum refinery (MFI = 0.7) and maleic anhydride-modified oligomer (MAPP - Licomont AR 504 by Clariant co.) with $M_n \sim$ 2900; MA-content~ 4 wt.%. were mixed for 2 min using a laboratory Brabender mixing chamber for 2 min. at the first stage. Then 7% wt. of organoclay (Cloisite 20A - Na^+ montmorillonite modified by dimethyl, dihydrogenatedtallow ammonium chloride by Southern Clay Co.) was added to the PP-MAPP - melt at a rotor speed of 60 rpm and set temperature of 190°C (PP-MAPP-Cloisite 20A). 10 min. mixing time was used in all experiments.

Characterisation

WAXS analysis of the nanocomposite layered structure was carried out with a DRON-2 X-ray Diffractometer with Cu-Kα radiation. Diffraction patterns were collected in the reflection-mode geometry from 2° to 10°2θ.

AFM studies were performed with a commercial scanning probe microscope Nanoscope IIIA and IV MultiMode (Digital Instruments/Veeco Metrology Group, USA) in tapping mode, under ambient conditions. Conventional etched Si probes (stiffness ~40 N/m, resonant frequency 160-170 kHz) were used. The amplitude of the free-oscillating probe, A_0, was varied in the 10-20 nm range, while the set-point amplitude, A_{sp}, ranged from 0.5 to 0.8 A_0. Imaging was conducted on the flat sample surfaces being prepared at –80°C with an ultramicrotome MS-01 (MicroStar Inc., USA) equipped with a diamond knife.

Thermogravimetrical Analysis (TGA) has been performed with a MOM Q 1500 instrument at the heating rates of 3, 5 and 10°C/min in air.

Kinetic analysis of the thermal degradation of the PP composites was carried out using Thermokinetics software by NETZSCH-Gerätebau GmbH.

RESULTS AND DISCUSSION

Structure Characterization

It is always necessary to carefully characterize the polymer structure in order to ensure a dispersion for the nanoclays in the polymers. XRD analysis and TEM provide some information on the nanocomposite structural morphology.

The diffraction patterns for nanoclay and nanocomposites are displayed in figure 1 (a). The Cloisite 20A itself has a single peak at around 3.6° with d-space of 2.4 nm (figure 1). The diffraction patterns for nanoclay and nanocomposites are shown in figure 1(a). The Cloisite 20A itself has a single peak at around 3.6° with d-space of 2.4 nm.

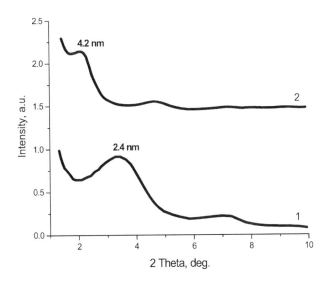

Figure 1. WAXS analysis for Cloisite 20A (1) and PP-MAPP-Cloisite 20A (2).

The shift of the clay basal spacing d_{001} from 3.6° to 2.2° in the PP-MAPP-Cloisite 20A sample suggests the intercalated nanocomposite sample has a higher d-space (4.2 nm) than that in the original clay (2.4 nm), it may have some exfoliated structures, and considering the smearing of the peak in the nanocomposite sample, the nanocomposite structure hasve not been well exfoliated (figure 2). However, the XRD can only detect the periodically stacked montmorillonite layers; for all these nanocomposites there exists a large number of exfoliated layers as well, which can be directly observed by transmission electron microscopy (TEM).

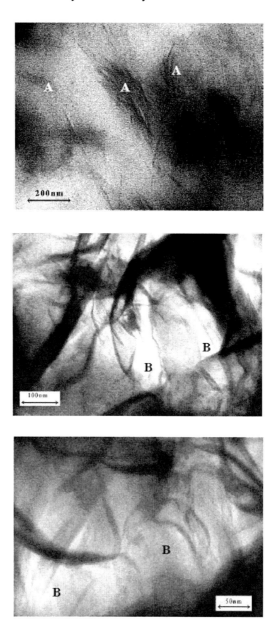

Figure 2. TEM photos with different magnification of PP-MAPP-Cloisite 20A where: A – stacks of layers (intercalated tactoids), B - exfoliated monolayers.

In figure 2 we present TEM images with different magnification which indicate the presence of intercalated tactoids (A) and exfoliated monolayers (B) coexisting in the nanocomposite structure. The intercalated structures are characterized by a parallel registry that gives rise to the XRD reflection of figure 1.

AFM studies indicate similar morphology characteristics for PP-MAPP-Cloisite 20A (figure 3). Height and phase images were simultaneously recorded for the polymer surfaces. The height image presents the surface topography, whereas the phase images provide a sharp contrast of fine structural features and emphasize differences in sample components. We presume the availability of exfoliated monolayer units (A) as well as more complex multilayered tactoids (B) (figure 3).

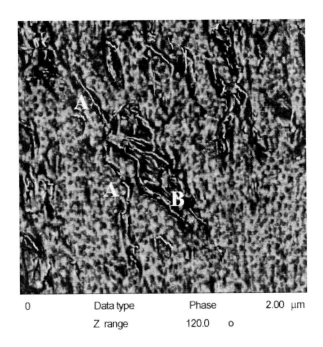

0	Data type	Phase	2.00 μm
	Z range	120.0 °	

Figure 3. AFM image of PP-mPP with 7% Cloisite where: A - exfoliated monolayer units, B - multilayered tactoids.

Thermal Degradation Study

TG analysis of PP and PP nanocomposite (PP-MAPP-Cloisite 20A) shows that when heating in air at 10°C/min, PP volatilizes completely, in two steps, beginning at about 300°C. The maximum rate is at 400°C through a radical chain process, propagated by carbon centered radicals originated by carbon-carbon bond scission (figure 4) [6]. Below 200°C, the hydroperoxidation on the C-H bonds, in which oxygen addition occurs to the carbon radicals created within the polymer chain by H abstraction, initiates radical-chain degradation of PP [7], whereas above 200-250°C, oxidative dehydrogenation of PP takes over [8]. Depolymerization and random scission by direct thermal cleavage of carbon-carbon bonds become possible in air as in nitrogen, above 300°C.

The stabilizing effect of $\Delta 50°C$ (figure 4b) of PP-MAPP-Cloisite 20A over neat PP, calculated with the maximum rate of mass loss, can be explain by means of the barrier effect of the silicate nanolayers which operates at the nanocomposite level against oxygen diffusion, shielding the polymer from its action.

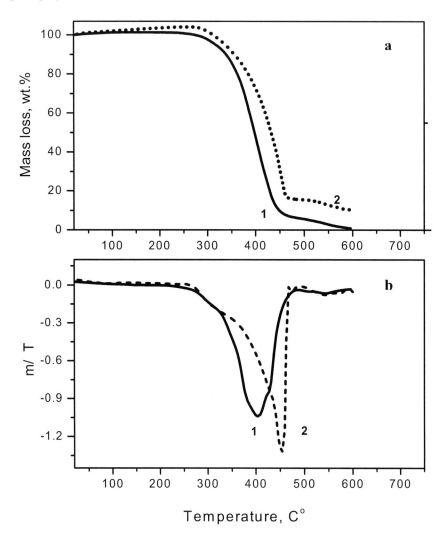

Figure.4. TG – (a) and DTG – (b) curves of PP (1) and PP-MAPP-Cloisite 20A (2) in air at the heating rate of 10°/min.

A char residue from neat PP is left at 450°C (5%), due to charring promoted by oxidative dehydrogenation. Then it slowly decomposes on heating up to 600°C in air (figure 4). On the other hand, thermal degradation of PP-MAPP-Cloisite 20A in air results in a much more stable char form which it does not oxidize even at 600°C (figures 4 and 5).

The silicate nanostructure executes the role of efficient barrier to oxygen diffusion towards the native polymer. The surface polymer molecules trapped within the silicate are thus brought into a close contact with oxygen and the catalytic - silicate layers to produce the thermally and oxidative stable carbonized structures (Scheme on figure 5).

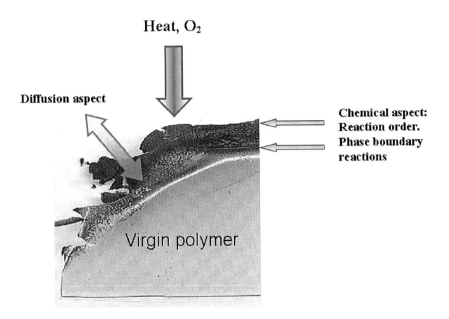

Figure 5. Scheme of the thermo-oxidative degradation of PP nanocomposite (PP-MAPP-Cloisite 20A).

Kinetic Analysis Using TGA Data

Kinetic studies of material degradation have been carried out for many years using numerous techniques to analyze the data. Most often, TGA is the experimental method of choice and the only technique explored here. TGA involves placing a sample of polymer on a microbalance within a furnace and monitoring the weight of the sample during some temperature program. It is generally accepted that material degradation obeys the basic equation (1) [9]

$$dc/dt = - F(t, T c_o, c_f) \tag{1}$$

where, t - time, T - temperature, co - initial concentration of the reactant, and cf - concentration of the final product. Equation $F(t, T, c_o, c_f)$ can be described by two separable functions, $k(T)$ and $f(co, cf)$:

$$F(t, T, c_o, c_f) = k(T(t) \cdot f(c_o, c_f) \tag{2}$$

The Arrhenius equation (4) will be assumed to be valid for the following:

$$k(T) = A \cdot exp(-E/RT) \tag{3}$$

Therefore,

$$dc/dt = - A \cdot exp(-E/RT) \cdot f(c_o, c_f) \tag{4}$$

A series of reactions types; classic homogeneous reactions and typical solid state reactions, is listed in table 1 [9].

Table 1. Reaction types and corresponding reaction equations,
$$dc/dt = - A \cdot exp(-E/RT) \cdot f(c_0, c_f)$$

Name	$f(c_0, c_f)$	Reaction type
F_1	c	first-order reaction
F_2	c^2	second-order reaction
F_n	c^n	n^{th}-order reaction
R_2	$2 \cdot c^{1/2}$	two-dimensional phase boundary reaction
R_3	$3 \cdot c^{2/3}$	three-dimensional phase boundary reaction
D_1	$0.5/(1 - c)$	one-dimensional diffusion
D_2	$-1/ln(c)$	two-dimensional diffusion
D_3	$1.5 \cdot e^{1/3}(c^{-1/3} - 1)$	three-dimensional diffusion (Gander's type)
D_4	$1.5/(c^{-1/3} - 1)$	three-dimensional diffusion (Ginstling-Brounstein type)
B_1	$c_0 \cdot c_f$	simple Prout-Tompkins equation
B_{na}	$c_0^n \cdot c_f^a$	expanded Prout-Tompkins equation (na)
C_{1-X}	$c \cdot (1 + K_{cat} \cdot X)$	first-order reaction with autocatalysis through the reactants, X. $X = c_f$
C_{n-X}	$c^n \cdot (1 + K_{cat} \cdot X)$	n^{th}-order reaction with autocatalysis through the reactants, X
A_2	$2 \cdot c \cdot (-ln(e))^{1/2}$	two-dimensional nucleation
A_3	$3 \cdot c \cdot (-ln(e))^{2/3}$	three-dimensional nucleation
A_n	$n \cdot c \cdot (-ln(e))^{(n-1)/n}$	n-dimensional nucleation/nucleus growth according to Avrami/Erofeev

The analytical output must fit measurements with different temperature profiles by means of a common kinetic model.

Kinetic analysis of PP compositions thermal degradation in air at heating rates of 3, 5 and 10°C/min was carried out using NETZSCH Thermokinetics software in order to provide extra evidence of the diffusion-stabilizing effect of the nanoclay structure (figure 6).

Model-free method evaluations were chosen as the starting points in the kinetic analysis of neat PP and PP-mPP with 7% Cloisite 20A for determining the activation energy in the development of the model. Ffigure 7 shows a corresponding Friedman analysis, where the activation energy is a function of partial mass loss change [10].

The curves show higher values at the beginning of the sintering process, i.e. at lower partial-mass-change values, and considerably higher values at the end of the process (a) and particularly (b). This indicates the presence of a multiple-step process.

First round analysis by the Friedman method indicates a complexity of the scheme for neat PP and PP-MAPP-Cloisite 20A thermal degradation in air [10]. The non-linear fitting procedure established the two - stage scheme for neat PP

$$A \rightarrow X_1 \rightarrow B \rightarrow X_2 \rightarrow C \tag{5}$$

and the triple - stage scheme for PP-mPP with 7% Cloisite 20A (figures 4a, 4b) [9,11].

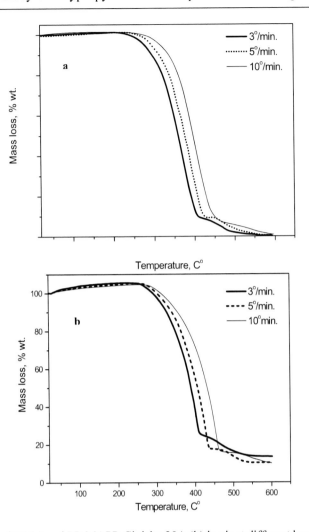

Figure 6. TG curves of PP (a) and PP-MAPP-Cloisite 20A (b) in air at different heating rates.

$$A \rightarrow X_1 \rightarrow B \rightarrow X_2 \rightarrow C \rightarrow X_3 \rightarrow D \qquad\qquad (6)$$

Taking these findings into consideration for neat PP, a fit was attempted using a nonlinear regression with model (5), where the nth-order (Fn) reaction type was used for all steps of the reaction (figure 8, table 2).

With this expanded model, an excellent fit is possible for all three measurements. The kinetic parameters are listed in table 2.

A more sophisticated model (5), based on different reaction types, was chosen for PP-MAPP-Cloisite 20A thermal degradation. The parameters are listed in table 3.

Taking these fittings for PP-MAPP-Cloisite 20A, a best approximation was attempted using nonlinear regressions with model (6), based on the best fit quality (correlation coefficient) (figure 9), where the one-dimensional diffusion (D1) reaction type was used for the second step of the reaction (figure 10, table 3), whereas the nth-order reaction models were chosen for the first and third steps, respectively.

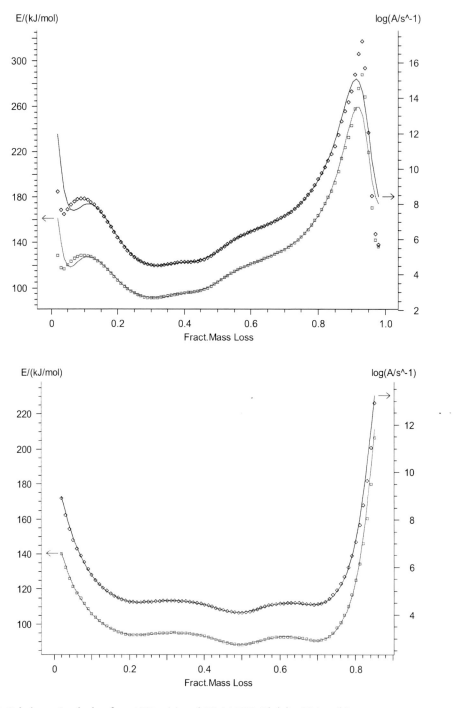

Figure 7. Friedman Analysis of neat PP – (a) and PP-MAPP-Cloisite 20A – (b).

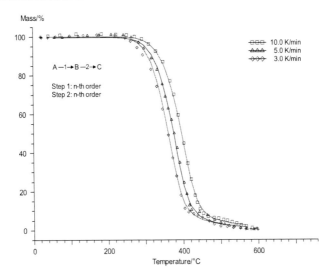

Figure 8. Non-linear kinetic modelling for neat PP.

Table 2. Kinetic parameters resulting from multiple-curve analyses (heating rates 3, 5 and 10 deg/min) with reaction model (A→X$_1$→B →X$_2$→C) from TG measurement of neat PP

Reaction models	Parameter	Value	Corr. Coeff.
(types, Xi)			
	$\log A_1$, s^{-1}	6.39	
	E_1, kg/mol	110.28	
	N_1	1.13	
F_n →F_n			0.9994485
	$\log A_2$, s^{-1}	9.85	
	E_2, kg/mol	151.64	
	N_2	2.59	

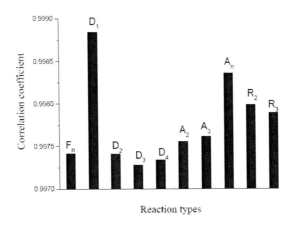

Figure 9. Fit quality between the multiple steps models. Correlation coefficients of different reaction types.

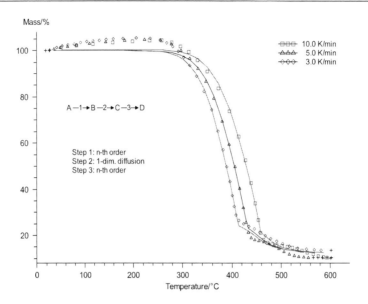

Figure 10. Non-linear kinetic modelling for PP-MAPP-Cloisite 20A.

Table 3. Kinetic parameters resulting from multiple-curve analyses (heating rates 3, 5 and 10 x/min) with different reaction models (A→X*1*→B →X*2*→C→X*3*→D) from TG measurement of PP-MAPP-Cloisite 20A

Reaction models (types, Xi)	Parameter	Value	Corr. Coeff.
	$\log A_1$, s^{-1}	6.33	
	E_1, kg/mol	113.40	
	n_1	1.16	
	$\log A_2$, s^{-1}	8.82	
	E_2, kg/mol	150.97	0.997415
$F_n \rightarrow F_n \rightarrow F_n$	n_2	2.46	
	$\log A_3$, s^{-1}	11.56	
	E_3, kg/mol	188.55	
	n_3	0.78	
	$\log A_1$, s^{-1}	6.90	
	E_1, kg/mol	113.42	
	n_1	1.21	
	$\log A_2$, s^{-1}	4.72	0.998841
$F_n \rightarrow D_1 \rightarrow F_n$	E_2, kg/mol	100.02	
	$\log A_3$, s^{-1}	12.04	
	E_3, kg/mol	199.85	
	n_3	1.17	
	$\log A_1$, s^{-1}	6.45	
	E_1, kg/mol	113.37	
	n_1	1.68	
	$\log A_2$, s^{-1}	6.23	
$F_n \rightarrow D_2 \rightarrow F_n$	E_2, kg/mol	118.43	0.997409
	$\log A_3$, s^{-1}	11.68	
	E_3, kg/mol	197.24	
	n_3	0.95	
	$\log A_1$, s^{-1}	6.49	
	E_1, kg/mol	113.62	0.997280
	n_1	2.04	

Table 3. (Continued).

Reaction models (types, X_i)	Parameter	Value	Corr. Coeff.
$F_n \rightarrow D_3 \rightarrow F_n$	$\log A_2$, s^{-1}	8.26	
	E_2, kg/mol	152.32	
	$\log A_3$, s^{-1}	11.84	
	E_3, kg/mol	197.06	
	n_3	0.94	
$F_n \rightarrow D_4 \rightarrow F_n$	$\log A_1$, s^{-1}	6.58	
	E_1, kg/mol	113.68	
	n_1	2.01	
	$\log A_2$, s^{-1}	7.23	0.997337
	E_2, kg/mol	138.94	
	$\log A_3$, s^{-1}	11.97	
	E_3, kg/mol	195.19	
	n_3	0.98	
$F_n \rightarrow A_2 \rightarrow F_n$	$\log A_1$, s^{-1}	6.61	
	E_1, kg/mol	114.40	
	n_1	2.10	
	$\log A_2$, s^{-1}	5.60	0.997557
	E_2, kg/mol	105.21	
	$\log A_3$, s^{-1}	12.03	
	E_3, kg/mol	199.34	
	n_3	1.23	
$F_n \rightarrow A_3 \rightarrow F_n$	$\log A_1$, s^{-1}	6.50	
	E_1, kg/mol	114.07	
	n_1	2.02	
	$\log A_2$, s^{-1}	4.81	0.997613
	E_2, kg/mol	95.25	
	$\log A_3$, s^{-1}	12.36	
	E_3, kg/mol	200.13	
	n_3	1.46	
$F_n \rightarrow A_n \rightarrow F_n$	$\log A_1$, s^{-1}	6.73	
	E_1, kg/mol	114.72	
	n_1	0.97	
	$\log A_2$, s^{-1}	4.75	0.998355
	E_2, kg/mol	97.73	
	$\log A_3$, s^{-1}	11.86	
	E_3, kg/mol	200.01	
	n_3	1.26	
$F_n \rightarrow R_2 \rightarrow F_n$	$\log A_1$, s^{-1}	7.10	
	E_1, kg/mol	114.89	
	n_1	1.27	
	$\log A_2$, s^{-1}	5.10	0.997984
	E_2, kg/mol	105.66	
	$\log A_3$, s^{-1}	12.13	
	E_3, kg/mol	200.34	
	n_3	1.76	
$F_n \rightarrow R_3 \rightarrow F_n$	$\log A_1$, s^{-1}	7.15	
	E_1, kg/mol	114.62	
	n_1	1.10	
	$\log A_2$, s^{-1}	5.22	0.997898
	E_2, kg/mol	108.92	
	$\log A_3$, s^{-1}	11.56	
	E_3, kg/mol	188.55	
	n_3	0.78	

These results show that the second step in the thermal degradation of PP-MAPP-Cloisite 20A is described by a one-dimensional diffusion (D1) reaction type which is liable for the overall process of the carbonization in nanocomposite polypropylene structure.

Flame Resistant Properties

The recent interest in the reported char-promoting functionalized dispersed nanoclays to yield nanocomposite structures having enhanced fire and mechanical properties, when the clays are present only at levels of 2~10%, prompts their investigation as potential fire retardants.

Because of its wholly aliphatic hydrocarbon structure, neat polypropylene by itself burns very rapidly with a relatively smoke-free flame and without leaving a char residue. It has a high self-ignition temperature (570°C), a rapid decomposition rate and hence has a high flammability. Polypropylene nanocomposites have attracted increasing interest in the flame retardant area in recent years due to their improved fire resistant properties [12-14]. It is suggested that the presence of clay can enhance char formation, providing a transient protective barrier and hence slowing down the degradation of the matrix [13,14] . Thus, the study of isothermal flash pyrolysis of PP composites under the temperatures higher 400-500 ^{0}C allows us to forecast their flammability.

The kinetic results of the present study provided the basis to predict the mass loss of material under isothermal pyrolysis conditions using the same thermokinetics software.

Figure 11 shows the partial reaction curves as a function of time with temperature (400 – 600^{0}C) as a parameter.

It is clearly seen that under conditions of polymer ignition and initial surface combustion, the mass loss for PP-MAPP-Cloisite 20A, and its rate, are noticeably lower than the adequate values for the neat PP. An improvement in flame resistance of PP-MAPP-Cloisite 20A over the neat PP happens as a result of the char formation providing a transient protective barrier. In the present study this phenomena was interpreted in terms of isothermal kinetic analysis.

Apart from this information, the graphs of mass loss rates (*dm/dt*) vs. time for neat PP and PP-MAPP-Cloisite 20A indicate the depression of the degradation (fuel) products under the isothermal pyrolysis conditions at 600^{0}C (figure 12). It is well known that the temperature of 600^{0}C corresponds to an incident heat flux of 35 kW/m^{2}; this being referred to as the real scale fire scenario [15].

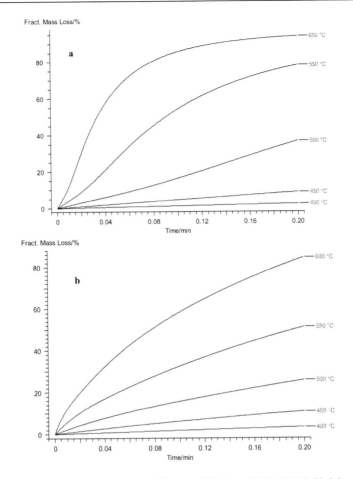

Figure 11. Fractional reaction vs. time (15 sec.) for neat PP (a) and PP-MAPP-Cloisite 20A (b).

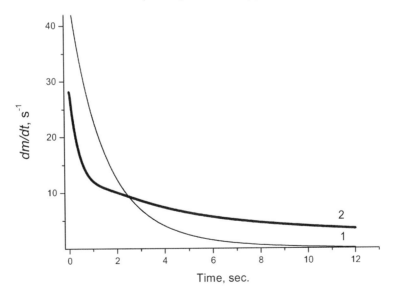

Figure 12. Mass loss rates vs. time for neat PP-MAPP-Cloisite 20A (2) under the isothermal heating condition of 600°C.

CONCLUSION

The kinetic data obtained by the dynamic TGA designate thermal stabilization effect of nanoclay structure into a polymer matrix, resulted in a one-dimensional diffusion process of catalytic-charring throughout the thermal degradation of PP nanocomposites. According to kinetic analysis, polypropylene nanocomposites demonstrated the transcendent thermal and fireproof behavior in relation to neat polypropylene.

ACKNOWLEDGEMENTS

This work was supported by the Russian Foundation for Basic Research, project N 04-03-32052. The authors are pleased to acknowledge Mrs. Natalia Erina from Veeco Metrology of LLC AFMs, Santa Barbara, Ca for supplying AFM data, and the Moscow division of NETZSCH-Gerätebau GmbH for the Thermokinetics software.

REFERENCES

[1]   Giannelis E, *Adv. Mater*, 8:29 (1996).
[2]   Gilman JW., Kashiwagi T, Nyden MR, Brown JET, Jackson C L, Lomakin SM, Giannelis E P, Manias E, *in Chemistry and Technology of Polymer Additives*, Chapter 14, ed by Ak-Malaika S, Golovoy A, Wilkie CA, p 249, Blackwell Science Inc., Malden MA (1999).
[3]   Zanetti M, Lomakin S, Camino G, *Macromol. Mater Eng*, 279:1-9 (2000).
[4]   Kojima Y., Usuki A., Kawasumi M., Okada A., Fukushima Y., Kurauchi T., Kamigaito O., *J. Mater Res*, 8:1185 (1993).
[5]   Zanetti M, Camino G, Reichert P, Mülhaupt R, *Macromolecular Rapid Communications.* 22:176-180 (2001).
[6]   Grassie N, Scott G, *in Polymer degradation and stabilization*, Cambridge University Press, Cambridge, p 275 (1985).
[7]   March J, *in Advanced Organic Chemistry*, McGraw-Hill Kogakusa Ltd, Tokyo, p.367 (1977).
[8]   Benson SW, Nogia PS, *Account of Chemical Research*, 12:233 (1979).
[9]   Opfermann J, *J. Thermal Anal Cal*, 60: 641 (2000).
[10]   Friedman H L, *J. Polym. Sci.*, C6:175 (1965).
[11]   Opfermann J, Kaisersberger E, *Thermochim Acta*, 11:167 (1992).
[12]   Lomakin SM, Zaikov GE, in Modern Polymer Flame Retardancy, VSP Int. Sci. Publ. Utrecht, Boston, p. 272 (2003).
[13]   Gilman J. W, *Applied Clay Sci*, 15:31 (1999).
[14]   Gilman G W, Jackson C L., Morgan A B, Harris R H, Manias E, Giannelis E P, Wuthenow M, Hilton D, Phillips S, *Chem. Mater*, 12:1866 (2000).
[15]   Babrauskas V, *Fire and Materials*, 19:243 (1995).

In: Textiles for Sustainable Development   ISBN: 978-1-60021-559-9
Editors: R. Anandjiwala, L. Hunter et al., pp. 227-236 © 2007 Nova Science Publishers, Inc.

Chapter 20

FIBRILLATION OF NATURAL RS – INCREASING THE SPECIFIC SURFACE FOR HIGH PERFORMANCE COMPOSITES

Nebel Kai and *Kohler Robert*

Institut für Angewandte Forschung, Reutlingen University

ABSTRACT

Bast fibers like flax and hemp are already applied in relatively large scale for technical products of moderate added value. Due to their comparatively high tenacity these fibers are mostly used for automotive parts. But the theoretical strength of the natural fibers is still far from being exploited. A first step to reach the true potential is a complete separation of the single fibers out of the fiber bundles by chemical processing, including the extensive removal of the plant glue of the middle lamella. It has been shown that the increased surface of fine single fibers leads to a considerably higher composite strength. By combining a chemical and a mechanical / hydro-mechanical treatment it is possible to produce finest fiber fibrils with a mean diameter in the range of 1 - 2 µm and a very high specific surface.

Keywords: bast fibers, fibrillation, specific surface, high performance composites.

INTRODUCTION

Although, the amount of natural fibers used for technical products, especially for composites, is actually increasing, the applications are still limited to commodity products. One main reason is the big variation of properties inherent to the natural products. On an average, the specific tensile strength of the strong bast fibers is comparable to glass fibers. But when measuring the tensile strength of single fiber, the best values found are much higher

---

* Alteburgstrasse 150, D-72762 Reutlingen; Tel. ++49 (0) 7121 271 549, Fax ++49 (0) 7121 271537, http://www-iaf.fh-reutlingen.de/; Kai.Nebel@FH-Reutlingen.de

than those of glass and almost comparable to aramide, whereas the low values are indeed ten times less. The reason for these big differences is the complex fiber structure containing highly crystalline cellulose fibrils embedded in a non-fibrous matrix of hemicellulose, lignin and pectin. In addition the fibers have defects from growth and from processing. The measured strength is in fact the superposition of the cohesion of the fibrils, their adhesion to the matrix and the kind and number of defects.

At present there is no process available to separate just the strongest single fibers from the bulk, and even if it were, the yield would be too much low to be economic. There are two well known facts in fiber science: 1. The tensile strength of fibers is increasing with fiber fineness, and 2. the tensile strength of fibers is decreasing with increasing distance between the test grips. The reason of both effects is the existence of flaws or defects in the fibers. The relations can be described by Weibull statistics accounting for the probability for the presence of defects. /Ehrenstein/ /Lee/.

Table 1.

Factors determining the mechanical properties of fiber-reinforced composites
Mechanical properties of components - Fibers - Polymer Composite structure - Fiber load (% - Vol.) - Fiber orientation - Fiber geometry (aspect ratio, critical length) Fiber-Matrix-Adhesion *Mechanical Factors* - specific interface - mechanics of boundary layer (interphase) *Chemical bonds* - secondary (v.d.Waals, Acid-Base) - primary (covalent / ionic: in special cases)

In addition to the fiber strength, the mechanical properties of composites are determined by multiple factors as shown in table 1.

Besides the fiber load, especially the aspect ratio and the fiber-matrix adhesion are predominant. The aspect ratio should at least be at least greater than 30, for the best reinforcement it should exceed a value of 100.

In the absence of primary bonds due to special adhesion promoters, the fiber-matrix adhesion is governed by secondary bonds at the interface and thus closely related to the specific surface of the fibers. Assuming a circular cross section of the fibers, the specific surface increases with the inverse of the fiber radius. The increase in composite strength when using finer fibers has often been demonstrated. /Kohler/ /Müssig/ An example is shown in figure 1a and 1b.

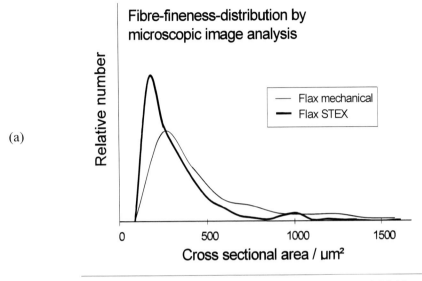

(a)

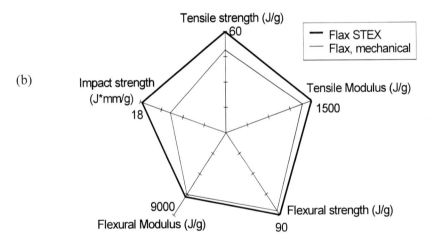

(b)

Figure 1. Fineness of Flax and mechanical profile of flax composite.

The basic idea to achieve improved fiber and composite properties is to disintegrate the naturally grown fibers, to get rid of the macroscopic defects and to separate the almost defect free crystalline fibrils. In addition the single fibrils expose a much higher specific surface leading to a greatly increased interfacial adhesion to the matrix.

Considering fibrous filter materials, it is also well known that finer fibers give much better separation efficiency.

The preparation of crystalline cellulose fibrils or "whiskers" and their use for enhanced composite strength has long been reported in literature [12-23]. Unfortunately the described procedures are quite complicated. They require several very time consuming and laborious steps and are therefore of little practical use.

As a consequence it was decided to dispense with the idea of a perfect fibrillation but instead search for methods applicable to large scale production.

The objective was to develop fibrillated fibers with a highly increased specific surface by using standard fiber finishing processes common in the textile and/or paper industry.

EXPERIMENTALS AND RESULTS

Mechanically decorticated fibers of flax and hemp were chosen as the raw material. The fibers used for fibrillation experiments were used as such or after steam explosion (STEX). STEX splits the fiber bundles into single fibers. Furthermore a major part of the hemicellulose and pectin is removed.

Screening experiments included chemical treatment of the raw fibers as well as steam exploded fibers with acids and bases. The various parameters and a typical processing sequence is given table 2.

Table 2. Typical processing sequence

1. Pre-wetting
2. Hydrocloric / sequestering scouring
3. Alkaline scouring
4. Neutralisation
5. Pulping or hollander Hollander processing

It turns out that the chosen chemical processes alone, even after steam explosion, were not sufficient to fibrillate the fibers. Therefore, after the chemical treatment the fibers were subjected to mechanical beating. A hollander beater, a laboratory blender and a pulper were used. The main factors are the beating time, fiber concentration and filling volume. Experimental design strategies have been used for the trials. But because of the many possible combinations of chemical and mechanical factors a great number of experiments is still necessary. Microscopy is the most meaningful for evaluating the results, but because of the small sample size numerous samples must be examined in order to obtain representative results. For routinely determining the fibrillation effect of a large number of samples a simple and rapid method was required.

Two techniques for assessing the fiber fineness and the specific surface proved very useful:

The freshly prepared fibrillated fiber suspension was immersed into a Schopper-Riegler freeness tester. The drainage of water through the settling fiber sheet is correlated to the fiber fineness.

The fiber sheets formed during the freeness test are carefully removed and dried, and then used for porometry measurements in a PMI Porometer. The information obtained is the "envelope surface" of the fibers, a relative measure of the specific surface. The principle of the method is shown in figure 2.

The fibrous sheet is tightly fixed in the porometer cell. The air flow across the structure is measured as a function of pressure.

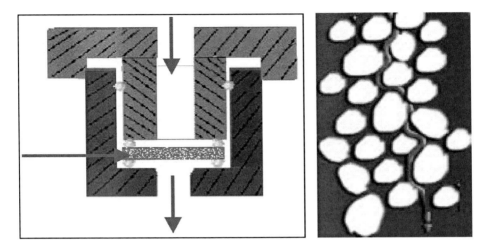

Figure 2. Principle of the Porometer.

Indeed, as shown ion figure 3 there is a good correlation between the envelope surface from porometry and the specific surface determined with the BET-method using nitrogen adsorption, as long as the fibers have similar surface structure. Different fiber types fall apart.

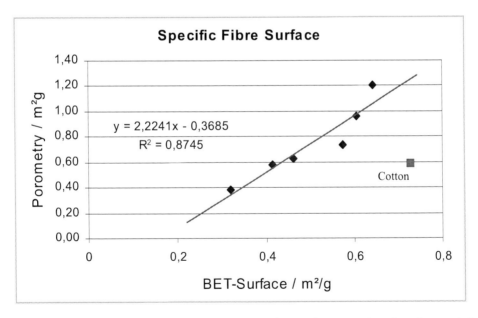

Figure 3. Correlation between Porometry envelope surface and BET-surface is quite good for the bastfibers flax and hemp (diamonds).

The intensity of mechanical beating is the lowest in the pulper, higher in the blender and very high in the hollander beater which also has some cutting effect.

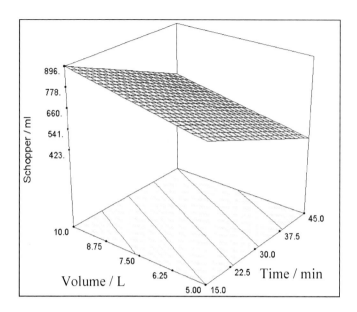

Figure 4. Beating in the hollander - The influence of fill volume and beating time.

With increasing beating time the drained volume of water is decreasing because the finer the fibers the denser the resulting sheet. Reduction of the filling volume increases the fibrillation effect.

By choosing the proper chemical and mechanical treatments, a relevant proportion of the fibers are fibrillated. The fibrils maintain a remarkable length and therefore a very high aspect ratio.

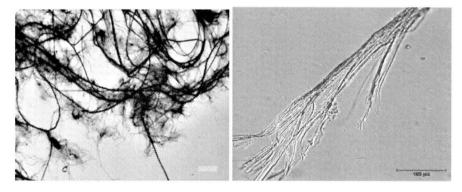

Figure 5. In the light microscope the thicker fibrils are clearly resolved, thinner ones are seen as a sort of "cloudy" environment around the fibers - Fibrillation often begins at the fiber ends forming a brush like tip.

More details than in the light microscope are revealed in the SEM (scanning electron microscope). Another observation is that the fiber "kinks", which are defects in the fiber structure originating from specific events during growth and more often induced by mechanical stress in the course of decortication and mechanical processing, are preferably attacked by hard chemical treatment. Because the chosen processes are not strong enough to result in a total fibrillation still unaffected single fibers are present. The significant length of the fibrils, their residual connection to the fiber core and the presence of many normal fibers have the strong tendency to entangle and clog together forming knots. Drying of the fibrillated fibers results in a partly irreversible spinning and entanglement of the fibrils.

The separation of single fibrils from such knots is almost impossible. Therefore, it is very important to keep the fibers in a diluted suspension, to avoid strong stirring and mechanical agitation. By a gentle movement of the suspension the entanglement can be reduced.

The best method for preparing composites is therefore the forming of wet-laid non-wovens directly from the diluted fiber suspension. After drying the fibrous sheets can be impregnated with thermoset resins and moulded in the hot press.

Alternatively thermoplastic fibers, such as polypropylene can be added to the suspension. The deposition on the screen results in homogenous hybrid sheets which are ready to be moulded in a hot press.

The composites with the fibrillated fibers show superior mechanical properties as demonstrated in figure 6.

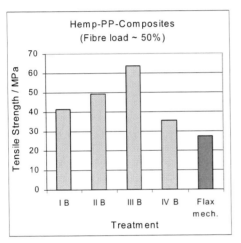
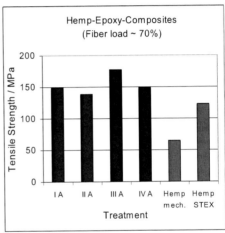

Figure 6. Mechanical properties of composites from fibrillated fibers prepared by different treatments.

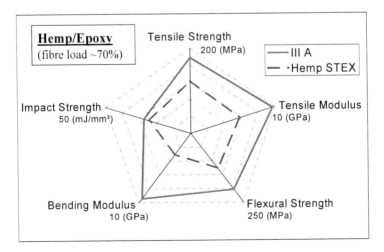

Figure 7. Property profile of composites from fibrillated hemp compared to STEX-hemp.

CONCLUSION

The mechanical properties of composites are greatly enhanced with increasing specific surface of the reinforcing fibers. In the case of natural fibers the first step is therefore to split the bast fiber bundles into high quality single fibers. This can only be achieved by chemical processing which also removes most of the non-fibrous substances hemicellulose, pectin and lignin. Although single fibers (e.g. from the steam explosion process) lead to greatly enhanced composite properties, their specific surface is restricted to a range of 0.5 - 1 m²/g. Furthermore the existence of defects in the fiber structure limits the maximum possible strength.

The separation of highly crystalline cellulose fibrils from the single fibers increases the specific surface and also eliminates many of the macroscopic flaws. A complete disintegration of the complex fiber structure needs a series of complicated and time consuming processing steps. It has been demonstrated that a partial fibrillation is possible by modified finishing processes, which can easily be carried out in any textile finishing line, and additional mechanical beating.

Although the fibrillation is restricted to the outer layers of the fibers, the specific surface available for bonding to the matrix is increased and composites made of these fibers show considerably improved mechanical strength. Because the fibrillated fibers have a high tendency to entangle and to form knots, the best procedure for preparing composites is not to dry the fibers but directly form wet-laid non-wovens.

ACKNOWLEDGEMENT

We are very grateful to the Ministerium für Ernährung und Ländlichen Raum Baden-Württemberg for the support toof this project.

REFERENCES

[1]   Ehrenstein, G.W. Faserverbund-Kunststoffe (Hanser, 1992).
[2]   Lee, SM. Handbook of Composite Reinforcements, (VCH, 1993).
[3]   Milewski, JV. Whiskers and Short Fiber Technology, *Polymer Composites,* Vol. 13, No. 3, (1992) 223-236.
[4]   De, SK; White, JR. Short fiber-polymer composites, Woodhead Publishing Limited, Cambridge England (1996).
[5]   Kohler, R; Wedler, M. Anwendung von Naturfasern in technischen Bereichen, mittex, Schweizerische Fachschrift für die Textilwirtschaft, Heft 3, S. 7-10, 1996.
[6]   Kohler, R; Kessler, RW. Einfluss der Aufschlussverfahren auf die Eigenschaften naturfaserverstärkter Kunststoffe. Proceedings of the International Wood and Natural Fiber Composites Symposium, 29.- 30. Juni, Kassel, (1998).
[7]   Kohler, R; Kessler, RW. Faseraufbereitung und Qualitätskriterien von Naturfasern für Verbundwerkstoffe Proceedings of 5. International Conference "Stoffliche Nutzung nachwachsender Rohstoffe", 28.-29.10., *Chemnitz* (1998).

[8]   Kohler, R; Kessler, RW. Designing natural fibers for advanced materials, Proceedings of the Fifth International Conference on Woodfiber-Plastic Composites, Madison Wisconsin, May 26-27 (1999) 29-42.

[9]   Kessler, RW; Becker, U; Kohler, R; Goth, B. Steam-Explosion of Flax - A superior Technique for Upgrading Fiber Value, *Biomass and Bioenergy,* Vol 14, No. 3 (1998) 237 - 249.

[10] Bos, HL; van den Oever, MJA. The large influence of flax fiber structure on composite strength Proceedings of the Fifth International Conference on Woodfiber-Plastic Composites, Madison Wisconsin, May 26-27 (1999) 79-85.

[11] J. Müssig. Influence of Fiber Fineness on the properties of Natural Fiber Composites Proceedings, 4. International Wood and Natural Fiber Composites Symposium, 10. - 11. April, Kassel (2002).

[12] Zimmermann, T; Pöhler, E; Geiger, T. Cellulosefibrillen für die Polymerverstärkung Proceedings NaroTech, 4. International Symposium "Werkstoffe aus Nachwachsenden Rohstoffen, Sektion 4, S4-5, 11. – 12. Sept., Erfurt (2003).

[13] Pöhler, E; Zimmermann, T; Geiger, T. Cellulose-Nanofibrils for Polymer Reinforcement – Poster, 5. Global Wood and Natural Fiber Composites Symposium, 27.- 28. April, Kassel (2004).

[14] Favier, V; Canova, GR; Cavaillé, JY; Chancy, H; Dufresne, A; Gauthier, C. Nanocomposite Materials from Latex and Cellulose, Polymers for Advanced Technologies, Vol. 6, No. 5, (1995) 351-355.

[15] Favier, V; Chancy, H; Cavaillé, JY. Polymer Nanocomposites Reinforced by Cellulose, *Macromolecules,* Vol. 28, (1995) 6365-6367.

[16] Helbert, W; Cavaille, J Y; Dufresne, A. Thermoplastic Nanocomposites Filled With Wheat Straw Cellulose s. Part I: Processing and Mechanical Behavior, *Polymer Composites,* Vol. 17, No. 4, (1996) 604-611.

[17] Hajji, J.-Y. Cavaillé, V. Favier, C. Gauthier, G. Vigier Tensile Behavior of of Nanocomposites from Latex and Cellulose s, *Polymer Composites*, Vol 17, Issue 4 (1996), 612-619.

[18] Dufresne, A; Cavaillé, JY; Helbert, W. Thermoplastic Nanocomposites Filled With Wheat Straw Cellulose s. Part II: Effect of Processing and Modelling, *Polymer Composites,* Vol. 18, No. 2, (1997) 198-210.

[19] Favier, V; Canova, GR; Shrivastava, SC; Cavaillé, JY. Mechanical Percolation in Cellulose Nanocomposites, *Polymer Engineering and Science,* Vol 37, Issue 10 (1997),1732-1739.

[20] Dufresne, A; Cavaillé, JY. Nanocomposite Materials of Thermoplastic Polymers Reinforced by Polysaccharide in Biopolymers – Utilizing Nature's Advanced Materials, Chapter 3, Syed H. Imam, R.V. Greene, B.R. Zaidi eds., ACS Symposium Series 723, (1999) 39-54.

[21] Matos Ruiz, M; Cavaillé, JY; Dufresne, A; Gérard, JF; Graillat, C. Processing and Characterization of New Thermoset Nanocomposites Based on Cellulose s Materiaux and Techniques, No. 7-8, (2000) 63-68.

[22] Matsumura, H; Sugiyama, J; Glasser, WG. Cellulosic Nanocomposites. I. Thermally Deformable Cellulose Hexanoates from Heterogeneous Reaction. *Journal of Applied Polymer Science,* Vol. 78, Part 13, (2000) 2242-2253.

[23] Matsumura, H; Glasser, WG. Cellulosic Nanocomposites. II. Studies by Atomic Force Microscopy. *Journal of Applied Polymer Science,* Vol. 78, Part 13, (2000) 2254-2261.

In: Textiles for Sustainable Development   ISBN: 978-1-60021-559-9
Editors: R. Anandjiwala, L. Hunter et al., pp. 237-246   © 2007 Nova Science Publishers, Inc.

Chapter 21

COMPARISON OF THE ALKALINE HYDROLYSIS AND DYEING PROPERTIES OF POLY (TRIMETHYLENE TEREPHTHALATE) AND POLY (ETHYLENE TEREPHTHALATE) FIBERS

Mahdi Nouri, Bahareh Mehrabli, Mina Mehratta and Sahar Beheshti

6th Km. of Tehran Road, Textile Department, Guilan University, Rasht, Iran;
mnouri69@guilan.ac.ir

ABSTRACT

Poly(trimethylene terephthalate) fiber has been commercialized at a competitive price competitive compared to with that of poly(ethylene terephthalate) fiber, and better understanding of the behaviour of these fibers is necessary for the textile industry. In this work, the alkaline hydrolysis and disperse dyeing properties of Poly (trimethylene terephthalate) (PTT) fiber are studied and compared with those of poly (ethylene terephthalate) (PET) fiber. For this purpose, C.I. Disperse red 302, C.I. Disperse Brown1 and C.I. Disperse yellow 42 were selected as low energy; high energy and medium energy disperse dyes, respectively. Dyeing was performed at 60, 80, and 96 °C and the rate of dye sorption was measured using a Cintra 10 UV visible spectrometer and finally the dyeing rate constant and diffusion coefficient were calculated at the different temperatures. The results indicated that the dyeing rate of PTT fibers is much greater than that of the PET fibers but for high exhaustion at 96 ° C it is necessary to use low or medium energy disperse dyes.

Alkaline hydrolysis is one possible way of modifying polyester fabrics. This treatment improves the handle, wettability, resistance to abrasion damage and soil release properties of polyester fabrics. Alkaline hydrolysis of PTT fibers is studied and compared with alkaline hydrolysis of PET fibers. The effects of certain treatment variables, such as concentration of sodium hydroxide and time of hydrolysis, are also studied. The rate of hydrolysis and strength loss indicated that the hydrolysis of PTT and PET fibers is not very different. The results are discussed on the basis of calculated hydrolysis rate constants.

Keywords: Poly (trimethylene terephthalate), poly(ethylene terephthalate), hydrolysis, sodium hydroxide, dyeing, disperse dyes.

INTRODUCTION

Poly Trimethylene Terephthalate (PTT) was introduced by Shell Cchemical Cco. as a commercial polymer, joining the polyester family which includes Ppoly Ethylene Terephthalate (PET) and Poly Butylene Terephthalate (PBT). PTT fiber, as a new textile fiber, has attracted immediate attention from both the fiber and textile industries.

From the industrial standpoint, using PTT fiber is not possible without knowing its behavior in textile processing. Dyeing and alkaline hydrolysis of polyester fibers are the most important processes in the textile finishing industry.

Disperse dyes are the most important dyes used in the dyeing of polyester fibers. Because of the high glass transition temperature (Ttg) of PET fiber, it can be dyed either at a temperature of 130°C or lower temperatures in the presence of a carrier. PTT fiber has a lower Ttg than PET fiber and can be dyed with a satisfactory rate of dyeing at 100°C.

The dyeing behavior of PET and PTT fibers with disperse dyes [4] and alkaline hydrolysis of PTT [2] have been reported. In this work a dyeing of PTT fiber with different energy level disperse dyes and alkaline hydrolysis of PTT fiber have been studied in more detail and compared with the dyeing behaviour and alkaline hydrolysis of PET fiber.

EXPERIMENTAL

Materials

75 denier PET yarn and 30 denier PTT yarn were used. The diameters of the PET and PTT fibers were 17×10^{-3} mm and 16×10^{-3} mm, respectively, being measured by means of an optical microscope. The Disperse dyes used for this study were Terasil Pink 3G (C.I. disperse red 302), Terasil Brown 3R (C.I. disperse brown 1) and Terasil Yellow WL (C.I. disperse yellow 42) representing low energy, high energy and medium energy level dyes, respectively. These dyes were supplied by a local distributor of Ciba, the sodium hydroxide, N, N dimethylacetamid and other chemicals used were of laboratory grade.

Methods of Treatment

Dyeing was carried out in a tow neck flask equipped with a condenser and thermometer in order to maintain a constant liquor to goods ratio and temperature during the dyeing process. Stirring of the dyeing bath was done with a magnetic stirrer. For the dyeing rate study, 1% dyestuff on the weight of fabric was applied and the liquor to goods ratio was 100:1 (initial dye concentration was 10 mg/g fiber). 0.5 mℓ/ℓ of acetic acid was added to the dye bath. The dye bath was heated to the required temperature (60, 80 and 96°C (the latter being the boiling temperature of water in the laboratory) before the introduction of the yarn.

Alkaline treatment of the yarns was carried out in a laboratory dyeing machine. The required amount of alkali solution was placed in the jars. The weighed yarn samples were immersed in the solution, and the sealed jars were placed in an oil bath. The liquor to goods ratio was 100:1. The bath temperature increased at the rate of 2.5°C/min. Following the alkaline treatment, the samples were rinsed with distilled water, neutralized with a solution of 1% hydrochloric acid and rinsed again. The samples were then dried at 50°C, conditioned at standard temperature and humidity and weighed.

Characterization

The dye sorption data were calculated from the changes in concentration in the dye bath during dyeing. A Cintra 10 UV-VIS spectrophotometer was used for the measurement of the dye solution concentration using the light absorbance of the dye solution based on the Beer-Lambert law. For each measurement, 0.5 mℓ of the dye solution was removed and the absorbance of the dye solution at the wavelength of maximum absorption was recorded, using 50% V/V of N, N dimethylacetamide aqueous solution as solvent.

The weight loss (WL) is expressed as relative WL according to the equation:

$$\%WL = ((W1-W2)/W1) \times 100 \tag{1}$$

Where, W1 and W2 are the weights of the samples before and after alkaline treatment, respectively.

The tensile tests were performed on a Micro250 Shirley tensile tester. The yarns were tested using a gauge length of 10 cm at a constant rate of elongation.

RESULTS AND DISCUSSION

Dyeing with Disperse Dyes

The rate of dyeing curves for C.I disperse red 302, C.I. disperse yellow 42 and C.I. disperse brown 1, at temperatures of 60, 80 and 96 $^\circ$C for both the PET and PTT yarns are given in figures 1, 2 and 3, respectively. The rate of dyeing at constant temperature provides kinetic information on the dyeing of the PET and PTT fibers. These figures show that, at all temperatures, absorption of disperse dyes by PTT fiber is much faster than that of PET fiber. This means that, at the same temperature and for the same time, a more disperse dye was absorbed by the PTT. The kinetic parameters of the dyeing, i.e., dyeing rate constant (K), and diffusion coefficient (D), were calculated from the dye sorption data and are summarized in table 1.

The dyeing rate constant was calculated using Equation 2 and the diffusion coefficient was calculated using Crank's rate equation (Equation 3) as follows:

$$c_t = K \sqrt{t} \tag{2}$$

where K is the rate constant and C_t is dye absorbed by the fiber at time t

$$\frac{C_t}{C_{inf}} = 4\left[\frac{D.t}{\pi r^2}\right]^{1/2} \tag{3}$$

where D is diffusion coefficient, C_{inf} is dye absorbed by the fiber under equilibrium and r is the radius of the fiber($r_{PTT} = 8.5 \times 10^{-3}$ mm, $r_{PET} = 8 \times 10^{-3}$ mm).

Plots of C_t and C_t/C_{inf} versus the square root of time were linear and dyeing rate constant K and diffusion coefficient D were obtained from their slopes, respectively.

The results in table 1 show that the dyeing rate constants for both PET and PTT fibers increase with increasing dyeing temperature and are much higher in the case of the PTT fiber. The results in table 1 also indicate that the dyeing rate constants are related to the energy level of the dyes, the low energy level dye having a much higher dyeing rate constant than the medium and high energy level dyes.

Table 1 compares the diffusion coefficients of the selected disperse dyes for the PET and PTT fibers. Diffusion coefficient is a function of the ease of penetration of the dye molecules into the fibers. Therefore, the higher diffusion coefficients of the disperse dyes for PTT fibers indicate easier penetration of these dyes into the PTT fiber. Easier penetration of disperse dyes into PTT fibers may be related to the lower glass transition temperature (Ttg) of the PTT fiber compared to that of the PTT and PET fiber. The Ttg of the PTT and PET fibers has been reported as 45-65 $^\circ$C and 70-80 $^\circ$C, respectively [1].

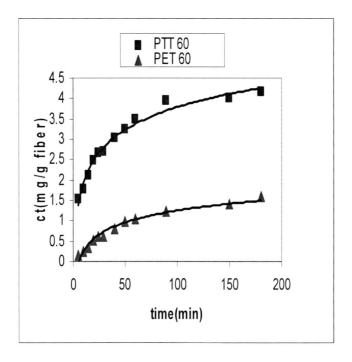

Figure 1. Continued

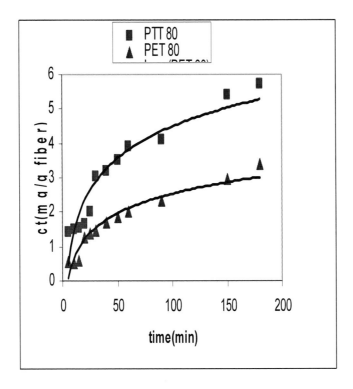

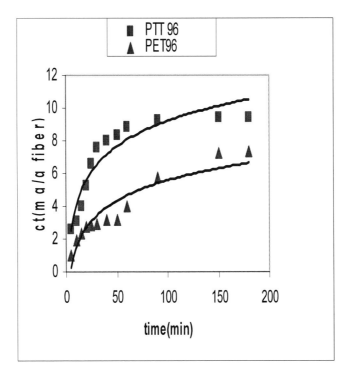

Figure 1. The rate of dyeing curves for Cc.Ii.disperse red 302 (low energy) at 60, 80 and 96 °Cc (initial amount of dye 10 mg/g fiber).

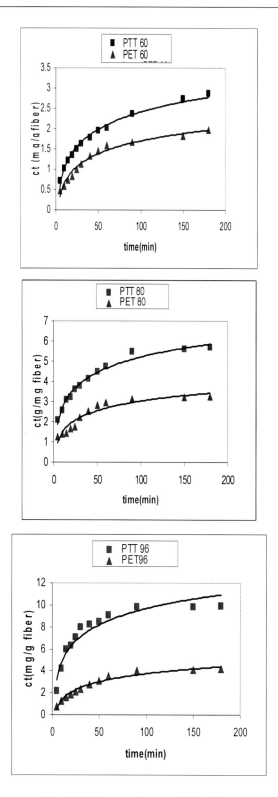

Figure 2. rate of dyeing curves for Cc.Ii.disperse brown 1 (mediume energy) at 60, 80 and 96 °Cc (initial amount of dye 10 mg/g fiber).

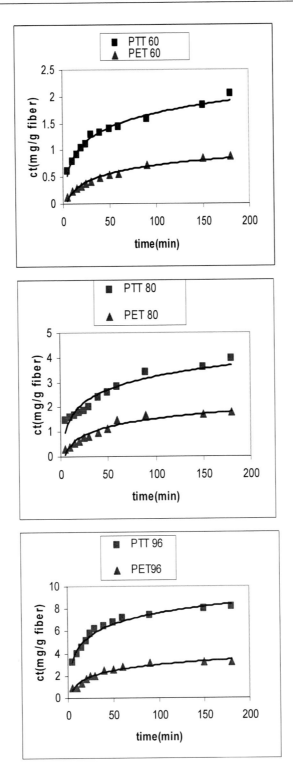

Figure 3. rate of dyeing curves for Cc.Ii.disperse yellow 42 (high energy) at 60, 80 and 96 °Cc (initial amount of dye 10 mg/g fiber).

The diffusion coefficients increase with increasing dyeing temperature because the segmental mobility of the polyester fibers increase with increasing dyeing temperature.

The results in figures 1-3 and table 1 indicate that, although the rate of dyeing of PTT fiber with disperse dyes is relatively high at 96°C, to achieve high exhaustion of the disperse dyes for the PTT fiber at 96°C, it is necessary to use low energy or medium energy level disperse dyes. When using high energy level dyes, exhaustion within a reasonable dyeing time will not be acceptable from an industrial standpoint.

Table 1. Dyeing Rate Constants and Diffusion Coefficients for Dyes C.I. Dispesre Red 302 (low energy), C.I. Disperse Brown 1 (mediume energy) and C.I. Disperse Yellow 42 (high energy) at Different Temperatures (initial amount of dye 10 mg/g fiber)

Fiber	Temperature °Cc	Energy Level	Diffusion Coefficient $(D\times10^8)$ mm^{2}min^{-1}	Rate Constant(K) mg g^{-1} min$^{-1/2}$
PTT	60	Low	4	0.53
		medium	2	0.41
		high	0.8	0.41
	80	low	10	0.85
		medium	7	0.73
		high	3	0.5
	96	low	31	1.48
		medium	29	1.48
		high	13	0.97
PET	60	low	1	0.27
		medium	0.7	03
		high	0.3	0.14
	80	low	3.6	0.54
		medium	3	0.45
		high	0.7	0.31
	96	low	19	1.2
		medium	7.2	0.61
		high	3.6	0.51

ALKALINE HYDROLYSIS

According to the present understanding of the hydrolysis of polyester fibers by alkali metal hydroxides, the hydroxide ions attack the electron deficient carbonyl carbon, resulting in the production of hydroxyl and carboxyl end groups at the fiber surface [3]. A low molecular segment of the chains is removed, resulting in a weight loss and reduced fiber diameter.

Figure 4 shows the effect of alkali treatment time on the weight loss of PET and PTT fibers using 30 and 60 g/ℓ sodium hydroxide, respectively, at 100°C. The rate of weight loss is the same for the PTT and PET fibers. For example, the estimated regression equation between %WL and time(t) with 60 g/ℓ sodium hydroxide is %WL= 0.1949t for the PTT fiber and %WL=0.1856t for the PET fiber at the same alkali concentration. These facts indicate the same trend in weight loss for both fibers.

Figure 5 shows the tensile strength of the PTT and PET fibers after hydrolysis with sodium hydroxide solution plotted against weight loss. This figure indicates a small decrease in the tensile strength of both the PTT and PET fibers with increasing weight loss. Although the properties and morphology of the PTT and PET fibers are different, the results for the rate of hydrolysis and tensile strength loss indicate the same mechanism operates for the alkaline hydrolysis of the two fibers. This may be due to the mechanism of the alkaline hydrolysis of polyester fibers which is a topochemical reaction and takes places at the surface of the fibers.

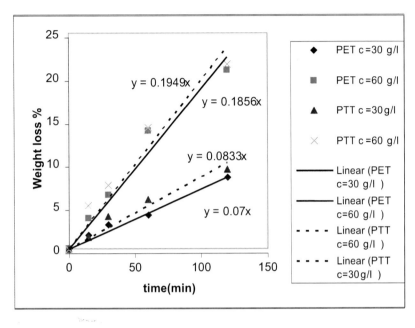

Figure 4. Weight loss of PTT and PET fibers at different treatment times.

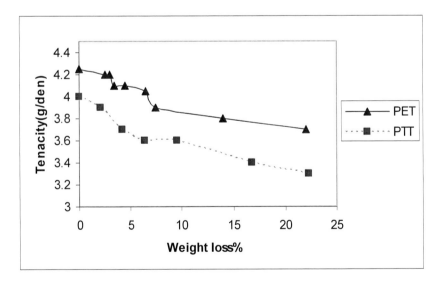

Figure 5. Relationship between tensile strength and weight loss for Ptt and PET yarns.

CONCLUSION

The kinetic parameters, namely the rate of dyeing constant and diffusion coefficient, were studied for the dyeing of PTT and PET fibers at 60, 80 and 96°C when dyeing with different energy level disperse dyes. The dyeing rate constant and diffusion coefficient were much higher for PTT than for PET fiber. The dyeing rate and diffusion coefficient were related to the energy level of the disperse dyes, being higher for the low energy disperse dyes. Although all the disperse dyes used had a good exhaustion for the PTT fiber at 96°C, to achieve satisfactory exhaustion within reasonable dyeing time, it is necessary to use low energy or medium energy level disperse dyes when dyeing PTT fibers at 96°C.

The alkaline hydrolysis of PTT and PET fibers at different alkali concentrations and treatment times indicated no significant difference in the rate of hydrolysis of the two fibers, implying the same mechanism for the hydrolysis of these two fibers.

REFERENCES

[1]   Dupeuble JC. Chemical Fiber International, 51, 43, 2001.
[2]   Kim JH ; Lee JJ ; Yoom JY ; Lyoo WS ; Kotek R. *J. of Applied Polymer Science,* 82, 99-107, 2001.
[3]   Latta BM. *Textile Research Journal,* 54, 7656-775, 1984.
[4]   Yang Y; Brown H; Li S; *J. of Applied Polymer Science,* 86, 223-229, 2002.

In: Textiles for Sustainable Development   ISBN: 978-1-60021-559-9
Editors: R. Anandjiwala, L. Hunter et al., pp. 247-261   © 2007 Nova Science Publishers, Inc.

Chapter 22

AGROBASED FIBERS OF BRAZIL AND THEIR COMPOSITES-AN OVERVIEW

K.G. Satyanarayana

CEPESQ – Centro de Pesquisa em Química Aplicada,
Universidade Federal do Paraná, Departamento de Química,
CP 19081, 81531-990, Curitiba – PR – Brazil. E-mail:kgs_satya@yahoo.co.in

ABSTRACT

Brazil has a number of abundantly available natural resources, such as lignocellulosic fibers (fibers of banana, coconut, curauá, sisal, pineapple) and natural polymeric materials (different types of starches and derivatives from sugarcane, rubber and cashew nut shell liquid). These are not utilized to their full potential. However, there have been many attempts made to find new uses for these resources, such as the development of composites, bearing in mind their biodegradability contributing to a healthy ecosystem, already established uses of these in automotive applications for interior parts in Europe and possibility for their use as structural components as well. This paper presents attempts made so far in Brazil for the better utilization of some of the plant fibers and natural polymeric materials available here through composite technology in the country.

Keywords: Lignocellulosic fibers, natural polymers, composites, biodegradable, compression moulding, structure and properties, automotive, societal applications.

INTRODUCTION

Lignocellulosic (LC) fibers have been the attractive fillers for different types of polymers, including rubbers, as well as for ceramic matrices. The reasons for this are their availability in most of the countries, although some of them are mainly abundant in the tropics. In addition, they have unique characteristics unequalled by many other reinforcing/filler materials in that they are biodegradable, contributing to a healthy ecosystem, low cost and exhibit reasonable characteristics, which may fulfill the economic interest of various industries. Also, LC fibers possess higher stiffness than glass fibers, which would be attractive for applications requiring stiffness, such as many of the automotive applications-car roofs, interior parts [35]. The development of these new materials may serve as the main provider of opportunities to improve the standard of living of the people particularly in developing and underdeveloped countries, while expanding the utilization of these abundantly available renewable resources. This would lead to the use of suitable local materials for local manufacturing or products, which meet the local demand, taking into account the local financial and technological capabilities.

Generally, the main research objectives for the use of such materials have focused on the synthesis and evaluation of the various properties of the products thus developed. The required form of fibers (short fibers/mats/fabric) for their use in composite preparation is normally obtained based on different concepts of textile processing. One of the long-term objectives of these attempts includes fulfilling the socio-economic responsibilities of the State. As a result of these attempts, a number of publications are available giving information on the properties of different LC fibers, their composite manufacturing and characterization as well as the development of products and the utilization. These are reviewed from time to time [3,24,38,Ref.3 in 40,41,43,45]. Information on bio-resources for composites and critical comparative assessments of composites made from LC fibers with those containing fibers have also been reported [13,18, 22, 26-28,52,53].

Brazil, one of the fast developing countries, has been on the forefront in terms of the utilization of its natural resources, such as LC fibers and natural polymers through the development of new materials. This is evidenced by the five successive International Conferences held in their country since 1996-97 on 'Natural polymers/fibers and their composites', the only country in recent times to do so [42]. A few books [22,27] exclusively on the lignocellulosic materials and their composites have also been published in Brazil. With about 235 Materials and Metallurgical Engineering groups working in the country and at least 28 working in the area of LC fibers, natural polymers and their composites, a number of papers have been presented at the conferences and published [2,4-17,19-23, 25,27,42,44,46-51,54]. A study of these reveal that R&andD efforts in this area in the country is still restricted to the preparation and characterization of composites; but concerted and coordinated efforts are needed to reach the level of some developing countries let alone Europe, which is in the forefront of such research and its application in daily life.

Taking cognizance of the foregoing, this paper gives an overview on the status of R&andD in Brazil in respect of the processing of the composites, their characterization and utilization to highlight the importance being given to the better utilization of LC fibers and natural polymers. This includes composites of both LC-synthetic polymers as well as those of the 'Green' variety, but does not cover wood flour/fiber reinforced composites. This is most important in view of the fact that LC fiber reinforced composites [LCFRC] have already established their use in automotive applications in Europe, and many LCFRC products are being exported to USA and other countries [References 3-8 in Ref.40]. In addition, the European Union has a directive for the 'end of life' of all new vehicles to use 95% recyclable materials by 2015 [Ref.9 in 40]. The latter may be due to the belief that it would notnt be long before LCFRC is used as structural components in automotives, these presently used only for the interior parts of cars [Ref.4 in 40]. This underlines the promise LC fibers containing composites hold for the future. It is hoped that the follow up of such initiatives will open up new avenues of research and potential markets for many of the agricultural resources leading to a whole spectrum of opportunities and challenges for many of the developing countries, such as Brazil, India and South Africa in particular and the world in general.

EXPERIMENTAL

Materials

Data on production and availability of a variety of LC fibers in Brazil along with some of their properties are given elsewhere [2, 11-13, 15, 20-22,27,30,32-40]. Major fibers used for composites are coir, sisal, pineapple, curauà, *Luffa Cylindrica,* piassava, sugarcane bagasse and rice straw [2,4,12,14,16,19,20-23,29,31-36,46-51,54]. These fibers have been used in the fiber form, mostly as short fibers. Blankets/mats of sisal fabric are produced by compression, using glue [10,19,23,32-39,]. Similarly, blankets of Luffa-cylindrical have been successfully tried with advantages in the preparation of molded composites by compression or resin transfer molding (RTM) [4,32-36,47,48]; sisal blankets also facilitate the preparation of such materials, wherein one can evaluate interference in the fiber/matrix adhesion [32-36]. Hybrids of LC with LC s and LC with glass fibers have also been used in some studiesd [10,25,29,32-36].

Similarly, both thermoplastics and thermosets synthetic polymers and natural polymeric materials, such as cassava starch, natural rubber, PHB and cashew nut shell liquid, which are available in good quantities [11,13,27,32,40] have been used in the preparation of composites. Research related to the preparation and characterization of some of these natural polymers and their appropriate blends, using a variety of techniques, for their use in composites, have also been carried out [7-9, 27,32-36,50]. Their use in a cement matrix has also been attempted by some of the researchers [14,29, 32-36,44].

Surface Modification of LC Fibers

It is well known that the purpose or principle of the surface modification of LC fibers is to (i) improve their wettability by the matrix by reducing their high polarity and hydrophilic nature whereby a strong interface between the fiber and the non-polar matrix can be obtained, (ii) reduce moisture absorption, (iii) and impart any special property and processability. A number of reviews are available on this topic [1, 3, 24, 27]. Researchers in Brazil have used most of these surface modifications, carried out elsewhere, for LC fibers for the preparation of polymer-LC fiber composites. They include physical, physico-chemical and chemical methods. The chemical methods used are acetylization, benzylation, treatments with isocynate compounds, silanes and other chemical reagents and grafting beside preliminary alkali treatment [mercerization]. These processes changes the hydrophilic surfaces to hydrophobic ones by condensation reaction, the fiber surface structure is being exposed to the insertion of compatible chemical groups with the matrix materials. The effects of the concentration of the chemical used and the time and temperature of the treatment have also been studied since all these parameters dictate the quality of the surface modification. In addition, some sizing agents or coupling agents have also been used to improve the adhesion between the fibers and the matrix. However, the best treatments are those which provide continuous covalent bonds between the cellulose surface and the macromolecular matrix, since they optimize the mechanical properties and reduce water absorption. Some new methods, such as selective oxidation of some units of lignin for interaction with furfuryl alcohol have been attempted [16,51]. The physico-chemical methods include the use of solvent extraction of different substrates to remove the impurities from the substrate, while the physical methods indicate the use of cold plasma, corona treatment, laser, vacuum-UV and γ-ray treatments. All these treatments bring about changes in structural and surface properties, including the surface energy of the fibers. However, no mechanical method [rolling, swaging, etc.] seems to be used by any one here. A number of experimental techniques, such as FTIR, XPS, elemental analysis, contact angle measurement, inverse GC, thermal techniques [DTA, TGA, DSC, etc] and optical and scanning as well as transmission electron microscopic methods, have been used to assess the effects of surface treatment on LC fibers [32-36].

Studies on Composites

Both synthetic and natural polymer based composites as well as cement matrix composites have been studied. The use of green coconut fiber with PVC has been reported [Robson et al in 36]. Similarly, studies on hybrid composites and eco-friendly 'green' composites have been carried out. Attempts have also been made to manufacture some products. Details of these are given below.

Preparation of polymer-based composites has been investigated, mostly using conventional manufacturing methods used elsewhere [40]. Compression molding technique seems to be favored, while extrusion followed by injection molding and other techniques have also been attempted. Both raw and modified LC fibers have been used with synthetic polymers whilst only a few groups have devoted themselves to the studies of natural polymers reinforced with natural fibers and recycled plastics [9, 17,25,31-36,40,42].

RESULTS AND DISCUSSIONS

Surface Modification of LC Fibers

It is observed that mercerization is the most favored chemical method followed by silane treatment and acetylation / benzylation. The effects of different surface modifications [alkali and IPA-Iso Propyl Acrilamide] of some LC fibers on their basic properties are shown in table 1.

It can be seen that the surface modification of LC fibers results in a decrease in density and moisture content and in an increase in crystallinity, while the tensile properties varied from fiber to fiber and from treatment. It is also associated with a lower weight loss, and higher thermal stability. These differences may also be attributed to differences in the chemical compositions of different fibers. Also, the degradation mechanism is affected due to the reduction of the hydrophilicity of the fibers, extraction of some of the components, such as hemicellulose and loss of volatile products.

Table 1. Property cChanges on sSurface modification of LC fibers [from 39,47-49]

Material	Treatment	Density [kMgm⁻³]	Tensile Strength[MPa]	Moisture Content [%]	Crystallinity Index [%]
Luffa-cylindrica	None	8200.82	-	8.0	59.1
Luffa-cylindrica	2%NaOH	11901.19	-	7.5	61.6
Luffa-cylindrica	3%N-IPA	11101.11	-	7.9	62.1
Sisal	None	12601.26	324.2	11.7	72.2
Sisal	2%NaOH	11901.19	375.4	11.2	76.2
Sisal	1%NaOH	-	366.2	11.3	-
Sisal	1%N-IPA	11801.18	331.2	6.5	75.6
Sisal	3%N-IPA	11801.18	256.4	6.7	77.8
Sugarcane Bagasse	None		222	9.5	47
Sugarcane Bagasse	Furfuryl alcohol		153	11.0	42

Some typical resulting microstructures, due to such modifications, are shown in figures 1(a and b), while figures 1 (c and d) illustrate their possible effect in composites.

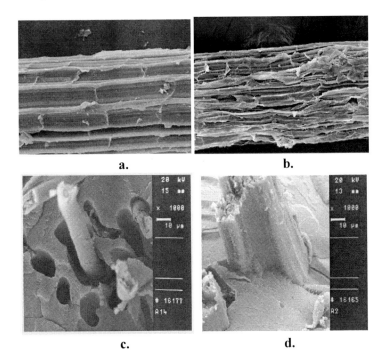

Figure 1. Photomicrograph of Curauá fiber (a) before (b) after the surface modification and (c) Broken interface indicating poor adhesion between cotton fiber and matrix, (d) Good interface showing better adhesion between jute fiber and matrix (With permission Rreprinted from Ref.35).

Synthesis and Characterization of Polymer Based Composites

Studies on Mono Composites

Tables 2(a-c) and figures 2(a-c) show some of the properties evaluated for different LC fiber-polymer composites in Brazil.

Table2(a). Properties of PP-LC fiber Composites [From 20,32-36]

Material	Tensile Strength [MPa]	Tensile Modulus [GPa]	Flexural Strength [MPa]	Flexural Modulus [GPa]	Un notched Impact Strength [J/m]
Bagasse-PP	27.00	5.42	47.79	5.14	58.22
Coir-PP(80/20)	9.25	0.45	9.23	0.43	90.34
Curauà-PP(50/50)	46.58	3.78	33.1	2.51	148.00
Jute-PP(50/50)	15.66	2.4	23.97	2.5	103.55
Ramie-PP(50/50)	34.67	3.43	29.33	3.02	117.62
Sisal-PP(60/40)	23.25	1.97	32.3	2.78	102.49
Luffa Cylindrica-PP	23.24	3.64	48.46	3.26	160.00

These results reveal the following:

a. Many of the composites showed improvement in strength over that of the matrix, while some did not, even with surface modification of the fibers. For example, sisal-polyester composites showed improved strength with surface treatments, while Luffa-polyester composites did not with any of the treatments [46]. Similarly, the impact strength of curauà and bagasse fiber-phenolic composites was higher (28 and 88 J/m, respectively) than those of their counterparts containing chemically modified fiber (15 and 71 J/m, respectively) [51]. On the other hand, short luffa-cylindrica-polyester composites prepared with mats treated with 2% NaOH with fiber contents between 24.4 and 36.3 v%, showed better tensile strength than those prepared with short-fibers even at higher volume fraction (46.6%) in the same conditions [48]. However, the strength properties of many of these composites containing surface modified fibers decreased rather faster on exposure to the environment (UV light) than those containing untreated fibers [19,35].

b. Thermal properties of composites evaluated through DTA/TGA/DSC, etc., also show improvement (see figure 2), with the thermal stability of the composites being higher than that of its constituents, which is attributed to the improved interaction between matrix and fiber.

c. Most of the composites with surface treated fibers showed decreased water absorption compared to untreated fibers, the extent of decrease varying with the nature of the surface treatment.

d. Partial substitution of non renewable materials, such as phenolics by renewable ones, such as lignin, showed improved strength properties as observed in coir-phenolic composites [36].

e. Curauà fiber–polymer composites showed overall higher strength and impact properties compared to other LC fiber composites, including ramie and jute, except for bagasse in respect of modulus and flexural strength [20,21,27].

f. Green coir-PVC composites exhibited no physico-chemical interaction between the constituents, but the Young''s modulus of the composites was higher than that of the PVC matrix when prepared by blending followed by extrusion by 154 and 179% (16.2 and 22.5% for the fibers respectively), and by 225% and 325% for those prepared by blending followed by mixing [36].

Table 2(b). Properties of some Polymer-LC fiber (with and without surface treated) Composites

System	Content (%) /Treatment	UTS (MPa)	YM (GPa)	Elong. (%)	FS (MPa)	FM (GPa)	IS (J/m)	Ref.34 and36
Curauà-Polyester	28.4v	53.1	4.99	-	85.3	-		Nestor in 34
Pineapple-Polyester	32w/10% NaOH	77.82-84.15	3.20-3.68	5.82-6.80		5.2-5.4	352-368	Sivam in 46
Luffa Cylindrica-Polyester	30/nil 30/5%NaOH	30 -	1.7 -	- -	- 46.4	- 3.22	-	Almeida et al in 34
Sisal-Epoxy	46v	211	19.7	1.9				Oksman in 34
Sisal (Untreated)-LDPE	30w/w	31.12	3.09	2	-	-	-	Kuruvilla et al in 34
Sisal-HDPE	30w/Plasma	23	2.75		29	2.49	105	Martin et al in 34

UTS: Ultimate Tensile Strength; YM:Young`s Modulus; FS:Flexural Strength; FM:Flexural Modulus; IS: Impact Strength(Unnotched).

Table2(c). Properties of Rubber [particle size~420µ]-LC fibers [34]

System	Content (%) / Treatment	Density (kMgm^{-3})	Young`s Modulus (MPa)	Elong. (%)	Moisture Absorption (%)
Matrix	None	1110.11	5.17	50.70	2
Sisal-Rubber	5-10/none	1.117-1.124	6.76-8.43	38,27-40.28	6
Sisal-Rubber	5-10/5-2/10% NaOH		7.51-13.35	31.51-43.68	6
Sisal-Rubber	5-10/ 10% NaOH+Acetylated		8.96-12.00	34.79-58.23	9

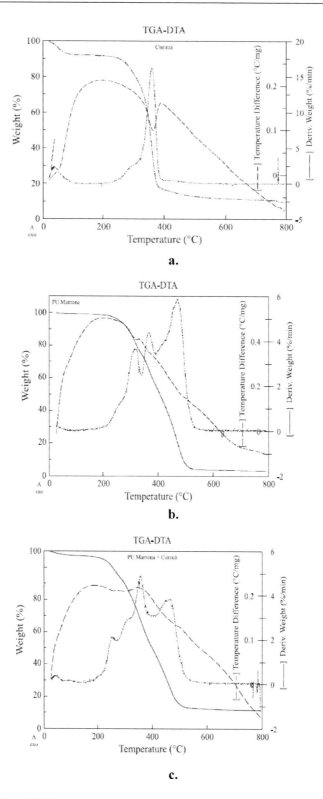

Figure 2. TG/DTG and DTA curves for (a) Curauá fiber (b) PU mMatrix ,(c) their cComposite (Reproduced with permission From: Ref. 25).

Studies on Hybrid Composites [10,19, 32-36]

Systems studied include sisal-glass, jute-glass, jute-cotton, luffa cylindrical-glass and jute-bentonite with indigenously available synthetic polymers [polyester and phenolic]. Woven fabrics of jute-glass, jute-cotton, and sisal-glass fibers and wood flour-sisal waste or short fibers have been used. Glass fibers up to 50 % by weight and bentonite up to 10 % by weight were used; even nano particles of clay with polyurethane-sisal have been studied [Pinto et al in 35]. Processing is done by mixing followed by compression moulding and/or casting in steel moulds.

In general, the hybrid composites of LC fiber and/or glass/LC fiber exhibit improved strength depending on the properties of fibers, their quantity, length and orientation as well as test angle [0,45 and 90°] as is evident from table 3, which shows strength properties obtained in some hybrid systems. Higher elongation in the case of sisal-glass system ise associated with extensive delamination at higher fiber contents, while the decrease in the properties with increasing test angle in the case of the jute-cotton system is attributed to the rigidity of the jute fibers, lower load transfer in the cotton direction and poor fiber-matrix adhesion in the case of cotton. These properties of the hybrid composites also suggest possible use of these as light-weight materials for structural applications.

Table 3. Properties of Hybrid LC Composites

	Orientation (Deg)/Test Direction	Tensile Strength (MPa)	Young's Modulus (GPa)	Elongation (%)	Refs: 33-36
Jute-Cotton-Polyester(70%)	L(0o) T(0o)	73.82 15.30	2.26 1.80	4.52 2.47	Kuruvilla in 34
Jute-Cotton-Polyester(50%)	L(0o) T(0o)	128.30 13.96	2.28 1.55	5.76 4.62	Kuruvilla in 34
Jute-Cotton-Phenolics(60%)	L(0o) [fabric type 10/4]	58.9	7.1	1.1	Carvalho in 35
Jute-Cotton-Phenolics(60%)	L(45o) [fabric type 10/4]	22.1	4.4	0.6	Carvalho in 35
Jute-Glass-Polyester(50%)	Jute Glass	51.1 230	3.30 8.2	3.9 6.1	Medeiros in 35
Sisal-Glass-Polyester(55%)	Sisal Glass	45.2 40.5	2.54 0.95	6.4 14.2	Medeiros in 35
25Sisal-0Bentonite-PolyUrethane(73%)	--	18.7	0.91	5.7	Pinto et al in 36
25Sisal-5Bentonite-PolyUrethane(73%)	--	24.4	1.26	5.5	Pinto et al in 36
Luffa Cylindrica(30%)-glass-polyester	--	83.9	2.51	-	Boynard et al in 33

Studies on `Green` Composites [9, 17,25,31-36,40,42]

Most of the studies are preliminary in nature, with the results indicating the potential of these composites. Systems studied include jute-castor oil based polyurethane, sisal-bentonite-castor oil based polyurethane cotton- and jute-, coir-phenolics obtained from CNSL and tannin, starch/PHB-wood pulp and sisal-natural rubber. Processing is done by the conventional techniques mentioned under the mono-composites. Curing procedures are followed in all cases. It was observed that tannin-jute composites exhibited [36] about 56% and 52% higher impact strength over the jute composites with phenolic and lignophenolic matrices, respectively, indicating good adhesion between the matrix and the fiber. On the other hand, coir-cashew nut based phenolic resin composites (3:1 on weight basis) prepared with different molding pressures (1-4 tons) showed [Kaz et al in 36] lower density (0.51-0.68Mgm^{-3}) and modulus of rupture values (3.6-5MPa) but comparable flexural properties with commercial particle board/chopped bagasse-gypsum boards, which are used in the building and furniture sectors.

Sisal (25wt%)-bentonite-polyurethane hybrid composites showed [Pinto et al in36] improved modulus (51.7%) up to 7% of bentonite, tensile strength (18.2% and 30.5%) and impact strength (33%) for 7% and 5% of bentonite, respectively, compared to the sisal-polyurethane composite. In addition, the tensile strength and modulus further improved, by about 10% with modifications of the bentonite with HCl and Dodigen, while impact resistance increased by 75.8% with modifications of the bentonite with HCl. However, these properties deteriorating on thermal aging at 110°C for all the composites, probably due to the oxidative degradation of the composite constituents. A limited study on malva fiber-rubber composites has also been reported [34].

Synthesis and Characterization of Cement Based Composites

Various systems studied include sisal-cement [Junior et al and Dantas in 36], bamboo pulp and wollstaonite-cement [Silva et al in 36], sisal and coir-cement [Filho et al in 34and35] and wood residues-cement [Beraldo et al in 35]. Mostly, the reinforcements are used in the form of fabrics. Processing of these composites is by conventional methods, such as hand laying, compression molding, Hatscheck process, etc. Generally, the incorporations of LC fiber showed improved properties, particularly toughness, which depended on the type of fiber, size (long or short), their volume fraction and arrangement [Filho et al in 35]. For example, coir-cement composites showed about 160% higher toughness compared to sisal-cement composite; the toughness of sisal fiber-cement composites, having both continuous aligned and random short sisal fibers (3v%), was higher by 15%, 93% and 195% over the random short (25 mm-2v%), aligned long (375 mm-1v%) and random short (25 mm-3v%) sisal fiber-cement composites; load at first crack for long aligned sisal fiber and also for random short (25mm) sisal or coir fiber containing cement composites was 180% higher than that of the matrix alone. Also, short sisal and coir fiber containing cement mortar composites showed 6 to 21% increase in splitting tensile strength compared to its counter part (0-40%) containing steel wire [Filho et al in 34]. Furthermore, the fibers transverse to the splitting plane showed best properties in terms of peak strain and energy absorption capacity. In the case of bamboo-wollstanonite-cement composites, improved toughness (~65%), modulus of rupture (22.4%) and Charpy impact strength (~47%) over the matrix were observed [Silva et al in 36].

The viability of these composites for some applications, such as silos and sheets for low cost housing, has been examined. An interesting suggestion was made about manufacturing silos of size 9m x 3m using such composites based prototype fabrication and evaluation of sisal-polymer composites silos of size 400x75x3mm after aging them in cement [Dantas et al in 36].

Product Development

Attempts have been made to fabricate some products using LC fiber-polymer composites, such as the proto-type of a chair made of coir-tannin-urea formaldehyde composite [36] and a helmet for cyclists (figure 4) made from a Castor oil based polyurethane-curauá fiber composite [25]. Another attempt has been made to assess the life cycle of some automotive parts made of a coir-natural rubber composite [Salazar et al in 34]. In the former case, a preliminary technical feasibility of producing the molded components has been reported, which indicated treatment with a natural adhesive was necessary to obtain good products.

In the latter case, an observation made about the fabrication of seats using the composite showed that it was comparable to its counter part made of polyurethane foams.

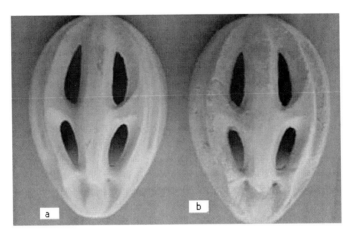

Figure 4. Helmets for cyclists (a) PU matrix,(b) Pu-20% Curauá composite [Reproduced with permission from Ref:25].

TEXTILE ASPECTS

As can be seen from the foregoing, researchers in Brazil have utilized LC fibers in composite technologies by adopting textile engineering principles. This encompasses (i) a variety of non-woven products and different production methods, (ii) homogeneous blending for yarns and non-wovens [opening, cleaning and blending], and in different forms [fabrics, blended yarns, non-wovens] through spinning/hybridisation, with the effect of an interlayer barrier, etc. One of the interesting studies deals with the use of appropriate warp/weft ratio in the jute-cotton hybrid woven fabrics. It is concluded [Kuruvilla et al in 34] that 30% cotton as warp and 70% jute as weft in polymer matrix would give better unidirectional properties, while 60(warp)/40(weft) of these fibers are good for bi-directional properties, both of which can be used as structural materials. Similarly, the use of proper methods of yarn spinning to obtain appropriate yarn linear densities [80-84 tex] for a wider assessment of textiles, chemico-mechanical processing of cut fibers, cording of fibers on the machine have also been attempted. However, there is still a need for detailed studies on the use of various aspects of textile engineering with LC fibers for their extended utilisation, which ultimately helps in generating employment. Some of the above aspects are to be considered along with the textile processes for overcoming moisture absorption, odor and fiber wetting, use of a needling system rather than weaving, preparation of fibers for spinning/blending, weaving of fibers and non-wovens of LC fibers, component dependent and non-dependent blending, which can be used for medium strength composites.

CONCLUSION

Being blessed with a number of natural resources of LC fibers and polymers, taking into account the R&andD and the potential applications of LC fiber incorporated composites around the world as well as resulting socio-economic benefits, Brazilian researchers have not lagged in their efforts to utilize these resources in composite technologies. Despite these efforts, leading to a number of publications in the area, there is a need for more concerted and coordinated efforts in the country to reach the level of R&andD and its applications related to LC fiber-composites as exists in some of the developing countries.

ACKNOWLEDGEMENTS

The Author thanks CNPq for the grant of the project funding, Dr.Mothe et al, Editor of Polimeros:Ciència e Tecnologia and Prof. E. Frollini, Editor of Ref.35 for giving permission to use the figures from their papers. Help by Mr. A.C. Gregario of Department of Quimica of UFPR for his ready help during the preparation of this paper.

REFERENCES

[1]   Abdelmouleh, M; Boufi, S; Belgacem, MN; Durante, AP; Ben Salah, A; Gandini, A. *Intern. J. Adhesion and Adhesives,* 2004, 24,43.

[2]   Alexandre, ME De O; Ladchumanandasivam, R; Caralho, LH de; Cavalcanti, in Proc. in 2nd International Conference on Textile Engineering (SINTEX-2004), Eds: R.L.Sivam et al, Sept.7-11, 2004, Natal, in CD-ROM, Paper Nos.TTN-H-001, Paper Nos.TTN-H-004.

[3]   Bledzki, AK; Reihmane, S; Gasson, *J. Appl. Polym. Sci.,* 1999, 59,1329; *Prog. Polym. Sci.,* 1999, 24,221.

[4]   Boynard, CA; d'Almedia, JRM. Polym. Plast. Technol. and Engg, 39 (3): 489(2000); J Appl Polym Sci., 87 (12), 1927(2003); *J. Mater. Sci. Lett.,* 1999, 18, 1549.

[5]   Campana, FSP; Frollini, E; Carvelo, AS. in Lignocellulosics-Plastics and Composites, Eds.A.L.Leao, F.X.Carvalho and E. Frollini, *DOP Publishers, Sao Paulo,* 1997, 163-180.

[6]   Caraschi, JC; Leao, AL. Mol. Cryst. and Liq. Cryst.; 2000, 353,149and449; in Proc. *Wood fiber-Plastic Composites,* Madison, 1996, WI, 251.

[7]   Carvalho, AJF de; Curvelo, AAS; Agnelli, JAM. Carbohydrate Polym, 2001, 45, 189, *Int. J. Polym. Mater.,* 2002, 51, 647.

[8]   Carvalho, AJF.de; Zambon, MD; Curvelo AAS; Gandini, A. *Polym. Degrad. and Stability,* 2003, 79,133.

[9]   Curvelo, AAS; Carvalho, AJF.de; Agnelli, *JAM. Carbohydrate Polym.,* 2001, 45, 183and212.

[10]   Curvelo, LH; Kuruvilla, J; Nobrega, MMS. in Anais do Simpósio Argentino de polímeros/SAP, Córdoba, Argentiana, 1999, 67.

[11]   Filho, PA; Bahr, O. *Appl.Energy,* 2004, 77(1), 51.

[12]   Frollini, E; Paiva, JMF; Trindade, WG; Razera, T; Tita, SP. *'Plastics and Composites from Lignophenols'* in Ref.28, 2004, 193-226.

[13]   Gandini, A. "Polymers from renewable resources", in Comprehensive Polymer Science, Suppl, Eds. S.L.Agarwal and S.Russo, Pergamon press, Oxford, 1990,1,527-570; " *Polymeric Materials Derived from the Exploitation of the Biomass"* in Ref.27.

[14]   Ghavami, K; Toledo, FRD; Barbosa, NP. *Cement and Concrete Comp.* 1999, 21, 39.

[15]   Guimaráes, JL; Satyanrayana, KG; Fernando, W. in Proc. 2005, FAO/ESCORENA, pp. 503-516.

[16]   Horaeau, W; Trindade, WG; Seigmund, B; Castellan, A; Frollini, E. *Polymer Degradation and Stability,* 2004, 86,567.

[17]   Iozzi, MA; Martins, MA; Mottoso, LHC. *Polimeros:Ciència e Tecnologia,* 2004, 14(2), 93.

[18]   Joshi, SV; Drazl, LT; Mohanty, AK; Arora, S. *Composites.* Part-A, 2004, 35(3), 371.

[19]   Kurvilla, J; Carvalho, LH de. Anais do5° Congresso Brasileiro de polímeros[ABPOL-99] , Águas de Lindóia, São Paulo, 1999, 693-698 and 834-839; IPCM-99, Berlin, 1999, 23-26.

[20]   Leao, AL; Rowell, R; Tavares, N. "Applications of Natural s in Automotive Industry in Brazil-Thermoforming Process" in *'Science and Technology of Polymer and Advanced Materials',* Eds. P.N.Prasad, J.E.Mark, S.H. Kandil and Z.H. Kafafi, Plenum Press, New York, 1998, 755-761.

[21]   Leao, AL; Tan, IH; Caraschi, JC. "in Proc. International Conference on Advanced Composites,(ICAC)", [Eds. Yasser Gowayed and Faissal Abdel-Haydy], Hurghada, Egypt, 15-18 December 1998, 557.

[22]   Leao, AL; Caraschi, JC; Tan, IH. in Ref.27., 2000, pp.257-272 .

[23]   Martins, GS; Iozzi, MA; Martins, MA; Mottoso, LHC Ferreira, FC. *Polimeros: Ciència e Tecnologia,* 2004, 14(5), 326.

[24]   Mohanty, AK; Misra, M; Drzal, LT. J.Polym.Environ., 2002, 10,19; Comp.Interfaces, 2001, 8 (5), 313; M*acromol.MaterandEngg.,* 2000, 276(3-4),1.

[25]   Mothe, CG; Araujo, CR de. *Polimeros:Ciència e Tecnologia,* 2004, 14(4), 274.

[26]   Narayan, R. "Biomass Resources for Production of Materials, Chemicals and Fuels" in *"Emerging Technologies for Materials and Chemicals from Biomass ",* Eds. R.M.Rowell, T.P. Schultz and R. Narayan, American Chemical Society, Washinton, DC, 1992, 1-5 and12-15.

[27]   Natural Fibers and Agro s Composites, Eds. L.H.S.Mottoso, A.L.Leao, and E. Frollini, *EMBRAPA Instrumentação, Agropecária, São Carlos,* (2000).

[28]   Natural s, Plastics and Composites, Eds. F.T. Wallenberger and N. Weston, Kluwer Academic press, USA, (2004).

[29]   Nobrego, MMS; Carvalho, LH de. Anais do VII SLAP, Lattabano, Cuba, 2000, 1,38.

[30]   Nunes, RCR; Visconte, LLY. in ref.27, 2000, pp135-157.

[31] Paiva, JMF; Trindade WG; Frollini, E. Polímeros: Ciência e Tecnologia, 1999, 9(4),170; *J. Appl. Polym. Sci.,* 2002, 83,880; *Polym. Plastics Techn. And Engg.,* 2004, 43(4),1187.

[32] Proc. First International conference on Natural Polymers and Composites (ISNaPol-1996-97), "Lignocellulosics-PlasticsandComposites", Eds.A.L.Leao, F.X.Carvalho and E.Frollini, (Eds.L.H.C. Mottoso, A.Leao and E.Frollini), DOP Publishers, Sao Paulo 1997, SP, Brasil.

[33] Proc. 2nd International Symposium on Natural Polymers and Composites *(ISNaPol 1998),* May 10-13, 1998, (Eds. L.H.C. Mattoso, A. Leao and E. Frollini), Atibaia, SP, Brasil.

[34] Proc.3rd International Symposium on Natural Polymers and Composites (ISNaPol 2000), May 14-17, 2000, (Eds.L.H.C. Mottoso, A.Leao and E.Frollini), Sao Pedro, SP, Brasil.

[35] Proc. 4th International Symposium on "Natural Polymers and Composites/ISNaPol 2002, 1- 4 September, 2002, São Pedro-SP, Brasil.

[36] Proc.5th International Symposium on Natural Polymers and Composites (ISNaPol 2004), Sept 12-15, 2004, (Eds.L.H.C. Mottoso, A.Leao and E.Frollini), Sao Pedro, SP, Brasil.

[37] Sanandi, AR. 'Natural s as fillers/reinforcements in thermoplastics' in An Introduction to low Environmental Impact Polymers, Eds. N.Tucker, M.Johnson and S.Humphreys, Rapra Technology ltd., UK,(2002).

[38] Sandro, AC; Mochnacz, S; Thais, HDS. *Plastico Industrial,* 2004, 67, 72. (in Portuguese)

[39] Satyanaryana, KG; Fernando, W; Guimarães, JL; Sandro, AC; Thais, HDS; Ramos, LP. *Metals, Materials and Processes,* 2005, 17(3-4) 183-194.

[40] Satyanarayana, KG; Gregorio, AC; Wypych, F. in 2nd International Conference on Textile Engineering (SINTEX-2004), [Eds: R.L.Sivam et al], Sept.7-11, 2004, Natal, in CD-ROM, Paper No.TIC-E-001.

[41] Satyanarayana, KG; Fernando, W; Ramos, LP; Sandro, AC; Thais, HDS. in Proc.5th International Symposium on Natural Polymers and Composites (ISNaPol 2004), Sept 12-15, 2004, (Eds.L.H.C. Mottoso, A.Leao and E.Frollini), Sao Pedro, SP, Brasil, Paper No.90.

[42] Satyanarayana, KG; Pai, BC; Sukumaran K; Pillai, SGK. in Hand Book of Ceramic and Composite - *Vol: I Structure and Properties,* Ed. N. P.Cheremisinoff), Pub. Marcel Dekker Inc., 1990, New York, 339-386.

[43] Savastano, H Jr; Warden, PG; Coutts, RSP. *Cement andConcrete Composites,* 2002, 22,379.

[44] Schuh, T.G. http//www.ienica.net/sseminar/schuh.pdf.

[45] Steal, GC; Tavares, MIB; DÁlmedia, *JRM. Polym and Polym. Comp.,* 2000, 8, 489.

[46] Tanobe, V; Mochnacz, S; Mazzaro, I; Thais, HDS; Sandro, AC. Proc. 58° Congresso Anual da Associação Brasileira de Metalurgia e Materiais - ABM, Rio de Janeiro - RJ 2003. (*in Portuguese*).

[47] Tanobe, V; Thais, HDS; Sandro, AC; Souza. G. in XV Congresso Brasileiro de Engenharia Química/COBEQ, Curitiba-PR, (2004), (*in Portuguese*).

[48] Thais, HDS; Mochnacz, S; Sandro, AC. *Polymer Testing,* 2003, 22(4), 375.

[49] Thiré, RMSM; Somão, RA; Andrade, CT. *Carbohydrate Polymers,* 2003, 54,149.

[50] Trindade, WG; Hoareau, W; Razera, IT; Ruggiero, R; Frollini, E; Castellan, A. *Macromol. Mater. Eng.,* 2004, 289,728.

[51] Wambua, P; Ivens, J; Verpoest, I. *Comp. Sci. andtechn.,* 2003, 63, 1259.

[52] Wool, RP; Khot, SN. 'Bio-based resins and Natural s', in ASM Hand Book, Pub: ASM International, 2000, Vol.21, 184-193.

[53] Yamaji, FM; Bonduelle A; Thais, HDS ; Koehler, HS; Reinert, AF. in Congresso em Ciência de Materiais do Mercosul, SULMAT 2004, Joinville/SC. (*in Portuguese*).

In: Textiles for Sustainable Development   ISBN: 978-1-60021-559-9
Editors: R. Anandjiwala, L. Hunter et al., pp. 263-274   © 2007 Nova Science Publishers, Inc.

Chapter 23

INFLUENCE OF CORONA TREATMENT ON LINEN FABRIC DYED WITH NATURAL DYESTUFFS

K. Schmidt-Przewoźna, R. Kozłowski and M. Zimniewska

Institute of Natural s, Wojska Polskiego 71b, 60-630 Poznan, Poland;
kasia@inf.poznan.pl, sekretar@inf.poznan.pl, gosiaz@inf.poznan.pl

ABSTRACT

The paper presents the analysis of differences of color obtained on linen samples, dyed with natural dyestuffs, with and without Corona treatment. We compared the color differences obtained on samples dyed with: Annatto Bixa orellana L., Tumeric Curcuma Longa L., Weld Reseda luteola L., Cochineal Dactylopius coccus Costa, Cutch Acacia catechu L., Madder Rubia tinctorium L., and Woad Isatis tinctoria L. After the process of natural dyeing, the samples showed a wide color range with a large palette of shades. The Corona treatment technology, applied during cellulosic fabric finishing, produces better conditions for natural dyeing, because of the improvement in hydrophilic properties.

Keywords: Corona, natural dyestuffs, mordants, linen, green products.

INTRODUCTION

The Institute of Natural s has participated in an EU research project CORTEX, which was coordinated by the University of Minho in Portugal. One of the Institute's tasks was to investigate efficiency of the Corona treatment when applied to linen fabrics and its effect on dyeing the fabrics with natural dyes. A Corona discharge is produced between two electrodes, with a high voltage and frequency of 20-40 kHz.

A *Life Cycle perspective* is absolutely essential for product development as optimization has to be achieved from an economical and quality standpoint. The main focus of eco-friendly products lies in finishing. However, such processes can not be considered without relation to the materials, yarn manufacturing, knitting and weaving. In our research we are interested in comparing eco-friendly technologies in natural dyeing and the creation of modern, ecological textile products. After a preliminary recognition identification of plants likely to possess dyeing potential we began applying these dyes on natural fabrics, such as, linen, hemp, silk, wool.

During the whole period of the research, hundreds of dyeing experiments have been done in order to find plants giving the widest range of colors, brightness of colors and which were also economical. Due to difficulties in obtaining several dyestuffs, a 'dyeing garden' was set up at the Institute in 2003. For the experiments, imported plants and those growing wild were also used.

One of the main objectives of the program is the creation of color-card for natural fibers, introduction of cultivated plants for dyeing and promotion of the results in modern dyeing technology. With the cooperation of the University of Minho in Portugal, about 120 dyeing experiments have been performed on linen fabrics to compare the results of dyeing with and without Corona treatment.

MATERIALS AND METHODS

For dyeing, two different kinds of 100% linen fabrics have been used.

Fabric 23122 - fabric A
Condition of Corona treatment
- Number of passages 3+3
- Power 1,51kW
- Speed 2,44 m/min

Fabric 42002 - fabric B
- Number of passages 6+6
- Power 1,51kW
- Speed 2,44 m/min.

Dyeing conditions of linen fabrics:
- temp. 95°C
- gradient 1°C/ 1 min.
- Time of dyeing 30 min.
- changes of temp to 50°C
- gradient 2°C/1 min. gradient 2°C/1 min.

In our treatments were used:
- mass of linen sample - 7g sample
- 150 ml dye bath
- natural dyestuffs

Equipment: laboratory dyeing machine: IBELIUS I L- 720

For comparing results of dyeing with and without Corona treatment 120 trials have been carried out using, six plant dyes and one insect dye. For dyeing, water extracts of the dyes were applied.

1. Cochineal Dactylopius Coccus Costa

Photo 1. Opuntia plant with Cochineal.

Cochineal is a traditional red dye of pre-Hispanic Mexico. This precious dyestuff was obtained from an insect that lives on the Opuntia plant. They required fast colors, i.e., those that would not fade derived from native cochineal for various shades of red, crimson, lilac, pink and violet. *Cochineal* is also the name of the *crimson* or *carmine* color *dye*. The coloring comes from carminic acid.

Table 1. Cochineal dyeing results on linen samples A. Samples 1-6 with Corona treatment and samples 7-12 without Corona treatment

Natural dyestuff	Mordant	color	result
Sample1-Corona	no mordant	light peach	bad
Sample2- Corona	0,2% alum	violet	good, special effect
Sample3- Corona	0.2% copper sulphate	lilac	good
Sample4- Corona	0.1 % citric acid	peach	good
Sample5- Corona	0.1 % alum	pink lilac	good, special effect
Sample6- Corona	0.2% alum	rose pink	good, special effect
Sample7	no mordant	grey lilac	bad
Sample8	0.2% alum	strong violet	good
Sample9	0.2%copper sulphate	lilac	good
Sample10	0.1 % citric acid	light peach	good
Sample11	0.1 % alum	pink	good
Sample12	0.2% alum	rose pink	good

Results

- The cochineal dyed samples showed good results in terms of color.
- Different mordants produce differences in colors.
- In treatments with mordants, such as; alum, copper sulphate and citric acid, the following colors were obtained:; lilac, dark lilac, violet, pink, rose, dark rose and peach.
- When dyeing with Cochineal it is not possible to obtain good colors without mordants.
- With the Corona treatment on Sample 2, 5 and 6 a special design effect resembling mélange was observed.

2. Madder Rubia Tinctorium L

Photo 2. Madder roots, INF plantation.

Madder Rubia tinctorium L., is one of the most ancient dyes. It was known 3,.000 B.C. as a source of red color. The roots of this plant contain alizarine, purpurin, rubian, rubiadin, ruberythric acid. Madder was cultivated in Europe, Middle East and Turkey. The Turkey-red and other shades are adjective dyes, different mordants producing many shades of
    red, pink, lilac, purple, brown, orange and black . [1,3].

**Table 2. Madder dyeing results on linen samples A. Samples 1-6
with Corona treatment and samples 7-12 without Corona treatment**

Natural dyestuff	mordant	color	Result
Sample1-Corona	no mordant	orange	Good
Sample2- Corona	no mordant	orange	Good
Sample3- Corona	0.2% alum	orange	Good
Sample4- Corona	0.2 % soda	orange	Good
Sample5- Corona	0.05% citric acid	light orange	Good
Sample6- Corona	0.1% alum+0.1% soda	yellow rose	Good
Sample7	no mordant	rose	Good
Sample8	special pretreatments	red	Good
Sample9	0.2% alum	rose	Good
Sample10	0.2 % soda	rose	Good
Sample11	0.05% citric acid	light orange	bad - uneven color spots

| Sample12 | 0.1% alum+0.1% soda | red | bad – uneven color |

Results
- Samples treated with Corona are more yellow.
- Samples dyed without Corona treatment are redder.
- Corona produced better results in terms of even dyeing.

3. Weld Reseda Luteola L

Photo 3. Weld – INF experimental plantation.

Reseda luteola L. is one of the oldest yellow plants and produces some of the most light-fast and wash- fast yellow shades. Weld is a typical mordant dye. The plant contains luteolin and apigenin. Weld produced colors: yellow, intensive yellow, old gold, olive green and gold colors. [1, 2].

Table 3. Weld dyeing results on linen samples A and B. Samples A 1-3 and B 4-6 with Corona treatment, and samples A 7-9 and B 7-12 without corona treatment.CORONA

Natural dyestuff	mordant	color	result
Sample1 Corona	no mordant	light yellow	good
Sample 2 Corona	0.2% alum	light yellow	bad
Sample 3 Corona	0.2% copper sulphate	yellow olive	good
Sample 4 Corona	no mordant	yellow	good
Sample 5 Corona	alum + soda	yellow	good
Sample 6 Corona	0.2% soda	yellow	good
Sample 7	no mordant	light yellow	bad
Sample 8	0.2% alum	light yellow	bad
Sample 9	0.2%copper sulphate	yellow olive	good
Sample 10	no mordant	yellow	bad
Sample 11	alum + soda	light yellow	good
Sample 12-Fabric B	0.2% soda	yellow	bad

Results

- Copper sulphate mordants in Weld dyeing produced the best yellow results.
- Good results were obtained also with a combination of alum and soda, without mordants, but the color was not very deep.
- The Corona treated samples were evenly dyed.

4. Tumeric – *Curcuma Longa* L

Photo 4. Tumeric.

Tumeric is the source of very deep and bright yellow color. The main producer of this plant was India, but it was also cultivated in China, South East Asia and tropical countries.

The dye is extracted from the fresh or dried rhizomes of the plant. Curcuma longa contain curcumin natural pigments. It is a substantive dye with good wash fastness and poor light fastness. Tumeric produced: bright yellow, yellow, old gold, green, gold and ochre colors. [1, 2]

Table 4. Tumeric dyeing results on linen samples A and B, samples 1-3 with Corona treatment and samples 4-6, without Corona treatment

Natural dyestuff	mordant	color	result
Sample 1-Fabric A	no mordant	gold yellow	good
Sample 2-Fabric A	0.2% citric acid	yellow	good
Sample 3-Fabric B	0.2 ferrous sulphate	dull yellow	good
Sample 4- Fabric A	no mordant	light sun yellow	good
Sample 5- Fabric A	0.2% citric acid	gold yellow	good
Sample 6- Fabric B	0.2 ferrous sulphate	sun yellow	bad – uneven color

Results:

- Corona treated samples were brighter and more saturated.
- Samples dyed without Corona treatment were yellow.
- The Corona treatment produced more even dyeing of sample 3 (with ferrow mordant).

5. Cuth Acacia Catechu L

Photo 5. CuthUTH *Acacia catechu* plant.

Catechu *Acacia catechu L.* is a purified extract of wood Accacia catechu. The plant of Accacia catechu is about 15 meters high. It is mainly composed of Catechu-tannic acid, with catechin, catechu red and quercetin. Natural Dye: different shades of brown [1, 2]

**Table 5. Cuth dyeing results – *Acacia catechu*, samples 1-6
with Corona treatment and samples 7-12**

Natural dyestuff	mordant	color	result
Sample 1-Fabric A	no mordant	light brown	good
Sample 2-Fabric A	0.2 ferrous sulphate	Dark brown	good
Sample 3-Fabric A	0.2% citric acid	tabac	good
Sample 4-Fabric B	no mordant (1/4dye)	brown	good
Sample 5-Fabric B	0.2% ferrous (1/4)	dark brown	good
Sample 6-Fabric B	0.2% citric acid(1/4)	light brown	good
Sample 7-Fabric A	No mordant	light brown	good
Sample 8-Fabric A	0.2 ferrous sulphate	dark brown	good
Sample 9-Fabric A	0.2% citric acid	tabac	good
Sample 10-Fabric B	no mordant (1/4dye)	brown	good
Sample 11-Fabric B	0.2% ferrous (1/4)	dark brown	good
Sample 12-Fabric B	0.2% citric acid (1/4)	light brown	good

Results:
- After dyeing with Cutch a wide range of brown colors was obtained.
- It produced homogenous dyeing.
- With the in Corona treatment (samples 1-6) a special design effect resembling mélange, was observed.

6. Annato Bixa Orellana

Photo 6. Annato *Bixa orellana* tree.

Annato Bixa orellana L., is a small tree belonging to the family Bixaceae, and which originated in tropical countries. These seeds are processed to obtain the orange-yellow pigments, bixin and norbixin. Colors: orange, light orange and peach. [1, 2].

Table 6. Annato dyeing results samples 1-6 with Corona treatment and samples 7-12 without Corona

Natural dyestuff	mordant	Color	result
Sample 1 - A Corona	no mordant	light peach	good
Sample 2 - A Corona	0.2% soda	Peach	good
Sample 3 - A Corona	0.2% citric acid	Orange	good
Sample 4 - B Corona	no mordant	Peach	good
Sample 5 - A Corona	0.2% soda	Orange	good
Sample 6 - A Corona	0.2% citric acid	light peach	good
Sample 7 - A	no mordant	light peach	good
Fabric 8 - A	0.2% soda	Peach	good
Fabric 9 - A	0.2% citric acid	Orange	bad- uneven color spots
Fabric 10 - B	no mordant	Peach	good
Fabric 11 - B	0.2% soda	Orange	good
Fabric 12 - B	0.2% citric acid	light peach	good

Results:
- Soda mordants in annatto dyeing produces the best orange colors.
- The color without mordants is good, but lighter than with soda.
- The color with the corona treatment is more orange, and without Corona it is more red.
- The Corona samples Corona treated samples were evenly dyed.

7. Woad Isatis Tinctoria L

Photo 7. Woad *Isatis tinctoria* L. INF plantation.

Woad *Isatis tinctoria* L. was a native of southeastern Europe, presumably either around Greece and Italy or southwestern Russia, but spread quickly throughout Europe in prehistoric times.

This plant became the dominant blue dye in Europe, especially in western Europe.

Dyer's Woad was formerly much cultivated in Britain for the dye extracted from the leaves.

Isatis tinctoria is a biennial plant that is a source of the blue dye chemical, indigotin,

The blue dye chemical indigotin, from indigo or woad, is the only natural "vat" dye. [1, 3].

Table 7. Woad dyeing results – *Isatis tinctoria* L. sample with Corona treatment and samples 2 and 3, without Corona treatment

Natural dyestuff	mordant	color	result
Sample1- A Corona	vat dyeing	navy blue	good
Sample2 – A 50% of dye	vat dyeing	blue	good
Samples 3 A	vat dyeing	navy blue	good

RESULTS AND DISCUSSION

A comparison of selected linen fabric samples dyed with and without Corona treatment is shown in the table below (table 11).

Table 8. Results of spectrophotometric analysis of samples of linen fabrics dyed with and without Corona treatment

Natural dyestuff	ΔL	Δa	Δb	ΔC	ΔH	ΔE	Remarks
Weld sample 5 sample11 alum and soda	0.55	-3.55	1.47	2.34	-3.04	-3.88	CORONA -slightly darker -less red -less yellow -more saturated and bright -significant hue difference for CORONA (an advantage)
Weld sample 3 sample 9 copper	-0.20	-0.46	-1.61	-1.56	0.61	1.69	CORONA -slightly darker -slightly less yellow -duller
Tumeric sample 3 sample 6 citric acid	-2.85	3.80	-0.49	-0.71	-3.77	4.78	CORONA - slightly darker - redder - brighter - significant hue difference
Tumeric sample 1 sample 7 no mordant	0.86	-3.43	17.3	17.22	-3.81	17.66	CORONA -less red -much more yellow -much brighter hue -difference so large that it is difficult to compare the samples (another hue obtained)
Annato sample 1 sample 6 no mordant	-0.77	3.43	1.07	1.88	3.03	3.68	CORONA -slightly darker -redder -slightly more yellow -very bright and saturated hue -quite large, easily noticeable change of hue
Annato sample 2 sample 7 soda	-0.61	-0.82	-1.5	-1.71	-0.1	1.81	CORONA -less red -less yellow - slightly less saturated color
Cochineal sample 5 sample 11 alum	-4.81	-1.83	-9.01	-3.49	-8.51	10.38	CORONA - much darker - slightly less red - less yellow - duller hue - very big difference in hue
Cochineal sample 2 sample 8 alum 0.2%	10.41	-10.35	2.34	-10.55	1.17	14.86	CORONA - much lighter - less red -less blue
Cochineal sample 3 sample 8 copper	1.53	-0.65	-0.46	-0.61	-051	1.72	CORONA - slight difference -slightly darker -minimally less red - minimally more blue - minimally duller

Table 8. (Continued).

Natural dyestuff	ΔL	Δa	Δb	ΔC	ΔH	ΔE	Remarks
Madder sample 1 sample 7 no mordant	0.34	2.81	8.11	6.96	-4.62	8.36	CORONA -redder -much more yellow -more saturated and bright hue -big difference in color
Madder sample 6 sample 12 alum soda	2.06	3.30	2.05	3.86	-0.46	4.40	CORONA -lighter -redder -more yellow -brighter - quite large difference in color
Cutch sample 2 sample 8 ferrow	-3.26	2.01	1.44	2.34		4.09	CORONA - lighter - less red - less yellow, less saturated - duller - quite large difference in hue
Cutch sample 1 sample 7 no mordant	0.3	-0.75	-0.77	-1.03		1.1	CORONA -slight difference in hue -slightly lighter -slightly less red
Woad	-0.49	0.09	0.45	0.46		0.67	CORONA - slight difference in hue -slightly darker -slightly redder -more blue - slightly brighter

L- lightness

a, b – coordinates of color

ΔC- differences in saturation

ΔH- hue differences

ΔE- total differences in color

CONCLUSION

- Fabrics treated with Corona were more evenly dyed and did not have lighter spots.
- In some samples, differences in hue and saturation were observed in comparison with the samples not treated with Corona.
- In the case of dyeing with Cochineal and Cutch, a melange effect appeared which is interesting from a designing point of view but needs further investigation in terms of dyeing results.
- Different mordants yield differences in the values the of the color parameters.
- During the experiments, a wide range of colors has been obtained, including several shades of yellow, orange, red, pink, violet green, brown and blue.
- The samples dyed with the addition of mordants displayed fair and to good resistance to washing, perspiration and light.

The tests have shown that naturally dyed linen fabrics are not only ecological products but also interesting for industry. Simplifying the dyeing process by means of the Corona treatment, eliminates the necessity of washing the fabrics, pre-treatment and guarantees more even dyeing.

Thanks to the application of the Corona treatment, it is possible to obtain "green" products with a lower amount of chemicals applied during processing, especially for natural dyed fabrics.

The technology of natural dyeing investigated at INF is an example of the Corona treatment applied during the cellulosic fabric finishing process, which produces better conditions for dyeing and bleaching, as a result of an improvement in hydrophilic properties.

ACNOWLEDGEMENTS

We express our appreciation for the cooperation in the EU research project CORTEX, which was coordinated by the University of Minho in Portugal. Special thanks also to: N. Carneiro, A. P. Souto and also to a group of young scientists working together on the CORTEX Project.

REFERENCES

[1]   Dean J. Wild Color. New York, NY: Watson Guptill Pub. By Octopus Publishing Group Ltd., 1999, pp.98, 100,111, 119,124

[2]   Gulrajani. ML; Gupta D. (1992). *Natural dyes and their Application to textiles.* Department of Textile Technology, Indian Institute of Technology, New Delhi, pp.15-24

[3]   Schmidt-Przewozna K. (2005). Historical Dyes in Poland and their Revival. In Jo Kirby. *Dyes in History and Archaeology*, JG Publishing: Archetype Publications, ISBN: 1-873132-29-8, pp.110-116.

In: Textiles for Sustainable Development   ISBN: 978-1-60021-559-9
Editors: R. Anandjiwala, L. Hunter et al., pp. 275-283   © 2007 Nova Science Publishers, Inc.

Chapter 24

DEVELOPMENT OF A NEW VAT DYEING PROCESS FOR CELLULOSE MATERIALS PRE-TREATED WITH CORONA

António Souto, Noémia Carneiro, Francisco Mendes and Paula Dias

Departamento de Engenharia Têxtil, Universidade do Minho,
Campus de Azurém 4800-058 Guimarães, Portugal;
souto@det.uminho.pt, noemiac@det.uminho.pt

ABSTRACT

Vat dyeing of cellulosic materials is shortened by means of the replacement of preparatory desizing and bleaching operations by a Corona discharge. The final dye oxidation using alkaline/hydrogen peroxide bath is reinforced in order to obtain a simultaneous effect in terms of the cleaning of the materials. Several vat dyes of different chemical classes were tested either by exhaustion or pad-batch and pad-steam processes and positive results were obtained concerning the yield of dyeing, hue and the brightness of the color. Significant economical and ecological benefits are possible in textile wet processing of cellulosic materials.

Keywords: plasma treatment, corona discharge, cotton , vat dyes, dyeing quality.

INTRODUCTION

During the history of the textile industry, dyeing houses are considered as being responsible for serious environmental damage and they were repeatedly requested to develop new dyeing processes which do not harm the environment or consumers.

The goal of every dyeing house is to obtain a dyed fabric having the best quality, in terms of fastness, reproducibility, levelness and high saturation at the lowest price and without pollution problems. To achieve all these, it is well known that a good preparation of the fabric is essential. Cotton fabric preparation requires de-sizing, alkaline boiling and bleaching before dyeing. This enables a uniform penetration of the dye molecules into the cotton fibers. The possibility of dyeing raw fabric has always been a challenge to the dyers.

Physical and chemical surface changes in cotton are observed after Corona discharge treatment. The increase in oxidation potential and the creation of channels through the cuticles are considered responsible for the variation in cotton properties after plasma discharge treatment, especially in terms of the absorption of water and wet treatment liquors [1,3-5,8]. Corona treatment involves the application of an electrical discharge of high voltage (around 10 000V) through the air between two electrodes, using frequencies around 40kHz, at normal atmospheric temperature and pressure, to dry cotton fabric. The Corona discharge treatment produces a uniform hydrophilicity of the fabric. In previous studies the improvement in the quality of fabrics treated with Corona and afterwards de-sized, boiled and bleached, or even mercerized, has been demonstrated [2,6,7]. The increase in hydrophilicity after Corona treatment enables the dyed cotton fabric to be dyed with vat dyes.

In this work, the ability to get a fabric perfectly dyed without any kind of chemical preparation is demonstrated, for dyeing with vat dyes by the exhaustion, pad-steam and pad-batch processes.

DESCRIPTION OF THE EXPERIMENTAL WORK

Materials, Equipment and Methods

Fabric
100% raw cotton fabric, plain weave, sized with starch (8% o.w.f), and the following characteristics: mass per unit area - 172.6 g/m^2; thickness - 0.48 mm; number of yarns/cm - 18 (warp) and 15 (weft); yarn count - 30.6 tex (warp) and 76.2 tex (weft).

Equipments
- *Corona* - The discharge was made in a SOFTAL laboratory prototype model "Lisboa", consisting of a ceramic electrode and a counter electrode with silicone coating, the width of treatment being 50 cm.
- *Long bath equipment* - A laboratory machine, model IBELUS IL-720, Labelus, with infrared heating, was used.
- *Foulard* - A Roaches padding equipment was used, the following conditions being used: speed of the fabric – 5.04 m/min; pressure of the rolls – 4.3 bar.
- *Steamer* - A laboratory machine, type DH, Mathis Laboratory Steamer, was used.
- *Reflexion spectrophotometer* - The model Spectroflash 600 plus from Datacolor was used for the evaluation of whiteness and tinctorial values.

Methods
- Preparation processes

Corona Discharge

The following conditions were used: power of discharge – 1.53 kW; speed of the fabric – 2.44 m/min; three passages for each side of the fabric to achieve perfect hydrophilicity.

Desizing

Table 1. De-sizing - impregnation processes (Pad-roll)

Bath recipe	Conditions	Washing
3.0 m ℓ/ℓ Lubifrol E 3.0 m ℓ/ℓ Enzilase U-50 Kieralon ED	Pick-up of bath 60-65% Bath temperature = 20 °C Temperature = 80 °C Duration = 360 minutes	With water (98°C) for 10 minutes With water (95°C) for 10 minutes With water (95°C) for 10 minutes With cold water

Bleaching

Table 2. Bleaching process

Bath recipe	Conditions	Washings
Liquor ratio – 1/20 2.0 m ℓ/ℓ H_2O_2 50% 3.0 m ℓ/ℓ NaOH 48% 0.4 m ℓ/ℓ Kieralon ED 0.3 m ℓ/ℓ Sequestrator S	Bath temperature = 100 °C Duration = 30 minutes	With water (90°C) for 10 minutes With water (70°C) for 10 minutes With cold water, until neutral pH

- Dyeing

Vat dyeing is made in substrates differently prepared:

I. Corona discharged
II. Enzyme de-sized

Liquor ratio – 1/20

Dyes:
a. Orange Anthraquinone carbazoles C.I. Vat Orange 15
b. Blue Indanthrone C.I. Vat Blue 4
c. Olive Green Benzathrone C.I. Vat Green 3

Table 3. Dyeing recipe

Dye concentrations	0.08% to 0.8%	1.0% to 2.5%	3.0% to 7.0%
$Na_2S_2O_4$	3g/ℓ	5g/ℓ	6g/ℓ
NaOH	10mℓ/ℓ	14mℓ/ℓ	16mℓ/ℓ
Dekol SN	2mℓ/ℓ		
Setamol WS	3g/ℓ		
Peregal P	1mℓ/ℓ		
$NaNO_2$	1g/ℓ		

Process

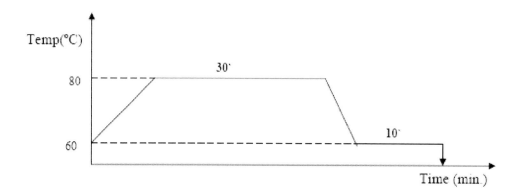

Oxidation after Dyeing

Table 4. Oxidation recipe and method

Bath recipe	Conditions	Washings
2.0 ml/l H_2O_2 200v 3.0 ml/l NaOH 48%	Bath temperature = 100 °C Duration = 30 minutes	With 0.5 ml/l Kieralon B and 1.,0g/l Na_2CO_3 (90°C) for 20 minutes With cold water

Quality Control

Starch Degree

Starch degree was tested with a solution of iode/potassium iodide and measured using the TEGEWA scale.

Hydrophilicity

Time of water drop absorption was measured according to AATCC-39-1980.

Whiteness

The whiteness was evaluated using the Berger formula. Twenty readings with aleatory distribution for the calculation of uniformity were made on the entire surface of the sample. The standard deviation of the readings was calculated.

RESULTS

Preparation of Cotton

In the first part of this work, several tests were carried out in order to study the possibility of Corona discharge replacing de-sizing, followed by an oxidative bleaching. Whiteness, hydrophilicity and starch removal were evaluated for the different preparation options:

Table 5. Whiteness (Berger)

	Sample treated with Corona + bleached	De-sized + bleached
Average	58.8	54.4
St. Dev.	0.5	0.8

Whiteness is very important when the final article has to be white or dyed to light colors. An improvement of 4.4 and a better uniformity are achieved when Corona discharge is applied to the fabric and it is then bleached.

Table 6. Starch removal (Tegewa scale)

	Sample treated with Corona + bleached	De-sized + bleached
Average	6/7	8

Better starch removal is obtained when de-sizing before bleaching than when the Corona treatment precedes the bleaching. Nevertheless, for fabrics to be dyed with vat dyes, the amount of starch remaining in the fabric (6/7) is not so important.

Table 7. Hydrophilicity (seconds)

	Sample treated with Corona + bleached	De-sized + bleached
Average	0.5	1.1
St. Dev.	0.04	0.3

In the preparation and dyeing processes, hydrophilicity is extremely important in order to allow good penetration of the bath liquors and thereby achieving good uniformity and yield for the dyed substrates.

The results in table 7 demonstrate the increase in hydrophilicity of the fabric as well as in its uniformity. The fabric with the Corona/bleaching preparation shows a better potential for dyeing with vat dyes than the fabric prepared according to the classical method (de-sizing/bleaching). These results led to trials involving Corona discharge treatment prior to dyeing and a bleaching after dyeing.

Exhaust Dyeing

The classical method of vat dyeing includes de-sizing, alkaline boiling and bleaching as preparatory processes, the dyeing requiring alkaline reduction to exhaust the dye, followed by oxidation to insolubilise the dye molecules.

Dyeing of fabric after hydrophilisation with Corona discharge was investigated, cleaning of the material taking place afterwards by oxidative means, simultaneously with oxidation of the vat dye molecules.

Samples of raw cotton fabrics were subjected to two different preparations:

I. Corona;

II. Enzymatic de-sizing.

Table 8. Tinctorial yield (K/S)

dyes	Sample treated with Corona (CV%)		De-sized sample (CV%)	
Orange 0.10%	0.53	(1.80)	0.19	(4.30)
Orange 0.25%	0.89	(1.68)	0.33	(4.29)
Orange 0.60%	2.39	(1.91)	1.29	(4.15)
Orange 2.00%	6.73	(1.54)	5.93	(1.79)
Orange 7.00%	13.49	(3.01)	13.28	(3.75)
Blue 0.10%	0.15	(3.39)	0.15	(3.39)
Blue 0.30%	0.21	(2.35)	0.20	(4.08)
Blue 0.70%	0.45	(8.54)	0.49	(9.86)
Blue 2.00%	8.56	(0.28)	7.49	(2.42)
Blue 5.00%	18.40	(1.79)	15.92	(1.49)
Olive Green 0.15%	0.34	(2.84)	0.34	(9.97)
Olive Green 0.40%	1.14	(2.22)	0.97	(3.71)
Olive Green 1.00%	2.69	(1.18)	2.04	(2.85)
Olive Green 3.00%	7.72	(2.28)	5.80	(3.03)
Olive Green 7.00%	14.89	(3.87)	12.31	(2.70)

Table 9. Color co-ordinates

Dye	Sample treated with Corona			De-sized sample		
Orange	L^*	C^*	h	L^*	C^*	h
0.10%	86,78	32,38	76,51	90,60	16,13	78,94
0.25%	84,44	40,50	74,60	88,16	25,19	75,29
0.60%	78,18	56,51	70,00	81,41	45,69	70,31
2.00%	70,19	71,34	66,51	71,12	69,66	66,65
7.00%	61,32	73,71	63,57	62,40	75,13	64,05
Blue						
0.10%	86,25	7,65	265,06	87,00	5,97	254,41
0.30%	80,43	15,23	261,66	82,20	11,43	260,55
0.70%	74,83	19,82	264,95	73,99	20,07	265,34
2.00%	36,80	39,55	280,30	38,42	37,99	278,68
7.00%	26,60	28,50	284,74	28,57	38,33	283,11
Olive						
0.15%	78,77	9,76	167,19	78,29	9,07	167,84
0.40%	65,09	12,89	167,84	66,17	11,30	168,79
1.00%	53,33	14,28	166,65	56,69	12,60	167,34
3.00%	34,48	14,18	164,88	41,86	13,80	165,34
7.00%	29,07	12,79	163,75	31,37	12,90	163,89

Note: All values are the average of four measurements.

The dyes applied by exhaustion gave better dyeing results when the substrate is pretreated by Corona discharge and oxidatively cleaned when the dye is insolubilised (except for the blue dyeing at 0.7%). The paler colors obtained with low concentrations of the orange dye are very positively affected in intensity and chroma, while the darker colors (blue and green) are favored in terms of these colorimetric parameters. The dye uniformity of the de-sized materials is much lower than that of the Corona discharge treated samples.

Continuous Dyeing

Table 10. Blue Dye (0.7%)

Colorimetric evaluation	Pad-Batch		Pad-Steam	
	Raw - Corona	De-sized	Raw - Corona	De-sized
K/S (St. Dev)	3.2 (0.04)	3.7 (0.06)	2.2 (0.04)	2.4 (0.06)
L*	50.1	47.8	54.8	53.9
C*	33.4	34.2	29.9	30.3
h	274.4	274.9	269.6	269.3

Table 11. Orange Dye (0.6%)

Colorimetric evaluation	Pad-Batch		Pad-Steam	
	Raw - Corona	De-sized	Raw - Corona	De-sized
K/S (St. Dev)	2.4 (0.07)	2.6 (0.1)	1.4 (0.07)	1.4 (0.14)
L*	77.8	77.2	79.5	80.2
C*	56.2	57.4	44.5	45.4
h	68.5	67.8	68.3	68.1

Table 12. Green Dye (0.8%)

Colorimetric evaluation	Pad-Batch		Pad-Steam	
	Raw - Corona	De-sized	Raw - Corona	De-sized
K/S (St. Dev)	4.3 (0.04)	5.8 (0.07)	2.6 (0.05)	3.0 (0.17)
L*	57.3	53.9	55.2	53.3
C*	37.4	39.1	38.4	39.8
h	184.6	185.9	185.1	184.9

For the three dyes, using either the Pad-batch or Pad-steam processes, no noticeable difference in hue is observed if the dyeing is made without previous de-sizing, but with a plasma discharge. The purity of the color is somewhat lower for the treated samples, but differences are small (1 to 3 %) and of little practical consequence. The differences in luminosity correspond to a lower yield in dyeing but, except for the green dye applied by the pad-batch method, no important decrease in intensity occurs when the de-sizing operation is omitted. In all cases, an increase in the uniformity of the dyed samples is obtained with the Corona discharge treatment.

CONCLUSION

In this paper, the results obtained using the Corona discharge treatment are compared with those obtained with the classical preparation of the fabrics. On average, the final properties show that the Corona discharge treatment can be considered a valid alternative to the traditional processes when dyeing with vat dyes, provided a final oxidation phase is also used to clean the substrate.

In exhaust dyeing, the Corona discharge treatment gives a perfect and more intense dyeing of the cotton fabric at a reduced costs (several times less), better color uniformity, the same fastness and a large reduction in pollution – in terms of the chemicals applied during the preparation of the fabric. Dyeing with the three main types of vat dyes show an increase in color intensity for the samples treated with Corona compared to those treated using conventional methods. During the final oxidation phase in the dyeing process, the natural color of cotton as well as vegetable impurities can be removed as well the vegetable impurities.

Continuous dyeing processes require more research in order to obtain higher color yields, but cleaner, more uniform and reproducible colors can be obtained.

One textile enterprise in Portugal has acquired an industrial Corona machine and an economic evaluation of the process, under industrial conditions, will be undertaken.

ACKNOWLEDGEMENTS

Authors want to acknowledge European Commission for the funding of the GROWTH project "Corona irradiation in textile finishing", G1RD-CT- 2002-00757.

REFERENCES

[1] Souto, AP; Carneiro, N; Knott, J; Kaufmann, R; Sevirich, B; Hocker, H. "Influence du Traitement Corona sur le Cuticule de la de Coton", 17° IFVTCC Congress, Vienn June, 1996.

[2] Souto, AP; Carneiro, N; Nogueira, C; Madureira, A; Rios, M; Fernandes, F; Dias, P. "Quality improvement and shortcut of preparation of cotton fabrics with Corona discharge", CIRAT-1; 3-5 December, Monastir-Tunisie, December, 2004.

[3] Carneiro, N; Souto, AP; Nogueira, C; Madureira, A; Rios, M; Fernandes, F; Dias, P. "Quality improvement and shortcut of preparation of Corona discharge cotton fabrics", submitted to publication.

[4] Carneiro, N; Souto, AP; Marimba, A; Ferreira, H. "Industrial Impact of Corona Plasmatic Treatments in the Wet Processing of Cotton Materials", World Congress on Textiles in the Millenium, Huddersfield – United Kingdom, 6-7 July, 1999.

[5] Carneiro, N; Souto, AP; Nogueira, C; Madureira, A; Krebs, C; Cooper, S. "Half bleaching of cotton materials using Corona discharge", submitted to publication.

[6]   Carneiro, N; Souto, AP; Nogueira, C; Rios, MJ; Madureira, A; Fernandes, F; Dias, P. "Developments in preparation and dyeing of Corona discharged cellulosic materials", World Textile Conference Autex 2005, Portoroz, Slovenia, June, 2005.

[7]   Carneiro, N; Souto, AP; Rios, MJ. "Evaluation of cotton fabric properties after mercerisation, using Corona discharge as a preparation step", 5th International Istanbul Textile Conference – Recent Advances in Innovation and Enterprise in Textiles and Clothing, 19-21 May Istanbul - Turquia, May, 2005.

[8]   Patent: PCT/PT/04/000008 – May (2004), "Continuous and semi-continuous treatment of textile materials integrating Corona discharge".

In: Textiles for Sustainable Development   ISBN: 978-1-60021-559-9
Editors: R. Anandjiwala, L. Hunter et al., pp. 285-291   © 2007 Nova Science Publishers, Inc.

Chapter 25

DIGITAL PRINTING ON SILK FABRIC

N. Surana [a] and R. Philip [b]

[a] Senior Lecturer, Home Economics Department,
University of Swaziland, Luyengo, Swaziland
[b] Lecturer, Fashion Design Department, Rai University,
Navi Mumbai , Belapur, India ; Telephone: +268 5283021;
Mobile: +268 6232775; Email: *nishdeep@agric.uniswa.sz*

ABSTRACT

Digital printing has taken over the paper printing industry and is now focused on the textile printing industry. In this study an attempt was made to print silk fabric using ink-jet printing technology and ink cartridges meant for paper. Since the fastness properties of such inks were poor an effort was made to fix the unfixed inks on to the silk fabric using steaming, curing and silicate padding processes. Steaming was found to give a desirable result. A water repellent finish was also applied to enable the graceful prints, available through digital printing, to be used for other end uses.

Keywords: digital printing, silk, steaming, curing, silicate padding.

INTRODUCTION

Digital printing is at present making rapid advances in the area of textile processing. It has successfully established a strong presence in applications, such as paper printing, transfer printing, banners, and the demand for production of printed fabric samples.

Despite its remarkable progress, digital printing is still at its infancy and considerable efforts are being made to increase the growth in this technology.

Digital printing is a high speed process where activities, such as creating a design, selection of colors, alteration of the selected design, printing of strike- offs and final production are carried out at great speed.

For a fabric to be digitally printed, three key components are necessary: suitable software, printing machine and ink. A design can be created using CAD software, and scanned images can also be used for printing. The software should be able to alter the images, to suit the customer needs, and send data to the printer. [2]

Ink-jet printers use a minimum of four print heads, one print head per color, for the cyan, magenta, yellow and black (CYMK) inks. Any color can be produced using the color space of the four colors. Drop-on-demand and Continuous ink-jet technologies form the basis of ink-jet printing technology. In the drop-on-demand technology the ink droplets are produced only when necessary while in continuous ink-jet printing the drops are produced continuously and printed only on selected locations. Bubble-jet or thermally activated ink-jet printing is another method where the droplets are ejected by a thermal pulse [2]. Ink-jet printing is currently largely used for office printing applications, with the leading technology being drop-on-demand. The low cost heads and trouble-free ink management are the main reasons for the wide acceptance of the latter. The second large area is industrial applications, where continuous ink-jet and piezo drop-on-demand technologies are used to attain higher resolution [5].

The ink, which is the third component, must be of very high quality because of the environment in which the printing occurs. The nozzles have tiny holes through which the inks have to flow consistently without clogging the nozzles. Hence, the manufacturer must have control over the relevant properties, such as viscosity, surface tension, conductivity, chemical stability, pH, physical stability, purity and foaming.

The present study was undertaken to investigate the printing of silk fabric with ink-jet cartridges meant for papers and evaluate the printed fabric for rubbing and wash fastness. The aim of the study was also to find techniques to fix ink and to apply water repellent finish to the ink-jet printed silk fabric. In this study, the conventional screen printing technology was compared with the digital printing technology.

MATERIAL USED

Fabric used: Silk (a blend of wild and spun silk yarns)
Paper used: Color Ink-jet Paper.
Printer used: Wide Format Ink-jet Printer (with drop-on-demand technology)
Chemicals used: Sodium hydroxide, sodium silicate, Finish NEC (resin), Destofil YL (softener), Cerol PA (softener), NUVA HPC (fluorocarbon), $MgCl_2$ (catalyst).
Instruments used: Crockometer, Launderometer, Padding mangle, Spray Tester.

METHODOLOGY

1. Printing of silk fabric with ink-jet cartridges used for paper
2. The silk fabric was digitally printed with the cartridges that were meant for printing paper, also, the same prints were printed on color ink-jet paper.
3. Testing the ink-jet printed silk fabrics

Rub fastness: The test was performed according to the IS: 766-1956 test procedure, using the Crockometer. The numerical ratings for staining of the undyed fabric used in the dry and wet rubbing tests were noted and evaluated by means of a Grey Scale [3].

Wash fastness: The test was carried out according to the IS: 3361-1979 test procedure, using a Launderometer. The numerical ratings for staining of the undyed fabrics and the change in color of the printed silk fabric were noted and assessed by means of a Grey Scale [3].

3. **Techniques used to fix the unfixed inks on silk fabric:**
➤ *Steaming*[6]:
(a) Preparation of the fabric:
The printed fabric was rolled in a newspaper to avoid creasing. This paper was further rolled inwards to lock the open ends of the paper. The roll was secured using a masking tape. The roll was wrapped in aluminum foil, leaving the bottom of the foil open for the passage of steam to fix the unfixed inks. The ends of the foil at the bottom were crumpled to form a stand, to avoid continuous contact with the base of the vessel.

(b) Preparation of the steamer:
A large base pan was filled with water and boiled. The sieve was placed in the pan without being immersed in, or touching, the water. The prepared fabric was kept on the sieve and the steamer was covered with a lid.

(c) Steaming:
The prepared fabric was steamed for 60 minutes. The fabric was left overnight to allow the ink to settle. The next day the fabric was rinsed.

➤ *Curing:*
The ink-jet printed silk fabric was cured at 140° C for 5 minutes and then rinsed [4].

➤ *Silicate Padding:*
The ink-jet printed silk fabric was padded in a solution (1 litre) containing 10ml sodium hydroxide and 10ml sodium silicate, with the help of an electrical padding mangle. The treated fabric was placed in a vacuum seal bag for 14 hours and then rinsed.

4. **Application of water repellent finish on the ink-jet printed fabric:**
➤ *Recipe of the water repellent solution:*
The recipe for water repellency was obtained from Century Textiles and the process was carried out at Century Textiles.

(a) Recipe:

Finish NEC (resin)	60kg	42g
Destofil YL (softener)	40kg	28g
Cerol PA (softener)	50kg	35g
NUVA HPC (fluorocarbon)	80kg	56g
$MgCl_2$ (catalyst)	6kg	0.3g
Total	*1000l*	*1l*

(b) Method:

A one litre solution was prepared as per the recipe above. The solution was stirred thoroughly to any lumps which had formed. The ink-jet printed fabric was then padded through the solution, dried completely and later cured at 140°C for 5 minutes.

A spray test was conducted to evaluate the water repellency imparted to the fabric, following the test procedure described in Booth J.E., 1968 [1]. The fabric was observed and rated. The mean rating of the five readings was taken.

5. **Screen printing on silk fabrics:**

To compare conventional screen printing technology, with digital printing technology screens were prepared. A three color design was chosen. The screens were prepared by following the standard screen printing procedure. The silk fabric was printed and the difference between conventional screen printing and digital printing was noted, along with the limitations and advantages of each one possesses.

RESULTS AND DISCUSSION

The results obtained were as follows:

1. **Digitally printed fabric using cartridges that were meant for printing on paper.**

It was observed that:

➢   The print on the silk fabric was not as sharp as on the color ink-jet paper. This could be due to the fibrous structure of the silk fabric, causing a spreading of the inks, thereby affecting the sharpness of the print.

Ink-jet printing on paper   **Ink-jet printing on silk fabric**

➢   Absorption could also have affected the sharpness of the prints. The silk fabric absorbed more ink than the paper. This was evident in that the digitally printed silk fabric the print is clearly visible at the back of the cloth which was not the case for the color ink-jet paper. This is due to the fact that these papers are specially designed to block deep penetration of the ink, resulting in excellent depth of shade and good sharpness. The color obtained on the silk fabric was comparatively dull.

Ink-jet printing on paper   Ink-jet printing on silk fabric

2. **Rub and wash fastness properties the**:
➤ *Rub fastness*: The dry rub fastness rating for the ink-jet printed silk fabric was found to be very good, while the wet rub fastness was extremely poor.
➤ *Wash fastness*: The change in color of the printed silk fabric was rated 1 which is extremely poor. The staining of the undyed fabrics of silk and cotton were rated 3 and 1, respectively which is moderate and extremely poor, respectively.

3. **Fixing the unfixed inks on to the printed silk fabric**:
➤ *Steaming*: On rinsing the steamed fabric, it was noted that slight color bleeding occurred. The prints were neither destroyed nor were the white spaces stained. Hence, steaming can be used to fix the unfixed ink on ink-jet printed silk fabric.
➤ *Curing*: When the cured sample was rinsed, the sample continued to bleed and the resultant fabric was left with no identifiable print. Hence, curing failed to fix the unfixed ink.
➤ *Silicate padding*: While the printed silk fabric was undergoing the padding process, the color began to bleed considerably and the prints on the fabric were completely destroyed. As a result, the silicate padding process cannot be used since it leaves the fabric in a state which is totally undesirable and unattractive for use.

4. **Application and evaluation of water repellent finish.**
➤ The printed fabric was passed through the padding mangle containing the water repellent solution. During the padding process, bleeding of the print took place, at the same time the sharpness and the background of the print affected. The fabric was dried and later cured, and then tested using a spray tester. The mean of the five ratings was taken. The water repellent finish was found to be successful, but the print was destroyed, making the process practically unacceptable.

5. **Comparison of conventional screen printing technology with digital printing technology:**
➤ *Screen printing technology*:
• Screens have to be prepared, one screen per color. Preparation of screens is a laborious process.

- There is high wastage, especially when screens are not properly made and when patterns are changed.
- Screen printing is a time consuming process.
- Selections of designs that can be screen printed are restricted, as very fine lines are extremely difficult or impossible to produce.
- Choices from the color range are limited as not all colors can be produced repeatedly.
- For printing, if the registration marks are not perfect, printing will be defective.
- A large table is essential for printing.
- It is an expensive process.
- The size of the repeat is restricted.

> *Digital printing technology*:
- The designs are created on a computer using CAD software. No screens are required.
- Digital printing is not a laborious process.
- Less wastage occurs, even if any pattern has to be changed.
- The overall process is not time consuming.
- There is no restriction for printing any designs, as the tiniest spot can also be printed by this technology.
- Unlimited choice of colors from the color range is made possible, as it can print as many colors as one desires.
- Production of defective pieces is almost nil.
- It is less expensive than screen printing.
- No repeat size restrictions.

CONCLUSION

It can be concluded from the above results that, for ink-jet printing, silk fabric must be given a pre-treatment to reduce ink absorption and spreading and to increase the depth of color and for better sharpness. Digitally printed silk fabric has poor fastness properties, although steaming as a post treatment gives acceptable results. The water repellent finish imparted to the printed silk fabric was found to be successful, but the print was destroyed, thus making this treatment unacceptable in practice. Digital printing is considered to have more benefit than screen printing in the long run. Further research to improve the fastness properties of digitally printed fabrics can have a tremendous impact in the Textile and Apparel industry.

REFERENCES

[1] Booth, JE. Principles of Textile Testing, (London: Butterworth and Co.), 1968, 325, 326.

[2] Clark, D. AATCC Review, 2003, 1, 14.

[3] IS: 3361 1979; IS: 766 1956, ISI Handbook of Textile Testing, New Delhi: Indian Standards Institution: New Delhi, 1982, 571, 572, 553.

[4] Prayag, RS. Technology of Textile Printing, Dharwad, L R Prayag, 1989, 62.

[5] Stefanini, JP. *Text Chem. and Col,* 1996, 28, 19-22.

[6] Vanables, J. The Silk Painting Workshop, Sterling Pub. Co. Inc, 1994, 122-124.

In: Textiles for Sustainable Development   ISBN: 978-1-60021-559-9
Editors: R. Anandjiwala, L. Hunter et al., pp. 293-309   © 2007 Nova Science Publishers, Inc.

Chapter 26

ECO-FRIENDLY NATURAL FIBER TEXTILES FOR SUSTAINABLE DEVELOPMENT

S. Thomas[1] and L.A. Pothen[2]

[1] School of Chemical Sciences, Mahatma Gandhi University,
Kottayam, Kerala, India, E mail: sabut552001@yahoo.com
[2] Department of Chemistry, Bishop Moore College, Mavelikkara,
Kerala, India, E mail: lalyaley@yahoo.co.uk

ABSTRACT

Composites of woven natural fibers in various polymeric matrices were prepared using different weave structures and different processing techniques, with special reference to fiber surface modification. The weave structure was found to have the maximum influence on the ultimate composite properties and also the fiber wetting characteristics. Composites were also prepared with a natural fiber combined with a synthetic fiber. Fabrics with maximum fiber orientation in the loading direction proved to be the best reinforcement to impart maximum properties. The impact response of the composites as a function of their weave structure was studied using different impact test methods and a different sample geometry. The values of the initiation energy and propagation energy, obtained from the force-time curves, were found to be the maximum in the case of composites with the weave structure where there is maximum number of fibers in the loading direction. Natural fiber textiles find application in geo-textiles and research in this area has also been reviewed.

Keywords: natural fiber, tensile behavior, impact behavior.

INTRODUCTION

Current environmental awareness is triggering a paradigm shift towards the use of cellulose fibers as reinforcement in various polymeric matrices. Different cellulose fibers have been studied by various researchers all over the world as reinforcement in various matrices. Cellulose content and micro fibrillar angle have been found to be the important parameters, which determine the effectiveness of these fibers as reinforcement in various matrices [1]. Sisal fiber obtained from the leaf of the sisal plant (*Agave sisalana*) has been proved to be a good reinforcement in various polymeric matrices [2].

Textile structural composites are finding use in various high performance applications [3, 4]. The increased interest in textile reinforcements is due to the enhanced strength, lower production cost and improved mechanical properties, which they offer, compared to their non-woven counterparts. Additionally, textile structural composites are associated with near net shape and cost effective manufacturing process. Another special feature of the textile reinforcement is the interconnectivity between adjacent fibers. This interconnectivity provides additional interface strength to supplement the relatively weak fiber/resin interface. In addition, woven fabric composites may be more damage tolerant in the case of a delamination. Formation of different textile preforms is an important stage in composite technology.

Lateral cohesion is also an important issue to be addressed in the preparation of the reinforcing elements, and woven reinforcements are a possible solution. Twisted yarns have been reported to increase lateral cohesion of the filaments as well as to improve the ease of handling [5]. However, by twisting yarns, possible micro damage within the yarn can be localized, leading to a possible decrease in the failure strength of the yarn. Whatever the fiber structure, fiber architecture has been found to influence the composite properties based on the morphological and structural parameters [6].

Even though reports on the usage of natural fiber as reinforcement in various matrices have been published, usage of natural fibers in the woven form is rare. Bledzki and Zhang have reported on the usage of jute fabrics as reinforcement for the preparation of composites [7]. Since natural fibers are generally not very long, twisting such fibers is generally necessary to produce yarns of the required length and properties. In fact, fiber twist induces normal forces between fibers and increasing inter-fiber friction gives yarn cohesion.

Composites were prepared using different natural fibers and also hybrids of natural and synthetic fibers using different processing techniques. Manufacturing methods frequently used for natural fiber thermoset composites are modified lay up/press molding, pultrusion etc. The resin-transfer molding (RTM) process has been used to produce high performance polymer composites. Research in this area has been in progress for many years [8]. Recently, RTM has been adopted as a manufacturing process for automotive structural components [9]. Resin impregnation is influenced by several factors, such as the chemo-rheological properties of the liquid resin, orientation or anisotropy of the fibrous pereform, mould temperature, resin impregnation pressure and surface characteristics between fiber and resin [10]. Oksman et al. have reported on the longitudinal stiffness and strength of unidirectional sisal-epoxy composites manufactured by the RTM process [11]. A detailed review by Mai et al. on the effectiveness of sisal fibers in thermoplastic and thermosetting matrices suggests the usage of the RTM technique for the preparation of composites [12].

MATERIALS AND EXPERIMENTAL

Woven fabrics of different natural fibers, such as sisal and banana, were prepared with different area densities and weave structure for the preparation of composites. In one set, fabrics differed mainly in the distance between the weft yarns. Details of the fabric used for reinforcement are given in Table 1. Two layers of the fabric-arranged in parallel were used as reinforcement in preparing the composite. In another set, alternate strands of glass and banana were used in the weft direction while twisted banana yarns were used in the warp direction. Details of the weave patterns are shown in figure 1. Composites were also prepared using banana fiber and glass fiber by weaving the two different fibers by hand. Banana fibers were used in the warp direction and alternate strands of banana and glass fibers were used in the weft direction.

Chemical Modification

Silane Treatment for Sisal Fibers

0.6 % of the silane was mixed well with an ethanol/water mixture in the ratio 6:4 mixed well and was allowed to stand for an hour. The pH of the solution was carefully controlled to bring about the complete hydrolysis of the silane by the addition of acetic acid. The fabric was dipped in the above solution and was allowed to remain there for 1-½ hours. The ethanol/water mixture was drained and the fabric was dried in air for half an hour followed by drying in an oven at 70 °C till the fabric was fully dry.

Treatment with NaOH

The sisal fabric was dipped in a 1% solution of NaOH for half an hour and then washed in very dilute acid to remove excess alkali. Washing was continued till the s were alkali free. The fabric was finally washed in distilled water and the washed s were then dried in anthe oven at 70 °C for three hours.

Thermal Treatment

Thermal treatment was carried out by keeping the woven fabric in anthe oven for 24 hours at 70°C. The fabric, directly from the oven was used for composite preparation.

Composite Preparation

Composites were manufactured using compression molding as well as with RTM. In compression molding, pre-weighed fabrics were kept in the mould and degassed polyester resin and curing agents were added to the fabric and the composites were kept under a pressure of 1 bar for 24 hours. RTM is a closed mould process where laminates are formed between two stiff mould halves. Two injection gates at the smaller side of the mould, 140mm apart, were used for injecting the resin. The pre weighed fabrics were placed into the mould cavity, the mould was closed and vacuum applied. Degassed polyester resin with curing agents was then injected into the mould cavity. The laminate size was 200x240x6mm. Three different pressures, 0.8 bar, 1 bar and 1.5 bar, were used for the preparation of composites. The laminates were allowed to cure in the mould for 4 hours and then taken out and post cured. Samples were cut for impact, tensile and flexural tests, starting from the gate regions.

The specimens were cut parallel to the weft yarns and a minimum of four samples was tested in each case, the average value being reported. The dart falling impact samples were cut from regions nearest the gate, followed by tensile and flexural. Charpy impact samples were cut from areas next to the region from where the flexural samples were cut. Tensile tests were carried out using a universal tensile tester according to ASTM D 638 M using dumb bell shaped samples (Instron model 4206). A clip on the extensometer with gauge length 50mm was used to measure the tensile strain to give accurate measurement of the tensile Young's modulus. Flexural strength was determined by testing the samples according to ASTM D 790. Four samples were tested in each case and the average value reported. To have an in depth idea about the failure behavior of the composites, SEM and optical micrographs of the failed samples were also taken.

Table 1. Details of the fabric used

Designation	Yarn spacing (weft)	Yarn spacing (warp)	Twist (turns per mm)	Area density (g/m^2)
Weave 1	5mm	5mm	10	2000
Weave 2	3mm	5mm	10	1500
Weave 3	1mm	10mm	10	2500

Figure 1. Details of the weave structures followed.

RESULTS AND DISCUSSION

The permeability of the various fabrics was measured. In addition to the weave geometry, the effect of chemical modification on the permeability of the fabrics was also noted. Hammond and Loos [13] have concluded from their studies that the test fluid has no significant influence on the permeability. The relative permeabilities of the three fabrics are shown in figure 2.

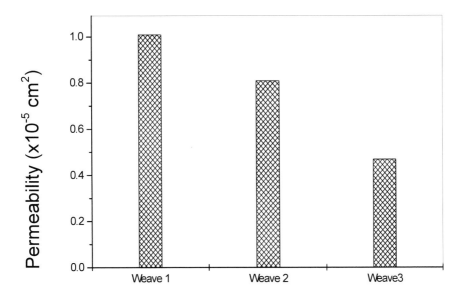

Figure 2. Permeabilities of the various fabrics.

In the case of woven fabrics, two types of resin flow occur through the fabric, one between the fiber bundles called the macro flow and the other within the fibers called the micro flow. These in turn are related to the capillary pressure in the fiber bundles. The lower permeability can be related to the greater capillary pressure in the fibers due to the decreased hydraulic radius which results from an increased fiber volume fraction. Figure 3 gives a comparison of the permeabilities of the fabrics after chemical modification.

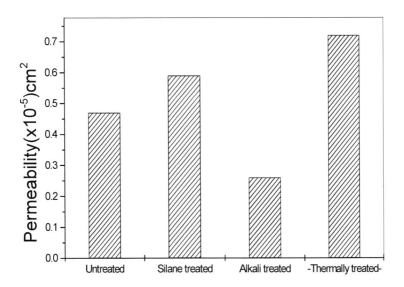

Figure 3. Comparison of permeability of the various fabrics.

Increased polarity improves the wetting and thereby the permeability. Except in the case of the alkali treated fabrics, the permeability of the treated fabrics is found to be higher than that of the untreated fabrics. The improved permeability in the case of thermally treated fabrics can be associated with the escape of moisture from the fabrics which lead to free resin flow through the micro and macro regions. In the case of alkali treated fibers, the rough surface morphology rather, than the polarity and the hydraulic radius, leads to a reduction in the flow rate leading to lower permeability values. Three different weave structures with area densities 1500, 2000 and 2500g/m^2 were used for the preparation of composites. Composites with an area density of 1500 are marked weave 2, those with an area density of 2000 as weave 1 and those with 2500 as weave 3. The tensile properties of the composites were found to be relatively unaffected by the change in pressure.

Tensile Properties

The tensile strength values obtained for the different weave structures and resins with different viscosities are given in Table 2, with the S.D. in brackets.

Table 2. Tensile strength values of the various composites

Sample	Tensile Strength(MPa) 0.8bar	Tensile Strength(MPa) 1bar	Tensile Strength(MPa) 1.5bar	Fiber volume%
Resin 1	29.5±3.6	29.5± 3.6	29.5± 3.6	0
Weave 1	20± 1	16± 3.3	19± 1	26
Weave 2	25± 3	24± 0.2	25± 6	22
Weave 3	45± 5	45± 3	54± 2	32
Resin 2	40± 4.6	40± 4.6	40± 4.6	0
Weave 1	28± 2	21± 3	25± 2	26
Weave 2	37± 3	30± 3	30± 1	22
Weave 3	53± 1.5	56± 4.2	50± 3.9	32
Resin 3	44± 4.7	44± 4.7	44± 4.7	0
Weave 1	28± 5	32± 3	29± 0.8	26
Weave 2	33± 1	37± 4	31± 2.3	22
Weave 3	67± 7	63± 2	57± 1.6	32

In the case of the woven reinforcements used in the present case, the arrangement of the yarns, together with the lower fiber volume fraction, gives rise to higher matrix regions. In woven fabric composites, cracks originate in the interstitial regions and the lower fiber volume, coupled with the weaving arrangement employed presently, give rise to more interstitial regions. Orientation of the fibers with respect to the loading axis is an important parameter, in determining composite properties. Composite strength and stiffness will be reduced when the fibers are not parallel to the loading direction. Interlacings points have been identified as one of the weakest points in most woven fabric composite systems. The interlacing points, in addition, have the tendency for more voids and fiber distortion at the interlace gap. These increased interstitial positions serve as crack initiation points. In a woven fabric composite, the interlacing point has been identified as one of the weakest points. The stress strain curves show progressive failure in the case of composites unlike the pure polyester sample. The progressive failure can be attributed to both shear failure as well as to progressive failure of the fabric because of the special fiber arrangement, which gives rise to lateral cohesion. The presence of interlacing gaps in the weft direction relates to the fiber distortion in the region during the molding process. This in turn pushes the 0° fiber to the transverse direction in order to fill the gaps, and this reduces the composite strength as the percentage of fibers, which are not parallel to the load direction, increases.

Flexural Properties

The flexural properties of the composites have also been compared. Figure 4 gives typical flexural load displacement curves for composites with the three weaving structures at a pressure of 0.8bar. The flexural strength is found to be maximum for weave 3.

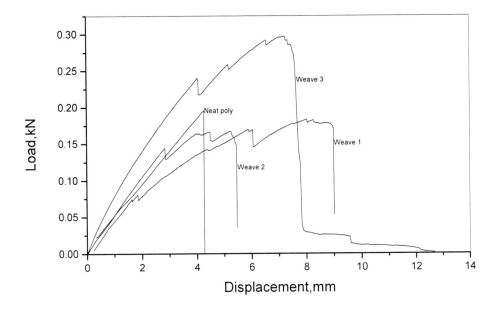

Figure 4. Flexural Load displacement curves of the various composites.

The abrupt failure of the composite can be related to flexural failure and when the load deflection curve decreases gradually to zero, shear failure can be assumed to be the predominant mode. A curve between these two forms can be believed to fail by a mixed failure mode. In the present case, the nature of the curve reveals a mixed failure mode in the case of composites with all the weave structures. However, the flexural strength is the highest in the case of composites containing weave 3. Figure 5 shows the flexural strength of the various composites.

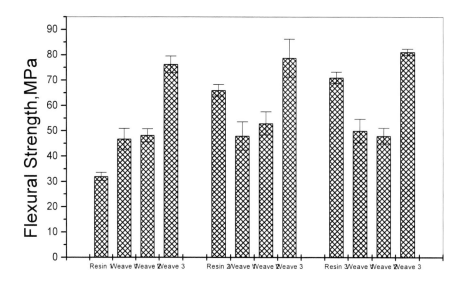

Figure 5. Flexural strength of the various composites.

The tensile modulus is found to be maximum for the thermally treated composite. The composite containing silane treated fabric exhibited lower modulus than the untreated composite. One possible reason for the decrease in properties is the change in the nature of the weave structure. Twisting of yarns has been reported to lead to a reduction in the ultimate failure strain [4]. In addition to this aspect, the twisted yarns, when subjected to various treatments, give a further reduction in the ultimate failure strength, the reason for which has to be investigated further.

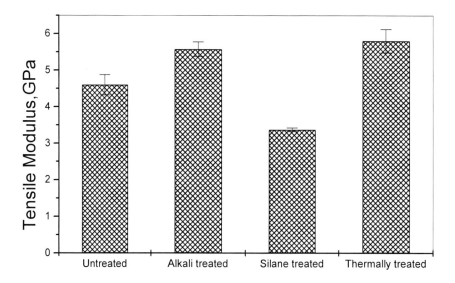

Figure 6. Tensile modulus of the variously treated composites.

The impact properties of woven sisal reinforced polyester composites were characterized by different impact test methods. Both conventional and instrumented Charpy impact tests were done. The instrumented Charpy impact tests were carried out on rectangular specimens measuring 120mm x 12mm, according to DIN 53453. The falling impact samples had a dimension 80 x 80 x 6 mm^3. A total of 5 samples were tested for each composition. A Ceast Fractovis instrumented drop weight impact tester with, a hemispherical tip (tip diameter = 20mm), was used for the falling impact test. The impact velocity was 6 m/s and the mass 3.174 kg. The impact velocity was kept at 6m/s to make sure that all samples, so that a comparison could be made of the energy required for breaking the samples. The samples were fully clamped by an annular support-ring and movable clamp mechanism. The diameter of both the support ring and movable clamp was 40mm. Samples were tested under two different velocities of 3.7m/s and 5.7m/s, respectively. Conventional Charpy impact tests were also done using a 7.5 J pendulum hammer. The higher energy hammer was used to make sure that all the samples break fully under impact.

Most composite materials are brittle and can absorb energy during elastic deformation and through damage mechanisms. Low velocity impacts can be treated as quasi static, the upper limit of which can vary from 1 to 10 of m/s. In low velocity impact, the contact duration is long enough for the entire structure to respond and in consequence, more energy is absorbed elastically. In fiber reinforced plastic laminates, the major modes of failure are those due to; a) matrix mode, b) delamination mode c) fiber mode and d) penetration. The neat polyester resin, in addition to composites with the three weaving structures was analyzed for their impact performance using different test methods. The mode of failure of the composite samples was investigated by looking at the impacted surface in all cases.

In the case of the dart impact tests, using plate specimens, depending on the weave structure employed, the nature of the impact-failed surface was found to be different. Whereas in the case of composites with weave 1 and weave 2, a series of rings, could be observed away from the point of contact. In the case of composites with weave 3, in addition to the series of rings, cracks parallel to the fibers could also be encountered. The main mode of failure could therefore be concluded to be due to matrix fracture.

In the dart impact tests performed, all the composite samples failed by cracks, which penetrated the whole sample. The impact force-time curves of the neat resin and the composites with different weave structures, under the drop weight impact tests, are compared in figures 7(a,b,c, d). The impact force-time curves reveal clearly the distinct threshold force at which damage increases in an unstable fashion in composites. Other authors have reported on the usage of damage force/energy maps in monitoring damage growth, in addition to predicting the onset of damage in fiber-reinforced composites.

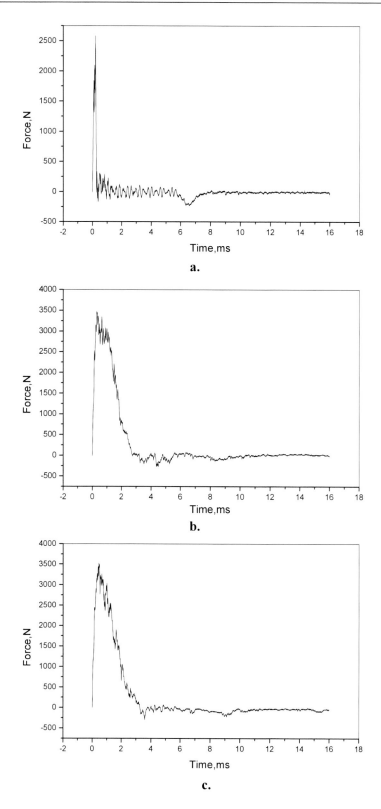

a.

b.

c.

Figure 7. Continued.

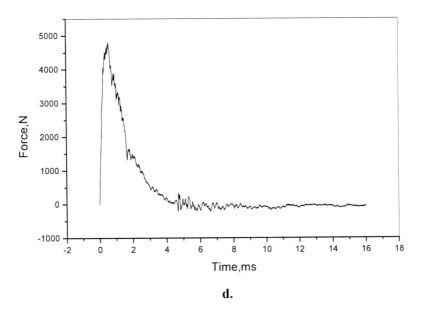

d.

Figure 7. The impact force/time curves of a) the neat resin and composites with b) weave 1 c) weave 2 and d) and weave 3.

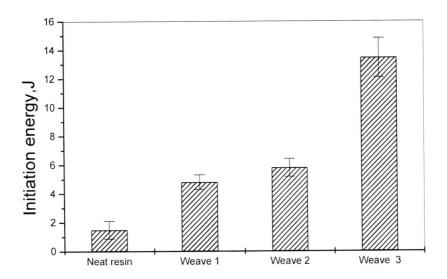

Figure 8. Crack iInitiation eEnergies of the various composites.

The impact force/time curve drops to zero immediately after reaching the peak in the case of the neat resin. This implies that all the impact energy is involved in crack initiation and there is practically no energy spent in crack propagation. However, in the case of the composite samples, the impact force-time curves exhibit a different nature, showing that considerable energy is employed in crack propagation. The energy required for crack propagation is also found to be dependent on the weave geometry, the highest value being in the case of composites with containing weave 3. From the force/energy diagrams, the threshold force at which damage increases in an unstable fashion in composites with the three weaving structure, is found to be different.

Based on the values obtained from the force-time curves, the threshold force at which damage increases in an unstable manner is found to be highest in the case of composites with weave 3 structure. The time required to reach the threshold force is also found to be the highest in the case of composites with weave 3. The crack damage in the post peak region is, however, relatively lower. Interestingly, the crack damage in the post peak region is more in the case of composites with weave 2 than in weave 1. The reason can be attributed to the special weave structure in which there are more interstitial positions and fiber undulations. The width of the base of the curve is broader in the case of composites with weave 3, showing increased energy absorption.

Figure 8 shows the variation of initiation energies of the various composites. It can be seen that maximum crack initiation energy was observed in the composite containing weave 3.

The damage force and energy maps have been found to be effective in monitoring damage growth in addition to the onset of damage. The crack initiation energy for the various composite samples, which corresponds to energy absorbed before the maximum load, obtained from the initial portion of the load/deflection curve, is compared in figure 9.

The initiation energy is found to be maximum for composites with weave 3 structure. The higher fiber volume combined with the lower undulation positions in the case of composites with weaves 3 structure can be the reasons for the higher crack initiation energy. As observed in the case of tensile and flexural properties, the higher number of fiber undulation positions and the resulting resin rich pockets serve as crack and failure initiation points for composites with weave 1 and weave 2.

The instrumented Charpy impact tests were also carried out according to DIN 53453 on rectangular specimens measuring 120mm x 12mm. Specimens were tested at two velocities, 5.69m/s and 3.75m/s. In both cases, samples broke into two under impact load. The load/displacement curve of the neat resin with velocity 3.75m/s is plotted in figure 9(a).

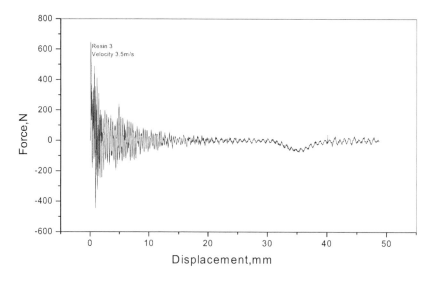

Figure 9(a). Force/displacement curve of the neat resin under impact.

The initial portion of the curve is expanded and given in figure 9b.

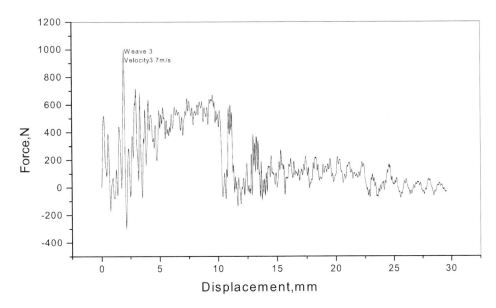

Figure 9(b). The initial portion of the load displacement curve expanded.

It is clear from the curve, that failure of the neat resin occur abruptly without any prior damage. The matrix cracks are found to be induced by a combination of tension and shear and occur because of a mismatch of properties between the fiber and the matrix. The shear bands are clear in the matrix rich regions. The SEM of the impact fracture surface is given in figure 10 and it shows the cracks at the interfacial region.

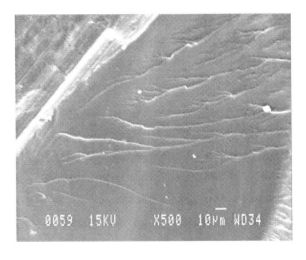

Figure 10. SEM of the impact fracture surface of the composite.

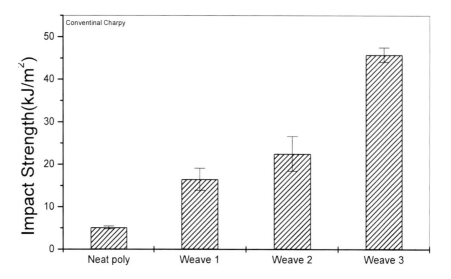

Figure 11. Impact strength of the composites (Charpy tests).

The composite samples were also tested using the conventional Charpy tests, the samples being the same dimensions as used in the instrumented Charpy tests. The values of the impact strength calculated from the conventional tests were found to be slightly higher than the ones calculated using the instrumented impact tests. Figure 11 shows the impact strength values of the various composites and the neat polyester tested using the conventional Charpy tests. However, in all cases, the impact strength and the total impact energy needed for the fracture of the material are found to be the highest in the case of composites containing weave 3. The impact strength values of the composites were also determined using the instrumented impact tests. Figure 12 represents the values of the impact strength determined using the instrumented impact tests. In the instrumented impact tests also, the impact strength value is found to be the highest for weave 3.

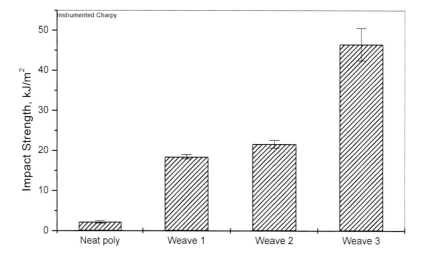

Figure 12. Impact strength using the instrumented impact test.

BANANA GLASS HYBRID COMPOSITES

Banana s were combined with glass s for developing composites with additional degrees of compositional freedom. The intrinsic nature of banana fiber is expected to improve the impact properties of the hybrid composite. Emphasis is given to optimization, which will minimize material cost. The tensile behavior of the various hybrid composites with varying fiber volume fraction is shown in figure .13.

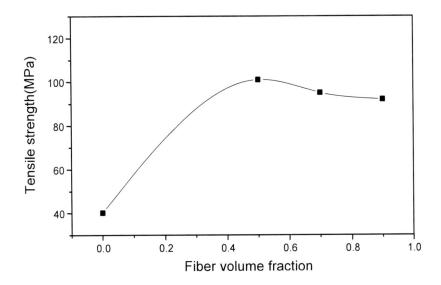

Figure 13. Effect of fiber volume fraction on the tensile strength of the composite.

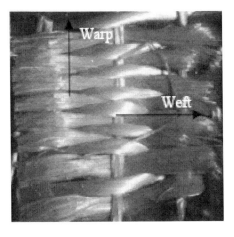

Figure 14. Weave structure in hybrid fabric.

Increase in the number of layers leads to more interstitial positions and more resin rich regions, the latter being the points where crack initiation occurs. These cracks propagate through the resin rich regions. This ultimately leads to crack initiation followed by delamination in the composites. The crack propagation pattern depends on the relative direction of crack path to fiber alignment. In other words, the fiber volume fraction and alignment of the fabric can affect the crack propagating pattern. In the pattern followed in the present case, the crack propagation is found to be from warp yarn to filling yarn through the matrix region. The weave structure is shown in figure 14.

Geo-textiles constitute a market which is currently dominated by synthetic fibers. However, the demand for products from natural, biodegradable fibers is increasing. These products decompose gradually after they have supported the establishment of deep-rooted plants, for example in slope protection projects. Geotextiles from hemp, alone or in blends with synthetic fibers, represent technically and economically attractive products.

Geo-textiles are another important field where natural fibers are finding great application. They are used mainly to prevent soil erosion as well as to reduce weed growth. For example, rooted aquatic plants are a natural part of the lake ecosystem and comprise a critical component of a healthy lake. They stabilize shorelines, oxygenate water, provide cover and spawning areas for fish, and provide habitat for aquatic invertebrates that are critical for juvenile fish growth. Uncontrolled plant growth, however, quickly can overtake swimming beaches, impede boating access around docks, limit angler success, and may result in an aesthetically undesired situation. When excessive vegetation growth affects the recreational and economic potential of a lake, it may be desirable to directly control rooted aquatic vegetation. Typically, this is accomplished through the application of herbicides. Bottom barriers, made of geo-textiles, however, provide an alternative method that avoids the environmental, health, social and economic concerns that can be associated with chemical treatments. *Bottom barriers* are sheets of synthetic or natural material anchored to the bottom of the lake to obstruct sunlight, which controls the growth of aquatic plants. The concept is comparable to using landscape fabric to control weed growth around ornamental bushes and plants in residential yards. Bottom-barrier treatments are intended for small areas of a lake and are most commonly installed in highly used areas such as swimming beaches, docks and boat ramps. The barrier can also be installed to create an edge habitat for predator fish, such as largemouth bass, bluegill and crappie. Predator fish that are popular with anglers commonly reside along weed edges. Bottom barriers increase the amount of edge habitat within a lake and may increase angler success. There is a variety of "bottom barrier" or "screen" products available that aim to suppress aquatic plant growth by reducing or blocking light. Like their polymeric counterparts, natural fiber geo-textiles are being synthesized primarily for erosion control application and these are comparatively inexpensive in Asian countries. Recent developments in the areas of ground stabilization and erosion control are causing engineers to take another look at fabrics from natural fibers for geo-textile application. In a project on the use of woven coir geo-textiles in Europe, coir based geo-textiles were used as an erosion control system, a reinforcement and a filtration material. On the basis of this experience, it had been concluded that woven coir fiber fabrics are most suitable for projects mentioned above. Most of the present day products are being developed with an eye on erosion control applications (for vegetative growth), particularly, because among naturals they have a much longer life. Their biodegradability has not yet produced uses for more permanent applications. In fact they are yet to be standardized, for their tensile behavior and their biodegradability characteristics. Keeping this in view, over the years many varieties of woven and non-woven products have been developed in India and are now commercially available

CONCLUSION

Natural fibers, in woven form, find application in various fields and have the potential for sustainable development. An important technological field where these textile fibers can be used is in composite preparation. The ultimate property of the composite depends on the weave structure. Better properties are observed in weave structures where there is minimum of crimp regions and in composites where there are minimum of interstitial positions. Natural fiber textiles find important applications in geo-textiles as well.

REFERENCES

[1]   Bledzki, AK; Zhang, W. [7] *J. Reinf. Plast. and Comp,* 2001, 20,14,2001.
[2]   Bueno, MA; Renner, M; Pac, MJ. [6], *J. Mater Sci,* 2002, 37, 2965-2974.
[3]   Butryn, TF. 36th International Sampe Symposium,[8] 1991, 15-18:546-55.
[4]   Hammond, VH; Loos, AC. [13] *J. Reinf. Plastics and Comp.* 1997, 161, 50-72.
[5]   Ishikawa, T; Chou, TW. [14] *J. Mater Sci,* 1982, 17 3211-19.
[6]   Joseph, K ; Varghese, S ; Kalaprasad, G ; Thomas, S; Prasannakumari, L ; Koshy P ; Pavithran C. [2] *Eur. polym,* 1996, J 32,10, 1243.
[7]   Li, Y ; Mai, YW ; Ye, L. [12] *Comp. Sci. and Tech,* 2000, 60, 2037.
[8]   Mukherjee, PS ; Satyanarayana, KG. [1] *J. Mater Sci,* 1984, 19, 3925-34
[9]   Naik, NK. [3]Woven fabric composites, Lancaster, PA: Technomic Publishing Co.,Inc, 1994.
[10]   Naik, NK ; Kuchibhotla, R. [5] *Composites.* Part A 2002, 33 697-708.
[11]   Oksman, K ; Wallstrom, L ; Berglund, LA ; Filho, RDT. [11] *J. Appl. Polym. Sci.* 2002, 84, pp2358-2365.
[12]   Pandita, SK; Falconet, D; Verpoest, I. [4] *Comp. Sci. and Tech,* 2002, 62, 1113-1123.
[13]   Patel, N; Rohatgi, V; Lee, L. *J. Polym. Compo,* [10] 1993, 14, 161-72.
[14]   Stover, D. *Adv. Compos.* March/April: [9] 1990, 60-80.

In: Textiles for Sustainable Development   ISBN: 978-1-60021-559-9
Editors: R. Anandjiwala, L. Hunter et al., pp. 311-317   © 2007 Nova Science Publishers, Inc.

Chapter 27

TRENDS AND DEVELOPMENTS OF THE WORLDWIDE TEXTILE INDUSTRY

Lutz Trützschler

Trützschler GmbH and Co. KG – Duvenstr. 82-92,
D-41199 Moenchengladbach – GER; lutz.truetzschler@truetzschler.de

Textile Industry

Ladies and gentlemen: We all live with, and from, the textile industry. How significant is this industry really today? The textile and clothing industry is one of the most important global employers and is of enormous economic importance for many national economies. Only tourism employs more people. Other industries, such as the car manufacturing industry, iron and steel or information technology, clearly rank in their importance behind the textile and clothing industry.

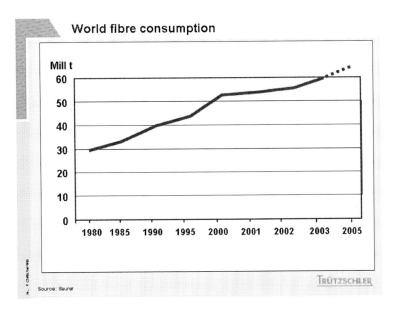

Source: Saurer

Worldwide textile consumption steadily increases between 2 and 3.5 % every year. This growth is generated almost automatically through the growth of the world population and increasing per capita consumption. Individual branches, such as web and technical textiles, even achieve two-digit growth rates.

On the other hand, hardly any other industry has had to endure such extreme structural changes like the textile industry. 40 years ago, Europe was still the main producer of textiles and clothing, today, however, it has slipped into niche market applications. Only specialists have survived.

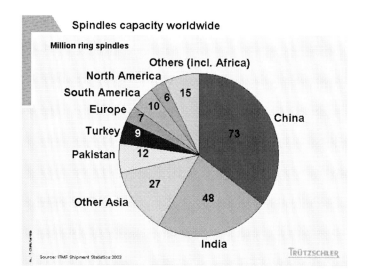

The Asian countries are the main producers today, primarily China, India, Pakistan and Turkey. We, Trützschler, specialize in machinery for the short-staple spinning mill. 2/3 of the worldwide spindle capacity is located today in just two countries, China and India.

What is the situation like here in South Africa? The South African textile and clothing industry has a long tradition. It is still one of the large employers and tax payers in the country today. Around 4% of the Gross National Product is earned in this sector.

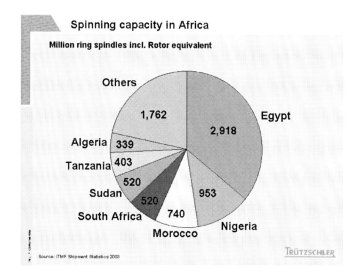

South Africa today represents the fourth largest spinning capacity on the continent. Only Egypt, Nigeria and Morocco are ahead of South Africa. South Africa, however, is able to demonstrate clear advantages compared with the three competing countries. The political and economic stability is far greater than in Nigeria and the level of modernization and thus efficiency of the production installations, far better than in Egypt and Morocco.

In this case, please consider that a high spindle capacity does not mean that they also produce. Looking at the fiber consumption in Africa gives as a completely different picture.

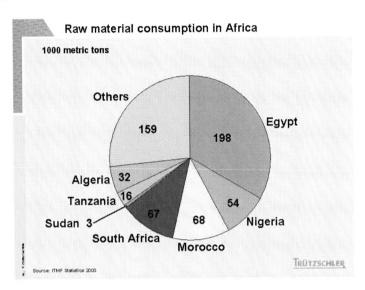

Raw material consumption in Africa

1000 metric tons

Others 159 — Egypt 198 — Nigeria 54 — Morocco 68 — South Africa 67 — Sudan 3 — Tanzania 16 — Algeria 32

Source: ITMF Statistics 2003

South Africa processes ca. 67 000 t fibers per year. They consist of ca. 77% cotton and 23% synthetic fibers. This puts South Africa, together with Morocco, in second place.

Spinning capacities less than 10 years old

	Ring spindles	OE Rotors
South Africa	43%	70%
Egypt	4%	5%
Morocco	7%	11%
Nigeria	3%	33%
Sudan	<1%	3%

Source: ITMF Shipment Statistics 2003

The discrepancy between spindle number and fiber consumption becomes clear when we look at the degree of machinery modernization.

Of today's spinning capacity, 43% of the ring spindles and 70% of the rotors are no older than 10 years. No other country in Africa comes even close to such a consequent modernization during the last 10 years. In Egypt, for instance, only 4% of the spindles are no older than 10 years, in Morocco less than 7%, and in Nigeria only 3%.

Just like the European countries or the USA, South Africa must find its way for the future. The structural changes have of course not passed the country by without leaving traces.

And thanks to the CSIR there are excellently trained experts in the country as well as strong application-specific research and development. This is a further plus with regard to the future of the country's textile and clothing industry.

However, the textile and clothing industry now has to tackle two major problems:

1. The rand is extremely strong against the US dollar and probably also over-valued. This makes export difficult.
2. More and more cheap textiles from China are penetrating the South African market.

In spite of this, South Africa could, from 1999 to 2002, increase textile exports by 73% and clothing exports by 160%. This positive development was, however, not continued in 2003 and 2004.

I see the chances for the textile industry in South Africa in a relatively strong home market, in high flexibility and specialization of trade, in well-trained technicians and specific market know-how for export into other African states.

The price pressure from the strong rand and cheap imports from China, however, forces the South African textile industry to make further rationalizations and cost reductions in production. State-of-the-art textile machines and new technologies can make a contribution in this respect.

And now we, the suppliers of these machines and technologies, come into play. Ladies and gentlemen, before I talk about our working relationship with the CSIR, please allow me to briefly introduce the company Trützschler:

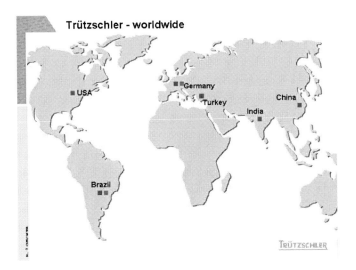

We are an internationally operating family business specializing in the development and manufacture of spinning preparation machinery. Today we are the global market leader in this field. We employ approx. 2300 people at 8 locations.

The roots of the company and the current head offices are in Mönchengladbach in Germany.

We primarily produce machines for fiber preparation in the short-staple spinning mill. These are blowrooms, cards and draw frames. In addition there are fiber preparation installations for web production and the development and production of card clothings. However, we also cover small niche markets such as e.g. tampon or cotton bud production as well as the production of medical products and cosmetic items with our product range.

But please now allow me to talk about the current events. Several weeks ago we were able to install here at our hosts today, the CSIR, an installation for development and training.

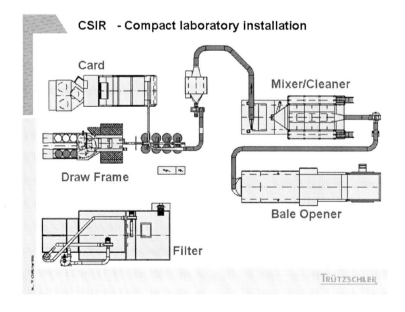

This is a typical laboratory installation. It comprises a bale opener, a combination of mixer and cleaner, a high-production card and a draw frame. A modern filter installation provides efficient dedusting of the material and keeps the ambient air clean.

The laboratory installation is suitable for processing all short-staple materials. The spectrum ranges from cotton through to manmade fibers, right up to hemp, sisal and flax. It is the processing of the last-mentioned fibers in particular, naturally in shortened form and in blends with cotton or manmade fibers, which is the immediate application area of this installation.

Before we could plan this laboratory installation in line with requirements, we carried out extensive trials together with specialists from this institute in our Technical Centre in Germany.

I am convinced that this laboratory installation will be another small building block for the successful future of the CSIR in research and teaching.

To conclude, I would like to congratulate the organizers on the excellent execution of this event. I am sure that it is also a building block for the successful textile future in South Africa.

ACKNOWLEDGEMENTS

Ladies and gentlemen, thank you very much for your attention.

My special thanks go to Dr. Rajesh Anandjiwala, who encouraged me to make this presentation. I have enjoyed both business relationships and personal friendships alike with this, your country, over decades. My regular trips to South Africa are always one of the pleasant aspects of my work in the worldwide markets.

In: Textiles for Sustainable Development   ISBN: 978-1-60021-559-9
Editors: R. Anandjiwala, L. Hunter et al., pp. 319-335 © 2007 Nova Science Publishers, Inc.

Chapter 28

INFLUENCE OF FABRICS CONSTRUCTION, LIGNIN CONTENT AND OTHER FACTORS ON UV BLOCKING

Malgorzata Zimniewska, Ryszard Kozlowski, Jolanta Batog, Justyna Biskupska and Anna Kicinska

Institute of Natural s(INF), Wojska Polskiego 71b, 60 – 630 Poznan, Poland;
gosiaz@inf.poznan.pl, sekretar@inf.poznan.pl

ABSTRACT

Ultraviolet (UV) radiation can cause erythema, sun allergies, faster skin ageing and skin cancers, especially melanoma, which is caused by damage to the chromosomes in the cells of the body. That is why there is a need for efficient protection against harmful UV radiation. And this should be an aim of the textile designer's activities to produce apparels with a high Sun Protection Factor (SPF). This can be achieved with apparel from bast fibers, such as linen and hemp, which also provide excellent comfort due to their high hygroscopicity, air permeability and other factors. The natural fibers, such as hemp and flax, contain in their chemical structure the natural pigment known as lignin, which is a natural UV absorber and ensures good sun protection. A study on the application of lignin, as UV blockers for fabrics, was conducted at the INF. The research has shown that changes in the level of lignin cause large changes in the UV protection properties of the linen fabrics. This paper also describes the influence of fabric structure, density, porosity, weight, surface mass, degree of interlacing and kind of weave on the level of UV protection. Different kinds of dyes applied to fabrics also play a very important role in ensuring good UV blocking. For example, some reactive, direct and VAT dyestuffs are characterized as good UV absorbers.

Keywords: UV protection, fabric, UV absorbers, sun protection factor, natural fibers, lignin.

INTRODUCTION

Ultraviolet rays are electromagnetic rays with wavelength longer than soft X-rays and shorter than visible rays as shown in figure 1. Of all the light projected onto the earth by the sun only 47% reaches the earth's surface,. It means that 34% beingis reflected by the atmosphere and 19% is absorbed. The amount of ultraviolet rays reaching the surface varies depending upon the season and time, weather conditions and geographical location.

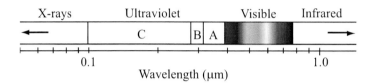

Figure 1. Electromagnetic radiation.

Electromagnetic radiation exists in a range of wavelengths, which are delineated into major divisions for our convenience. Ultraviolet B radiation, which is harmful to living organisms represents a small portion of the spectrum, from 280 to 320 nanometer wavelengths as illustrated by Robert Simmon [4].

There are three categories of UV radiation:

- UV-A, between 320 and 400 nm
- UV-B, between 280 and 320 nm
- UV-C, between 100 and 280 nm

UV

UVA	UVB	UVC
400-320 nm	320-280 nm	280-100 nm
max: represents 98.8% of UV reaching the earth	max: represents 1.1% of UV reaching on the earth	Almost zero UVC reaches the earth
Can penetrate ozone layer	Mostly absorbed by ozone in stratosphere, but it is increased by damage to the ozone layer	Absorbed by ozone at high altitude
Penetrates indoors through windows. Sunlamps and salon UV lamps use UV-A	Harm to the human body is more obvious	

Some of the dangerous radiation removed in the stratosphere is absorbed by the O_2 molecules there. Radiant energy wavelengths (λ) must be shorter than 242 nm to have enough energy to break the O-O bond, and UV-C radiation falls within this range.

UV with $\lambda < 242$ nm

$$O_2(g) \longrightarrow 2O(g) \hspace{3cm} (1)$$

UV radiation can also provide the energy to break the bond between oxygen atoms in ozone (O_3) molecules. Because less energy is needed to break a bond in the O_3 molecule than to break the bond in the O_2 molecule, the UV photons which break the bond in O_3 are associated with longer wavelengths. The O_3 molecules will absorb UV radiation of wavelengths from 240 nm to 320 nm.

UV with λ from 240-320 nm
$$O_3(g) \longrightarrow O(g) + O_2(g) \tag{2}$$

Thus, oxygen molecules (O_2) and ozone molecules (O_3) work together to absorb high-energy UV radiation. O_2 molecules absorb UV radiation with wavelengths less than 242 nm, and O_3 molecules absorb radiant energy with wavelengths from 240 nm to 320 nm. Wavelengths between 240 to 320 nm can cause problems, including skin aging, skin cancer and crop failure. Because O_2 does not remove this radiation from the atmosphere, it is extremely important that the ozone layer be preserved.

In recent years the process of ozone layer protection has been disturbed. Large emissions of chlorides into the atmosphere are caused by freon produced by mankind, volcanoes eruptions and forests fire, as well as evaporation from the oceans. Releasing one oxygen radical from an ozone molecule, chloride combines with ozone to create oxygen molecules. By this reaction, the ozone layer is becoming thinner and more ultraviolet rays reach the earth surface, passing through the so created "ozone hole".

The Skin

A certain level of ultraviolet radiation is needed for proper human existence and life on the earth. The UV rays synthesize vitamin D (which prevents rickets). People use UV radiation for sterilization and disinfection. An appropriate amount of sunbathing promotes circulation of blood, invigorates metabolism and improves resistance to various pathogenic bacteria.

However, it is important to sunbathe wisely. Both the UV-A and UV-B rays can cause stable changes to the skin. Packed with energy, UV-B rays are responsible for the lovely and nice suntan so sought after. That is why they are often called "leisure" ultraviolet rays. But these rays are also responsible for burning red - a degradation of fibers in the dermis. When destroying chromosomes, these rays can also cause skin cancer. The UV-B rays, with its high energy, do not penetrate skin as well as UV-A rays do. The latter penetrate easily and that is why they cause damage, before it is realized. We are exposed to such rays almost constantly as they penetrate through clouds and glass. The changes in the skin are irreversible with no possibility of noticing the exposure.

When the human skin is exposed to ultraviolet rays, a biosynthesis of melanin occurs. Melanin is a brown or black pigment, which protects the skin and body from the negative influence of intensive sun irradiation. The melanin pigments filter the ultraviolet rays of the sunlight and thus prevent damages to the deeper skin layers. But these dark pigments do not reduce UV rays completely.

Radiation of shorter wavelengths, namely 290-320 nm, designated as UV-B, causes damage at the molecular level to the fundamental building block of life— deoxyribonucleic acid (DNA).

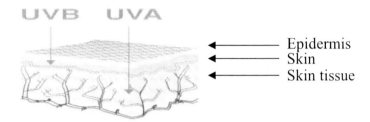

Figure 2. Ultraviolet rays effect on skin.

DNA readily absorbs UV-B radiation, which commonly changes the shape of the molecule in one of several ways. The illustration below shows one such change in the shape due to exposure to UV-B radiation. Changes in the DNA molecule often mean that protein-building enzymes cannot "read" the DNA code at that point on the molecule [4]. As a result, distorted proteins can be created, or cells can die.

UV Index

The UV index means the maximum expected level of the half-hour UV radiation dose reaching the earth's surface between 11.00 a.m. and 2.00 p.m., depending upon the conditions of the weather and ozone layer.

The UV index is a measurement of the amount of skin damaging UV radiation that is reaching the earth's surface. It ranges from 0 (at night) to 15 or 16 (in the tropics at high elevations under clear skies). The higher the UV index, the greater the dose rate of skin and eye damaging UV radiation. Values reaching 9 – 12 UV index values signifies the need for complete sun protection.

UV PROTECTION BY TEXTILES

The extent to which a woven or a knitted fabric transmits, absorbs, or reflects UV radiation determines its sun protection properties. The transmission, absorption and reflection are in turn dependent on the fiber, fabric construction (thickness and porosity) and finish [5]. The barrier or protection factor of flat textile products against the ultraviolet radiation is described according to international standards: British Standard [2] and Australian Standard [1].

Table 1. UV Index and Sun Protection Reference

UV index	Exposure Risk	Sun bathing limit	Protection method
0~2	Light		Cap or umbrella
3~4	Low		Cap or umbrella
5~6	Moderate	30minutes	Cap or umbrella Sun block Sunglasses Stay in a cool place
7~9	Excessive	20minutes	Cap or umbrella Sun block Sunglasses Stay in a cool place Long sleeve clothes Stay indoors from 10:00am to 2:00pm
10~15	Dangerous	15minutes	Cap or umbrella Sun block Sunglasses Stay in a cool place **Long sleeve clothes** Stay indoors from 10:00am to 2:00pm

Table 2. UPF Classification System

Range of UV protection	UPF	Ranking of UV protection	UV reduction [%]	UV transmittance [%]
15 – 24	15, 20	Good	93.3 – 95.9	6.7 – 4.2
25 – 29	25, 30, 35	Very good	96 – 97.4	4.1 – 2.6
40 – 50, 50+	40, 45, 50, 50+	Excellent	97.5 and more	Less than 2.5

The standard prescribes a method to test for UV radiation transmittance (%) through a dry textile product. Closely associated with this is the index of reduction of the ultraviolet radiation.

UV transmittance [%] = 100% - reduction [%]

The value of the transmittance factor gives direct information as to what percentage of UV radiation reaches the skin through the clothing. The relationship between the percent reduction of UV radiation and the UPF for a given clothing fabric is shown in figure 3.

This relationship is non-linear. Till the value of UPF reaches 15, the reduction in radiation increases rapidly, then it slows down and becomes insignificant at higher UPF values. Thus, for instance, doubling the UPF from 20 to 40, will not double the reduction in radiation, which impact only changes from 95% to 97%. It is, therefore, assumed that a clothing fabric with an UPF of 15 provides sufficient protection to the skin of the wearer.

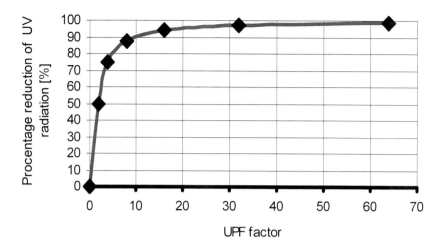

Figure 3. Relationship between percent reduction of UV radiation and UPF [7]. Source: "Sun protection by numbers.more or less" Robin Marks, University of Melbourne, Australia.

The following factors determine the effectiveness of garments in reducing the UV:

Fiber Properties

Among the natural fibers, hemp, flax and grey cotton show good protection against UVR as their natural pigments, lignin, waxes and pectins act as UV absorbers. The horizontal cut section of hemp fibers is in the shapes of irregular triangle, polygon and irregular circle. The molecular structure is loose, with more prism and whorl. Hence products made from hemp rs are able to dissipate sound waves and optical waves. The inspection report of the Physical Institute of the China Academy of Science reported proved that moderate hemp cloth can stop 95% ultraviolet rays. In comparison, scoured and bleached cotton offer poor protection. Wool provides maximum protection, while silk is intermediate between the two fibers [9]. Acrylic has a low UPF due to the dipole interactions of the nitrile group. The delustrant, TiO_2, modifies the reflection and absorption of the UV rays by the fiber, leading to increased scattering. Dull, pigmented viscose fibers (such as ENKA SUN by Akzo Nobel/Lenzing), for example, show lower transmittance (high absorption) than lustrous fibers.

Fabric Composition

Lightweight, loosely woven fabrics, which are normally preferred in hot outdoor situations, ironically provide minimum protection. The UPF improves as the weave becomes tighter and the fabric weight increases. The porosity and cover factor of the fabric have been shown to be the important factors in sun protection. Less UV passes through compact woven or knitted fabrics. As shown below, the smaller the spacing between the individual fiber strands the higher is the UV protection [8].

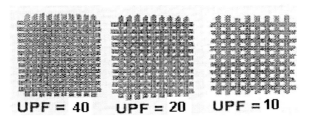

Figure 4. UPF for fabrics with different density.

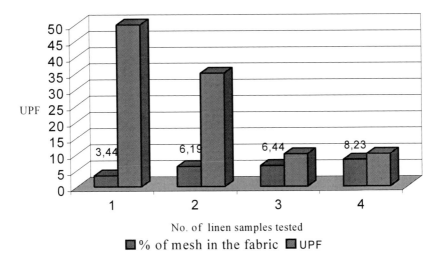

Figure 5. 'Mesh' size and UPF of 100% flax (linen) fabrics.

As shown in figure 5, linen fabrics with a low mesh percentage, i.e. fabrics with a compact construction and dense structure, provide excellent protection against the harmful ultraviolet radiation and their UPF is very high [10].

It is possible to improve the crease resistance and handle of flax and hemp fabrics by liquid ammonia treatment. The ammonia treatment imparts to these fabrics a pleasantly soft handle, makes them more resistant to creasing and easier to care for. The treatment with liquid ammonia (a two-step process) produces, among other things, a compacting of the fabric structure, of which a side effect is a significant improvement in the fabric's ultraviolet protection factor.

Figure 6a, 6b and 6c show the radiation passing through the same hemp fabric after successive stages of treatment [10].

Color: Many dyes absorb UV radiation. Darker colors of the same fabric type (black, navy, dark red) will usually absorb UV more strongly than light pastel shades and consequently will have a higher UPF rating.

The following table shows the effect of color on the UPF of some fabrics with identical weave and weights. This should be taken as a guide only, as specific fabrics may have different characteristics [8].

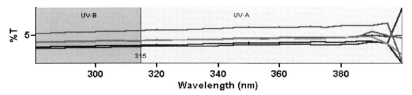

(a) Unfinished hemp fabric; UPF = 15, max penetration: 0.058

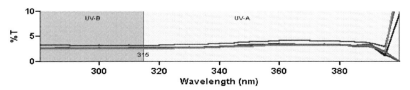

(b) Hemp fabric after ammonia treatment; UPF = 30; max penetration: 0.033

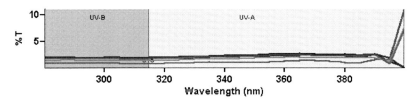

(c) Hemp fabric after final treatment; UPF = 50; max penetration: 0.0020

Figure 6. UV transmittance through hemp fabric [%].

Table 3. UPF of cotton and PES fabrics

Cotton	UPF	Polyester	UPF
White	12	White	16
Sky Blue	18	Light Green	19
Black	32	Dark Red	29
Navy	37	Black	34

Moisture content: Many fabrics have lower UPF ratings when wet. The drop in UPF rating depends on the type of fabric and the amount of moisture it absorbs when wet.

J. Neves studied the influence of degree of interlacement of dry and wet woven fabrics on the UV protection [6]. They tested fourteen different structures of 100% cotton fabric grouped into three main groups: plain, twill and satin, weaves. His results are illustrated in figures 7 to 9.

The satins offer better UV protection than than twills and these offer better protection than the plain weaves. The structures presenting the lower levels of protection are those with a lower average connection coefficient - ACC (Total of connecting or cross-over points in both warp and weft by the total number of connecting squares). "Z" structure among the plain weaves has a higher level of ACC and provides lower solar protection. Neves [6] explains that the more interwoven structures have more shrinkage areas (corresponding to the thread interlacing) which can create preferential interlacing channels of ultraviolet radiation.

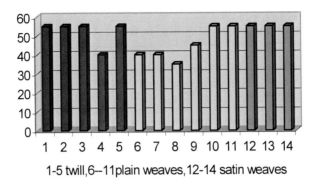

1-5 twill,6--11plain weaves,12-14 satin weaves

Figure 7. UPF of the dry undyed structures.

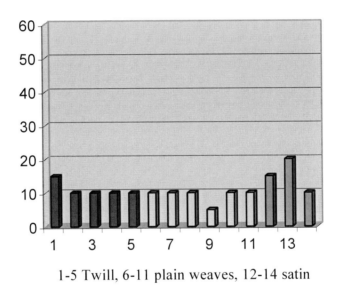

1-5 Twill, 6-11 plain weaves, 12-14 satin

Figure 8. UPF of wet (pick up of 132%) undyed structures.

Figure 9 shows a significant decrease in UPF for wet fabrics. Neves [6] pointed out that the degree of solar protection offered by dry fabrics increases after dyeing them to different colors (except white) and after optical brightening. Wet and dry fabrics in any color offer excellent UPF, when the percentage of dye is 1 or 3% [6].

Tension: Stretching a fabric may cause a decrease in the UPF rating. This is common in knitted or elasticized fabrics and care should be taken to select the correct size for the wearer.

Design: As well as considerations of fashion and comfort, selecting garments that are sensibly designed for sun protection can make a large difference to overall UV exposure. Garments that provide greater body coverage offer more protection. A shirt with long sleeves and a high collar offers more protection than a short sleeve shirt without a collar. Loose fitting garments give better protection than garments which are worn close to the skin and also may be more comfortable to wear on hot days. A legionnaire style cap with a flap protects the ears and back of the neck. A broad-brimmed hat shades the face and neck.

Condition: Unless otherwise stated, UPF ratings are performed on fabrics that are "new". The UPF rating of many cotton based fabrics can improve over their "new" rating after they have been washed at least once. Shrinkage in the fabric closes small gaps between the threads and allows less UV to pass through. However, old, threadbare or faded garments may have a lower UPF rating.

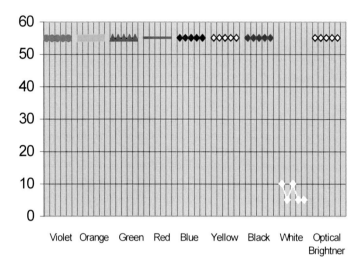

Figure 9a.UPF of dry twill fabrics - according to color.

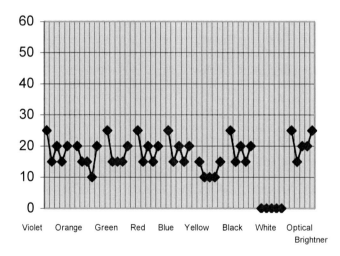

Figure 9b. UPF of wet twill fabrics – according to color.

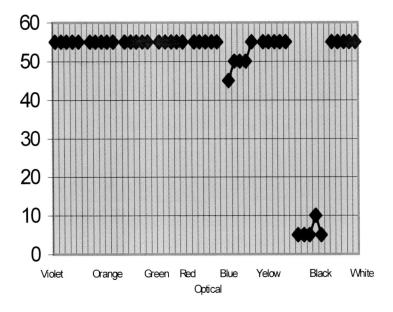

Figure 9c. UPF of dry plain weave fabrics – according to color.

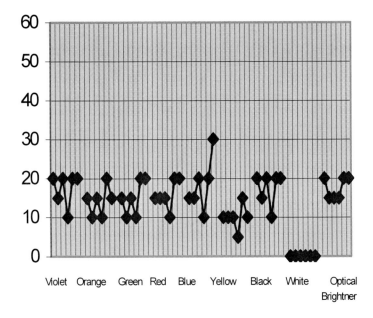

Figure 9d. UPF of wet plain weave fabrics - according to color.

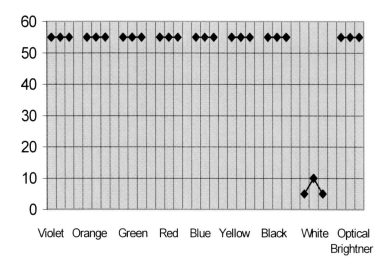

Figure 9e. UPF of dry satin fabrics – according to color.

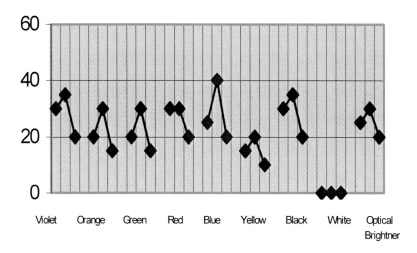

Figure 9f. UPF of wet satin fabrics - according to color.

There are two possibilities for reducing UV transmittance by fabrics - reducing the porosity through modification of construction or improving the absorption and reflection properties of the fabric.

FABRIC CHEMICAL PROCESSING

UV Absorbers

Some fabrics are treated to improve the UPF rating. This is usually done if the base fabric has a low natural resistance to UV. Treatment with a UV inhibitor, generally during manufacture, can result in a fabric with a higher UPF rating which still retains the comfort properties of the original fabric.

Many dyes absorb UV and therefore increase the UPF rating of the fabric. Some UV absorbers behave like colorless dyes. They bond to the fabric in a similar way, and have a permanency comparable to colored dyes. Recently there has been interest in adding UV absorbers to commercial washing powders.

Transmission through the fibers can be effectively reduced by the use of selected dyes, fluorescent whitening agents and by means of UV absorbers. These products have chromophoric systems which absorb very effectively in the UV region, enabling them to maximize the absorption of UV radiation on textiles. These key approaches are discussed further below.

Application of Dyes

As the spectral region of all dyes extends into the UV region (290-400nm), all dyes act as UV absorbers. Studies show that for a given color, the darker the shade, the higher is the protection [9]. In general, navy, black and olive shades would show a better protection. Some recent studies report an increase in the UV protection of cotton textiles, when dyed with selected direct, vat and reactive dyes. Figure 10 shows the structures of some such dyes. However, extensive research with dyes of different colors and structures only confirms that the UV absorbing capacity of each dye is unique and hence it is very difficult to generalize.

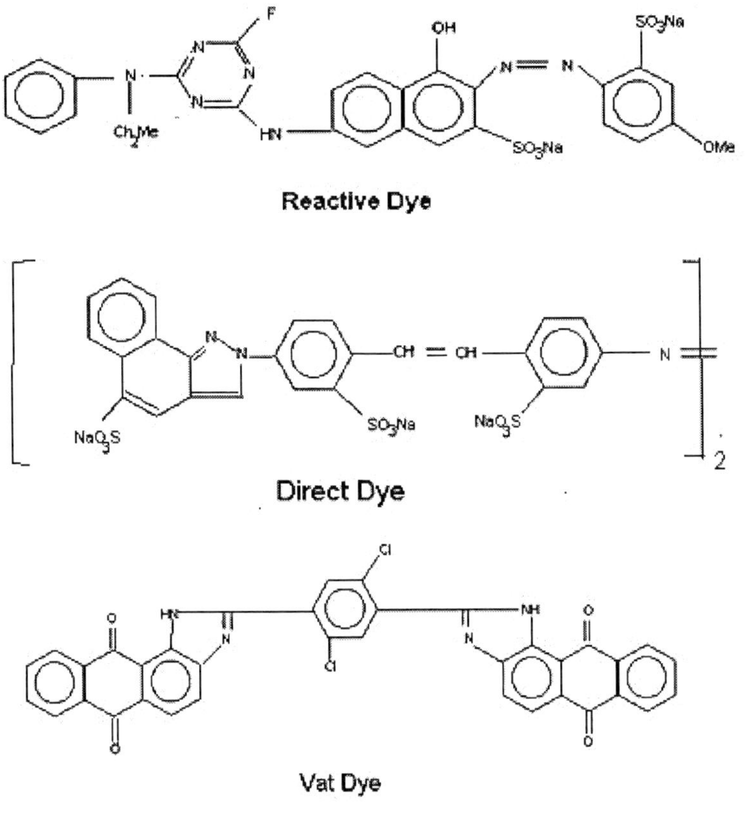

Reactive Dye

Direct Dye

Vat Dye

Figure 10. Structures of some dyes with good UV absorption.

Application of Fluorescent Whitening Agents (FWAs)

FWAs are applied to fabrics during laundering to enhance the ir whiteness by inducing fluorescence by UV excitation and visible blue emission. Most FWAs have excitation maxima in the range of 340-400 nm and hence have been known to improve the UPF of textiles. However, the efficiency of FWAs can be affected adversely by use of some UV blocking agents, depending on the respective absorption patterns of the two compounds.

In general, the improvement in UV absorption by FWAs is an interesting and positive contribution to UV protection by summer clothes, though in many cases it does not achieve the desired levels of protection.

Finishing with UV Absorbers

UV absorbers include all organic and inorganic compounds which preferentially absorb UV radiation [9]. These compounds have negligible absorption in the visible region and consequently have a high light fastness. UV absorbers have to be distributed mono-molecularly in the substrate for maximum effect. Besides, they should meet other criteria such as:

- absorb effectively throughout the UV region (280-400nm)
- be UV stable
- dissipate the absorbed energy in such a way so as to cause no degradation or color change in the medium they protect.

UV absorbers act on the substrate in several ways - by converting electronic excitation energy into thermal energy via a fast, reversible intermolecular proton transfer reaction; functioning as radical scavengers; and, functioning as singled oxygen quenchers.

Chemistry of UV Absorbers

All organic UV absorbers applied industrially to textile materials during wet processing are derivatives of one of the three structures given below [9]:

- o-hydroxybenzophenone
- o-hydroxyphenylbenzotriazole
- o-hydroxyphenyltriazine

Of the inorganic substances with UV absorbing characteristics, titanium dioxide deserves special mention for all common fibers except acrylics. UV absorbers are now available that are like colorless dyes and can be applied with dyes during most of the dyeing methods. Separate application procedures are not required. Care is needed only when they are applied with fluorescent whitening agents (FWAs). Australian researchers have worked out a finish technology that substantially increases the UPF of light garments. Clariant is marketing the technology under the name Rayosan. The dyer or finisher can apply the Rayosan process on yarn, knitwear or woven fabrics, using the traditional textile finishing processes and equipment. Products are available for use on cellulosics, polyamides and wool (with reactive dyes) and for PET and acetate fibers (with disperse dyes). These products reportedly, have no negative effect on the optical brighteners, as they do not absorb the UV required for the excitation of fluorescence. Ciba Geigy is marketing UV absorbers for different substrates under the brands Cibafast and Cibatex. These can also be applied to the fabric by either exhaust or pad batch method. Tinofast Cel is a new product capable of giving a UPF of 40+.

Non-reactive UV absorbers, based on oxalic anilides, triazine or triazol compounds, salicylic acid esters, substituted acrylonitrile or nitrilo-hydrazones, emulsifying agents, water and polysiloxanes, have also been reported.

Application of Polymeric Coatings

Lately, several Japanese companies have come out with specialized coatings for providing UV protection [9]. Ipposha Oil Industries of Japan has developed a homopolymer/copolymer based high molecular weight coating for imparting prolonged light resistance and UV screening to fabrics. Toyota RandD Laboratory has also used polymers to impart improved UV shielding and abrasion resistance properties to textiles. The process is based on dispersing organic alkoxy silanes, inorganic or organic salts or alkoxides of Ti, Mg, Al, Si etc, and inorganic or organic polar solvents followed by moulding. Toray Industries has developed an immersion technique for making antibacterial UV-blocking fabrics. A polyester fabric was immersed in ethanol containing 3% ferulic acid, dried and heated at $190^{\circ}C$ to give a fabric showing antibacterial activity against Streptococcus aureus and UV absorption of up to 98.5%.

INFLUENCE OF LIGNIN CONTENT ON UV BLOCKING

The natural fibers, such as hemp and flax, contain in their chemical composition the natural pigments, called lignin, which are natural UV absorbers and ensure good protection against UV. Hemp fibers have an additional ability to dissipate sound waves and optical waves thanks to special horizontal cut section shape - irregular triangle, polygon and lumbarcircle.Their molecular structure is loose and more prism and whorl like *(Inspection report of the Physical Institute of China Academy of Science).*

Lignin is a three-dimensional aromatic polymer with phenolic and alcoholic hydroxyl groups. Lignin, together with cellulose and hemicellulose, is the main structural polymer in the cell walls of higher plants. Lignin content of flax fibers is between 0.6 – 5.0 % and of hemp fibers between 3.5 – 5.5%. Some amount of lignin is removed from the fibers during the initial processes of fiber preparation.

Lignin is one of the most abundant, renewable natural products on earth and is produced as a by - product of the pulping process in tremendous quantities every year.

According to their chemical characteristics, commercially available lignin can be organized into three categories: lignosulphonates, Kraft lignin and sulphur-free lignin (organosol lignin, soda lignin, hydrolysis lignin, steam explosion lignin and oxygen delignification lignin).

Lignin have many traditional applications (binders, concrete plasticisers, dyestuff dispersants) and application in the areas of health and hygiene (animal feed, biostabilisers, cosmetics, nutraceuticals) [3].

Studies on new possibilities of using lignin as UV blockers for fabrics were conducted at the INF. Different kinds of lignin solutions were used for the tests:

- Solution of organosolv lignin – polymeric organosolv lignin material isolated from a commercial pulp mill using mixed hardwood. ‚Solution of hydrolytic lignin – polymeric autohydrolysis lignin material isolated from a commercial hydrolysis pilot plant using predominantly sugar bagasse.

The samples of linen fabrics contained different levels of lignin on their surface after being treated in lignin solutions.

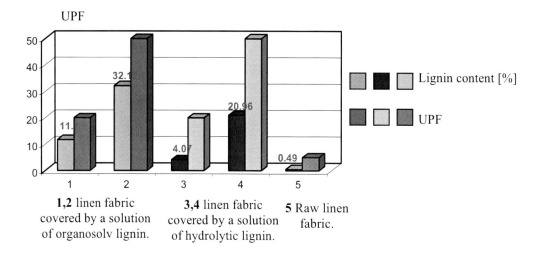

Figure 11. Levels of lLignin and UV protection for linen fabrics.

Tests of UPF for raw linen fabrics treated only by solvent, which were used for obtaining lignin solution, were also conducted. The tests were performed for checking if the use of solvent can influence UV blocking.

The UPF of linen fabric treated by both kinds of solvent: organosolv and hydrolytic was 0.

CONCLUSIONS

1. There are many ways of obtaining good UV protection by textiles, for example by careful selection of the fabric structure and construction, using UV absorbers, etc.
2. The application of lignin for UV protection appears to be a very good solution for UV problems. Lignin is a natural polymer and its application to textiles does not

decrease the hygienic properties of clothing which is important, particularly during summer.

3. Thanks to the use of lignin instead of chemical UV absorbers, makes it possible to reduce the use of chemicals during the finishing of textiles, thereby increasing environmental protection.

4. The next step in this study is the application of nano-structure lignins as UV blockers for fabrics. It is possible to obtain better physico-mechanical properties of linen fabrics by means of nano-structure lignin.

REFERENCES

[1]   Australian/ New Zealand Standard AS / *NZS* 399: 1996 Sun protective clothing – Evaluation and classification

[2]   British Standard BS7914: 1998 Method of test for penetration of erythemally weighted solar ultraviolet radiation through clothing fabrics

[3]   R.J.A. Gosselink; E. Jong, A. Abächerli; B. Guran, "Activities and Results of the Thematic Network Eurolignin"in 7th *International Lignin Institute Forum.* Barcelona Spain 2005, pp. 25-30

[4]   J. Allen; 2001 Ultraviolet Radiation: How it Affects Life on Earth www. earthobservatory.nasa.gog/Library/UVB/ September 6

[5]   J. Loy; the CEO of ARPANSA. Australian Radiation Protection and Nuclear Safety Agency (ARPANSA).

[6]   M. Neves; NEVES, "The influence of Interlacement Degree of Woven Fabrics on the Ultraviolet Protection Factor" in 3rd *AUTEX Conference*, 2003, Gdansk Poland

[7]   R. Marks Sun Protection By Numbers. More Or Less. *The Status Quo.*

[8]   Resource Guide for UVR Protective Products RMIT University www.arpansa.gov.au /uvrg/900.htm

[9]   D. Gupta Development in the Field of UV Protection of Textiles Department of Textile Technology Indian Institute of Technology. www.resil.com/articles/ articledevuvprot.htm

[10] M. Zimniewska, "Linen and Hemp Fabrics as a Natural Way of Sun Protection" in Proceedings of 2nd Global Workshop of the FAO European Cooperative Research Network on Flax and other Bast Plants. Bast Plants in the New Millennium. Borovets Bulgaria, 2001, pp. 332-341.

In: Textiles for Sustainable Development   ISBN: 978-1-60021-559-9
Editors: R. Anandjiwala, L. Hunter et al., pp. 337-347   © 2007 Nova Science Publishers, Inc.

Chapter 29

EFFECT OF CORONA TREATMENT ON FINISHING PROCESSES OF LINEN FABRICS

Malgorzata Zimniewska[1], Ryszard Kozlowski[1], Noémia Carneiro[2], António Souto[2], Romana Marszalek[1] and Eugeniusz Mazur[1]

[1] Institute of Natural s, Wojska Polskiego 71b,
60 – 630 Poznan, Poland; gosiaz@inf.poznan.pl, sekretar@inf.poznan.pl
[2] Universidade do Minho, TecMinho, Campus de Azurem
da Universidade do Minho, 4800-058 Guimarães,
Portugal; noemiac@det.uminho.pt

ABSTRACT

The application of Corona technology in the finishing processes of cellulosic fabric is an innovation in the European textile industry. A Corona discharge is created between two electrodes at high voltage and frequency of 20 – 40 kHz and affects the surface of a fabric running continuously in the discharge field at ambient pressure and temperature. This paper presents the newest results of research on the properties of linen fabrics before and after Corona treatment. Fabrics after Corona treatment have novel and better properties, also making finishing processes much easier. The quality of fabrics after Corona treatment can be improved in important aspects related to the safety of with users. The wettability of cellulosic fabrics improves significantly after Corona treatment. A new "in-line" step of Corona treatment in the finishing process allows the elimination of initial washing without a detrimental effect on the quality of the finished fabric, enabling good results to be obtained in bleaching and evenness of dyeing for some kinds of dyestuffs. Corona treatment provides better end-use properties at lower cost and with less harm to the environment.

Keywords: Corona discharge, linen fabrics, finishing process, quality of fabrics, bleaching, dyeing, end-use properties.

INTRODUCTION

A Corona discharge is created between two electrodes at high voltage and a frequency of 20 – 40 kHz. It affects the surface of a continuously running substrate at ambient pressure and temperature. For natural fibers, such as cotton and linen, superficial changes are sufficient to obtain good effects in textile finishing processing and on material properties. Some molecules on the surface of the material is changed when the material is treated by Corona discharge. Active groups, such as free radicals, are produced in the molecules [1].

After Corona treatment, the creation of channels for water penetration occurs, together with the oxidation of fatty matters — the mechanism responsible for a very rapid increase in hydrophilicity. This fact is decisive in wet finishing processes, including the desizing, alkaline treatment, bleaching, dyeing, printing and finishing of linen materials. The INF conducts studies on Ccorona technology applied to linen fabrics within the framework of European Project Cortex in cooperation with the University Minho, Portugal [1].

MATERIALS AND METHODS

A typical linen fabric, usually utilized for shirts, was used for the study. The mass of the fabric was 150 g/m^2 and densities of warp and weft were 210 and 192 threads per dm, respectively.

Conditions of Corona Treatment

- Number of passages: 3+3=6
- Velocity: 2.44m/min
- Power of discharge: 1510 watt
- Width of treatment: 0.5 m
- Corona dosage= 6x 1510/2.44x0.5 = 7388 W.min/m^2

The first Corona treatment applied to the linen fabrics under laboratory conditions did not give satisfactory results. The increase in the absorption ability of the fabrics caused by the Corona treatment did not ensure the expected savings in the bleaching and dyeing processes. Further trials were conducted under industrial conditions on a new prototype machine. The changes of treatment conditions, from the laboratory to the industrialtechnical, improved the process efficiency.

Properties of Linen Fabric Bbefore and Aafter Corona Treatment

Corona treatment applied to linen fabrics caused an improvement in their water sorption ability and hygroscopicity [2]. It is especially visible in the case of linen fabric treated under industrial conditions. The hygroscopicity was measured according to the Polish Standard PN-80/P-05635 and the rate of water sorption according to the Japanese Standard No. 59/L 1096-

199 (Ffigures 1 and 2). Bending stiffness of the tested fabric decreased after Corona treatment, particularly when using the industrial method. Apart from beneficial changes in the linen fabric properties, the Corona process can also cause some reduction in abrasion resistance. Nevertheless, when treated under the industrial conditions, the reduction is not as great as that obtained when treated by the laboratory method.

Polish Standards PN-73 / P-50101 and PN-EN 22313 were used for crease recovery and bending stiffness measurement, respectively [3].

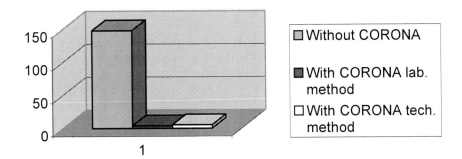

Figure 1. Rate of water absorption by Drop method [s].

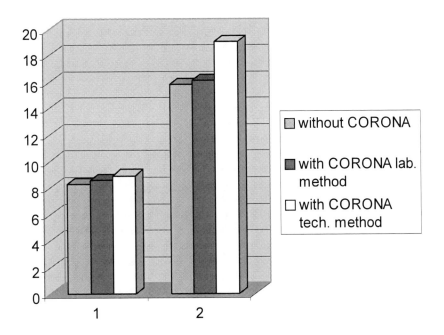

Figure 2. Hygroscopicity of fabric [%].

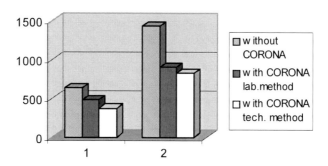

Figure 3. Bending stiffness [mg.cm].

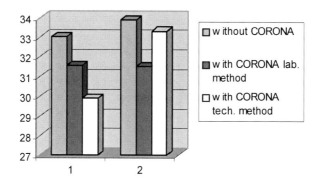

Figure 4. Crease recovery [%].

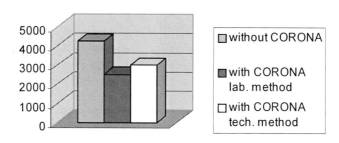

Figure 5. Abrasion resistance by the Martindale method [Number of cycles].

Effect of Corona Treatment on the Finishing Processes of Linen Fabrics

The properties of linen fabric treated by Corona under the industrialtechnical conditions appeared better than those of fabric treated under the laboratory conditions and were considered satisfactory. For this reason, only the technical industrial method was subsequently studied.

The linen fabric was twice used for finishing trials: firstly as a raw material and secondly after Corona treatment.

During the study, the grey linen fabric was prepared by alkaline boiling with the following contents in the bath:

Na_2CO_3	-2.5 g/dm^3
Sulfaton UNS	-2.0 cm^3/dm^3

Conditions of the process:

15 min.   60 min.
40 °C $\longrightarrow$ 80 °C $\longrightarrow$ 80 °C

Rinsing: hot, warm and cold water

The grey linen fabric, so prepared, was used for the finishing processes, such as bleaching, dyeing, printing and flame retardundancy, together with the same fabric treated with Corona.

Testing the Add on

The experiments were conducted using the Mathis two-roller horizontal padding machine. The wet samples were tested after padding twice. The add on is the ratio of the increase in sample weight after padding to the dry weight of the sample, expressed in %.

The temperatures of the bath were:

1. For bleaching - 25^{0}C,
2. For dyeing - 18^{0}C,

Table 1. Effect of Add on

	Kind of bath	Add On [%]
Raw linen fabric	Bleaching bath	96,8
Boiled linen fabric		97,2
Linen fabric after Corona treatment		117,4
Boiled linen fabric	Dyeing bath	62,9
Linen fabric after Corona treatment		64,0

The cold pad batch bleaching method, applied to the linen fabric prepared with and without Corona treatment, did not give satisfactory results. Nevertheless, interesting results in the case of dyeing, printing and flame retardundancy were obtained.

Dyeing with Reactive Dyes by Cold Pad-Batch Method

The dyeing experiments were conducted on desized and Corona treated fabric. The fabric was impregnated using the Mathis two-roller horizontal padding machine.

The bath temperature was 18 °C and the degree of padding 70%.

The dyeing bath chemicals were:

Remazol brillant blueu BB	-20 g/dm^3
Leonil SR	-2 g/dm^3
Urea	-50 g/dm^3
Water-glass	-110 g/dm^3
NaOH	-10 g/dm^3

After padding, the strips of fabrics were wound onto rollers wrapped with foil, and then conditioned for 24 hours. After this, the fabrics were rinsed in water according to the following sequence:

- Cold water
- Warm water 60^{0}C
- Hot water 90^{0}C
- Hot water 90^{0}C+ Locanit S 2 g/dm^3
- Warm water 60^{0}C
- Cold water.

When the fabrics were dried, the comparative calorimetric analysis was carried out using the photocolorimeter d/8-D65UV, working in the CIELAB mode. The colors of the desized (control) and Corona treated fabrics were measured.

The colorimetric analysis of the Corona-treated linen fabric showed significant differences compared to the desized fabric.

Printing with Pigments

The printing process was carried out using a laboratory flat film printer supplied by Zimmer. The prints were applied to both desized and Corona treated fabrics.

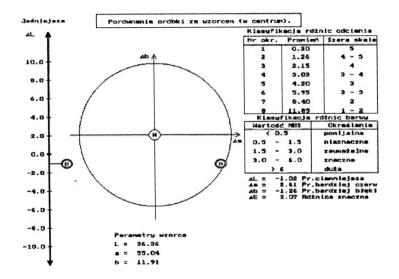

Figure 6. Comparison of color differences; Control– boiled fabric; Tested – fabric treated by Corona.

The composition of the printing paste was:

Poloprint ruby	- 10 g/kg
Mirox HP	- 40 g/kg
Binder ATB 9231	- 100 g/kg
Antispumin DNF	- 5 g/kg

After printing, the fabrics were dried, initially at room temperature and finally in a laboratory drier at 140°C for 5 min. It should be emphasized that the Corona-treated fabric showed good water absorption, resulting in a good printing effect.

Penetration and Uniformity of Reactive Printing

The following three samples of linen fabric were used for the reactive printing process:

- Fabric without treatment
- Fabric washed with wetting agent (ECE) for 30 minutes at the boil
- Fabric prepared by alkaline boiling, as mentioned above

Printing recipe:

Water:	717 g/kg
Lanitex S	16 g/kg
Lanitex L10	17 g/kg
Soda solvay	26 g/kg
Urea	150 g/kg
Ludigol	75 g/kg

Reactive dye – Procion Blue P3R

Conditions of the process:

Substrates (without treatment, washed, boiled)

↓

Corona treatment (with and without Corona treatment)

↓

Printing

↓

Fixation (150°C - 5 min.)

↓

Washing

Application of Paste for Lower Penetration	Application of Paste for Maximum Penetration
Speed -30m/min Number of Blade Passages: 1 Blade Pressure - 3 Bar	Speedy - 20 m/min Number of Blade Passages: 2 Maximum Blade Pressure - 6 Bar

SAMPLES:

- Without treatment (A) ⎰ Without Corona treatment / Corona (3+3)

- Washed (B) ⎰ Without Corona treatment / Corona (3+3)

- Boiled (C) ⎰ Without Corona treatment / Corona (3+3)

RESULTS

The penetration of printing paste was evaluated by means of reflectance measurements on the front and reverse sides of the printed fabric. The uniformity of printing was evaluated by means of the standard deviation of twenty reflectance measurements on the reverse side.

Lower penetration

Samples		Penetration Degree (%)		Uniformity St. Dev.
Without treatment A	Without Corona treatment	58,4	+ 7,7	6,5
	With Corona treatment	66,1		4
Washed B	Without Corona treatment	67,9	+ 17,7	7,7
	With Corona treatment	85,6		2,9
Boiled C	Without Corona treatment	65,8	+ 25,7	6
	With Corona treatment	91,5		3,8

For the boiled sample treated with Corona, the higher value of degree of penetration was obtained due to higher hydrophility of the substrate. All the samples showed better penetration of the printing paste when pre-treated with Corona treatment.

The uniformity on the reverse side of the printed fabric, determined by the standard deviation of reflectance data, was compared for each pair of printed samples A, B and C, with and without Corona discharge. In every case, uniformity on the reverse side of the fabric was higher for samples subjected to the Corona discharge.

Maximum penetration

Samples		Penetration (%)
Without treatment A	Without Corona treatment	99,23
	With Ccorona treatment	100,0
Washed B	Without Corona treatment	97,32
	With Corona treatment	98,00
Boiled C	Without Corona treatment	97,34
	With Corona treatment	97,28

Flame Retardant Treatment and Flammability Test

The following four types of linen fabric were prepared for the test:

- raw linen fabric
- raw linen fabric treated with Fobos M2T- a polycondensation product based on urea polyborates and polyphosphates
- boiled linen fabric treated with Fobos M2T
- prepared with Corona and treated with Fobos M2T

Flame retardant treatment:
The samples of fabrics were treated in an aqueous solution of Fobos M-2T at a temperature of 40°C. The samples were dried and conditioned.

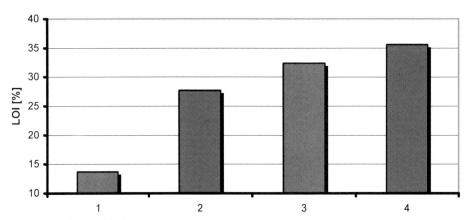

1. raw linen fabric
2. raw linen fabric treated with Fobos M2T
3. boiled linen fabric treated with Fobos M2T
4. Corona linen fabric treated by Fobos M2T

Figure 7. Oxygen Index (LOI) of linen fabric.

The flammability tests (LOI method) were performed limiting the LOI method according to the ISO 4589 standard. The flammability tests were performed on untreated and Corona treated fabrics. Flammability tests were also performed for samples after immersion in a water bath at 40°C.

CONCLUSION

*   The trials on the degree of aAdd oOn showed that the absorption of the linen fabric after Corona treatment is the highest in comparison to raw and desized fabrics, also in the case of bleaching and dyeing.
*   The colorimetric analysis of the Corona treated fabric showed considerable differences relating to the desized fabric.
*   The color uniformity of dyed fabric, with and without Corona treatment, is similar. It can be concluded, that it is possible to replace the boiling / desizing process by the Corona treatment.
*   The printed Corona treated fabric showed good water absorption which results in good printing of the paste, particularly in the case of pigment printing. However, testing prints for resistance to wet abrasion showed that the prints on Corona treated fabric are 0.5 degrees less resistant.
*   Results of flammability tests showed that the efficiency of the flame retardant treatment applied to linen fabric prepared with Corona is better than that for the linen fabric subjected to boiling. It means that there is a possibility to replace boiling with Corona treatment as a preparatory process for linen fabric.

- For the reactive printed fabric, the differences in penetration and uniformity for the prepared (washed and boiled) samples are very evident. These were obtained using printing conditions to achieve the maximum penetration effect (higher blade pressure, lower speed). Corona discharge contributes to the improvement in penetration and uniform printing on the reverse side of the printed fabrics.

REFERENCE

[1]   Report of CORTEX GROWTH PROJECT of 5th EU Framework Programme. 2005. *Corona Irradiation in Textile Finishing*

[2]   Kozlowski, R; Zimniewska, M; Carneiro, N; Souto, A; Mazur, E; Biskupska, J. Effect of Corona Treatment on Physical Properties of Linen Fabrics in Global Workshop of The FAO European Cooperative Research Network on Flax and Other Bast Plants: *Bast Fibrous Plants For Healthy Life,* 2004, Republika Srpska

[3]   Kozlowski, R; Zimniewska, M; Mazur, E; Biskupska, J. Modification of Linen fabrics by Corona Irradiation, 2004, II Simposio Sobre Fibras Naturales Aprovechamiento Integral Y Aplicaciones Textiles *FIBRATEX* Havana Cuba.

PART IV
APPLICATION OF NANOTECHNOLOGY

In: Textiles for Sustainable Development
ISBN: 978-1-60021-559-9
Editors: R. Anandjiwala, L. Hunter et al., pp. 351-356   © 2007 Nova Science Publishers, Inc.

Chapter 30

NANO-CELLULOSIC FIBERS, PREPARATION, PROPERTIES AND DIRECTIONS OF APPLICATION

Laszkiewicz Bogumil[*], *Kozlowski Ryszard*[*] *and Kulpinski Piotr*

* Institute of Natural Fibers, ul. Wojska Polskiego 71b,
60-630 Poznan, Poland; Technical University of Lodz,
ul. Zeromskiego 116, 90-543 Lodz, Poland;
blaszkie@mail.p.lodz.pl, sekretar@inf.poznan.pl

ABSTRACT

Cellulose fibers, non-woven fibers networks and cellulose membranes were obtained by means of the electrospinning process. The diameters of the fibers were in the sub-micron range. To obtain the spinning dope, cellulose was dissolved in an N-methylmorpholine-N-oxide/water system. Cellulose solutions, containing 2% of the polymer, were electrospun onto the grounded coagulation bath.

Keywords: nanofibers, cellulose, electrospinning.

INTRODUCTION

Electrospinning has been recognized as an efficient technique for the preparation of polymeric nanofibers. In recent years, more than one hundred polymers and copolymers have been successfully applied for the preparation of nanofibers. Most of the polymers were electrospun from a solvent solution [1] but only a few were spun from molten polymers [2]. To obtain the nanofibers by electrospinning, from a polymer solution, a solvent that is sufficiently polar and volatile must be applied. In addition there are still some important factors, such as molecular weight of polymer, polymer concentration, applied voltage, surface tension of polymer solution, and its electric conductivity, which are crucial to the process of fiber formation [3, 4]. The process of electrospinning for natural polymers appears to be even more complicated. Concerning, for example, the cellulose properties, there are several efficient solvent systems [5,6,7], but only a few could be successfully used for the electrospinning process [8,9]. For more than a decade, the Department of Man-Made Fibers of the Technical University of Lodz, in cooperation with the Institute of Natural Fibers, has carried out studies on the preparation of cellulose fibers using a direct solvent, such as N-methylmorpholine-N-oxide (NMMO) [10, 11, 12]. This excellent solvent can be used, not only for producing standard cellulose fibers but also can be successfully applied for obtaining the cellulose nanofibers. Although the electrospinning of cellulose nanofibers is not very difficult, the fact that NMMO is not volatile which creates some problems related to the coagulation process or the collection of the fibers which should be solved.

MATERIALS AND EQUIPMENT

The cellulose solutions were prepared mainly from the spruce cellulose, with the following characteristics:

α-cellulose	93.40%	Fe	3.0mg/kg
Ash	0.11%	Moisture	7.3%
Resins and fats	0.13%	Viscosity	23.6cP
DP	534		

In order to get more details about the cellulose used, the polydispersity of molecular weight was determined by gel chromatography and FTIR spectra were generated.

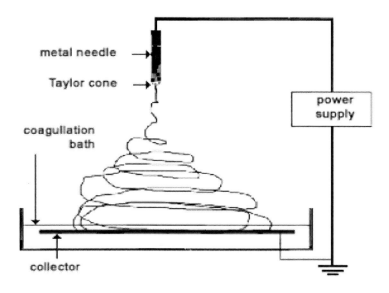

Figure 1. Scheme of the apparatus for electrospinning of cellulose nanofibers.

The preparation of the spinning solution, i.e., the dissolution of cellulose in NMMO, was carried out at a temperature of 90-95°C for a period of time not exceeding 60min. As a solvent, 50% water solution of NMMO was used. The final concentration of the cellulose in the spinning dope was 2%. The process of electrospinning was carriedying out on the apparatus shown in figure 1. The spinning solution obtained by the above mentioned method was delivered to the electrospinning zone by a metal needle heated to about 105°C. During the spinning process, the electrical potential difference between the surface of the spinning solution drop and the collector was around 10 kV. The distance between the metal needle and the surface of the collector was about 13cm.

As a collector of the fibers, the surface of the liquid coagulation bath was used.

RESULTS

The electrospinning process of fibers, from the polymers dissolved in the volatile solvent systems, is relatively simple as a result of one very important fact, namely the solvent evaporates during the formation of the fibers, hence so the solidified fibers can be directly collected from the spinning zone. Because NMMO is not volatile, the collection of the spinning jet, still containing solvent, leads to obtaining a membrane like product being obtained rather than fibers. To solve the problem of the coagulation of the spinning jet, a surface of water as the collector was utilizedapplied. Based on the experiments, the composition of the coagulation bath is one of the main factors, which have a great influence on the shape of the final product. Changing the parameters of the coagulation bath makes it possible to obtain products in different forms i.e. fibers, films or nonwovens.

When the process of collecting the spinning jet was carried out on the surface of water, the solidification was relatively slow and a thin film was obtained (figure 2). This appeared to be caused by two factors, namely the quite high water surface tension and the rate of spraying of the new layers of jet spinning solution. It appears that the rate of the removal of NMMO from the jet lying on the surface of the water is relatively slow, which contrasts with the relatively fast process of spraying the new layer on to the bath surface. This results in the deformations of the fibers and their sticking together.

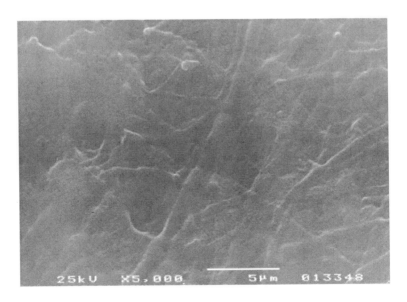

Figure 2. Cellulose film obtained by the electrospinning process.

Changing the properties of the coagulation bath, by the introduction of a surfactant or by using a different liquid (methanol etc), results in the lowering of the surface tension and increasing the rate of removal of NMMO from the jet. In this case, fewer fibers stick together (figure 3).

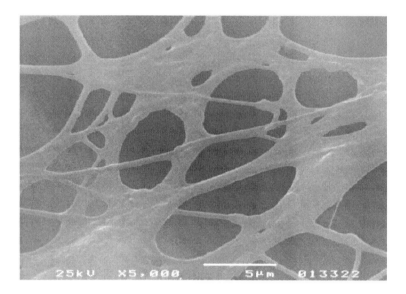

Figure 3. Cellulose nanofibers formed on the surface of the coagulation bath with a lower surface tension.

Concerning nanofibers, the best results were achieved when the movement of the surface of the coagulation bath was continuous. In this case, the jets of the spinning solution were continuously removed from the spinning zone. Movement of the liquid surface prevents the jets from sticking together and results in single nanofibers having a diameter between 150 – 350nm (figure 4).

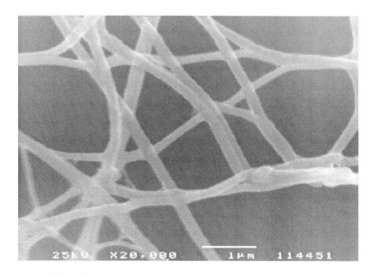

Figure 4. Cellulose nanofibers formed on the moving surface of the coagulation bath.

Using the electrospinnig method, it is also possible to spread the cellulose nanofibers on a commercially available textile fabric (figure 5).

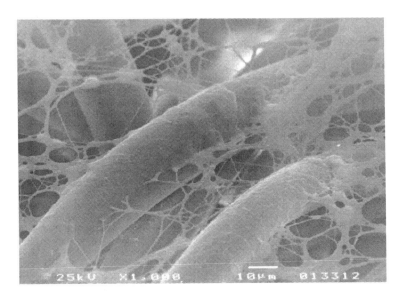

Figure 5. Cellulose nanofibers spread on the a fabric.

Due to the high flexibility of the NMMO process and the relative simplicity of preparing a homogenous solution and also the good quality of the fibers obtained by the NMMO method, there are vast possibilities for modifying the mixture composition and conditions of dissolution. It is also possible to obtain spinning solutions and fibers having a high content of nanomodifiers.

CONCLUSION

1. The NMMO method makes it possible to obtain a homogenous cellulose solution.
2. A cellulose solution in NMMO containing 2% of polymer is suitable for the electrospinning process.
3. The apparatus for obtaining cellulose nanofibers is relatively simple.
4. The parameters of the electrospinning process can be changed within a wide range to obtain the desired properties and morphology of the nanofibers.
5. The diameters of the cellulose nanofibers, obtained by means of electrospinning, arefall within the range of 150 and 350nm.

REFERENCES

[1]   Huang, Z-M.; Zhang. Y.-Z.; Kotaki, M.; Ramakrishna, S. *Composites Science and Technology*. 2003, 63, 2223-2253.
[2]   Larrondo, L.; Manley, R. ST J. *J. Polymer Science: Polymer Physics Edition.* 1981,19,909-20.

[3]   Shin, Y. M.; Hohman, M. M.; Brenner, M. P.; Rutledeg, G. C. *Polymer.* 2001, 42, 9955-9967.

[4]   Demir, M. M.; Yilgor, I.; Yilgor, E.; Erman, B. *Polymer.* 2002, 43, 3303-3309.

[5]   Turbak, A. F.; Hammer, R. B.; Davies, R. E.; Partnoy, N. A. *ACS Symposium Series.* 1977, 58, 12.

[6]   Phillip, B.; Schleicher, H.; Wagenknecht, W. *ACS Symposium Series.* 1977, 48, 278.

[7]   Rogovin, Z. A.; Galbrajch, *L. S. Faserforsch. Textiltech.* 1977, 28, 1.

[8]   Frey, M.F.; Song H. 225th ACS National Meeting, New Orleans, 2003.

[9]   Liu, H.; Hsieh, Y-L. *J. Textile Apparel*, Technol Manage 2001, vol. 1. Special issue: The Fiber Society Spring 2001 Conference, Raleigh NC.

[10]   Laszkiewicz, B. Manufacture of cellulose fibers without carbon disulphide, Lodz 1997, monograph in Polish.

[11]   Laszkiewicz, B.; Kowalewski, T.; Kulpinski, P.; Niekraszewicz, B.; Czarnecki, P.; Rubacha, M.; Peczek, B.; Jedrzejczak, *J. Polish Appl.* Pat. No. P-362101 (2003).

[12]   Kulpinski, P.; Laszkiewicz, B.; et al. *EP Appl. Pat.* No 04460033.6 (2004).

In: Textiles for Sustainable Development   ISBN: 978-1-60021-559-9
Editors: R. Anandjiwala, L. Hunter et al., pp. 357-362   © 2007 Nova Science Publishers, Inc.

Chapter 31

CONTINUOUS YARNS FROM ELECTROSPUN NANOFIBERS – RECENT DEVELOPMENTS

Eugene Smit, Ulrich Büttner and Ron D. Sanderson;

UNESCO Associated Centre for Macromolecules and Materials,
Department of Chemistry and Polymer Science,
Stellenbosch University, Private Bag X1,
Matieland 6702; asmit@sun.ac.za, rds@sun.ac.za

ABSTRACT

Electrospinning is a versatile, simple and cost-effective technique for making continuous nanofibers of various synthetic and natural polymers with many potential applications in fields such as high-performance filters, tissue engineering scaffolds, wound dressings, composite reinforcement and other smart and functional textiles. Until recently, electrospun fibers were typically obtained as non-woven webs. A break-through development in our laboratorys allowed the production of continuous yarns of electrospun nanofibers by electrospinning onto a liquid reservoir collector. In this paper, this technique for making continuous yarns from electrospun nanofibers and recent developments in nanofiber yarn research will be discussed.

Keywords: nanofiber, electrospinning, yarn.

INTRODUCTION

Electrospinning, a simple method for making continuous nanofibers of various natural and synthetic polymers, has been receiving increasing attention in recent years from researchers in the fields of nano- and biotechnology [1].

In this versatile method, high voltage (5-20 kV DC) is applied to a small droplet of polymer solution. The repulsive electrostatic forces between the molecules in solution lead to a micro-jet of polymer and solvent that shoots out of the droplet towards a grounded collector electrode. At a short distance from the droplet, jet instability sets in; this leads to a rapid whipping of the jet. This rapid whipping leads to evaporation of the solvent and the formation of a polymer fiber, which in turn stretches and thins to form micro- or nanofibers that collect on the grounded electrode in a randomly oriented non-woven web.

The potential application of electrospun nanofibers in tissue engineering scaffolds, wound dressings and high performance filter fabrics has also led to an increased interest from the textile science community. The biomimicking nature of porous nanofiber webs have been shown to lead to better cell adhesion in artificial tissue scaffolds [2], while the high specific surface area and controllable porosity of non-woven nanofibers webs lead to increased filtering efficiency [3].

Until recently, one of the main limitations of the electrospinning technique was that the fibers could only be obtained as randomly oriented non-woven webs, or relatively short tows of aligned fibers.

From a textiles production point of view, electrospun fibers ideally have to be obtained as uniaxially aligned fiber bundle yarns or continuous nanofilament yarns. This will allow the use of traditional textile techniques like weaving and knitting for large-scale production of nanofiber textiles. In addition, knitting and embroidery with nanofiber yarns will enable the production of complex 3-dimensional textile constructions for tissue engineering and other applications where fiber alignment and orientation play a significant role.

We recently reported a method for making continuous uniaxial fiber bundle yarns from electrospun fibers [4].

In this paper, we briefly review the process and then take a closer look at the hurdles that still need to be overcome in order to make a nanofiber yarn that can be used in standard textile production processes. We also discuss some of our most recent work in this direction.

REVIEW AND DISCUSSION

The Yarn Spinning Process

In this process, most of the standard electrospinning apparatus is used: a polymer solution is fed to the tip of a capillary, where a droplet forms, and a high voltage is applied to the solution.

Instead of electrospinning onto a solid, grounded collector electrode, the fibers are spun onto a grounded non-solvent bath. A non-woven web of fibers forms on the surface of the bath. When the web is drawn over and through the liquid, the fibers align in the drawing direction. The surface tension of the residual non-solvent on the fibers draw them together in a cylindrical yarn as it is lifted off the bath surface and collected onto a take-up roller. The process setup is illustrated in figure 1.

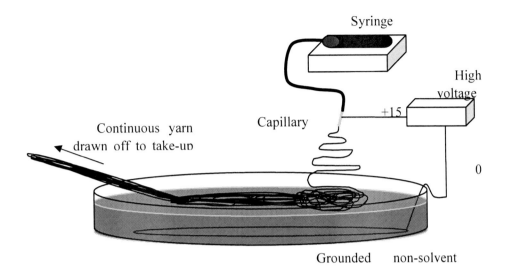

Figure 1. Continuous nanofiber yarn spinning setup.

Yarn Characteristics

The yarns obtained through this process exhibit high degree of fiber alignment, as can be seen from the SEM photographs in figure 2. The arrows in the photograph on the left point out bent loops of fibers that can be observed in all yarns made through this process.

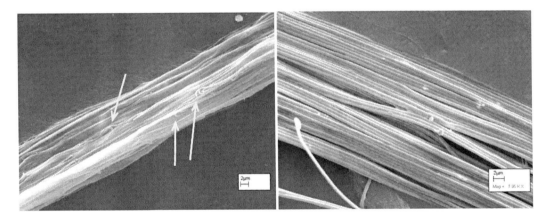

Figure 2. Yarns from electrospun nanofibers.

The bent loops of fibers are caused by the loops made by the electrospun fiber as it falls onto the non-solvent bath. As the fiber web is drawn across the liquid surface, the fiber loops get entangled and remain in the yarn. In essence, the yarn made through this process, using a single spinneret, consists of a single fiber that wraps and loops upon itself thousands of times per specific length of yarn.

A cross-section image (figure 3) shows that single-spinneret yarn contains thousands of looped fibers per cross-section. The average diameter of yarns made with a single-spinneret setup is 20 to 40 μm, depending on the rate at which the yarn is drawn off.

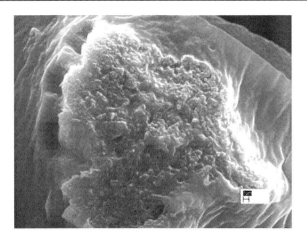

Figure 3. Yarn cross-section.

Increasing Yarn Processibility

Four basic characteristics of the yarns made through this process need to be improved before industrial weaving and knitting with these fibers can become viable. These are:

- Yarn thickness,
- Elasticity and tensile strength, and
- Rate of production.

Increasing Yarn Thickness

The yarns made through this process, with a single-spinneret setup, have average diameters of 20 to 40 μm. This makes them too fine for any industrial mass-production process. Initial work on making the yarns thicker have focused on two principles:

- Reducing the rate at which the yarn is taken off the spin bath, and
- Combining yarns from multiple spinnerets.

Although reducing yarn take-up speed did succeed in increasing yarn diameter, it was accompanied by a marked reduction in fiber alignment, as can be observed in figure 4 below. The reduction in fiber alignment is caused by a reduced drag-alignment effect from the spin-bath liquid since fibers fall on top of other dry fibers instead of the liquid surface.

In addition to increasing yarn thickness, the combination of yarns from multiple spinnerets opens the door to the manufacture of multi-functional composite yarns that contain fibers of various polymers. The work on this approach is still ongoing and we hope to report on further progress in the near future.

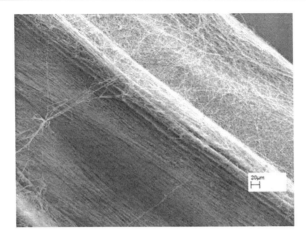

Figure 4. Thick nanofiber yarn with reduced fiber alignment.

Increasing Yarn Elasticity and Tensile Strength

The lack of fiber twist, and the possibility for entangled fiber loops to slip when force is applied to the yarn, leads to unpredictable elasticity and low tensile strength. These undesirable properties can possibly be overcome by the application of a 'spin-sizing agent' or similar coatings that keep fibers together during processing and which can be washed away in a final post-processing step. Figure 5 below shows SEM photographs of nanofiber yarn and ribbon structures that have been treated with water-soluble poly(vinyl alcohol). Initial studies show a significant increase in the tensile strength of these structures over their untreated counterparts.

Increasing the Rate of Production

The rate of production with a single spinneret setup is approximately 180m yarn/hour. This low production rate is obviously only suitable for lab-scale production. However, it is directly related to low rates of nanofiber production in the electrospinning process in general and numerous groups in the field are currently working on increasing nanofiber throughput through approaches that include multiple spinneret designs and needle-less designs. A breakthrough design for high-throughput electrospinning in general, will very likely lead to a similar advance in nanofiber yarn output.

CONCLUSION

Nanofiber yarns will find numerous applications in future medical-, smart- and functional textiles. The process described here utilizes the ease-of-use and all the flexibility of the electrospinning process in order to make continuous nanofiber yarns. Although certain technical hurdles still need to be cleared before these yarns are industry-ready, the options are numerous and the aims are within reach.

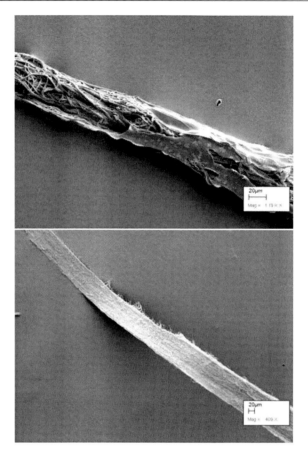

Figure 5. Nanofiber yarn partially coated (topleft) and nanofiber ribbon permeated (bottomright) with water-soluble poly(vinyl alcohol).

REFERENCES

[1] Huang, Z-M; Zhang, Y.-Z; Kotaki, M; Ramakrishna, S. A review of polymer nanofibers by electrospinning and their applications in nanocomposites. *Composites Science and Technology,* 2003, 63, 2223-2253.
[2] Kwon, IK; Kidoaki, S; Matsuda, T. Electrospun nano- to microfiber fabrics made of biodegradable copolyesters: structural characterstics, mechanical properties and cell adhesion potential. *Biomaterials,* 2005, 26, 3929-3939.
[3] Grafe, T. and Graham, K. Polymeric Nanofibers and Nanofiber Webs: A New Class Of Nonwovens. *International Nonwovens Journal,* 2003, 12, 51-55.
[4] Smit, E; Büttner, U; Sanderson, RD. Continuous yarns from electrospun fibers. *Polymer,* 2005, 46, 2419-2423.

In: Textiles for Sustainable Development   ISBN: 978-1-60021-559-9
Editors: R. Anandjiwala, L. Hunter et al., pp. 363-371   © 2007 Nova Science Publishers, Inc.

Chapter 32

NANOTECHNOLOGIES FOR MODIFICATION AND COATING OF FIBERS AND TEXTILES

T. Stegmaier, M. Dauner, V. Arnim, A. Scherrieble, A. Dinkelmann and H. Planck

Institute of Textile and Process Engineering Denkendorf (ITV),
Germany; (Institut für Textil- und Verfahrenstechnik (ITV) Denkendorf,
Deutschland); Koerschtalstrasse 26, D-73770 Denkendorf;
Tel.: +49 (0)711 9340 – (0) 219; Fax.: +49 (0)711 9340 – 297;
e-mail: thomas.stegmaier@itv-denkendorf.de,
website: www.itv-denkendorf.de

ABSTRACT

Using nanotechnology in spinning and surface treatment of fiber based materials is a great chance to change physical and chemical properties in a large scale. At ITV Denkendorf the focus in research and development is on following subjects:

- Spinning of nanofibers using electrospinning
- Activation of natural and artificial fibers and textiles by atmospheric plasma at high production speed
- Coating of fibers/textiles with very thin layers using atmospheric plasma treatment, based on the polymerization of gases in plasma reactors
- Development of the biomimetic Lotus-Effect on textiles for an extremely self-cleaning effect by using only water

Keywords: nanotechnology, nanofibers, electrostatic spinning, atmospheric plasma, Corona, bionic, biomimetic, self-cleaning, Lotus-Effect.

INTRODUCTION

The term "nano" is not clearly defined. In the following the nanometer range is considered as $\leq 0.1\ \mu m$. Nanosized systems can be applied to fibers or textile structures in different ways:

In spinning of fibers it is of interest:

- to reduce the fiber dimension down towards fiber diameters between 2-100 nm
- to get nano structures in the fiber bulk by working with nanofillers (e.g.: pigments, TiO2, ZnO, clay) or with nano phase separating systems in the polymer
- to modify the surface in a topographical way (e.g. profile fibers) or in a chemical way

In the processing of fibers it is of interest to apply coatings using;

- nanoscaled thickness, e.g. for optical effects
- nanofillers or the phase separation technology and self-organizing mono layers
- special additives for desired topographical and chemical properties

In the following some areas of nanotechnology are introduced in which ITV Denkendorf is involved.

PRODUCTION OF NANOFIBER NONWOVENS USING ELECTROSTATIC SPINNING

Porosity and pore size are crucial properties of filter media, which determine efficiency as well as pressure drop and permeability. Small pore sizes at high porosity of a textile filter media are dependent upon the fiber size. A reduction of the pore size below the fiber diameter reduces the porosity greatly and diminishes the permeability. This means the filtration efficiency increases with reducing the fiber diameter.

The diameter of natural as well as of synthetic fibers usually ranges from 10 to 20 µm, micro fibers and bi-component splitted fibers can be as fine as 3 to 7 µm. Melt blow and flash spinning end up with 1 µm fiber diameters [Dauner 2004], with even finer glass fibers being produced in sub-micrometer range; but for many filtration applications they should not be used.

The Electrostatic Spinning

The basic design of electrostatic spinning and its realization in most of the research laboratories are very simple (figure 1). A polymer solution is fed to a nozzle by a defined low pressure. An electrical field is applied between the nozzle and a collector (rotating mandrel or a conveyor belt). Independently from the polymer, solvent and concentration of the solution, a proportion of voltage to nozzle-carrier distance of 1 kV/cm is practical. Usually the nozzle diameter is about 100 μm.

The mechanism leading to nano fibers are multiple splaying similar to lightening [Reneker 1995]. In addition, in the so called "whipping", after leaving the nozzle the primary fiber stays stable on the way to the carrier as long as surface tension, electrical charging and external influences (like friction in air) stay in equilibrium. Any perturbation leads to a deviation of the fiber until a new equilibrium is reached. At constant margins (feeding and winding speed) a stretching of the fiber results. Here again, a draw ratio of one hundred can be easily achieved reducing the diameter from 1 μm to 0.1 μm.

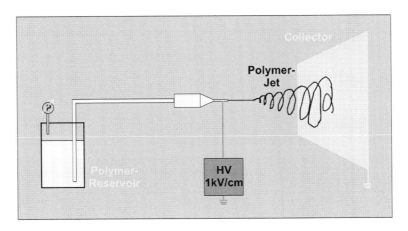

Figure 1. Apparatus for the electrostatic spinning "Whipping" mechanism.

Polymers and Solvents

Amorphous polymers are leading to very regular nonwoven structures by the electro spinning process. Yet, according to own experiments, and supported by literature data nano fibers could be produced only from crystallite forming polymers. As a further requirement for the electrostatic spinning, the polymer should be polar.

Regular structures in the μm scale were produced from different polyurethanes and from co-polyesters (e.g. figures 2 andto 3). The production of micro porous surfaces is of interest, as it could be shown as well for polylactides [Bognitzki 2001]

Using solutions from polyethylenoxide PEO, polyvinylalcohole (PVA), polyacrylonitrile (PAN) as well as from polyimide fibers in the nanometer scale were produced. The fiber diameter can be measured only by scanning electron microscope with limitations.

As with the polymers a high polarity of the solvent improves the electrostatic process. Furthermore, a high electrical conductivity of the solvent is required for the production of nano fibers [Böbel 2003].

PVA and PEO are favorites for experiments as they can be processed from aqueous solutions and no special safety considerations have to be made, neither regarding toxicity nor explosivity. Besides that water is highly polar and best suitable for electrostatic spinning (Their use for filters is limited, of course).

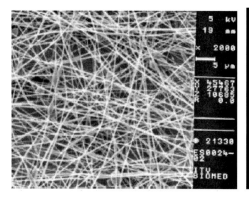 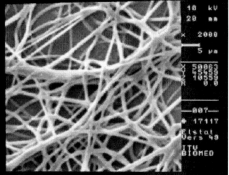

Figure 2. Polyvinylalcohole in water, 1 kV/cm   fFigure 3: Polyurethane, CHCl₃/MeOH, 1
kV/cm.

The appropriate concentration of the solutions depends on the polymer, its molecular mass and the solvent:

- Fibers do not form at very low concentrations.
- High concentrations hinder the feeding of the solution and its filtration.
- Good results are obtained from 5 to 20 Vol.-%, with best results in between.

Productivity

Usually spinning productivity is more or less proportional to the spun fiber diameter. This is particularly valid for melt blowing of 5 to 1 μm fibers, as well as for the solution blown and the electrostatic spinning processes.

By means of electrostatic spinning, nano fibers are produced only at very low throughput. A crucial limitation is the rate of solvent evaporation. If the remaining solvent content is too high, the fibers will be resolved at the carrier.

At ITV Denkendorf provisions to increase the productivity are under investigation .

"COLD" PLASMA TREATMENT BASED
ON CHEMICAL VAPOR DEPOSITION

Possibilities and Advantages

If the energy supply in a plasma system is controlled to keep the gas temperature in the range of room temperature, it is called cold or low temperature plasma. The main advantages of plasma treatments with such a system are:

- Modification of surface properties without changing the properties of the fiber bulk
- Dry process with a minimized consumption of chemicals
- Elimination of traditional drying processes

- Highly environmentally friendly process
- Availability of the processes for nearly all kinds of fibers.

Plasma treatment changes fiber properties such as friction coefficient, surface energy and antistatic behavior. The modification of the Corona technology by coating both electrodes with dielectric material (Dielectric Barrier Discharge = DBD), the use of an intermitting electrical power supply and the addition of different gases greatly increase the application field of plasma technologies for the textile industry (figure 4).

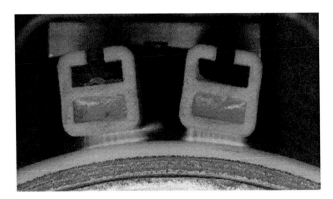

Figure 4. Dielectric barrier discharge.

Surface Activation and Hydrophilic Modification

For hydrophilic treatment of textiles, open or half open plasma units are suitable (figure 5). Their construction consists of two or more rod like ceramic-coated high voltage electrodes located in front of a roller shaped ceramic-coated electrode. The textile is guided through the small gap between rod and roller electrode. The set up of the unit is easy; the process speed depends on the textile surface area and the extension of the plasma zone in the direction of movement. A typical speed is 2 m/min to 10 m/min. A scale-up of this technology for the treatment of wide goods and to high process speed is comparatively easy.

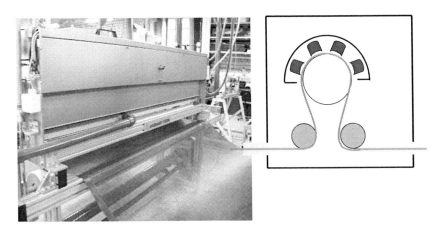

Figure 5. Half opened plasma unit with 2 m working width.

A wide range of tests involving industrial partners have demonstrated the potential use, especially for:

- Increasing the adhesion up to 200% for laminating, coatings, taping
- Considerable improvement in wetting and penetration of coating systems into the core of yarns and textile constructions
- Increasing lifetime of coated textiles due to better encapsulated yarns and therefore better protection from the environment

Hydrophobic and Oleophobic Coating by Chemical Vapor Deposition

For coating plasma systems based on polymerization of gases encapsulated units are necessary. A simple gas lock avoids the entry of air into the reactor chamber, even during continuous processing. The generation of water- and oil repellent layers by plasma polymerization, using gaseous fluorocarbons in a continuous process, was successful achieved by ITV Denkendorf [Arnim 2003]. Tests with industrial users show its potential in terms of;

- a change of hydrophobicity / oleophobicity to different degrees and
- the application oriented functionalisation, e.g. different degrees of water absorbence.

SELF-CLEANING SURFACES BASED ON THE LOTUS-EFFEKT®

By learning about the principles and functions of nature, new products and innovative properties can be developed. ITV Denkendorf is working in basic and applied science in networks with highly experienced botanic institutes, chemical companies, textile producers and end-users in different fields, with respect to bionic ideas [Stegmaier 2004]. The main focus for nano technologies is currently on the development of the Lotus-Effect on textile structures.

The characteristic behind the synonym Lotus-Effect is the capacity of surfaces to be cleaned completely using only water, for example in the form of rain. This capacity is often called a self-cleaning effect, as there is no need for cleaning agents or additional mechanical action. This characteristic was discovered and investigated on natural surfaces of plants, like leaf (figure 6) and blossom surfaces, but also on animal surfaces. The most famous and probably the most ideal representative from the plant world is the lotus plant that acts as the eponym.

The most important reason for the Lotus-Effect in nature is protection against pathogenic organic contamination, such as bacteria or spores. Through hydrophobic, nano- and micro-scaled structured surfaces, the contact area of water and dirt particles is largely minimized. SEM -Pphotographs show the double structured surface of the natural example – the lotus leaf. These result in extremely high contact angles that let water droplets roll off at the slightest inclination and removes dirt particles lying loosely on it, thus leaving behind a clean and dry surface.

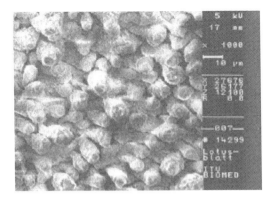

Figure 6. SEM-Photograph of the lotus leaf surface.

Based on textile materials, there is a high potential for a number of applications for such self-cleaning properties. This includes out-door applications, such as textile roofs for airports and railways, sunscreen textiles, out-door clothing, but also indoor applications, which come into contact with water (figure 7, 8).

Figure 7. Contaminated water drop on cleaned fabric with Lotus- Effect.

Figure 8. Honey droplet on a fabric with Lotus-Effect.

At ITV Denkendorf, research and development work is done to generate the Lotus-Effect on textiles and to have a permanent effect according to requirements:

- Especially the staining resistance is a very important criterion for out-door clothing and will lead to a reduction in laundering costs.
- According to the desired durability, the mechanical abrasion resistance of such a surface can be on different levels.

Ongoing research and development tasks regarding the modification of fibers, examination and development of textile formation, surface treatment, coating with new nano-structured chemicals, application methods and durability tests.

The durability of this superhydrophic surface has to be measured according to the demands of the product. Awnings, tested for 1000 h sunlight in the Xenon test and 2000 cycles of moving in/out, exhibited better self cleaning behavior compared to the reference-sample with conventional FC finishing [Keller 2004].

The ability for regeneration of once damaged surfaces, which is of course provided to plants by growth, plays an important role in the further development of long lasting self cleaning technical surfaces.

ITV Denkendorf coordinates activities for the technical implementation of the Lotus-Effect on textiles in cooperation with Prof. Wilhelm Barthlott of the Nees-Institute for Biodiversity of Plants, University of Bonn.

In April 2006 a sign of approval for the Lotus-Effect was introduced to the textile industry (figure 9), [Scherrieble 2006]. After fulfilling the requirements in the test procedures the sign of approval can be used for a textile product to demonstrate the attractive property of self cleaning to the customers.

Figure 9. Sign of approval for the Lotus-Effect on fiber based products.

REFERENCES

[1]   Scherrieble, A.; Arnim, V. v.; Reichardt, S.; Stegmaier, T.; Planck, H.: "Nachgewiesene Wirkung – Die Prüfkriterien des Gütesiegels" Paper on the Denkendorf Nano-Forum „Selbstreinigende Textilien – Das Gütesiegel für Textilien mit dem Lotus-Effekt", SI-Centrum Stuttgart, 6. April, 2006.

[2]   Arnim, V. v., Dinkelmann, A.; Stegmaier, T. „Functionalication of Textiles in Atmospheric Plasma "Paper on the International Symposium on "„Coating and Surface Functionalisation of Technical Textiles", 29.-31,. January 2003, Denkendorf.

[3]   Bognitzki, M; et al. Nanostructured fibers via electro spinning; *Adv. Mater.* 13 (1), p. 70-72, 2001.

[4]   Böbel J, Entwicklung von nanostrukturierten Oberflächen für das Tissue Engineering auf Basis des Elektrospinnens; *Studienarbeit,* DITF/Universität Stuttgart, 2003.

[5]   Dauner, M. Production of nano fiber nonwovens using electrostatic spinning 7. Symposium Textile Filter, *Chemnitz,* 02./03.03.2004.

[6]   Keller, H.; Dielemann, C.; Ebenau, A. Deloplments for the Lotus-Effekt® finishing, Lecture on the workshop Nanotechnology for the textile industry, ITV Denkendorf in cooperation with Gesamttextil e.V., 19. February, 2004.

[7]   Reneker, DH; Chun, I. Nanometer diameter fibers of polymer, produced by electro spinning; *Nanotechnology.* 7, p. 216-223, 1995.

[8]   Stegmaier, T.; Milwich, M.; Scherrieble, A.; Geuer, M.; Planck, H. Bionik Developments based on Textile Materials for Technical Applications, Lecture on the Bionik 2004 – International Conference, Hannover Messe, 22-23, April 2004.

In: Textiles for Sustainable Development   ISBN: 978-1-60021-559-9
Editors: R. Anandjiwala, L. Hunter et al., pp. 373-383   © 2007 Nova Science Publishers, Inc.

Chapter 33

ELECTROSPINNING AND STABILISATION OF POLY(VINYL ALCOHOL) NANOR WEBS WITH ANTIMICROBIAL ACTIVITY - ABSTRACT NO: 58

Wiebke Voigt, Helga Thomas,
Elisabeth Heine and Martin Möller
DWI e.V. and Institute of Technical and Macromolecular Chemistry,
RWTH Aachen; Pauwelsstraße 8, D-52056 Aachen,
Germany; voigt@dwi.rwth-aachen.de

ABSTRACT

In the present work the formation of antimicrobial nanofiber webs via electrospinning was studied underat environmentally acceptable conditions, thus excluding the use of hazardous organic solvents for the preparation of spinning solutions. Antimicrobial activity was attained by generation of PVA-fibers with incorporated spherical silver nanoparticles. Therefore aqueous PVA solutions with silver nitrate were electrospun followed by UV-irradiation to reduce silver ions to elemental silver. Special attentionregard was given to (i) the influence of spinning and solution parameters on the resulting fiber diameter, (ii) the stabilisation of the resulting nanofiber webs towards aqueous surroundings by crystallisation of the PVA and (iii) the antimicrobial functionality of PVA-silver nanofibers.

Keywords: antimicrobial nanofibers, polyvinyl alcohol, silver nanoparticles, water-insolubility, crystallinity.

INTRODUCTION

Nanofibers are accessible by the electrospinning process which demonstrates a simple, inexpensive and versatile way of nanofiber production. The electrospinning technique requires three basic components (figure 1): a high voltage supply, a spinneret (usually a syringe with a needle filled with the polymer solution or melt) connected to the high voltage supply and a grounded or oppositely charged target [1-3]. The high voltage (typically 5 – 30 kV) creates an electrically charged jet of the polymer solution, which is stretched and whipped on the way to the target. During this stage, the solvent evaporates leading to the formation of nanometer-sized fibers which are collected on the target as a nonwoven fiber mat. The target can be provided with a carrier material for fiber collection. Besides that, the target can take different shapes [4] according to requirements. For generating carrier free fiber webs a grounded frame can be used as target. A syringe pump feeds the polymer solution at a constant and controllable rate to guarantee reproducible results.

Influencing parameters of the electrospinning process include process parameters (electric field, distance between electrode and target, flow rate, needle geometry) and system parameters (polymer concentration, viscosity, polymer, solvent, surface tension, ionic strength, pH value) [1,3,5,6]. Environmental factors, such as humidity, temperature and air velocity in the electrospinning chamber can also affect the formation of the nanofibers. Examination of these parameters by variation provides the possibility of optimisation of fiber morphology and therewith receiving achieving the desired fiber properties [7-9].

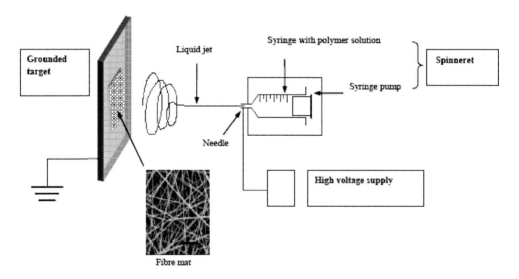

Figure 1. Basic setup for electrospinning.

AlThough being firstly described in a patent by Formhals in 1934 [10], the electrospinning process has attracted only scant attention in its early beginning. With increasing interest in nanotechnology electrospinning has gained exponential research interest in the last decades and several research groups (in particular Reneker's group, University of Akron, Ohio, USA) have demonstrated the formation of a large variety of polymers by the electrospinning technique. A broad range of pure and blended natural and synthetic organic as well as inorganic polymers have already successfully been spun allowing the production of various nanofiber webs for different application areas. The latter is supported by the possibility of using nanofiber webs as carrier material for subsequent fixation of various substances to fiber surfaces as well as for their direct implementation into the fiber. The large surface area of nanofiber webs allows (i) a rapid absorption of hazardous molecules (provided that the polymer contains reactive sites) or (ii) a rapid release of active substances which can be added to the spinning solution. Further the dirt holding capacity is correspondingly increased with the surface area of the fibers, being of special interest for filter media, e.g. for air filtration.

As a consequence of multiplication of microorganisms under at certain conditions, it is intended to inhibit uncontrolled growth of microbes on the surface of filter materials. This can be obtained by the addition of disinfectants e.g. organic agents (quaternary ammonium compounds, triclosan etc.), metalorganics (e.g. organometallic compounds) as well as inorganic additives (silver halides, elemental silver, cadmium compounds etc.) [11,12], either as individual additives or as polymers with special antimicrobial functions. Whereas antimicrobial polymers are supposed to generate nanofibers underat certain conditions, non-polymeric compounds can be used as add-on to the spinning solution.

The latter are represented e.g. by silver and silver ions already established as an aseptic in a wide area of applications particularly in medicine e.g. in unguents / tinctures or in wound-dressing materials [11]. Especially the excellent antimicrobial activity of silver nanoparticles [13] raises expectations for the development of antimicrobial nanofibers. Ag-nanoparticles act as a reservoir which continuously releases silver-ions over a long period of time due to corrosion of the outer silver layer. Thus there is no uncontrollable burst-release of silver ions. In comparison to that, antimicrobial additives consisting of silver salts show an uncontrolled short-term effect depending on their solubility in the surrounding medium [12]. Silver nanoparticles are antimicrobial effective already atin very low concentrations due to their high surface area and, in opposition contrast to silver salts they show no further discolouration [12,14]. Reduction of silver ions by application of reducing agents as ascorbic acid or by photochemical reaction with UV-light, leads to the formation of elemental silver.

Young et al. prepared nanocomposite polypropylene (PP)-fibers with permanent antibacterial effect by co-extrusion of PP and PP/Ag master-batches using general conjugate spinning [15]. For generation of the master batches they mixed PP chips with nano-sized silver powder. Yang et al. first generated PAN-nanofibers containing silver nanoparticles by electrospinning [16]. Antimicrobial cellulose acetate fibers with silver nanoparticles generated by electrospinning process were prepared by Son et al. adding silver nitrate to the spinning solution and generating silver nanoparticles by subsequent UV-irradiation after electrospinning [17]. Using silver and silver ions respectively, as add-on to the spinning solution to produce silver nanoparticles within the surface of the fibers illustrates an adequate and simple way to generate antimicrobial effective nano-sized fibers.

PVA was used as spinning material because of its good chemical and physical properties, such as like chemical resistance, high melting point and its biological compatibility. It is offered in a broad range of degrees of polymerisation and hydrolysis. Additionally, it is an inexpensive, non-toxic material which is water soluble. As a consequence of water solubility aqueous spinning solutions of PVA can be prepared [7,18,19] and electrospinning can be performed at environmentally friendly production conditions. Electrospun PVA-fibers are completely soluble in water [18,19]; for stabilisation of the fibers towards aqueous surroundings the fibers have to be modified by physical or chemical cross-linking.

Yao et al. stabilised electrospun PVA-nanofibers by post-treatment with methanol against water dissolution. These methanol-treated nanofiber webs show an increased crystallinity, presumably due to removal of residual water within the fibers by the alcohol which allows the formation of intermolecular hydrogen bonds [18]. PVA-nanofibers were also water stabilised by annealing with poly(acrylic acid) (PAA), leading to an esterification of PAA with PVA [19].

IBut in particular, the crystalline nature of PVA suggests the possibility of "physical" cross-linking [20] and thus, of stabilisation of PVA-fibers towards aqueous solutions. Annealing of electrospun PVA-fibers and therewith increasinge in their crystallinity offers one adequate possibility of water stabilisation.

In this study, water stable, antimicrobial PVA-nanofibers were generated. For obtaining antimicrobial activity the fibers were equipped with Ag-nanoparticles by subsequent UV-irradiation of electrospun PVA / AgNO$_3$ fiber webs. Water stability was achieved by heat treatment i.e. to increase the fiber's crystallinity.

EXPERIMENTAL PART

Materials

PVA (M$_W$ 86.000-124.000 g/mol, degree of hydrolysation: 98-99 %) was supplied by Sigma-Aldrich, Triton-X-100 and silver nitrate by Merck. All reagents were of analytical grade and used as received.

Preparation of the Spinning Solutions

PVA-powder (8 wt.-%) was mixed with distilled water and stirred at 80 °C until the polymer was completely dissolved. After cooling the polymer-solution to room temperature (RT), Triton-X-100 (0.25 wt.-%) was added and the solution was stirred for further 30 min at RT.

The generation of PVA-fibers with integrated silver nanoparticles was performed by addition of silver nitrate (0.5 wt.-%) to the PVA-solution before electrospinning and subsequent irradiation of the electrospun fiber with a UV-lamp (Osram, 300 W) for 4 hours.

Electrospinning

Electrospinning was performed underat environmental conditions using the setup already described in figure 1. A syringe was filled with the polymer solution and a high voltage, generated from a high voltage supplier (KNH34 / P2A, Eltex) in the range of 10 kV to 30 kV (regularly 17 kV), was applied to the needle (ID 0.8 mm). A syringe pump (Pilot A2, Fresenius Fial Infusion Technology) was used for providing a constant feeding rate (0.5 mL/h). The distance between spinneret and target was usually 15 cm unless otherwise noted. A grounded aluminium plate with a fixed aluminium foil was used as collector, except for DSC, the samples were collected by means of a grounded metal frames (figure 2) in order to obtain free-standing fiber mats.

Electron Microscopy

The fiber morphology was investigated using a scanning electron microscope (SEM) (Carl Zeiss / S 360). For the determination of fiber diameters a common image analysis program was used. Images from fibers with integrated Ag-nanoparticles were taken with field emission scanning electron microscope (FESEM) (Hitachi / S 4800).

Antimicrobial Testing

Antimicrobial activity of the PVA-fibers with Ag-nanoparticles was tested by using an adapted patch test with *E.coli*. The samples were sterilised (30 min at 110°C) and after that inoculated with *E.coli* (DSMZ 498). After exposure of the samples for 3 h at 25°C and 90 % relative humidity in a climate chamber, samples were contacted for 15 min under standardised conditions with the inoculated site onto nutrient agar plates and removed again. Thereafter, the nutrient agar plates were incubated overnight at 37°C.

RESULTS AND DISCUSSION

Formation of PVA-Fibers with Incorporated Ag-Nanoparticles

Electrospinning of an aqueous solution of PVA (8 wt.-%) in the presence of small amounts of Triton-X-100 (0.25 wt.-%) and silver nitrate (0.5 wt.-%) leads firstly to the deposition of very fine-structured white-coloured fiber mats. During subsequent UV-irradiation the colour of the fiber mats turns from white to slightly yellow (figure 2a) indicating the formation of Ag-nanoparticles by reduction of silver ions to elemental silver. As shown in figure 2b, the nanosilver containing fiber webs consist of very homogenous nanofibers with an average diameter of 390 nm.

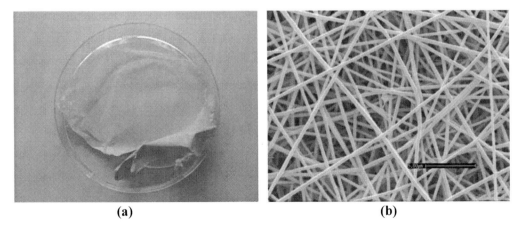

(a)   (b)

Figure 2. (a) Image of a light yellow-coloured PVA fiber-mat with Ag-nanoparticles (b) SEM-image of (a).

At higher magnification, uniformly distributed Ag-nanoparticles with diameters ranging from 3 - 10 nm can be detected within the surfaces of PVA-nanofibers as shown in the FESEM-images of figure 3. Furthermore, larger-sized silver particles are formed on the fiber surface showing average diameters of up to 100 nm (figure 3a). The latter indicates an additional aggregation of silver nanoparticles during spinning and UV-post-treatment, respectively.

a.   b.

Figure 3. FESEM-images of PVA-fibers bearing silver nanoparticles (3a,b) as well as silver aggregates (3a).

Antimicrobial Activity of PVA-Fibers with Ag-Nanoparticles

Antimicrobial tests demonstrate that PVA-fibers with incorporated Ag-nanoparticles significantly inhibit growth of *E.coli* in comparison to pure PVA-fibers. This can be taken as indication for the release of Ag^+-ions from the nanosilver particles in the fibers which are well-established for their propensity in inhibiting microbial growth. The images in figure 4 represent results of a patch test and demonstrate the antimicrobial effect of the PVA/Ag-nanofibers. After contacting the inoculated fiber webs bacterial colonies grow (figure 4a), whereas after contacting the nanosilver containing PVA-fiber webs the colony growth was almost completely inhibited (figure 4b).

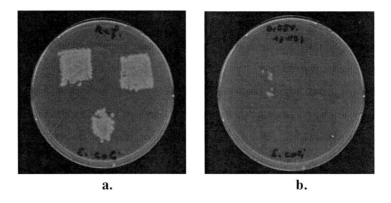

a.   b.

Figure 4. Antimicrobial effect (patch test) of PVA-nanofibers with Ag-nanoparticles against *E.coli*, growth of *E.coli* after contacting inoculated (a) PVA-fibers and (b) PVA-fibers with Ag-nanoparticles.

Influence of Spinning Conditions and Concentration of Agno₃ on the Fiber Diameter

The diagrams in figure 5 present the influence of the process parameters, voltage and feeding rate, on the resulting fiber diameter of PVA-fibers as well as on the variation width (standard deviation) of fiber diameters. The applied voltage exerts a great influence (figure 5a). At a value of 5 kV, the electric field is too low for overcoming viscosity and surface tension of the polymer solution to form a jet; the PVA solution just drops down. Increasing of the voltage up to 25 kV led to a constantly increase of the fiber diameter; after that at 30 kV the diameters tend to decrease accompanied by less homogeneity. Generally, a higher voltage ejects more fluid in a jet, resulting in a larger fiber diameter [1], but some studies showed opposite trends [3]. However, the effect of the voltage on the diameter seems to involve other parameters. Ruthledge and his co-workers developed a theoretical model in which the final diameter arises from a force balance between surface tension and electrostatic charge repulsion [8]. The forces that determine the jet diameter might be related to the flow rate, the electrical field strength and the surface tension [3,8]. The feeding rate of the polymer solution is also an important influencing parameter. At increasing feeding rates, the fiber diameter is reduced (figure 5b); but then, the diameter arises and at high feeding rates ≥ 1 mL/h bead formation appears.

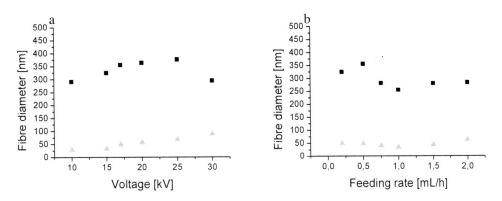

Figure 5. Influence of (a) voltage and (b) feeding rate of the polymer solution on the fiber diameter (■) and its variation width (▲) of PVA-nanofibers.

The concentration of silver salt added to the spinning solution and the spinning parameters also strongly interact with the resulting diameter of silver-bearing PVA-nanofibers. As shown in figure 6, the resulting fiber diameter tends to increase with the concentration of silver nitrate in the polymer solution. The addition of silver nitrate in a concentration range of 0.1 – 0.75 wt.-% followed by irradiation leads to a slight diameter increase. By addition of silver nitrate to the spinning solution, the conductivity linearly increases with the concentration of added salt (figure 6) and therefore results in an increased net charge density of the jet. The whipping instability is thus enhanced and the jet should be stretched under the stronger force, resulting in a fiber diameter reduction [3]. Instead of the expected diameter reduction with increasing AgNO₃-addition, a slight diameter increase was detected for the irradiated samples. However, the observed diameter increase was not significant.

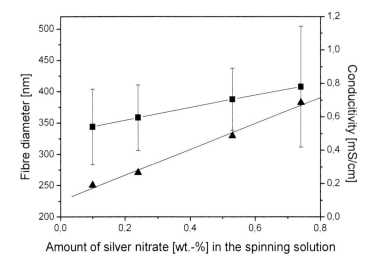

Figure 6. Fiber diameter (■) and conductivity (▲) in dependence on the amount of silver nitrate added to the spinning solution.

Figure 7 presents the variations in diameter of PVA / Ag-fibers for the two different process parameters. The influence of voltage and feeding rate show comparable results as those obtained for pure PVA-fibers. Differences can be found in fiber morphology with regard to inhomogeneity. Compared to pure PVA-fibers (figure 5), the fiber webs show generally more inhomogeneity and irregularity detectable by significantly higher variation widths of the fiber diameter. In summary, the fiber diameter and the fiber quality must be optimised by careful adjustment of the different process parameters and we could not observe a clear and simple correlation for generating optimal fiber fineness.

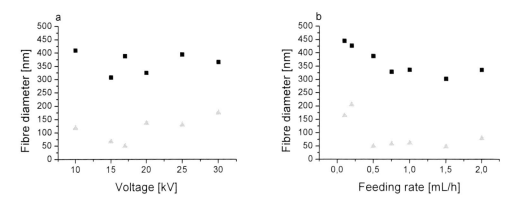

Figure 7. Influence of (a) voltage and (b) feeding rate of the polymer solution on the fiber diameter (■) and its variation width (▲) of PVA / Ag-nanofibers.

Stabilisation of the PVA Fiber Webs Ttowards Aqueous Conditions

Electrospun PVA-fibers are completely uinstable in water. However, due to demanding water stability for several application areas a stabilisation of PVA-nanofibers is required. Water resistance of PVA can be performed by increasing the degree of crystallinity which is well established to be achieved by annealing of highly hydrolysed PVA samples. Furthermore , PVA is stabilised by heat-treatment due to the formation of crosslinks during intermolecular dehydration. Decrease in crystallinity can be caused by thermal degradation, including dehydration and depolymerisation [20].

Initial trials indicate that an annealing temperature of 150 °C is optimal for stabilisation of PVA-nanofiber webs. For the heat-treated samples, a pronounced water stability of PVA- and PVA-nanosilver-fiber webs (figure 8) is achieved as indicated by withstanding an immersion in water over a time period of 1 h. But in contrast to pure PVA-fibers, those with silver show low swelling (figure 8b) presumably caused by a disturbance of the crystallisation process by the Ag-nanoparticles.

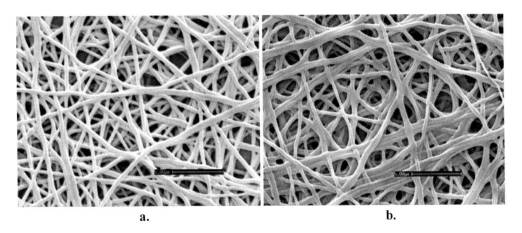

a.   b.

Figure 8. (a) PVA-fibers heat-treated at 150°C for 10 min, immersed 1 h in water, (b) PVA-fibers with Ag-nanoparticles heat-treated at 150°C for 25 min, immersed 1 h in water.

CONCLUSION

Electrospinning generally presents a straightforward and simple method for generating ultra-thin fibers from a wide range of polymers from their solution or melt. Whereas most of the processes described are based on polymers dissolved in organic solvents, the present work demonstrates the possibility of using environmentally friendly aqueous polymer solutions as well as the subsequent stabilisation of the resulting nanofiber webs towards humid environments. Water stabilisation of the PVA-nanofiber webs was performed by heat-treatment which is associated with an increase in crystallinity. In order to obtain antimicrobial activity PVA-nanofibers with integrated uniformly distributed spherical Ag-nanoparticles were prepared by UV-irradiation of the electrospun fiber webs obtained from PVA / AgNO$_3$-solutions.

ACKNOWLEDGEMENTS

The authors wish to thank Forschungskuratorium Textil e. V. for financial support of the research project (AIF-No. 14324) provided from funds of Bundesministerium für Wirtschaft und Arbeit (BMWA) via a grant of Arbeitsgemeinschaft industrieller Forschungsvereinigungen "Otto von Guericke" e.V. (AIF). We further wish to express our gratitude to Hitachi High-Technologies Europe GmbH, Krefeld for performance of the field emission scanning electron microscope studies on FESEM S 4800.

REFERENCES

[1]   Huang, Z. M., Zhang, Y. Z., Kotaki, M., and Ramakrishna, S. (2003). A review on polymer nanofibers by electrospinning and their applications in nanocomposites. *Composites Science and Technology*, 63, 2223-2253.

[2]   Jayaraman, K., Kotaki, M., Zhang, Y., Mo, X., and Ramakrishna, S. (2004). Recent Advances in Polymer Nanofibers. *Journal of Nanoscience and Nanotechnology*, 4 (1/2), 52-65.

[3]   Li, D., and Xia, Y. (2003). Electrospinning of Nanofibers: Reinventing the Wheel?. *Advanced Materials*, 16, 1151-1170.

[4]   Dalton, P. D., Klee, D., and Möller, M. (2005). Electrospinning with dual collection rings. *Polymer*, 46, 611-614.

[5]   Fang, D., Hsiao, B. S., and Chu, B. (2003). Multiple-Jet electrospinning of non-woven nanofiber articles. *Polymer Preprints*, 44(2), 59-60.

[6]   Thomas, H., Heine, E., Wollseifen, R., Cimpeanu, C. and Möller, M. (2005). Nanofibers from natural and inorganic polymers via electrospinning. *International Nonwovens Journal*, Fall 2005, 12-18.

[7]   Bhattacharya, A., and Ray, P. (2004). Studies on Surface Tension of Poly(Vinyl Alcohol): Effect of Concentration, Temperature, and Addition of Chaotropic Agents. *Journal of Applied Polymer Science*, 93, 122-130.

[8]   Fridrikh, S. V., Yu, J. H., Brenner, M. P., and Ruthledge, G. C. (2003). Controlling the Fiber diameter during Electrospinning. *Physical Review Letters*, 90(14), 144502-1-144502-4.

[9]   Son, W. K., Youk, J. H., Lee, T. S., and Park, W. H. (2004). The effects of solution properties and polyelctrolyte on electrospinning of ultrafine poly(ethylene oxide) fibers. *Polymer*, 45, 2959-2966.

[10]   Formhals, A. (1934). *US Patent*, 1-975-504.

[11]   Hillen, E., Rohlf, U., Frunder, B. (1995). CD Römpp Chemie Lexikon. Stuttgart, Thieme.

[12]   Rent a Scientist GmbH (2002). Schutz vor Bakterien und Viren, nano-Silber. *Technologie Transfer Magazin RandD waves*, 1. Available from: URL: http://www.rent-a-scientist.com/pdf/magazin1_2002.pdf

[13]   Sondi, I., and Salopek-Sondi, B. (2004). Silver nanopartcles as antimicrobial agent: a case study on E. coli as a model for Gram-negative bacteria. *Journal of Colloid and Interface Science*, 275, 177-182.

[14] Sun, Z., Zeng, J., Hou, H., Kissel, T., Wendorff, J. H., and Greiner, A. (2003). Functional nanofibers and nanotubes via electrospinning: chemical modifications for selected applications. *Polymer Preprints,* 44(2), 76-77.

[15] Yeo, S. Y., Lee, H. J., and Jeong, S. H. (2003). Preparation of nanocomposite fibers for permanent antibacterial effect. *Journal of Materials Science,* 38, 2143-2147.

[16] Yang, Q. B., Li, D. M., Hong, Y. L., Li, Z. Y., Wang, C., Quiu, S. L., and Wei, Y. (2003). Preparation and characterization of a PAN nanofiber containing Ag-nanoparticles via Electrospinning. *Synthetic Metals,* 137(1-3), 973-974.

[17] Son, W. K., Youk, J. H., Lee, T. S., and Park, W. H., (2004). Preparation of Antimicrobial Ultrafine Cellulose Acetate Fibers with Silver Nanoparticles. *Macromolecular Rapid Communications,* 25, 1632-1637.

[18] Yao, L., Haas, T. W., Guiseppe-Elie, A., Bowlin, G. L., Simpson, D. G., and Wnek, G. E. (2003). Electrospinning and Stabilization of Fully Hydrolyzed Poly(Vinyl Alcohol) Fibers. *Chemistry of Materials,* 15, 1860-1864.

[19] Zeng, J., Hou, H., Wendorff, J. H., and Greiner, A. (2004). Electrospun poly(vinyl alcohol)/poly(acrylic acid) fibers with excellent water-stability. *e-Polymers,* no. 078, 1-8.

[20] Finch, C. A. (1973). Polyvinyl alcohol Properties and Applications. New York, Wiley.

PART V
MARKET, FUTURE OPPORTUNITIES AND GENERAL

In: Textiles for Sustainable Development   ISBN: 978-1-60021-559-9
Editors: R. Anandjiwala, L. Hunter et al., pp. 387-395   © 2007 Nova Science Publishers, Inc.

Chapter 34

COTTON'S ROLE IN SUSTAINABLE TEXTILES

L. Hunter

Divisional Fellow, CSIR and Head: Department of Textile Science,
Nelson Mandela Metropolitan University, P.O. Box 1124,
Port Elizabeth, 6000, South Africa

ABSTRACT

Globally, cotton remains by far the most widely produced and consumed natural fiber, also being a close second to polyester in terms of global fiber consumption. Cotton has been grown and utilized since time immemorial and this paper discusses some of the aspects which have played, and will continue to play, a role in cotton globally being a very important part of sustainable textiles.

Keywords: cotton consumption trends, cotton R&D needs, cotton technology, per capita fiber consumption, sustainable cotton.

INTRODUCTION

It never ceases to amaze that some people refer to textiles as a "sunset industry", implying it is a dying or declining industry. One can, however, very simply turn this misconception into the truth by referring to the fact that when the sun sets in one country, or region, it is in fact already rising in another country or region. Taking a global perspective, total textile production and consumption have been increasing over hundreds of years due to the growth in world population as well as in per capita fiber consumption, about half of the growth in world textile production being due to population growth and the other half due to per capita growth. New applications for textiles are continuously being found, this adding to the growth in overall per capita consumption. World textile fiber consumption is expected to reach some 67×10^9 kg in 2010, with that of cotton exceeding 25×10^9 kg (figure 1). Therefore, far from being a "sunset industry", or what is implied by that term, the textile industry globally is a growing and dynamic one, which is often used by poorer and developing countries to launch their economies and move them from developing to developed countries.

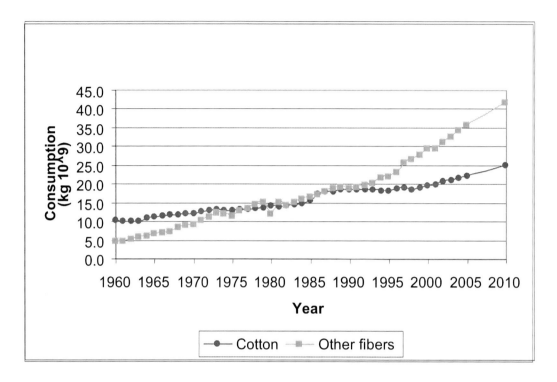

Figure 1. Global consumption of fibers.

What has been happening over time, particularly over the last few decades, is that man-made fibers have increased their share of the global market, and textile fiber production and textile manufacturing, particularly of commodity textiles, have been shifting around the globe to where the most favorable conditions apply, these mostly being in developing countries, where low labor costs and other favorable conditions prevail. In facing the contraction, and in some cases, the demise of their traditional textile industry, the developed countries have changed their focus from commodity textiles to high value "niche" products, technical textiles and high-tech and speciality textiles.

There is little chance within the foreseeable future for global textile production and consumption to decrease, in fact the opposite is more likely, as has been the case for many millennia. The key question is therefore, not the sustainability of textiles per sé, but rather the sustainability of one fiber or application or sector vis-à-vis those of another "competing" fiber, application, region or country. With respect to cotton, its share of global textile consumption has dropped from close on 70% in 1960 to less than 40% today (figure 2) although the total consumption of cotton more than doubled during this time (figure 1). Cotton's declining share of the global textile market is accounted for by the corresponding growth in the increased share of man-made fibers, more notably polyester. Clearly there are constraints in global cotton production, including its competition with other agricultural crops, notably edible crops, for arable land, particularly in the light of the growing world population and the associated demand for food and this will become increasingly important if the world population continues to grow at the present pace.

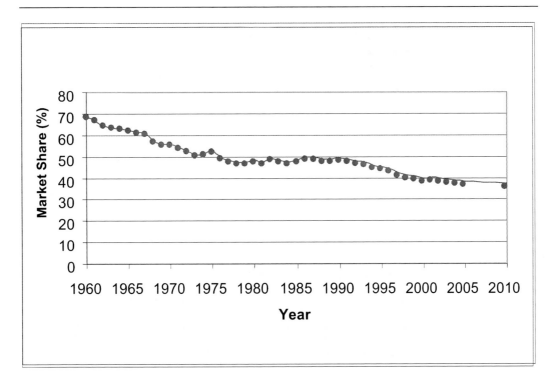

Figure 2. Market share of cotton.

The key question, relevant to this paper, and conference, is "what has sustained, and will sustain, cotton's very prominent position in the global textile scenario"?. In discussing this, "macro" issues, such as global trade agreements, WTO rules and regulations, quotas, subsidies etc, will not be considered, since there are many imponderables and unknowns involved, each justifying a paper, if not a thesis, in their own right. It has, for example, been stated [1] that the elimination of quotas under Multi Fiber Agreement (MFA) increased global cotton consumption by 500 m kg by the end of 2005. The elimination of quotas in January 2005 in place for over 30 years, has shifted textile and apparel production to China and other low-income developing countries, and will intensify competition and lead to lower prices, increasing pressure on the entire cotton pipeline, but benefiting the consumer. In a global free market system it boils down to the global competitiveness of products, companies, countries and regions although the issue of "level playing fields" is increasingly coming to the fore, and it is conceivable that non-tariff barriers (e.g. environmental and labor related) could increasingly be introduced.

In this paper, a global view of cotton in terms of its sustainability will be addressed, the overriding factor being the market demand. It is a complex matter to define what determines the market for a particular product, but rather simply stated, it ultimately revolves around the issue of "perceived value for money". In this context some very profound and complex issues are involved, notably production and manufacturing costs, product costs, product attractiveness (i.e. market perception), competing products, renewable resources and environmental aspects, continuous innovation etc, some of these factors being interrelated.

COTTON'S POSITION

Global per capita consumption of cotton has been virtually constant since 1960 (figure 3), presently being the highest in developed countries (e.g. 16 kg per capita in the USA), but the growth and potential are greatest in developing countries, notably China, India and Pakistan (where it is presently only about 2 kg), the per capita consumption of cotton in Africa being only about 1 kg [1].

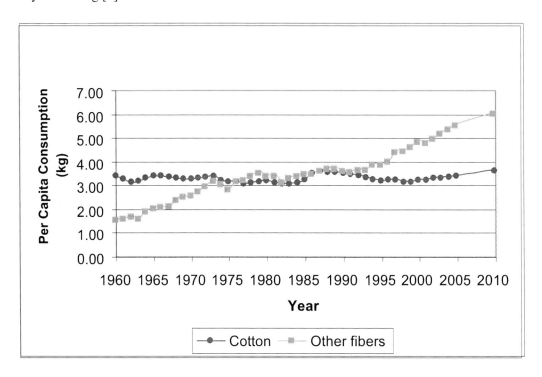

Figure 3. Per capita consumption of fibers.

Globally cotton is one of the most important and widely produced agricultural and industrial crops, being grown in more than 100 countries on some 2.5% of the world's arable land, making it second only to food grains and soybeans. Cotton represents one of the very few "cash crops", which is particularly important to small farmers in developing countries, cotton cultivation contributing to food security and improved life expectancy in the rural areas of a number of developing countries. Some 150 countries are involved in the imports or exports of cotton and 100 million family units are directly engaged in cotton production, and a total involvement in the cotton sector is about 350 million people, with also providing employment to millions more people in allied industries [1]. Global world cotton production is valued at some $30 billion. In addition to its importance as textile fiber, notably apparel and household textiles, where it accounts for more than 50% of fiber consumption, it is also used in industrial textiles and by products, from cotton seed and stalks, provide edible oil for human consumption, also soap, industrial products, firewood and paper and high protein animal feed supplements. Cotton oil is the fifth largest edible oil consumed in the world [1].

Over the past 50 years, cotton production has quadrupled. Since the 1940s, virtually the entire increase in cotton production has resulted from increased yields rather than from increased cultivation areas, increasing from some 230 kg/ha 50 years ago to some 700 kg/ha today (figure 4).

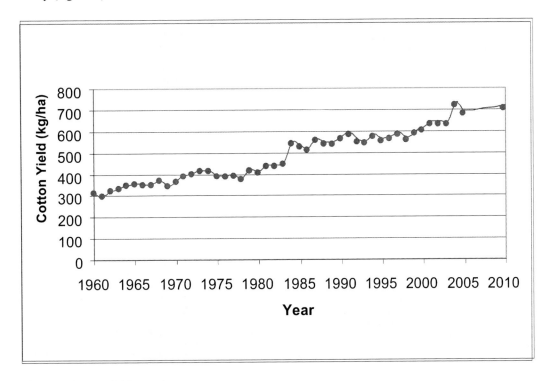

Figure 4. Cotton yield over time.

New technologies, notably biotechnology, have impacted greatly on cotton production and processing. The main achievement of biotechnology has been the decreased dependence of cotton production on insecticides and increased resistance to herbicides. Developing countries accounted for some 60% of cotton production at the start of the 1980s, today accounting for 66%, that in the former USSR falling from 19% to 7% over the same period. China has become the largest producer of cotton, followed by the USA, India and Pakistan. These four countries alone account for some 70% of world production. Africa, on the other hand, accounts for less than 1% of world production. Should subsidies (support), to cotton growers be removed, this situation could change dramatically, particularly with respect to cotton production in countries, such as the USA where it could drop by one third and in the EU by 25% [1].

Farming and harvesting practices and costs depend greatly upon the country and region. Countries which have an abundance of land and labor favored manual planting and harvesting etc., whereas countries with abundant capital, sophisticated RandDR&D and infrastructure etc., favor mechanization and automation at the expense of labor. The average total cost of cotton production is about $1.77 per kg, at a net cost of some $1.14 per kg of lint, cost of production being highest in the US and Europe and the lowest in Asia, South America and Australia, net cost being $1.48 per kg in USA and $3.72 in Europe, that in Africa being $1.4 per kg which is above the world average [1]. Costs of ginning, economic costs and fixed costs account for most of the variation in costs. International cotton prices have declined in real terms over the last six decades because of advances in technology. The cost of cotton production for most producers is around \$1.10 to \$1.30/kg which is what the price of cotton has dropped to this decade, having been around \$1.50 during the 1970s, 1980s and 1990s [1].

Cotton supply and demand are sensitive to price, its inflation adjusted price having decreased from about US \$9/kg in 1950 to \$1.10 today. Price decreases in competing man-made fibers will put increasing price pressures on cotton; the price of cotton (Outlook A Index) is expected to average around \$1.10/kg between 2005 and 2015 [1].

Relevant information on cotton production, exports, price and related matters can be accessed at the following websites [1]:

www.icac.org.
www.USDA.Grow/Nass/
www.ERS.USDA.gov/Briefing/cotton
www.FAS.USDA.gov/cotton
www.cotlook.com
www.ITMF.org
www.LCA.org.uk
www.ciworldreport.com/newswire

REQUIREMENTS FOR SUSTAINABLE COTTON

General

The most important advantages of cotton over its main competitors in the synthetic fiber arena include:
- Its unequalled "against the skin" comfort;
  - ➢ softness
  - ➢ moisture absorbency
  - ➢ wicking
  - ➢ "non-allergenic"
- Natural appearance
- Renewable resource
- Bio-degradable

Disadvantages include:

- Use of agro-chemicals (e.g. herbicides and pesticides)
- Contamination
- Quality variation
- Price fluctuations
- Wrinkle propensity
- Relatively long pipeline

It is important that RandDR&D continues to be directed towards reducing, or preferably eliminating, the above disadvantages, without adversely affecting the advantages (i.e. the desirable properties).

RESEARCH AND PROMOTION

There is little doubt that both research and promotion play an important role in maintaining, if not increasing, the market share of any product, it being estimated that research and promotion have increased cotton consumption by 300 x 10^6 kg since 1998 [1]. We live in an age where customers are becoming increasingly demanding in terms of what they expect of a product, including improved performance, novelty, comfort, style, design, 'ease-of-care", value for money and environmental friendliness. An important element in the survival, if not growth, of a product revolves around promotion, which in the simplest terms creates a desire in the customer to purchase the product at a price which provides adequate financial returns to make the entire pipeline financially viable and sustainable.

Research and innovation are important factors in imparting the desired properties to cotton products. Examples of successes in this context include "wash–and-wear"/"easy-care" and flame resistance. It is indisputable, that cost-effective and focused research is required if cotton is to maintain its place in the global textile market. This would need to cover growing, harvesting, processing, (mechanical and chemical), application and end-use performance, with due consideration being given to global developments in technologies which impact on cotton as well as the environmental impact, and the optimum and cost-effective utilization of technologies, both new and existing. The question which continuously crops up is "who should do and pay for cotton research", since there are many stake holders and concerns which have a direct interest in the welfare and survival of the cotton industry. These include growers, ginners, cotton textile processing companies, cotton machinery manufacturers, chemical suppliers, government etc.

Very similar considerations apply to promotion, the question once again revolving around who should pay for promotion and should it be generic or product related. The answer to both the above questions is quite simply that, to a lesser or greater extent, the research and promotion should be funded by all interested parties and that unnecessary duplication should be avoided at all costs.

In certain areas, such as the standardization of cotton testing for trading and other purposes, collaborative efforts are the preferred, if not essential, approach. Good examples of this include the International Textile Manufacturers Federation (ITMF) International Committee on Cotton Testing Methods and its working-groups, the International Cotton Advisory Committee (ICAC) Commercial Standardization of Instrument Testing of Cotton (CSITC) and its Expert Panel (formed in December 2003) and the USDA Universal Cotton Standards, as well as the role which the USDA Check Tests and Bremen Round Trials play. In this respect, the move by the ICAC towards an international laboratory certification scheme is also highly commendable. Research relating to sectoral and public good should be funded by government, if not fully then at least in part.

Commercial cotton related machinery and instrument research and development represent a very good example of cost effective and successful efforts. To quote but one of many examples, namely the development and commercialization of high volume (HVI) testing of cotton some 30 years ago, with today close on some 2000 systems being in place in over 70 countries, in theory able to test each bale of cotton produced worldwide. There can be no argument that the worldwide trend towards the objective instrument characterization of cotton fiber quality and its utilization in cotton pricing, trading and optimized processing and utilization will continue and be an important component in ensuring that cotton maintains its position in the global fiber market.

Areas R&andD needs to continue to address include:

- Bio-technology: In 2010, 50% of cotton production is expected to be biotech cotton, and this will be produced on 40% of the area planted, biotech cotton presently accounting for about 30% of cotton exports. It is also claimed to have substantial advantages for small growers in developing countries.
- Environmentally friendly production and processing, including organic cotton, the latter fetching considerable price premiums at present.
- Quality improvement (finer, longer, stronger, cleaner etc), by breeding and genetic engineering.
- Complete instrument characterization of cotton fiber quality and utilization
- Universal and standardized cotton fiber testing, including calibration and test methods, as well as the certification of test laboratories for benchmarking, trading and arbitration purposes.
- A more cost-effective and economical cotton pipeline, from grower to end-product
- Product innovation and enhanced cotton product qualities, including multi-functionality, easy-care, wrinkle resistance, flame resistance etc.
- The optimized and cost-effective utilization of new technologies for cotton, for example, air-jet and friction spinning, fabric objective measurement (Kawabata and FAST), air-jet weaving, multi-phase weaving, non-wovens, nano-technology, composites etc.
- The accurate prediction and optimization of processing behavior and performance, including spinning performance and yarn and fabric properties, from fiber properties, using knowledge based systems (e.g. expert, artificial, neural networks, fuzzy logic).

It is important that RandDR&D and end-use applications for cotton be focussed on those areas where cotton has a distinct benefit, presently or potentially, in terms of price and/or performance.

The reader is referred to reference 1 for a far more comprehensive treatment of the subject.

ACKNOWLEDGEMENTS

The Author is highly indebted to Mr Terry Townsend, Executive Director of the ICAC, for much of the information used in this paper. Information and assistance provided by Cotton S.A. is also gratefully acknowledged.

REFERENCE

[1]   Townsend, T. Chapter 19, "Economic and Cost Considerations", in *"Cotton: Science and Technology"*, (Editors: Dr S. Gordon and Dr Y-L. Hsieh), Woodhead Publishing Ltd., 2006To be published.

In: Textiles for Sustainable Development   ISBN: 978-1-60021-559-9
Editors: R. Anandjiwala, L. Hunter et al., pp. 397-403   © 2007 Nova Science Publishers, Inc.

Chapter 35

RAW MATERIALS BASED ON LINSEED OILS FOR POLYURETHANE SYNTHESIS

R. Kozłowski [b], J. Pielichowski [a], A. Prociak [a], M. Marek [a] and K. Bujnowicz [b]

[a] Cracov University of Technology, Department of Chemistry and Technology of Polymers Krakow, Poland, pielich@usk.pk.edu.pl
[b] Institute of Natural Fibres, Poznan, Poland, sekretar@inf.poznan.pl

ABSTRACT

Polyols based on vegetable oils can be used for obtaining polyurethane polymers including elastomers, fibers, foams with the properties required for various applications.

The method used for making vegetable oil based polyol is a two-step process. In the first step unsaturated vegetable oil react with the hydrogen peroxide to epoxidized oil. In the second step the epoxidized oil is converted by the hydroxylation reaction with alcohols into the polyols. The nucleophiles required to the ring opening reaction of the epoxide compounds might be also polyfunctional alcohols. A new method to obtain vegetable oil based polyols in two step process, in which ethylene glycol was used as a ring opening of modified triglicerides, has been investigated. The mechanical properties of the blown polyurethane polymers with linseed-based polyol are better in comparison with competitive products based on petrochemicals polyols.

Keywords: raw materials, polyols, polyurethanes, linseed oil.

INTRODUCTION

In times of high prices of oil the studies of materials based on renewable resources are very important. The products based on renewable resources usually are better eecologically compatible when compared with petrochemical-based substances [1]. Therefore the world vegetable oil consumption grows up. World vegetable oils consumption in 2003 is shown in figure 1.

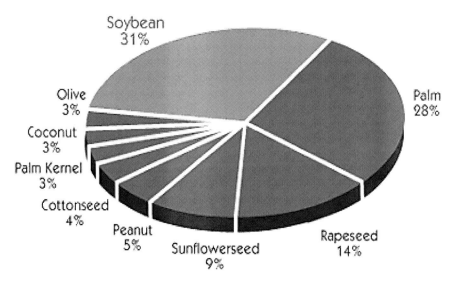

Figure 1. World vegetable oil consumption – 2003.

Vegetable oils are triglycerides, i.e., esters of different fatty acids and glycerol. The composition of the fatty acids contained in the vegetable oils determines the further use of the oils. Fatty acids in oils are mostly unsaturated, causing the oils to be liquid, while fats are solid at room temperature [2]. The most important unsaturated fatty acids in linseed oil are:

- oleic acid (C18:1) $CH_3(CH_2)_7CH=CH(CH_2)_7COOH$
- linoleic acid (C18:2) $CH_3(CH_2)_4CH=CHCH_2CH=CH(CH_2)_7COOH$
- linolenic acid (C18:3) $CH_3CH_2CH=CHCH_2CH=CHCH_2CH=CH(CH_2)_7COOH$

Oleic is dominant acid in oils with lower unsaturation (olive, peanut, canola) while linoleic acid is predominant in corn, soybean and sunflower oils. Linoleic acid exists in linseed, soybean oils (figure 2) [2, 3].

Double bonds in fatty acids are not very reactive except oxidation reactions that are used for drying in oil-based coatings. In order to make oils reactive, it is necessary to introduce functional groups, usually at the position of double bonds [2].

One of the methods for obtaining polymers from renewable resources is catalytic reaction of linseed oil with urea [4, 5]. It was found that in special conditions the linseed oil reacts quantitatively with urea:

$$ROCOCH_2CH(OCOR)CH_2OCOR + 2\ NH_2CONH_2 \xrightarrow{cat,Temp}$$
$$NH_2OCOCH_2CH(OCOR)CH_2OCONH_2 + 2\ RCONH_2$$

or in directly, in a two-stage reaction, in homogeneous system

$$C_4H_9OH + NH_2CONH_2 \xrightarrow{cat,Temp} C_4H_9OCONH_2 + NH_3$$
$$ROCOCH_2CH(OCOR)CH_2OCOR + 2\ C_4H_9OCONH_2 \xrightarrow{cat,Temp}$$
$$NH_2OCOCH_2CH(OCOR)CH_2OCONH_2 + 2\ RCOOC_4H_9\ ).$$

These studies allow for obtaining products capable of modifying properties of resins, changing for instance hydrophobic properties, elasticity, solubility, etc. [3].

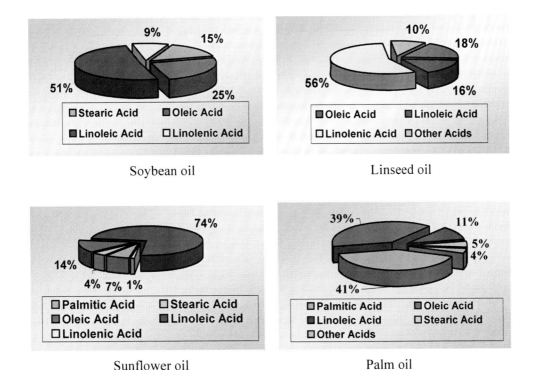

Figure 2. Fatty acids in vegetable oils.

In polymer applications epoxides, polyols, and dimerizations products based on unsaturated fatty acids, are used as plastic additives or components for composites or polymers like polyurethanes.

In the experimental part characteristic of linseed oil derivative polyol is presented and influence of this polyol on the mechanical and heat-insulating properties of rigid polyurethane foams blown with environmentally friendly agents.

EXPERIMENTAL

Preparation of Polyol

The method of making linseed oil-based polyols was two-step process. In the first step unsaturated linseed oil reacted with peroxyacid to form epoxidized oil. Through the epoxidation, the double bonds of the triglycerides were transformed into oxirane rings. In the second step the epoxidized oil was converted into the polyols using ethylene glycol. The characteristic of the new polyol product is shown in table 1.

Table 1. Properties of Linseed Polyol

Properties	Value
Hydroxyl number (mg KOH/g)	333,5
Acid number (mg KOH/g)	< 1
Viscosity (mPa·s at 25°C)	964
Colour	yellow

Preparation of Foams

Linseed polyol because of its suitable properties was added to rigid polyurethane foam formulations. The investigations were carried out with four different formulas (table 2). The first and third presented formulas were prepared on the base of petrochemical polyol mixtures (Alfapol TD-34, Alfapol G-1000, Alfapol RF-551) as the reference system. The second and fourth formulas consist of polyol mixture including 50% wt. of linseed oil–based polyol. The foaming processes were carried out using two different blowing agents: cyclopentane and HFC-365/227 (93 wt.%1,1,1,3,3-pentafluorobutane and 7 wt.% 1,1,1,2,2,3,3-heptafluoropropane) In both formulas (1 and 2) cyclopentane was added but in the last two HFC-365/227 was applied.

The rigid foams were prepared by mixing A and B components. Component A contained mixtures of polyols, catalyst, water, surfactants and a blowing agent. Component B (polymeric isocyanate -PMDI) was added to component A and the mixtures were stirred for 10 s with an overhead stirrer. Then prepared mixtures were dropped into the mould.

The polyurethane foams were conditioned during 24 hours, before being cut to analyse cell structure and measure their density, compressive strength and thermal conductivity coefficient. The mechanical properties of the foams were estimated versus vertical and horizontal directions.

Table 2. Formulations of the Rigid Polyurethane Foams

Component, g	Foam 1	Foam 2	Foam 3	Foam 4
Mixture of petrochemical polyols	100	50	100	50
Linseed oil-based polyol	-	50	-	50
Water	1,5	1,5	1,5	1,5
Surfactants (SR-321)	1,5	1,5	1,5	1,5
Catalyst (Texacat DMCHA)	1,9	1,9	1,9	1,9
Cyclopentane	12	12	-	-
HFC-365/227	-	-	24	24
Suprasec DNR (PMDI)	124,8	118	124,8	118

RESULTS AND DISCUSSION

The foam properties versus vertical and horizontal directions were estimated. The mechanical properties of the foams with linseed oil-based polyol are higher in comparison with competitive products based on petrochemical polyols. Results of compressive strength measurements, realised perpendicular and parallel to the direction of the foam rise, are shown in figure 3.

The cellular materials with apparent densities ca. 40 kg/m^3 were formed. The density of samples, prepared using different foam systems, was similar, but the maximum value was noticed for second formula (polyol mixture including 50% wt. of linseed oil–based polyol and cyclopentane as a blowing agent). Heat-insulating properties of the foams were very good, the λ-values are presented in figure 4. The insulation efficiency of the products with linseed oil-based polyol was ensured by the proper cell structure of foams and the use of the new generation, physical blowing agents.

The mechanical properties, density and thermal conductivity of the PUR correspond to used physical blowing agent and cell structures.

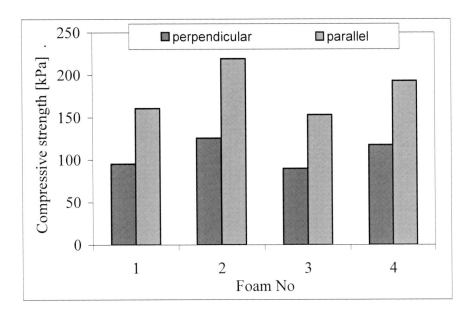

Figure 3. Compressive strength of foams.

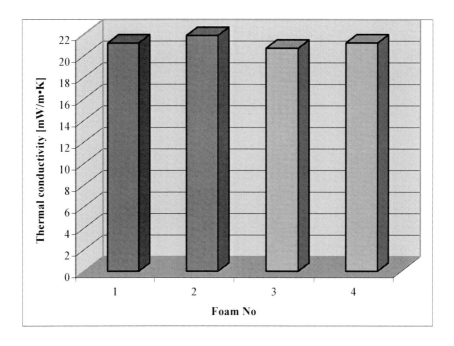

Figure 4. Thermal conductivity of foams.

CONCLUSION

1. Our investigations show the possibility to obtain environmentally friendly materials such as the rigid polyurethane foams using the linseed oil-based polyol.
2. Novel foams have comparable heat-insulating properties to the reference material.
3. New polymers from renewable resources can be useful matrix component for composites reinforcement by natural fibers.
4. Taking into account that many countries in the world have a vast potential regarding cultivation of oil plants, positive results of this study may result in a new source of modern, sustainable, more ecological polymers like polyurethane foams.

REFRENCES

[1]   Hill, K. 12q Fats and oils as oleochemical raw materials, *Pure Appl. Chem., Vol.* 72, 2000, pp. 1255-1264.
[2]   Petrovic, Z; Guo, A; Javini, I; Zhang, W. "Plastics and Composites from Soybean Oil" In: *Natural Fibers, Plastics and Composites,* F. T. WALLENBERGER, N. WESTON, eds. Kluwer Academic 2004.
[3]   Bujnowicz, K; Kozlowski, R; Pielichowski, J; Wirpsza, Z. "Polymers from Natural Fatty Acids" In: Modern Polymeric Materials for Environmental Applications, *Vol.1,* K. Pielichowski, eds., 1st International Seminar, 2004, Krakow, Poland.

[4]   Kozlowski, R; Pielichowski, J; Wirpsza, Z; Bujnowicz, K; Przepiera, A. "Polymers from Linseed Oil", in The Proceedings of the 3rd Global Workshop "Bast Fibrous Plants for Healthy Life", 2005, Banja Luka, Bosnia and Herzegovina.

[5]   Kozlowski, R; Pielichowski, J; Wirpsza, Z; Bujnowicz, K. Polymers from Natural Fatty Acids, The Proceedings of the 10th Internationanal Conference for Renewable Resources and Plant Biotechnology, Magdeburg, Germany, June 7-8, 2004.

In: Textiles for Sustainable Development   ISBN: 978-1-60021-559-9
Editors: R. Anandjiwala, L. Hunter et al., pp. 405-412   © 2007 Nova Science Publishers, Inc.

Chapter 36

IMPROVED PROFITABILITY THROUGH INDUSTRIAL UPGRADING OF BAST FIBERS IN SOUTH AFRICA

Martin Tubach, Gerhard Mayer and Rainer Alex

Institut für Angewandte Forschung, Reutlingen University; Alteburgstrasse 150, 72762
Reutlingen, Germany; Tel. ++49 (0) 7121 271 1401, Fax ++49 (0) 7121 271 1404,
http://www.iaf.fh-reutlingen.de/; Martin.Tubach@fh-reutlingen.de

ABSTRACT

The development, production and use of products, which are economically, ecologically and socially sustainable, represent the central theme for the route into the 21st Century. Non-renewable resources are becoming more and more scarce and thus more expensive. Businesses, which are today developing and implementing innovative solutions within the area of renewable resources, are achieving a strong competitive position in the worldwide market. Bearing this in mind, the real potential of hHemp and fFlax is not yet exploited. A low motivation of farmers to grow bBast fibers crops can be explained by volatile profitability of cultivation and mechanical refining. Through implementation of a new refining step into the process chain the fibers value is upgraded, which improves fiber fineness, evenness and purity. The STEX treatment (Steam Explosion) can be considered as a key technology in Bast fibers processing in order to enter higher value applications in textile and non-textile markets. The economic outlook for a fiber upgrading business using the STEX is good. This can be shown by an operational business calculation. The paper gives a clear picture of the attractiveness of the related industries. In the operational calculation a STEX business is investigated in detail as a producing company with real investments, sales and costs. A good internal rate of return can be expected. A sensitivity and a scenario analysis of parameters with the greatest influence ("critical values") show robust results.

Keywords: bast fibers, upgrading, economy, business model, profit.

INTRODUCTION

Agriculture, agro-processing, clothing and textiles are, beside automotive, tourism and others, political priority growth sectors in South Africa. Flax and Hemp offer excellent opportunities. They have not yet been fully exploited for high added value applications, such as use in bio based natural textiles and high performance fibers. There are few practical applications, although today's know-how in fiber purification, modification and application allow forof a large array of viable bio based products. A promising combination of such growth sectors must include farming, basic processing, upgrading and manufacturing as well as the focus on production efficiency, quality control and marketing actions.

MARKETS

In Europe, there is an increasing demand for natural fiber commodities in the field of automotive applications. Nevertheless, due to the low prices of raw materials and products income remains unsatisfying for the European farmers. Daimler Chrysler relies heavily on natural fibers. The Mercedes-Benz E-Class, for example, uses 21 natural fiber/plastic components weighting a total of 20.5 kilograms (41 pounds).

DaimlerChrysler is using natural fibers with extremely high tensile strength from the abaca banana plant in the standard underbody cover for the spare-wheel compartment of the 3-door version of the Mercedes-Benz A-Class model. After using natural fibers, such as flax, hemp, sisal and coconut, in the interior of Mercedes-Benz passenger cars and commercial vehicles for many years, a component in the exterior of a car is now being used for the first time. DaimlerChrysler research engineers patented a novel mixture of polypropylene (PP)-thermoplastic and abaca fibers in 2002.

wwwsg.daimlerchrysler.com.

The demand in the textile industry for refined s is still limited due to a lack of adequate supply and high prices resulting in low sales quantities for farmers and manufacturers. Bearing in mind the most obvious ecological challenges e.g. growth of population, future energy demand, green house effect and destruction of the ozone layer, profitability and sustainability in agriculture and industry should not be considered as contradictory in principle, but rather as a must in the future.

OBJECTIVES

In order to extend the use of natural fibers and to establish a robust economic value chain in South Africa, we recommend the creation of an interdisciplinary network including farmers, fiber refining companies and upgraders, closely connected to spinning and weaving firms as well as to manufacturers of innovative, technical applications. Through implementation of a new refining step, the fiber value is upgraded, which improves fiber fineness, evenness and purity. A totally new fiber can be produced with a better cost/benefit ratio. The technical feasibility and the economic benefits have been clearly shown in several projects and case studies. Therefore fiber upgrading is a key technology in Bast fiber processing in order to enter higher value applications in the textile and non-textile industry. Fibers deriving from the STEX process (Steam Explosion Treatment), as an example for wet processing, meet these requirements and offer a wide range of different applications. STEX can be considered as the missing technological link between the current supply in the fiber sector and the market demand for tailor-made raw materials. The economic outlook for a fiber upgrading business using the STEX process (in the following called STEX business) is good. This can be shown by an operational business calculation. /Kessler/Kohler/Tubach/

TECHNICAL DESIGN

The proposed processing line uses bales from decorticated Hemp and Flax fibers deriving from traditional decortication plants from national production or overseas suppliers. After opening the bales fibers can be cut, according to specific requirements. A step cleaner removes dust and shives as well as adherent impurities. After impregnation with a light alkaline solution and reducing agents, fibers are subjected to a steam vessel. Saturated steam, at about 10-15 bars and 160°C, degrades the middle lamella of the fiber bundles within 10-15 minutes and due to the sudden release of the pressure, the material is mechanically separated into single fibers. This technique provides fine fibers which can be spun on a traditional cotton line to finer yarns in the range of 20-25 Nm. Finer fibers also perform a lot better in natural fiber reinforced composites, as each individual fiber contributes to the overall strength. A further disintegration at a higher severity of the treatments results in a total disintegration of the supramolecular structure and produces pulp. After removing the water soluble impurities in a washing range, optional disc opening and drying, fibers are utilized in the traditional textile or/and demanding technical applications e.g. high performance composites.

/Nebel/Kessler/

The following figure shows the production line.

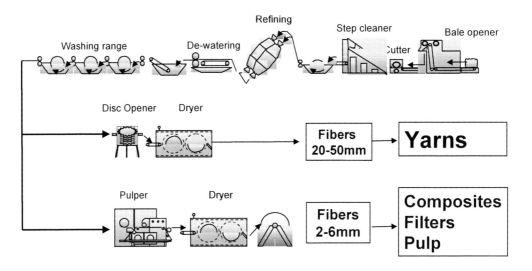

Figure 1. Production line for steam exploded bast fibers.

ECONOMICAL FOCUS

On the basis of a complete production line, we demonstrate that a profitable system in Bast fiber processing for investors is possible with fair and competitive prices to the farmers, processors and manufacturers. The focus is to produce clean and tailor-made short fibers at a cotton price level but without the usual disadvantages of bBast fibers e.g. inhomogeneity due to morphological variations and broad distribution of the chemical composition.

The basis for all calculations are conservative assumptions of South African price levels for property, investment, labor, raw materials, energy, chemicals, water etc.. Unfortunately it was difficult to obtain authentic on-site data. But it was possible to work out the economic range of quantities, prices and costs. As a next step all data must be verified.

/Tubach/Kessler/
Boundary conditions are:

- SME is located in South Africa
- Subsidy free investment
- Fair income for farmers (600 €/t decorticated fibers)
- Competitive price for users (1.8 €/kg steam exploded fiber)
- Attractive Internal Rate of Return on Investment (IRR) for investors (~25% before Tax)

RESULTS

Bast fibers are upgraded in a virtual average scale pilot plant (STEX technology) with an investment for property, plant and equipment of €6.1 m € and a capacity of 6,000 t/yr. The calculation gives a detailed and complex economic view of the production step with promising prospects: The internal rate of return on investment (IRR) is 26 % before tax. This is fairly good for an SME in the fiber business and the rate should attract potential investors. All assumptions along the different processing steps are realistic or slightly conservative in order to obtain reliable results. The following figure shows the most important economic characteristics for investors in the STEX technology. It demonstrates the critical factors for IRR before tax. For more clarity, all variables of less importance are suppressed.

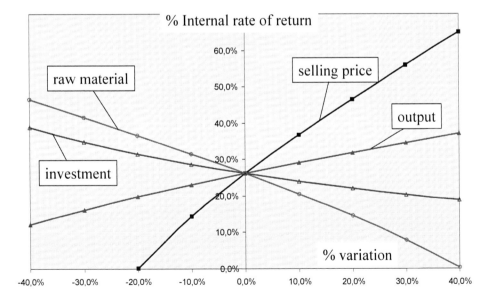

Figure 2. Sensitivity analysis: Internal rate of return depending on the critical variables "selling price", "output", "investment" and "raw material price". Model calculated and diagrams created by ProWi-Software ©, Prof. Dr. G. Mayer, www.prowi.de.

The intersection with the ordinate shows the IRR without variations (26%). Any variation of parameters brings about significant changes of the rate. In particular an increase in "output" and "selling price" influences the rate favorably, whereas increases in "investment" and "raw material price" affect in adversity. These parameters have the greatest influence and must be considered as the critical factors regarding the rate of return. The model shows that the calculated business can be considered as a robust business. Fluctuations in the range of +/-15% can be compensated.

Moreover the question is, will the market accept these fluctuations? Any variation of the critical value "selling price" will influence the demand from the textile industry significantly. A calculated price of €1.8 €/kg for short fibers guarantees a high demand from national and overseas spinning mills. But in order to stimulate national fiber production at the same time, the raw material price should not be below the world market price level of around €600 €/t. In order to keep the fiber price at the lowest possible limit and to satisfy investor's expectations of IRR before tax >25%, the optimum of the production scale is around 5000-5.600 t/yr.

The next figure illustrates that even smaller production scales can, under certain conditions, result in the same IRR. Smaller production scales can be compensated for, primarily by either higher selling prices or lower costs for raw materials. For example: if production decreases to 3000 t/yr. and if investors want to gain the same 26% IRR before tax they would have (in principle) the possibility to increase selling price (~ +18%) or decrease raw material price (~ -35%) which is hardly realistic, or choose any combination along the 3000 t/yr line. A decrease of the production scale to 4000 t/yr. can still be compensated for, by slight reductions in raw material prices. But this means that (1) national fiber farming should be extended up to 7000-8000 t raw fibers/yr. corresponding to 4000 to 5000 ha. depending on fiber yield *and* that (2) a highly economic decortication step can be established successfully at the same time. Slightly increasing the selling price level should be possible, if marketing actions are able to develop a strong African label for textiles. Any reduction of scale less than 5000 t/yr,. however, will strongly influence the market.

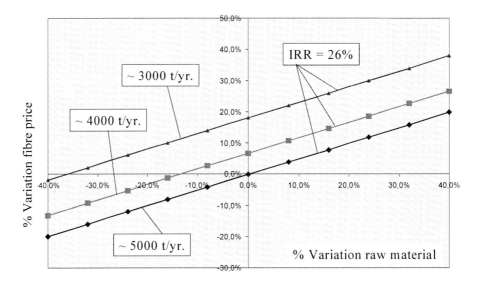

Figure 3. Scenarios of 3 different production scales with corresponding variations of selling and material price for an IRR of 26%.

The next figure shows the distribution of product costs (€1800 €/t). Raw material and auxiliary materials e.g. steam, chemical, electricity etc. influence the product cost most accounting for 62% of the product cost. Wages have not that large an influence on costs as may have been presumed. Even variations of +/-20% will not shift costs to significant higher or lower values. Assessing fiber quality is the key issue for the economical success. Different lots, varieties, preparation methods, harvesting time and retting degrees vary according to "natural" variations. The raw material can only be optimally processed if the whole process is adjusted to the input quality.

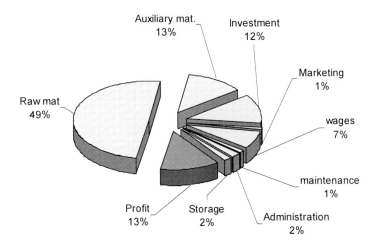

Figure 4. Distribution of production costs.

Details of the virtual pilot scale plant (STEX) for upgrading mechanical decorticated fibers in South Africa are as follows:

- Investment: €6,1 m €
- Capacity: 6000 t/yr. steam exploded fibers
- Output: 5000 t/yr.
- Planning horizon: 10 years (together 50,750 t; €91.35 m €)
- Assumed cost of capital (cost of capital): 11% before tax
- Pay back time (including cost of capital): 5.22 years
- Pay back output (including cost of capital): 23,967 t corresponding to €43.141 m €
- Calculated Internal Rate of Return on Investment (IRR): 26,2% before tax at the end of the planning horizon
- Selling price: €1800 €/t
- Raw material price: €600 €/t decorticated fiber
- Marketing costs: €0.5 m €

REFERENCES

[1]   Kohler, R; Wedler, M. Anwendung von Naturfasern in technischen Bereichen, mittex, Schweizerische Fachschrift für die Textilwirtschaft, Heft 3, S. 7-10, 1996.

[2]   Kohler, R; Kessler, RW. Einfluss der Aufschlussverfahren auf die Eigenschaften naturfaserverstärkter Kunststoffe. Proceedings of the International Wood and Natural Composites Symposium, 29.- 30. Juni, Kassel, 1998.

[3]   Kohler, R; Kessler, RW. Faseraufbereitung und Qualitätskriterien von Naturfasern für Verbundwerkstoffe Proceedings of 5. International Conference "Stoffliche Nutzung nachwachsender Rohstoffe", 28.-29.10., Chemnitz 1998.

[4]   Kohler, R; Kessler, RW. Designing natural s for advanced materials, Proceedings of the Fifth International Conference on Woodfiber-Plastic Composites, Madison Wisconsin, May 26-27 (1999) 29-42

[5]   Mayer, G. ProWi ©, Software für Produkt-Wirtschaftlichkeit und Produktions-Lebenszyklus-Controlling, http://www.prowi.de

[6]   Kessler, RW; Becker, U; Kohler, R; Goth, B. Steam-Explosion of Flax - A superior Technique for Upgrading Value, *Biomass and Bioenergy,* Vol 14, No. 3 (1998) 237 - 249.

[7]   Nebel, K; Ruehle, A; Selcuk, R; Haryanto, A. Prerequisites on Hemp s for the Production of fine Yarns by Cotton Spinning Proceedings of the International FAO Conference Bast s Plants on the Turn of Second and third Millennium, 18.-22.09.2001 Shenyang, China, III/10

[8]   Alex, R; Nebel, K; Tubach, M. Economical Considerations on Cultivation, Processing and Use of Hemp and Flax in Germany, Proceedings "Bast Fibrous Plants on the Turn of Second and Third Millennium, 18-22. September, 2001, Shenyang, China

[9]   Kessler, R; Nebel, K; Werner, H. Adaptive chemical processing for tailor made traditional linen, Proceedings of the 1st Nordic Conference on Flax and Hemp processing, 10-12 August, 1998, Tampere, Finland, p. 159-171R.

[10]   Kessler, RW; Kohler, R. New strategies for exploiting Flax and Hemp In: *Chemtech,* 12, 1996, p. 34-42

[11]   Alex, R; Kessler, RW; Kohler, R; Tubach, M. (2004). Economic trends along the value chain. Proceedings of the "Bast Fibrous Plants for Healthy Life", The Third Workshop (General Consultation of the FAO European Cooperative Research Network on Flax and other Bast Plants, Banja Luka, Bosnia and Herzegovina

[12]   Alex, R; Debowski, G; Mayer, Th; Ströher, MA; Toonen, J; Tubach, M. Intelligentes Management einer Wertschöpfungskette in der Bastfaserverarbeitung Proceedings "Produktion, Verarbeitung und Anwendung von Naturfasern", 10.-11.09.02, Agrartechnik Bornim, Potsdam, Deutschland.

In: Textiles for Sustainable Development ISBN: 978-1-60021-559-9
Editors: R. Anandjiwala, L. Hunter et al., pp. 413-419   © 2007 Nova Science Publishers, Inc.

Chapter 37

FLAX CANADA 2015:
GOING BEYOND THE STATUS QUO

Alvin Ulrich

161 Jessop Avenue, Saskatoon, Canada S7N 1Y3; aulrich@biolin.sk.ca

ABSTRACT

In 2004 the federal government of Canada initiated a program to focus resources on one crop in Western Canada that has a large potential for creating more added value industries domestically. Flax was the chosen crop and this new initiative is called Flax Canada 2015. This program attempts to focus funding from several agencies and private sector companies to expand the potential for flax in the broad areas of: (1) human nutrition, (2) animal nutrition, (3) fiber, (4) industrial uses, and (5) breeding/agronomy. Many of the fundamentals are in place for this program to create significant benefits for Canada. The program concept is a good one but there are an assortment of constraints that may prevent program components from reaching their long term potential.

Keywords: Flax Canada 2015, R and D, industry development, strategic plan.

INTRODUCTION

Canada is the world's largest exporter of flaxseed (i.e., linseed) for crushing. Annual planting of flax varieties for oilseed ranges from 700,000 to 900,000 hectares and total production of flaxseed varies from 600,000 to 1,100,000 tonnes annually. Planting of flax varieties for fiber is less than 50 hectares and is, at the present time, restricted to research trials.

More than 90% of Canada's production of flaxseed is exported in the form of whole seeds and the major markets are Belgium, Netherlands, USA and Japan. The majority of this seed is crushed in the importing countries. The majority of oil thus produced is used in industrial applications (e.g., linoleum, wood stains and finishes, printing inks, mould release agents); the majority of the meal produced in the crushing process is used for livestock feed near the crushing plants. The market for industrial uses for flaxseed oil (i.e., linseed oil) has been quite stagnant for several decades and the increased demand for some linseed oil based industrial applications has been generally countered by a reduction in other traditional industrial uses (e.g., increased linseed oil use in linoleum has been countered by decreased linseed use in paints and stains).

At the farm level, average per hectare yields of flaxseed have also remained almost the same (i.e., 1,100 to 1,300 kg/ha) for several decades although individual farmers who grow flax every year as part of their crop rotation often experience yields 50% or more above these average yields. Flax is often a neglected crop. It is often seeded last because it suffers less from late planting than most other crops. Mature flax crops can also withstand rain and snow better than other mature crops and hence another reason to plant flax last, even though early seeding generally produces the highest yields of flaxseed. Many farmers plant flax only when the flaxseed price is unusually high relative to other crop prices.

Canada normally accounts for 70% to 80% of the world trade in flaxseed. The price of flaxseed on the world market fluctuates more than many other crops and every four to six years there is a significant jump in prices. This happened most recently in the 2004/05 crop year. On August 20th, 2004 an unexpected early frost destroyed almost 40% of the flax crop. Following this frost, farm flaxseed prices rose from a range of C$280 to C$325 per tonne in August 2004 to a range of C$550 to C$625 per tonne in May 2005. Such high prices encourage farmers who have not grown flax for a number of years to plant flax. Given their inexperience, flax is often planted too deep and/or in a poor seedbed and/or weed control is not very good. This, in turn, often produces a crop that gives a lower than average yield. In contrast to this, there are farmers who plant flax every year and in certain areas of Western Canada flax can be found every year. These farmers and areas tend to have higher than average flax yields but a significant amount of production always comes from farmers who get into and out of flax production every couple of years.

The biggest single factor that farmers do not like about flax is "the straw problem." The flax crop is harvested with the same machines and in the same manner as most other crops in Western Canada. The major part of the plant is cut and passed through a "combine". This machine both threshes the straw and separates the straw from the seeds. The straw inside the machine is severely beaten and shaken to extract quickly as much seed as possible. The straw is then chopped and spread by the combine as it passes out of the machine. However, flax straw often cannot be chopped easily by a combine. In such cases, the straw chopper on the combine is turned off and the straw is allowed to fall in a row behind the combine. Often a farmer using the tillage machinery commonly available, cannot easily work this straw into the soil by the next planting season. If this is the case, farmers often burn the straw in the rows that were dropped by the combine or rake it into large straw piles and then burn it. Most farmers do not like the extra work and unpleasantness of flax straw burning. In addition, near urban areas more and more non farmers complain about the smoke and particulate matter that blows into such areas when flax straw is burnt.

By using conventional seeding and harvest methods for oilseed flax, potential straw production would range from 400,000 to 1,200,000 tonnes annually depending on such factors as weather conditions, actual area seeded, harvesting method, straw collection method and the agronomic practices and varieties that were used. In the last 50 years, not more that 15% of the straw produced has been used for commercial processing purposes, and end products have been restricted to use in speciality papers (i.e., cigarette and currency papers) and low end plastic composites.

For many years, two companies, Schwietzer-Mauduit Canada and Ecusta s, have been responsible for most of the straw that is collected and processed into speciality paper. They have part-time straw buyers (often retired farmers) who, each year, try to find areas that have relatively tall oilseed straw with good fiber content. Experience has shown them that the best areas for straw change from year to year because of changing localized weather conditions during the growing season. The flax straw left in rows after combining in the selected fields is normally round baled shortly after harvest, although some is always left until the following spring before it is baled. Farmers receive a "courtesy payment" of C$5 per tonne for fall baled straw and about C$10 per tonne for spring baled straw. It should be pointed out that the processors also pay all the costs to get the straw from a loose row of straw in the field to stacks of bales at the processing plant. Hence, a processor's total costs for courtesy payments, field inspection, baling, hauling and stacking would be C$30 to C$50 per tonne by the time the straw is stacked beside the processing facility. Typical "salvaged" straw yields would be about 0.5 to 0.6 tonnes per acre (i.e., 1.25 to 1.50 tonnes per hectare) by simply baling straw left after the combine.

This straw is, for the most part, under-retted, broken into inconsistent lengths, and contains many seed holders. It is good for pulping, low end plastic composites, biofuel, animal bedding, windbreaks, duck nesting sites and water erosion prevention; however, it has too much physical damage, too little retting and too many seed holders to be transformed into fiber for higher end uses.

RECENT DEVELOPMENTS

In the past decade, there has been a rapid increase in people's interest in the possible health benefits of flaxseed and its components for human and animal use. This has been spurred on by a variety of research efforts into the various effects that inclusion of whole flaxseed, ground flaxseed, flaxseed oil and flaxseed meal components can have on humans, domesticated animals and fish species. The list of these studies could, by now, fill a small book. A few examples include the Flax Council of Canada's *Flax A Health and Nutrition Primer* by Diane Morris [1], J.S. Drouillard *et al*'s work on the feeding of flaxseed and flaxseed products to cattle [2] and Cunnane and Thompson's *Flaxseed in Human Nutrition* [3]. These are by no means the most important or most recent research results regarding the beneficial effects of using flaxseed and its derivatives in human and animal nutrition. By chance, they are all on the author of this paper's shelf at this time and contain many references. A little searching would turn up multitudes of such publications. This type of research has shown that there are, in most cases, significant health and monetary gains to be made by including flaxseed or its components in diets of humans, domesticated animals and fish. The result has been a rapid increase in the amount of flaxseed that is "ground" for nutritional use instead of being "crushed" to produce linseed oil for industrial purposes. Some people in the seed trade have estimated that more than 15% of the Canadian flaxseed crop is now ground instead of being crushed and that, if this trend continues, it could be more than 80% within the next ten years.

This optimistic forecast is coupled with the expectation that total demand for flaxseed could be three or four times the level it is today. Are such increases possible? A simple example may help illustrate this point. Cattle in feedlots eat 70 to 80 pounds (32 to 36 kilograms) per day of feed. Cost effective rations containing flax could easily contain 5% by weight of flaxseed. This would mean that each feedlot animal would be consuming about 1.7 kg of flaxseed per day. Canada's annual average production of flaxseed is about 900,000 to 1,000,000 tonnes per year. At the dietary inclusion rate just mentioned, Canada's total flax crop could supply the flax needs for 530,000,000 to 590,000,000 "cattle days" or 1,450,000 to 1,600,000 cattle fed for 365 days in a year. If the average feedlot animal spends 180 days in a feedlot, the number of cattle that could get flax in their ration would roughly double to about 3,000,000 cattle per year. In 2005, there were, in total, almost 18,000,000 cattle in Canada and over 80,000,000 in the USA. Thus, if only a small portion of North American cattle have flax included in their ration because trials show that it is economically beneficial to do so (and most cattle feeding trials to date have shown this to be the case), the demand for flaxseed for inclusion in North American cattle diets could easily consume the present total flaxseed production of Canada by many fold! Similar calculations can be made in reference to diets for North American pigs, chickens, dairy cows and farmed fish. It is staggering to think that most of the world's domesticated animals and fish are not in North America. Will they also start consuming flaxseed?

Humans do not have the potential to consume flaxseed in the same volume as domesticated animals and fish; however, they incur health care costs that are many magnitudes larger than those of other animal species. If the inclusion of flaxseed or its components can be shown to reduce the incidence of major and widespread conditions like diabetes, cancer and cardiovascular disease, there will be many opportunities to make private financial gains from flax related products, not to mention the reduced health costs that society as a whole would enjoy. Thus both private and public funders of R&andD have an incentive to develop added value products that will build upon the apparent health maintaining properties of flaxseed and its components and will certainly increase the demand for flaxseed and its derivatives for human health and nutrition.

The projected demand for flaxseed in animal and human nutrition bodes well for rapid increases in the consumption of flaxseed in the future. Will farmers be willing to grow more flax? This, of course, depends on the profits that can be made from growing flax relative to the profits that can be made from growing other crops. The main non-monetary constraint to farmers growing more flax is the "straw problem." If we could turn flax straw from a problem to a new revenue source, it would make it so much easier to get farmers to cultivate increased areas of flaxseed and produce many times more flaxseed for the potential new value adding industries concerned with animal and human health and nutrition.

Fortunately, the last decade has seen several companies and groups conduct research and/or commercialization activities in Canada focused on the production of higher end fiber and shive from both oilseed and fiber flax varieties. These have included both Canadian and foreign based companies. Much has been learned and new, large scale developments are expected within the next couple of years. Nevertheless, further research is needed to reduce the risk of such first time ventures and to facilitate the scale up and commercialization of techniques, processing systems and markets.

Some of the more significant advancements have included the development of a NIR based system to rapidly estimate the bast fiber content of unretted intact straw. The database of observations needed to give good estimates took at least four years to develop but it is enabling researchers to develop a whole new understanding of why bast fiber content varies so much in flax in Western Canada. It will also help flax breeders develop oilseed flax varieties with enhanced bast fiber content and will help commercial operators select fields and areas of flax that have enhanced bast fiber content. Initial work with fiber flax varieties gave new insights into how to better manage oilseed flax to improve both the quality and quantity of fiber that can be produced from oilseed flax. For instance, harvesting with a stripper header, drum mowing or rolling the resultant de-seeded standing straw, allowing it to ret and then raking and baling it up can result in not only a doubling of straw yield but a great improvement in the average fineness, length and cleanliness of the fiber that is extracted from oilseed flax straw. Selection of existing oilseed varieties that tend to have relatively higher fiber content, heavier seeding rates coupled with better seed distribution and later seeding dates can also produce even further significant increases in straw and fiber yield with only small increases in cost.

Another advancement included the construction of the first phase of a flax straw, fiber and shive processing pilot plant in Saskatoon by the Saskatchewan Flax Development Commission and Biolin Research with private and public funding in 2004/05. The results have shown that Canada has the potential to be a very large supplier of a wide spectrum of flax fiber types ranging from roughly cleaned fiber for paper making to high end textile fibers.

FLAX 2015: GOING BEYOND THE STATUS QUO

In 2004 the federal government of Canada initiated a program to focus resources on one crop in Western Canada that has a large potential for creating more added value industries domestically. Flax was the chosen crop and this new initiative is called Flax Canada 2015 (FC 2015). This program attempts to focus funding from several agencies and private sector companies to expand the potential for flax in the broad areas of:

1. human nutrition,
2. animal nutrition,
3. fiber,
4. industrial uses and
5. breeding/agronomy.

In 2005, committees are drawing up R&andD strategies and funding requirements to advance each of these focus areas or "pillars." Implementation will then take place from 2006 to 2015. Rough goals for 2015 include raising the total value of flax related products at the farm gate from C$300 million to C$1,500 million annually. Additionally it is estimated that through the implementation of FC 2015's human and animal nutrition, fiber and industrial development strategies, C$15 billion of value per year will be contributed to Canada's health care system and those industries involved in renewable resources and sustainability.

Healthcare is a major Canadian issue and expense, with the national health care bill estimated to be roughly C$1.4 trillion by 2015. In 2005, some Canadian provinces are spending as much as 50% of their total budget on health care alone. The situation is worsened by the fact that 7 out of 10 Canadian provinces have deficit budgets. The need to reduce healthcare costs is a significant priority in Canada and the inclusion of flaxseed and its components in human diets appears to offer a significant way to decrease health care costs. If implemented, FC 2015 will focus on securing the clinical data necessary to ensure that flaxseed and/or its components becomes part of Canada's health agenda.

The draft FC 2015 plan targets the development of increased flax usage in aquaculture and swine diets. Aquaculture is growing at a rate of 8-10% annually and the industry is experiencing a shortage of suitable protein and lipid feed sources. Requirements of salmonoid species for omega 3 fatty acids (which, in the past, have come mainly from fish meal) can be met by flax derived products better than from most other plant based sources. The swine industry has been targeted because of the high use of antibiotic growth promoters (AGP) relative to other non-poultry species. Initial research work has shown that the inclusion of flax hulls and flax oil in swine rations can give the type of results often seen when AGP are used but without the negative image associated with AGP.

Currently flax straw and fiber are, with few exceptions, a waste product of flaxseed production. FC 2015 would target the development of those things that are necessary to turn this waste product into a revenue source. These would include the development of an assessment and grading system for flax straw, fiber and shives, alternative retting technologies and further development of one or more pilot plants. The initial focus would be on developing fiber suitable for use in specialty papers, plastic composites and textile use. Longer-term goals include the development of fiber for insulation, higher end textiles, filtration products and fiber based consumer product manufacturing. In addition, greenhouse gas reduction, due to the expected reduction in the burning of flax straw, will help eliminate a portion of the Kyoto "deficit" that Canada is facing.

Linseed oil is used in the manufacture of floor coverings (i.e., linoleum) as well as paints and stains. The FC 2015 goals for industrial oil use includes assistance to develop a Canadian linoleum industry, an expansion of the current linoleum market and development of flax oil feedstocks for fuel bio-additives, polymer resins and conjugated linoleic acid.

The four just described "pillars" are supported and intimately related to flax agronomy and plant breeding. In this area, FC 2015 wants to support the development of higher yielding, disease resistant, agronomically adapted cultivars. It also wants to support the development of cultivars with value-enhancing traits like novel fatty acid profiles, improved flax meal characteristics and/or improved bast fiber properties.

CONCLUSION

In 2005, FC 2015 committees representing the five just described pillars met frequently and commissioned a number of studies to help define the potential benefits and the existing constraints to greatly enlarging flax based industries and their potential value adding components. Draft documents have been written and these are being turned into a comprehensive overall plan that would have several phases over the next ten years. The program concept is a good one but there are assortments of constraints that may prevent program components from reaching their long term potential.

One of the biggest of these is lack of certainty as far as future funding and the political commitment that may or may not go along with such funding. Many of FC 2015's goals are long term in nature. Politicians come and go and political priorities change. Even though the long term goals of a program may be extremely large for the country as a whole, the benefits may be spread out so thinly to millions of beneficiaries that no one is a big enough stakeholder to ensure that sufficient publicity and lobbying are done to keep funding for the program flowing until the longer term objectives are met. It is common for industry people and civil servants to be transferred or to move to other areas of work. The change of several key people can bring broad-based, multi-faceted, multi-year, projects like the proposed FC 2015 program to a point of bureaucratic and industry constipation. If funding slows down over an extended period of time (even if unintentional), key personnel can move on and the initiative can fizzle out and become yet another report on a shelf of many reports.

The initial announcement of FC 2015 was accompanied by statements that FC 2015 would focus C$5 million to C$10 million annually, over a ten year period, on flax. The organizers of the FC 2015 concept assumed that this total would include "re-focusing" funds already being spent on flax and hence that the Federal government would only have to supplement existing funds by a few million every year. Unfortunately most people outside the FC 2015 organizing group assumed that the C$5 million to C$10 million annually that was talked about was all "new" money coming from the Federal government. This has, at least temporarily, resulted in traditional funders of flax based research projects, to reduce or totally stop funding flax related projects because "everything will get funded with all that new FC 2015 money". Unfortunately the Federal government has no intention of replacing all the funds that were previously committed to flax related research with funds from FC 2015.

To date, the initial FC 2015 pillar committees and the overall steering group appear quite motivated, meetings have been held, plans have been drafted and further funding requests are being made. Only time will tell if this method of targeting a specific crop will be the new way to stimulate and benefit the agriculture, heath and environmental sectors or if it will end up being just another bureaucrat's dream.

REFERENCES

[1]   Morris, DH. Flax A Health and Nutrition Primer, Flax Council of Canada, Winnipeg, Canada, 2003.

[2]   Drouillard, JS; Good, EJ; Gordon, CM; Kessen, TJ; Sulpzio, MJ; Montgomery, SP; Sindt, JJ. "Flaxseed and Flaxseed Products for Cattle: Effects on Health, Growth Performance, Carcass Quality, and Sensory Attributes," in *Proceedings of the 59th Flax Institute of the United States*, Flax Institute, North Dakota State University, Fargo, North Dakota, USA, pp. 72-87, 2002.

[3]   Cunnane, SC; Thompson, LU. Editors, Flaxseed in Human Nutrition, AOCS Press, Champaign, Illinois, USA, 1995.

INDEX

D

employment, 4, 22, 33, 258, 390

emulsifying agents, 333

encouragement, x

energy, 22, 27, 33, 40, 41, 44, 138, 190, 200, 218, 237, 238, 240, 241, 242, 243, 244, 246, 256, 293, 301, 303, 304, 320, 321, 332, 366, 407, 408

energy consumption, 41

energy recovery, 40, 190

energy supply, 366

England, 51, 179, 210, 234

entrepreneurs, 4, 26, 34, 35

environment, 17, 33, 41, 133, 161, 162, 232, 252, 275, 286, 337, 368

environmental awareness, 90, 293

environmental conditions, 186, 376

environmental factors, 75

environmental impact, 393

environmental protection, 335

enzymes, 84, 322

equilibrium, 240, 365

equipment, 28, 33, 44, 82, 84, 88, 89, 175, 190, 191, 276, 333, 409

erosion, 308, 415

ethanol, 28, 295, 333

ethers, 14

ethylene, 88, 237, 382, 397, 399

ethylene glycol, 397, 399

ethylene oxide, 382

EU, 74, 209, 263, 274, 347, 391

Europe, 26, 74, 81, 134, 247, 248, 266, 271, 308, 312, 382, 391, 406

European Commission, 282

European Community, 73, 74

European Parliament, 144

European Union, 54, 248

evaporation, 321, 358, 366

evidence, 212, 218

excitation, 332, 333

execution, 317

expectations, 22, 375, 410

experimental design, 3, 4

expertise, 4, 82, 84

experts, ix, 314

exploitation, 22

exports, 26, 28, 314, 390, 392, 394

exposure, 88, 201, 202, 203, 204, 207, 208, 252, 321, 322, 327, 377

external influences, 365

extraction, 5, 21, 24, 25, 26, 27, 28, 40, 76, 95, 96, 250, 251

extrusion, 41, 250, 253, 375

F

fabric, 4, 13, 16, 17, 18, 19, 33, 54, 81, 83, 84, 85, 87, 88, 103, 114, 147, 148, 174, 175, 176, 177, 178, 179, 182, 184, 185, 199, 200, 201, 202, 205, 208, 238, 248, 249, 255, 263, 264, 271, 274, 275, 276, 277, 279, 282, 283, 285, 286, 287, 288, 289, 290, 294, 295, 296, 297, 298, 300, 307, 308, 309, 319, 322, 323, 324, 325, 326, 327, 328, 330, 331, 333, 334, 337, 338, 339, 341, 342, 343, 344, 345, 346, 347, 355, 369, 394

fabrication, 134, 182, 256, 257

factor analysis, 66

failure, 175, 194, 294, 296, 299, 300, 301, 304, 305, 321

family, 24, 238, 270, 315, 390

family units, 390

farmers, 4, 22, 53, 55, 118, 390, 405, 406, 407, 408, 409, 414, 415, 416

FAS, 392

fat, 97

fatty acids, 102, 398, 399, 418

FDA, 148

feet, 135

fertilization, 64

fiber bundles, 76, 77, 78, 80, 194, 227, 230, 234, 297, 408

fiber content, 3, 4, 6, 39, 76, 119, 124, 190, 191, 192, 193, 194, 196, 201, 205, 209, 252, 255, 415, 416

fibers, ix, 3, 4, 5, 6, 13, 14, 15, 16, 18, 21, 22, 24, 25, 26, 27, 28, 29, 30, 32, 33, 34, 39, 40, 41, 43, 45, 46, 47, 50, 51, 53, 54, 57, 58, 59, 60, 74, 76, 77, 78, 80, 81, 83, 84, 87, 89, 90, 95, 96, 97, 101, 102, 103, 104, 105, 106, 110, 117, 118, 124, 126, 133, 134, 135, 136, 137, 138, 139, 140, 141, 142, 143, 144, 147, 148, 149, 150, 153, 176, 178, 182, 183, 184, 186, 189, 190, 193, 194, 198, 200, 201, 202, 203, 207, 208, 209, 227, 228, 229, 230, 231, 232, 233, 234, 235, 237, 238, 239, 240, 244, 245, 246, 247, 248, 249, 250, 251, 252, 253, 255, 256, 257, 258, 264, 276, 293, 294, 295, 297, 298, 301, 308, 309, 313, 317, 319, 321, 324, 331, 332, 333, 338, 351, 352, 353, 354, 355, 356, 357, 358, 359, 360, 361, 362, 363, 364, 365, 366, 367, 370, 371, 373, 374, 375, 376, 377, 378, 379, 380, 381, 382, 383, 388, 390, 392, 397, 402, 405, 406, 407, 408, 409, 410, 411, 417

fibrillation, 227, 230, 232, 234

field trials, 77, 80

filament, 46

fillers, 190, 247, 260

films, 353

filtration, 308, 364, 366, 375, 418

P

S

T

U

V

W

X

Y

Z